The Complete Guide To A Show Car Shine

Written by: Mike Phillips

Autogeek.net

www.Autogeek.net
A Division of Palm Beach Motoring Group

Copyright

First printing February 2013

Trademarks

ISBN 978-0-615-54046-7

Printed and bound in the U.S.A.

Printed by:

Commercial Printers, Inc.
Fort Lauderdale, FL
877-423-8492 ext 235

Acknowledgements

We are grateful to all of you that contributed to the development of this manual, provided technical information and/or certain pictures and illustrations.

Important

Term, conditions, features, service offerings, prices, and hours referenced in this manual are subject to change without notice. We at Palm Beach Motoring Accessories, Inc. are committed to bringing you great printed and online services through Autogeek.net and AutogeekOnline.net. Occasionally, we may decide to update our online services and change our service offerings, so please check www.Autogeek.net for the latest information, including pricing and availability, on our products and services.

PBMG
Palm Beach Motoring Group

7744 SW Jack James Road
Stuart, FL 34997

www.autogeek.net
www.autogeekonline.net
www.palmbeachmotoring.net

1-800-869-3011

Table of Contents

I wrote this book to help people better understand how to polish their car's paint. For me, polishing paint is the fun part. Swapping out engines, replacing brakes, even simple tune-ups and oil changes are the dirty routine things. While important and necessary, these aren't what most people consider fun and are better described as just plain old knuckle-busting work.

On the other hand, spending a Saturday afternoon washing and waxing your pride and joy is a time to relax and unwind on the weekend, while performing preventative maintenance and having fun. The key to having fun is getting good results. This is where knowledge comes into the equation. You see modern clearcoat paints tend to be hard, thin and delicate in that they are easily dulled and scratched.

For these reasons, it's important to have a little knowledge about the paint you're working on, the products you're using and most importantly, the process. The paint polishing process is where the magic happens, it's where you take a diamond in the rough and turn it into a glistening gemstone.

Perfecting your technique, with help from the information contained inside this how-to book and reinforced by interaction on the AutogeekOnline.net discussion forum will ensure you get professional results the first time and every time. The members of our discussion forum and I are always available as a resource to see you through to success in your garage. You can even take what you learn from this how-to book and start a detailing business, earning money either part time, or if you wish, full time.

When it comes to washing and waxing your car, there is nothing more disappointing than to wipe off the final application of wax, only to reveal a finish that looks only marginally better than before you started. This how-to book will ensure this never happens to you.

The trend for the last 20+ years has been for everyone from car enthusiasts to professional detailers to switch over to machine polishing instead of trying to do all the polishing steps by hand. An electric polisher is more efficient when working on any type of paint as you always get better results faster. That said, you really need some background information about the different types of popular polisher options available today.

In this updated version of my first how-to book I'll walk you through how paint works and how to work on it through all stages of the detailing process. For example how to wash a car or even wipe a car carefully using a spray detailer and a microfiber towel so you don't accidently instill swirls and scratches into the paint. These skills are just as important as knowing how to use any electric polisher because after you polish the paint to perfection you'll still need to know how to expertly wash

and dry it and then maintain it. (Or you'll be back to square one).

I will walk you through the different types of electric polishers available and how they work and how to use them to create a show car finish on your own vehicles or for your customers if you detail cars for a hobby or for a part time or full time car detailing business.

Different strokes for different folks
Some of you may look at your car merely as a means of transportation. You are mostly interested in learning how to best protect your investment. Some of you may look at your car as an extension of your personality; you see it as an escape from the daily grind of living in a complicated world. You have a passion for polishing paint and you take it as serious as a heart attack. You want to know everything you can about the products and process you're using and how to get the best results possible from your time, money and efforts. The term "second best" is not in your vocabulary.

Polishing paint is an art form
To achieve a flawless finish, you need to know a lot more than what the directions on the label of a can or bottle of wax can tell you. Like the saying, "wax-on, wax-off", from the movie The Karate Kid, there's more to it than simply wiping wax on and off.

You need to combine knowledge and experience, as well as the right products and tools with the human elements of care and passion. You need to genuinely care about what you're doing and have a passion for the craft. When all these things come together, polishing paint becomes an art form as you truly create a work of art.

Information is the true secret to a show car finish
I believe you will find the information in this how-to book to be very different from anything else you have ever read in any bother book, magazine article or even on any website related to the topic of car detailing.

Over the years, I've helped thousands of people with their different paint polishing projects. While demonstrating at car shows or teaching classes, I'd explain how paint works, how polishing products work and the different types of procedures that go with them. Afterwards, I would always be asked the same question that usually goes like this:

Hey Mike, is any of this information written down anywhere?

Until now, the answer was always "no".

Most of the information shared in this book is from my own experiences, gained from polishing just about every type of surface under the sun, in every imaginable condition.

Some of the information shared in this book comes from people I have met over the years including painters, detailers, do-it-yourselfers and the hundreds of thousands of friends I've made on detailing discussion forums and who have attended my detailing classes.

I'm confident that after reading this book, you will be ready to tackle any detailing project that comes your way.

Let the polishing begin!
Mike Phillips

Early Painting Technology

■ Paint History

Karl Benz, of Mercedes-Benz, was awarded the first patent for what we call the automobile in 1885. However it wasn't until Henry Ford introduced the Model T in 1908 that the general public began the transition from riding a horse to driving a car.

It was a decade later before enough people had purchased a car for it become established as the new mode of transportation. If we use the general year of 1910, only two years after the Model T was introduced, and fast forward to today, (as I write this, it's the year 2013), in general terms, we've only been driving cars for approximately 100 years out the entire known history of human existence. In context, we've only been driving cars for a very short time.

For the largest portion of this 100 year history of the car, most of our cars had single stage paints. It's only been since the 1980s that car manufacturers starting switching over to modern basecoat/clearcoat paints.

When cars were first introduced in the late 1800s and early 1900s it was a new industry and as such, there were no specific manufacturers of car paints (because cars didn't exist).

Car manufacturers borrowed coatings from the furniture industry. This would include shellac, varnish and lacquer paints. Early cars used a lot of wood, so these coatings prevented the wood from rotting and the steel from rusting. As the car manufacturing industry grew, paint companies introduced paints specifically for the needs of auto manufacturing assembly lines (high production output) and for the specific

In This Section:

- Paint History
- Basecoat/Clearcoat Paint Technology
- Not a Miracle Coating
- Not An Invisible Force Field
- Paint Is Thin
- Paint Is Hard
- Difficult To Work On By Hand
- The Practical Differences Between Single Stage Paints And Clear Coat Paints
- Clearcoat Failure
- Swirls – The Number One Complaint
- Single Stage Paints – Oxidation
- Paint Hardness Of Softens – Polishable & Polishability
- Hard Paint Or Soft Paint?
- Paint Systems
- Paint Types Affect Paint Hardness
- How To Test For Single Stage Or Basecoat/Clearcoat Paint Systems
- Tinted Clears
- How To Test For Single Stage White Paint

needs of vehicles themselves. This included characteristics to both protect the surface from deterioration and provide a beautiful finish.

■ Basecoat/Clearcoat Paint Technology

Most cars manufactured from the 1990s though today have what's called a basecoat/clearcoat paint system. The top coat is a clear layer of paint which provides gloss and durability to the basecoat layer, which is the pigmented (colored) layer of paint.

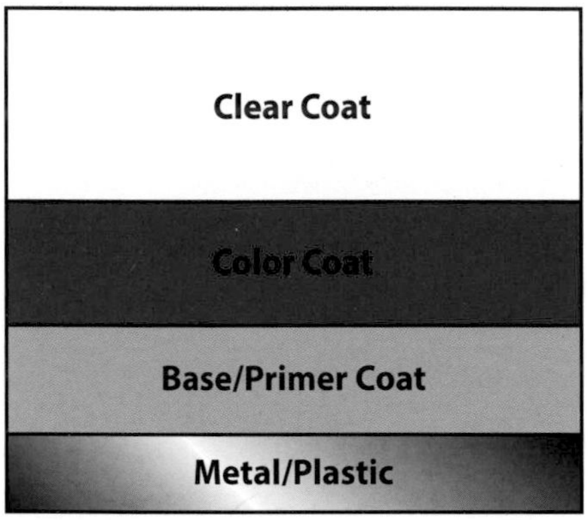

■ Not A Miracle Coating

Some people think the clear layer is some kind of miracle coating that doesn't need to be routinely polished or waxed. That's simply not true. The top clear layer of paint is just that: it's paint with no pigment, but it's still paint.

■ Not An Invisible Force Field

The clear layer of paint is not an invisible force field that repels anything that comes near it. Clearcoat paint still needs to be maintained just like old fashioned single stage paint; it must be washed, clayed, polished and protected on a regular schedule to maintain a showroom-new appearance.

■ Paint Is Thin

The factory paint on new cars, trucks and SUVs is thin. How thin? Generally speaking, the top coat layer, the layer you can polish and wax, averages around 2 mils thick. If you like to measure using microns, this would be 50.8 microns. Let me help you to understand just how thin this is by

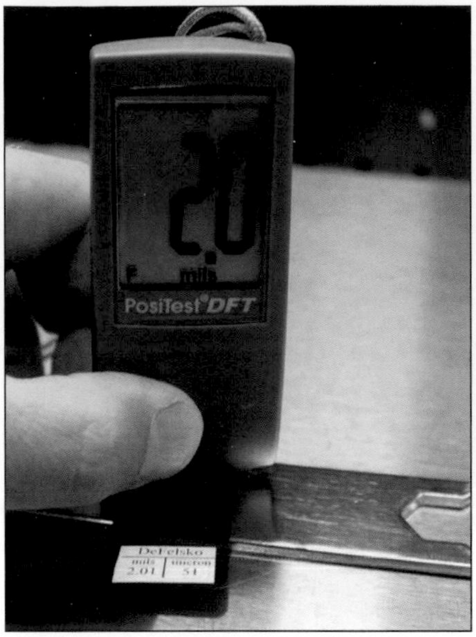

using a simple Post-it Note.

In the picture above, I'm measuring a test shim that comes with the Defelsko PosiTest DFT Coating Thickness Gauge to ensure accuracy. The tool is ready to use out of the box and does not need to be calibrated. If you want to calibrate it just to make sure, it's very simple: simultaneously click the two side buttons three times and it will automatically zero out

After you do this recalibration, you'll want to test the measuring accuracy. You do this using an object with a known measurement, like the included test shims.

There are a lot of paint thickness gauges on the market and they range greatly in price. But like any quality tool, you get what you pay for. The Defelsko PosiTest is called a 3% gauge, which means it's very accurate. Most gauges are 5% gauges and while the difference between 3% and 5% may seem minimal, when you're working on a coating that's already thin to start with, accuracy is of the utmost importance.

What you see, (pictured right) is a reading of 0.0 mils after I recalibrated the gauge. After recalibrating it, I measured a test shim that measures 2.01 mils from the factory. The 1 in the 2.01 stands for one ten thousandth of a millimeter. This test gauge, like most test gauges, doesn't read to the hundredth thousandth of a millimeter measurement. When measuring the thickness of paint, accuracy to the one ten thousandth of a millimeter is not as important.

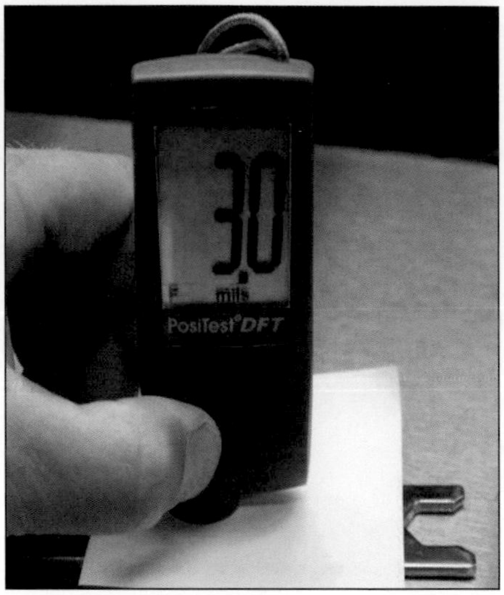

Here I'm measuring a standard Post-it Note. The reason I'm measuring a Post-it Note is because most of you reading this will have access to one. I took 5-6 measurements and the average was 3.0 mils.

Keep in mind that the average clearcoat is approximately 2.0 mils. I'm talking about just the clear layer, not the color coat, or primer or e-coat, etc. The clear layer is the part you can work on and the coating you need to take care of in order to maintain the finish over the service life of the car.

The next time you have a Post-it Note, feel it between your fingers and

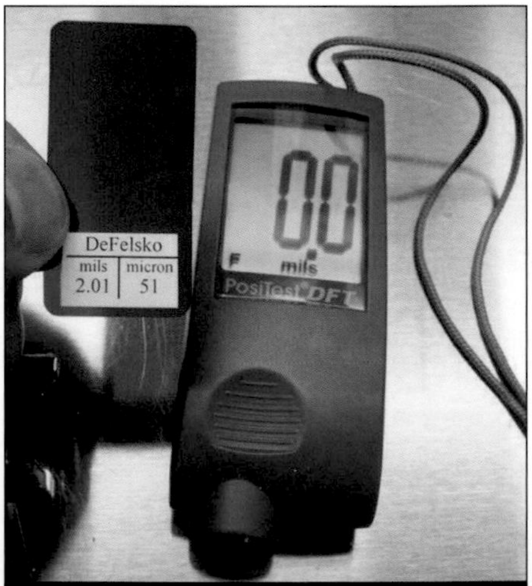

Pictured is a DeFelsko Paint Thickness Gauge for measuring total film build.

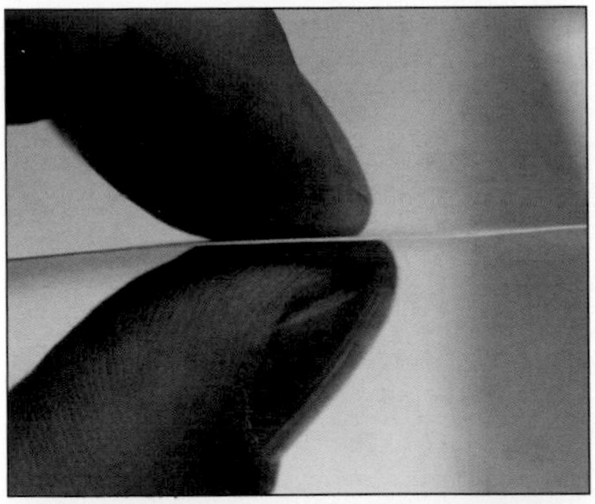

understand that the thickness is thicker than the average clear layer of paint on a modern car, truck or SUV. In other words, paint is thin!

With this in mind, there's not a lot of room to make mistakes. Hopefully, understanding how thin your car's paint is will drive home the importance of obtaining knowledge before attempting to polish or correct the paint. Understanding how thin your car's clearcoat finish is drives home the points made in this article:

📖 *Use the least aggressive product to get the job done*

■ Paint Is Hard

Compared to paint systems from just a few decades ago, modern basecoat/clearcoat paints tend to be harder than traditional single stage paints. It's this hardness factor that makes paint more difficult to work on.

All my detailing classes start with a PowerPoint presentation in which we go over the principals of machine polishing paint. This way, students get head knowledge before moving onto hands-on training. You would never go to a heart surgeon who has never been to medical school, would you? In the same way, before you go out and start working on your car's hard and precious thin paint, it's a good idea to learn a little bit about the material itself.

■ Difficult To Work By Hand

From the time of the Model T to the cars of the 1970s, it was easy to work by hand and get some pretty good results with no problems because the paint systems were softer and easier to polish.

All you have to do to see why machine polishing is so popular is to go out into your garage with a modern compound or polish and try to remove swirls by hand and leave a better looking finish than when you started. You'll find out really fast that working on paint by hand is more work than most people are prepared for. Besides being a lot of work, it's difficult to get good results by hand as you can't duplicate the power or the action of an electric polisher. It is easy to get show car results by machine with a little bit of head knowledge on what I call the three Ps. That is, you need to know a little bit about **paint**, (the finish you're working on), **products**, (these would include paint care products like compounds, polishes, waxes), and **process** (that's the actual manner or method in which you use your hands or polishers to apply the products to the paint).

Polishing paint by hand is frustrating and you'll quickly discover that as soon as you get started. The next step in the natural progression of car care as a hobby or profession is to correct, polish and wax your vehicle using an electric polisher.

■ The Practical Differences Between Single Stage Paints And Clearcoat Paints

I've worked on thousands of cars with single stage paint and have conducted many extreme makeovers in which the project car had single stage paint. The opportunity to work on cars with single stage paint is becoming rarer as all modern vehicles feature a clearcoat paint system. I'll outline some of the practical differences between singles stage paints and modern clearcoat paints.

Early Mustangs had single stage paint while modern Mustangs have a basecoat/clearcoat paint system.

Clearcoat paints were introduced to production cars in the USA starting in the early 1980s. Since that time, technology has continually improved to create automotive paint systems that will last a long time and provide a beautiful finish with great gloss and clarity.

The oldest factory clearcoat finish I've ever worked on was an all original 1980 Corvette when I was the guest speaker for the 2007 National Corvette Restoration Society at their National Convention in Boston, Massachusetts.

I gave a presentation on machine polishing paint at their national convention. Afterwards, the owner of an all original 1980 Corvette (the owner purchased this Corvette new and has never had the car repainted), asked me to show him how to remove swirls. Since the owner had not yet progressed to machine polishing, I first demonstrated how to remove swirls by hand. Afterwards, I demonstrated how to remove swirls using the Porter Cable DA Polisher.

The clearcoat used on this 1980 Corvette was soft and it was easy to remove the swirls and scratches by hand or machine. Anyone with detailing experience that has worked on new Corvettes knows that the current paint technology is very hard. This just demonstrates that since the introduction of modern clearcoat paint systems in the early 1980s, paint technology is continually changing and improving. I'm sad to say it's not getting thicker however.

The next oldest original factory basecoat/clearcoat finish I've buffed out is this 1982 Corvette, which is still in very good condition with no signs of clearcoat failure. Above you can see it in my driveway after I detailed it.

It was owned by April aka "The Vette Lady" and she gave me the Johnny Lightening version of her car.

The point is I've been teaching machine polishing classes since 1988 and have had the opportunity to work on paint systems from the 1920s all the way to a brand new 2012 Mercedes-Benz CLS63 AMG. I've seen the changes in paint technology first-hand as both a detailer and a detailing instructor. One of the primary changes I've seen take place is the clearcoat hardness factor.

The hardness factor is both a good thing and a bad thing. These new high-tech paint systems are incredibly durable as far as coatings goes, but they are also incredibly hard to work on by hand.

■ Clearcoat Failure

Since clearcoat paint systems have become the standard for automotive finishes, we now have entire generations of people that have only owned cars with basecoat/clearcoat paint systems; they have never owned or worked on a car that has a single stage paint system.

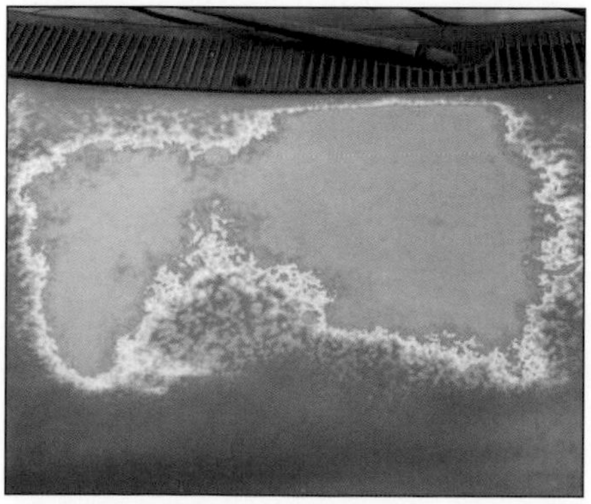

From time to time, a new member will join our forum, Autogeekonline.net, and ask for help removing oxidization from their car's finish. More often than not the problem with their car's clearcoat is not oxidation but rather clearcoat failure.

Clearcoat paint systems will deteriorate over time when exposed to too much sun without proper care. This occurs throughout the entire matrix, or thickness, of the clear layer of paint, meaning you can't fix it by abrading the surface. Abrading the surface simply removes damaged paint and uncovers more damaged paint. If you continue abrading the paint you will get down to the basecoat or pigmented layer of paint. The pigmented layer of paint is naturally dull and will not polish to a clear, high gloss. This deterioration of the clear layer is called clearcoat failure and the only solution is to repaint the affected panels or the entire car.

The cool thing about old single stage paint systems is they don't suffer from clearcoat failure since there is no clear layer of paint. Single stage paint systems oxidize and oxidation is easy enough to fix that anyone can do it.

■ Swirls – The Number One Complaint

Swirls are among the most common defects present in clearcoat finishes. Besides being ugly and unsightly, these scratches make the surface hazy and this dulls your view of the color coat under the clearcoat.

Swirls can be removed because they

Clearcoat finish before removing swirls

Clearcoat finish after removing swirls

are topical. Like oxidation, they are in the upper surface of the layer of clear paint. All you have to do is use a compound or an abrasive polish to remove a little paint from the surface. This will level or flatten out the surface again and thus remove the visual appearances of swirls.

■ Single Stage Paints = Oxidation

Single stage paint systems tend to oxidize very easily. They still get swirls and scratches, but in the real world

Before removing oxidation

After removing oxidation

the noticeable problem is the dullness and fading caused by oxidation. True oxidation is easy to remove, making restoring a show car shine easy.

If after reading all of the above you're wondering,

If single stage paints tend to be more user-friendly to work on for the average person, why do car manufacturers use basecoat/clearcoat paint systems?

Good question!

The primary reason the Original Equipment Manufacturer (OEM) industry switched paint systems was due to new laws and regulations from the Environmental Protection Agency (EPA) and other governmental regulatory agencies.

The new basecoat/clearcoat paint systems emit less VOCs (Volatile Organic Compounds) into the air, making them safer for the environment. Another benefit is that modern finishes will tend to last longer over the service life of a car because clearcoat paint systems offer greater hardness and dramatically improved resin technology.

■ Paint Hardness Or Softness – Polishable & Polishability

Most people talk about paint being either hard or soft. Better words for describing the hardness of softness of paint are polishable and polishability

- ***Polishable** - Capable of being polished*
- ***Polishabilty** - To the degree a surface or coating can be polished*

Polishable, in the context that I use it, refers to how easy or difficult it is to remove below-surface defects from the paint.

Polishable is a range between:

- ***Too Hard** – Extremely difficult to level paint in an effort to remove below-surface defects.*
- ***Too Soft** – So soft that just the act of wiping the paint with a clean, soft microfiber polishing towel can instill swirls and scratches.*

The best paint systems are somewhere between these two extremes. This would be a paint system the average person can work on. By this I mean a paint system soft enough that defects can be removed but hard enough to resist scratching through normal maintenance procedures while still providing long service life.

■ Hard Paint Or Soft Paint?

When you go to work on your car in your garage, the best thing you can do is what we call a Test Spot. This is where you'll test the products, pads, and procedures to see if they'll remove the defects and restore a show car finish. This is called dialing-in your paint polishing process.

Dialing-in a process means starting out with the least aggressive products you have available. If your test spot reveals that your first choice for products are not working effectively enough or fast enough, you can always try again substituting a more aggressive product, pad or both.

Once you determine a combination of products that will remove the defects and restore a show car shine to your expectations, then all you have to do is duplicate this process over the rest of the car. Your test spot will prove your paint polishing process either works or it doesn't.

If the result from your test spot works and looks great to your eyes then you can tackle the rest of the car without wasting your time using a product, pad and/or process that isn't working. I started writing on the Internet about how to do a test spot back in 1994, that's nineteen years ago. I believe it's very important to learn how to do a test spot and to practice this the first time you work on any vehicle.

If your first test spot doesn't work then you continue testing until you dial-in a pad, product and process that works. If you run into trouble, the best thing you can do is to join the AutogeekOnline.net discussion forum and start a thread describing the issues you're seeing. Our forum community will chime in and help you to dial in a process that works.

Asking questions on a discussion forum regarding your vehicle's paint system can be a good way to get other people's opinions on the matter. If they have the same car with the same factory original paint, then their opinion can be even more valuable. That said, the best way to find out is to go out into your garage and try a couple of products first-hand and find out for yourself how difficult or easy it is to remove defects from the paint.

You Need Experience
The more cars you work on, the more experience you'll gain with a wider range of paint systems. You'll soon be able to gauge if the paint on a car is hard or soft after doing a few test spots. The harder the paint the more difficult it will be to remove swirls, scratches and water spots. The softer the paint the easier it will be to remove swirls, scratches and water spots. You'll know immediately whether your vehicle's paint is hard or soft after performing a test spot.

Nothing beats first-hand experience. Your personal skill level will have a huge influence on your success or failure and can actually mislead you regarding polishability of the paint. For example, if you're new to machine polishing and are still honing your skills and technique, then removing swirls and scratches out of soft paint may seem difficult to you. Put someone with a lot of experience in the same garage with the same car and they may find the paint is soft and show you just how fast and easy it is to remove swirls and scratches.

I know the above to be true after almost two decades of teaching people that are brand new to machine polishing how to detail cars, and more specifically how to use a DA polisher. Technique is more important than the products and pads you're using. You can have the best products and the best tools available but if your technique isn't exactly right, you won't get the results that you're after.

In order to really know if the paint on any car is hard or soft, you must have as much experience as possible working on a wide variety of paint systems.

So get experience!
Go out into your garage and do some testing on your car's paint. Dial-in a process that works to your satisfaction and lock into your memory how the paint reacted. That way when you detail your car in the future, you'll know exactly what products and processes gave you great results.

■ Paint Systems

There are about a dozen major automotive paint manufacturers in the world that supply paint systems to both the OEM and the refinishing industry.

Paint Systems Vary
Different car manufacturers and body shops use different paint systems. These can vary greatly and because technology is always changing, even paint systems from a single paint manufacturer can vary greatly.

Every time you work on a car, you're working on a specific paint system. Because the chemistry between paint systems can be very different, polishing characteristics can vary greatly.

Even identical models from any particular car manufacturer can have paint that is completely different (harder or softer) from year to year. Try to avoid generalization in regards to paint hardness. Instead, test each car you work on and gain experience.

■ Paint Type Affects Paint Hardness

Clearcoats
The hardness of a clearcoat finish is determined primarily by the type of resin used to make the paint. Other factors include catalysts, hardeners, solvents and other additives as well as the drying or baking process used to cure the paint.

Single Stage
The hardness of single stage paint is determined primarily by the type of resin and other ingredients used to make the paint, as well as the type of pigment used to give the paint color. Different pigments can be soft or hard, altering the overall hardness of the finish.

■ How To Test For Single Stage OR Basecoat/Clearcoat Paint Systems

Chances are very good that if you're working on a car less than 10 years old, you're working on a basecoat/clearcoat finish. Even though the majority of cars manufactured since the mid-1980s come with a clearcoat finish, I still get asked how to check.

Here's a simple way to test the paint on your car to find out if it's a single stage paint or a basecoat/clearcoat finish.

It's easy to see...
With a true single stage paint system, it's very apparent because you'll easily see the colored paint residue building up on the face of your buffing pads.

To test for a single stage paint system, try to find a white colored polish (if you're working on any kind of pigmented or colored paint), and a

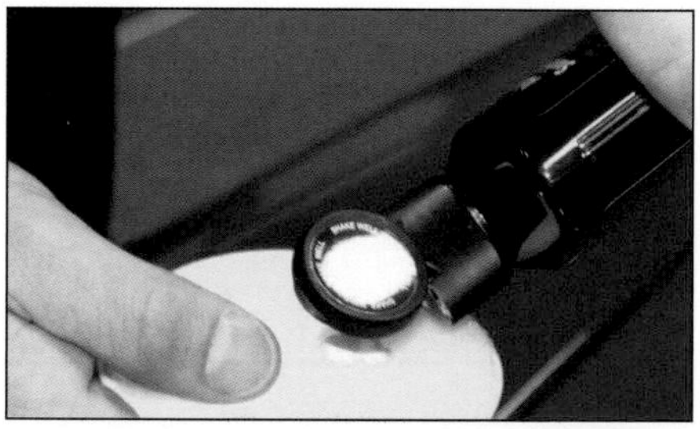

light or white colored applicator pad. Pour some polish onto a clean applicator pad.

Use an ample amount of polish for plenty of lubrication as you're going to want to push firmly if no visible oxidation is present (as was the case on this 1956 Pontiac Starchief). Then using firm pressure, apply the polish in an overlapping circular motion to a small section of paint.

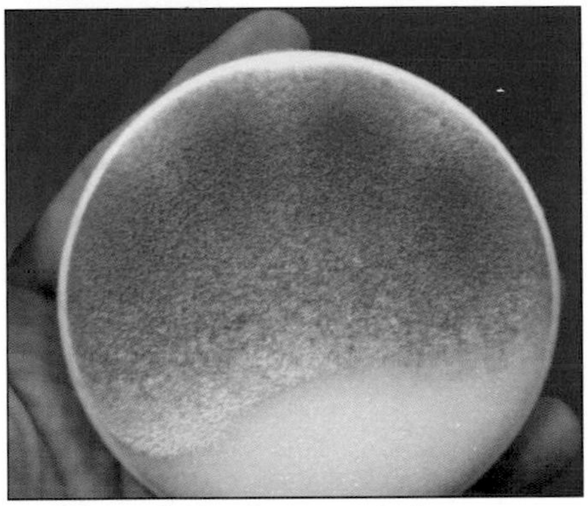

Confirmed Single Stage Paint
As you can see, red pigment is coming off the car and onto the applicator pad, so we're working on red single stage paint. If the pad remained yellow with some white polish on it, this would be an indicator of a basecoat/clearcoat paint system.

■ Tinted Clears

Some car manufacturers use a tinted clear for the top coat of paint over the clearcoat finish. The car has a basecoat/clearcoat finish, but the very last layer of clear paint has color added for a special effect. This can be a little misleading and make someone think they're working on a single stage paint when in fact they're not. The biggest visual indictor of a tinted clear is when you test as shown above. If you're machine polishing the paint, you will only see a little color coming off the surface, not a lot.

My friend Rene's 2001 Camaro is painted Red Jewel Tint and you can see a "little" red coming off on a Cyan Hydro-Tech Pad as we were buffing it

out for a how-to video with Matt Steel and me.

■ How To Test For Single Stage White Paint

Testing white paint can be just a little trickier, because so many abrasive polishes are white in color. This makes it hard to see if the test results are white paint coming off, or just the color of the polish.

Tips for testing white paint
If you're testing white paint, try to use a colored polish with a dark colored cloth (so you can confirm that you're removing white paint and not just seeing the color of the polish or the color of the cloth). Most people have old t-shirts that are blue, red or black that can be cut up for testing purposes.

Pinnacle Advanced Finishing Polish not only works fantastic as a finishing polish, but it's also gray in color.

Interestingly, it's possible to find white single stage paints on newer vehicles manufactured in the last twenty years. Due to the ingredients used in white single stage paint, it is very hard and durable and will hold up to exposure to the elements as well as normal wear and tear without a clear layer of paint

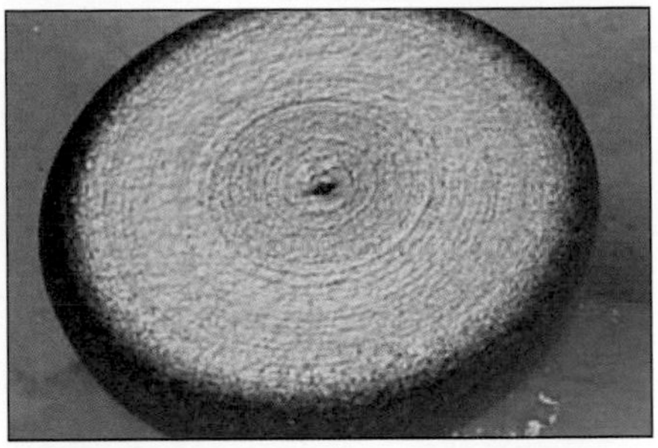

over it. It normally costs less to spray a car using a single stage paint system rather than a basecoat/clearcoat system in a production environment due to reduced costs in labor, time and materials.

Mismatched Panels
I buffed out a 1956 Rolls Royce a few years ago and it had been repainted using a basecoat/clearcoat paint system. I tested on the hood and confirmed it was a basecoat/clearcoat paint system. Like I recommend in this how-to book, I started buffing on the highest point of the car and then moved downward and tackled the hood. Next up was the trunk lid; I discovered by the volume of white paint on the face of my buffing pad that the entire car was clearcoated except the trunk lid, which had single stage paint.

So it's completely possible to find cars like this that have two types of paint. It may all look the same from a distance but as soon as you polish each panel, you might find that it has two paint systems.

Lesson learned
The lesson here is if you're in doubt, simply perform the aforementioned test and find out for sure. ■

■ Washing Your Car – The Most Important Step

Washing is the most important step there is when it comes to machine polishing your car's paint. You need the car to be surgically clean for two primary reasons:

1. To properly evaluate the surface
Whether you want to create a true show car finish or just wash and wax your car to maintain the factory finish, you need to evaluate the condition of the paint. In order to do this, it needs to be thoroughly clean and dry. When evaluating the condition of the paint, you're going to inspect it visually (in good lighting) and you're going to feel the paint with your sense of touch. For both of these steps, it's vital that the paint is completely free of contaminants.

2. To ensure all loose dirt, road grime and any abrasive particulates are removed
To make sure you don't put swirls into the paint while you're machine buffing, start by making sure there's no dirt or any abrasive particles on the car.

■ 2 Approaches To Washing Your Car

The idea behind washing your car is to remove any built-up dirt, road grime or other loose surface contaminants from the exterior finish, trim, windows and other components.

There are two very different approaches to washing your car. The condition of your car's paint is what determines how you approach the washing process.

1. Aggressive Approach – Washing before a detailing session. (neglected paint)

2. Careful Approach – Washing after a detailing session. (show car finish)

Let's take a look at each approach...

■ Aggressive Approach – Washing Before A Detailing Session

When washing a neglected finish, the priority is getting the car as clean as possible. It's okay to wash a neglected vehicle a little more aggressively to get it surgically clean because any defects you instill during the washing process will be removed during the correction steps.

Your goal is to ensure that you've removed as much loose dirt from the car as possible so that dirt particles won't enter into the decontamination step or any of the machine polishing procedures.

In This Section:

1956 Ford F150 - Show Car Quality Finish. This picture was taken right after I machine polished and machine waxed the paint. To prevent re-instilling swirls and scratches into the black mirror finish this truck must be washed and dried as carefully as humanly possible using the best car washing products that can be obtained. "Best Truck" Award at 2009 Grand National Roadster Show.

Air currents
Spinning buffing pads create air current on the surface. It's possible for loose dirt particles to be drawn between the paint and the pad potentially inflicting swirls and scratches throughout the entire finish. For this reason, it's vitally important to thoroughly wash and rinse the car and clean your pad often. As you're machine polishing, after you work a panel, take a moment to inspect paint that you've polished to catch any problems as soon as possible. If not discovered quickly, one tiny abrasive particle of dirt accidently caught between your pad and the paint can potentially inflict swirls into the entire finish.

I can tell you from experience that if you do a stellar job of washing the car, your chance of having any problems in the buffing steps are almost zero.

■ Careful Approach – Washing After A Detailing Session

If the finish on your car is in excellent condition, then you want and need to increase the level of care used while washing the car. Your priority is to avoid instilling any swirls, scratching or marring back into the paint. Anything that touches the paint must be clean, soft and gentle. While washing, you must focus on the task at hand and use expert technique.

■ Paint Decontamination – Iron X

This is an advanced procedure that I personally use and recommend. Paint decontamination is where you chemically wet the painted body panels after washing and rinsing to remove any embedded airborne chemical compounds and ferrous particles that may contain iron. This requires a special product like Iron X – a specialized spray-on iron remover.

Any corrosive substances like acid rain or contaminants containing iron including iron particles from things like brake dust and rail dust penetrate into the paint and cannot always be completely removed by washing or claying. It's also possible for some iron particles to be removed by clay. However, they can embed into the clay itself and inflict swirls and scratches into the paint as the clay is rubbed over the surface.

Iron particles can be seen on white paint because they oxidize and turn into orange rust dots. On medium and dark colored cars you cannot see the damage being caused by iron particles. If iron particles and other corrosive alkalis or acid substances are not removed they will continue to eat into your car's precious, thin clearcoat causing irreversible damage. The time to decontaminate your paint is before you see any signs of damage. By the time visible signs of damage appear, it's too late to undo the damage and a new paint job is costly.

How to remove iron particles out of paint
The safe way to remove any iron contaminants off your car's painted body panels is to chemically dissolve the iron into a water soluble mixture that can then be safely rinsed off. This same type of procedure is also popular for decontaminating wheels where iron brake dust particles are a huge problem.

CarPro offers a number of products that are safe for both car paints and wheels that decontaminate these areas of your car during the wash process. Due to the fact that the iron particles undergo a chemical reaction, the best time to use CarPro decontaminating products is when washing a car using the Traditional Car Wash procedure because this way you can thoroughly flush the resulting residues off the surface.

You can use CarPro Products for decontaminating paint, clear bras, plastics and wheels. My approach is to get the best bang for your buck by washing and rinsing any and all loose dirt off the surface and then drying the surface before using the CarPro products.

Why?
By removing the loose dirt first and then rinsing and drying the surface, the CarPro products can focus completely on dissolving and removing the corrosive substances and iron particles. When you use the products on a dirty car, the dirt and road grime can dilute the strength of the active ingredients. If you leave water standing on body panels or wheels, the water will also act to dilute the concentrated active ingredients. So my approach is to first wash, rinse and dry the vehicle and then apply one of the various CarPro

products and then rewash and rinse the wheels and vehicle.

While this does add more time to the washing process the value and importance of these extra steps comes back to the fact that the clear layer of paint on your car is thin to start with and a little extra maintenance is a better option than a repaint. Repainting your car is not only costly but it's a time-consuming process, especially when you consider you will be without your car for some period of time and you must make other arrangements for transportation. Then there's always the hassle of finding a reputable body shop to do the job right the first time and not return your car filled with swirls from their buffing process after the new paint is sprayed which, I'm sad to say, is the norm in the body shop industry.

Here are the current offerings by CarPro (pictured below) at the time this chapter was written with a brief description for each product. The simplest and most straightforward product is the Iron X spray which you can use on both your car's paint and wheels.

Iron X – Powerful Iron Filings & Contaminants Cleaner
This is a thin liquid and is applied using a pump spray bottle to remove iron particles off of paint, plastic, glass and wheels.

My comments...
This is the simplest and easiest Iron X product to use and a good product to start with if you're new to Iron X products.

Iron X Paste – Super Strong Iron & Brake Dust Remover
This is a thicker, gel version of the original spray-on Iron X and the thicker consistency enables the product to cling and dwell on non-horizontal surfaces to allow it to work longer.

Iron X Snow Soap – Triple Action Iron Remover, Car Shampoo and Pre-Wash Foam
This is a thick rich gel that works really well in Foam Guns and Foam Cannons to wash a car. Foam tends to cling and dwell to surfaces longer than a soap wash solution giving the active ingredients more time to work. This formula also includes a degreaser for preparing neglected cars for a detailing session.

Tar X – Powerful Tar & Adhesives Remover
CarPro Tar X is a bug and tar remover made of natural solvents extracted from orange peels. Tar X safely lifts grease, tar, asphalt, insects, tire marks, adhesives, traffic film and any other stubborn contaminants.

TR.IX- Powerful Tar & Iron Remover
This is a strong degreaser, cleaner, tar remover and iron remover for virtually any exterior automotive surface.

CAUTION: Iron X products should not be used on chrome, bare metal parts, brake calipers, wheel balancing weights, or SMART paint repairs. Mask off these areas. Avoid letting Iron X dry on any surface.

Question: When do you use an Iron X product?

Answer: *When using the Traditional Car Wash Approach because the residue must be thoroughly rinsed off using water.*

Some of the Iron X products are specifically for removing iron filings and should be used after you first use a normal car wash soap to remove loose dirt and road grime from body panels or wheels. Some Iron X products are actual car wash soaps and replace your normal car wash soap. Read the directions for each of the products and then choose the product that best suits your detailing needs.

NOTE: All Iron X products need to be completely rinsed off the surface and for this reason work best when using the traditional car wash procedure using a water hose for the rinsing step.

■ Four Ways To Wash Your Car

There are four popular approaches to washing and cleaning cars. Below are descriptions of four different approaches, followed by the products they can be used with.

1. Traditional Car Wash
A traditional car wash is simply the more traditional method of using a hose and bucket to wash your car. This system works well, but it also uses a lot of water and in some geographical areas, this may not be allowed. Note: Iron X works best with this style of car wash procedure.

2. Waterless Car Wash
A waterless car wash is a high lubricity pre-mixed spray detailer used to heavily saturate a panel. The panel is then carefully wiped to remove any dirt or road grime. The key to working safely with a waterless car wash is to use plenty of clean, microfiber polishing towels. After one becomes contaminated, switch to a clean towel so you don't simply transfer dirt removed from one panel to another.

3. Rinseless Car Wash
A rinseless car wash is a cross between a traditional car wash and a waterless car wash. Like a traditional car wash, you're still going to use water, but only a couple of gallons. Like a waterless wash, instead of rinsing your wash

solution off, you'll work panel by panel, wiping each panel to a dry shine using microfiber drying towels like the Guzzler Waffle Weave Microfiber Drying Towel.

4. Spray Detailers
Spray Detailers are for removing:

- Light Dust
- Fingerprints
- Smudges

As long as your car only has a light accumulation of dust, you can clean or wash your car using a spray detailer.

■ How To Use A Traditional Car Wash

Tools Needed:

- Car Wash Soap
- Wheel Cleaner
- Iron X (optional)
- Tire Cleaner
- Wash Mitt, Sponge or Brush
- Wheel Brush
- Tire Brush
- Drying Towels or Chamois
- Metro MasterBlaster Sidekick
- Spray Hose
- One 5-Gallon Bucket – It's optional to use the Two Bucket Method
- Grit Guard Inserts

Buckets
A good wash bucket holds up to 5 gallons of car wash solution. You don't necessarily want to fill the bucket with 5 gallons of water but instead, use 3-4 gallons of water leaving some room at the top of the bucket. You want more than 1 or 2 gallons because you want an adequate volume of water to enable you to move your wash mitt, sponge or brush around to allow gathered dirt to loosen and fall of the bottom of the bucket.

Single Bucket Wash Method
The single bucket wash method is the most common way people wash their cars and it's pretty straight forward. Get a clean bucket and add about 4 gallons of water. Then, measure and add your car wash soap and mix thoroughly.

My Comment…
I use the single bucket method to wash wheels and tires.

Two Bucket Wash Method
In this method, one bucket contains your wash solution and the second bucket contains clean rinse water. To use the two bucket method, gather some wash solution and use it to wash a single panel. Instead of placing your

mitt back into the soapy water bucket, you first rinse the mitt in the clean water bucket to remove the majority of dirt. After rinsing, squeeze a little water out and then start the process over again by dipping the mitt into the soap solution bucket.

My comment…
For washing the body panels of a car, I always use the two bucket method.

Grit Guard Inserts
My good friend Doug Lamb invented these back in 1989 and I've been using one ever since I was introduced to these ingenious and beneficial tools. The Grit Guard Insert is as the name implies – it is a plastic insert that fits into the bottom of a 5-gallon bucket that will trap the dirt that comes off your wash mitt. The design includes a plastic grille that dirt and other abrasive particles can fall past to rest in the bottom of the bucket. The grille is suspended about two inches off the bottom of the bucket by four vanes. These vanes help to trap dirt particles by preventing the water at the bottom of the bucket from swirling around. This stops dirt particles from rising back above the grille where they could potentially get back onto your wash mitt.

Single Grit Guard Insert

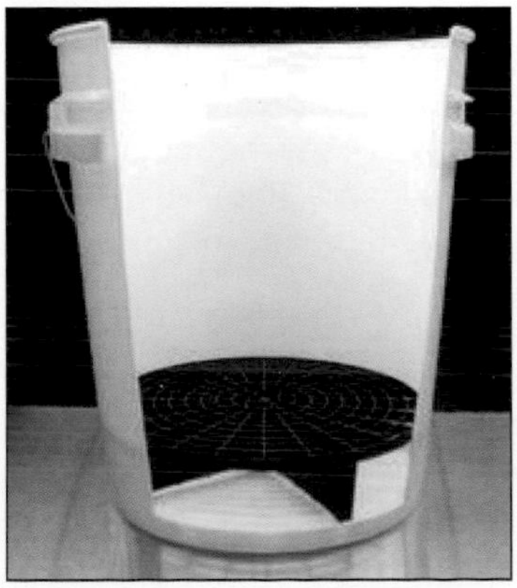

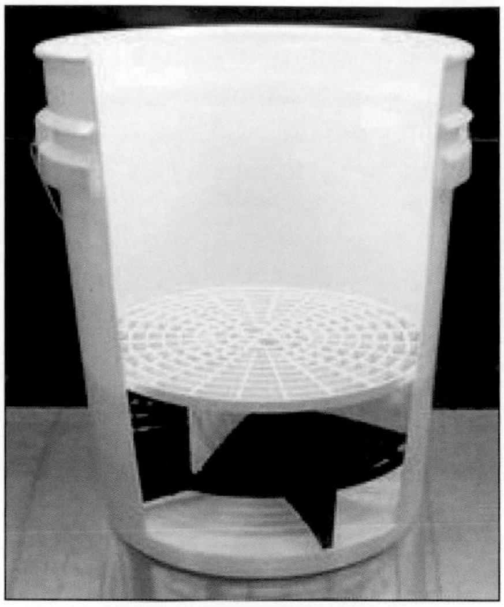

Dual Grit Guard Insert
- Twice the distance to keep removed dirt off your wash mitt.

My comment…
Once you use a Grit Guard Insert and see all the dirt it traps onto the bottom of the bucket, you'll never want to wash a car without one again.

Best Practice
Don't scrub your car's paint. By this I mean you only need to make a few passes over each square inch of a body panel. This will loosen the bond any dirt or road grime has on the paint, allowing it to freely rinse off.

People watching
If you watch the average person wash their car, you'll see they don't focus on the task at hand. This leads to rubbing their wash mitt back and forth, over and over again to the same area. There's no reason to do this. If there was dirt on the surface and you did effectively loosen it, rubbing your wash mitt back and forth over and over again just grinds the dirt into the paint. This needlessly instills swirls and scratches into the paint. Focus on the task at hand and only rub your wash mitt over each section for a few passes and then move on to new territory.

Tips & Techniques
For as long as I can remember, everyone that writes about how to wash a car says the same thing:

Start washing at the top and work your way down

I totally disagree.

Why? *Water spots!*

If you start at the top, wash and rinse all the body panels, you now have a wet car that needs to be dried off before the water dries and potentially leaves water spots on and even in the paint. In case you don't already know, water spots, especially Type II Water Spot Craters are one of the worst paint defects there is and also one of the more difficult types of paint defects to remove. Removing Type II Water Spots usually means compounding the paint and removing a measurable amount of the precious clear layer of paint that we already learned is thin to start with in Chapter 1 Car Paint Overview.

If you dry the body panels to prevent water spots on the paint and then wash the wheels and tires you can't help to get water spatter back onto the body panels while washing and rinsing the wheels and this means drying the body panels a second time. Guess what… I hate doing things twice!

Allow me to share my method…

Start at the bottom and then move to the top
Start at the wheels, tires and wheel wells, and after these are washed and rinsed, then start at the top and work your way down. When rinsing your wheels and tires, you can't avoid getting water splatter on the surrounding paint. If you still have to wash the body panels of your car, this won't matter. You don't have to repeat any steps and this will save you time as well as help you to avoid water spots on your car's paint.

The order in which you wash your car is relative
It doesn't matter if you start up high or down low – the goal is to get the car clean while avoiding water spots. The old-fashioned approach means moving incredibly fast to try to wash and rinse the wheels before water dries on the body panels or continually re-wetting the car to keep the panels wet so the water doesn't dry before you can chamois it off.

How to wash your car KISS style!
(KISS stands for Keep it Simple Simon)

Water Filtration Systems
Another way to avoid water spots is to first filter the water to remove any minerals or dissolved solids as well as corrosive substances that can spot or etch the paint.

Avoiding Type I and Type II Water Spots
The two most common questions I get are, *How do I remove water spots off paint?* and *How do I remove swirls and scratches out of paint?* The sad news is, both repairs typically mean using either a medium cut polish or an aggressive compound to level the paint in order to remove these types of defects. Of course, we already talked about the issue of how thin factory paint is to start with and there's not very much of the clear layer of paint to work with for these types of paint defects.

Water Filtration Systems remove both dissolved minerals and corrosive substances out of the water so that if the rinse water is not removed and instead dries on the paint, it won't leave any Type I or Type II water spots. (Type II Water Spots are the worst).

The CR Spotless Water Deionization System is one such water filter system that removes all the dissolved minerals and corrosive substances for the rinsing step which helps you to avoid water spots when washing your car.

Step-by-Step How-To Wash Your Car using the Traditional Car Wash

Work in this order, using the optional steps for decontaminating with Iron X. (You can skip the Iron X steps)

1. Wash and rinse wheels and tires
2. Optional: Decontaminate wheels using Iron X
3. Wash and rinse car body – Start at the top and work down
4. Decontaminate car body with Iron X
5. Dry the car body panels and glass
6. Dry wheels, and tires – Use dedicated wheel towels

Step 1. Wash & rinse wheels & tires

Personal Safety First: Wear appropriate safety gear, including safety glasses and protective gloves. Make sure the wheel is cool to the touch and work in the shade out of direct sunlight. Never spray water on hot wheels or brakes.

- **Step 1:** Spray wheels and tires first with a strong blast of water to remove any loose brake dust, dirt and road grime.

- **Step 2:** Spray wheel cleaner onto wheel. Follow the manufacturer's recommendations for dwell time to allow cleaner to penetrate and loosen brake dust, road grime and dirt.

Important: Wash one wheel and tire at a time
Only spray your wheel cleaner onto one wheel at a time. If a mistake is made by using the wrong type of wheel cleaner, you will only damage one wheel, thus preventing further damage to others.

Some people make the mistake of spraying all of their wheels at once. They figure this will make it easier and faster because while they're working on the first wheel, the wheel cleaner will be going to work loosening and dissolving brake dust and road grime on the other wheels and tires. The problem is if you have mistakenly purchased the wrong wheel cleaner and you spray all four wheels with it, by the time you realize the damage is being done, it's usually too late.

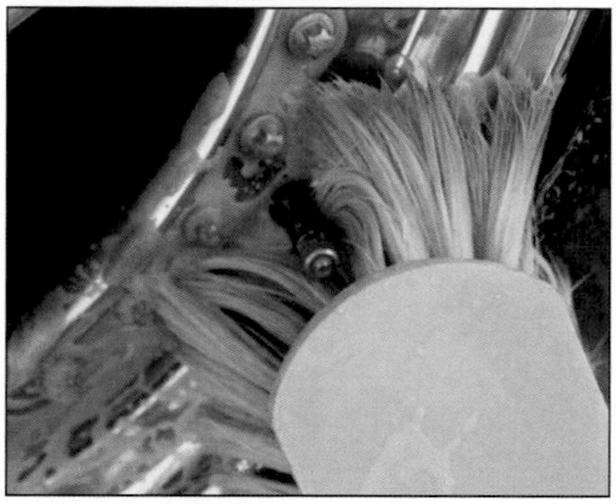

- **Step 3.** Agitate with a wheel brush that is safe and appropriate for the type of wheel. The 8 inch Montana Original Boar's Hair Wheel Brush is safe for all wheels and the bristles do a good job of getting into intricate areas to agitate wheel cleaners for perfectly clean wheels.

- Use a Daytona Speed Master Wheel Brush to clean behind the wheel, hard to reach areas and intricate wheel designs.

- Use a Lug Nut Brush to clean lug nuts and the barrel around the lug nuts.

- **Step 4:** Spray wheel with strong blast of water

- **Step 5:** Spray tire with tire cleaner *Follow the manufacturer's recommendations for dwell time to allow cleaner to penetrate and loosen road grime and dirt. Agitate tire with a tire brush with stiffer bristles for good cleaning.*

- **Step 6:** Spray tire with a strong blast of water and then re-spray both wheel and tire.

Repeat the process on the rest of the wheels and tires.

Step 2. (Optional) Decontaminate wheels using Iron X

BobbyG, a good friend and loyal Autogeek.net customer, provided this helpful tip when I posted my article about how to keep it simple when washing your car:

How To Wash Your Car KISS Style

Tip from BobbyG
A while back there was a discussion on the best way to use Iron X to clean wheels and there were three camps or opinions on the best practice.

***Camp 1** - Spray Iron X directly onto dry, dirty wheel.*

***Camp 2** - Wash wheel and tire, then rinse then spray Iron X onto clean, rinsed wheel.*

***Camp 3** - Wash wheel and tire, then rinse, then DRY off water and then spray on Iron X*

I was in Camp 2 because I believed that by removing the road grime, (an oily coating), and the brake dust first, you enable the Iron X to do its job more effectively to get the most bang for your buck. The people in Camp 1 thought the Iron X was too costly to allow to possibly drip off the wheel with the excess water after washing and rinsing first.

Camp 3
BobbyG's technique was a tweak to

my technique and that is to wash the wheel and tire first, thus removing the oily road grime and brake dust but then pat the wheel dry using a clean utility towel so there would be no excess water left on the wheel to flush the freshly sprayed-on Iron X off the wheel and onto the ground where its decontaminating ability is wasted.

Camp 3 for the win!
I agree with BobbyG and wanted to share his tip and give him credit for an incredibly easy tweak to my technique so you can get the best performance out of Iron X while getting the most bang for your Iron X bucks.

Using Iron X
First, pat the washed and rinsed wheels dry using a clean wheel towel.

Now spray the Iron X onto the wheel to remove any Iron Particles (if any).

The Red Bleeding Effect
Everyone wants to see the red bleeding effect from the Iron particles being dissolved and in the process turning the water red. Actually, seeing no red water bleeding off the wheel is a good sign because it means your wheels are not contaminated. If the wheels are contaminated and they have a clear layer of paint on them, this would mean

iron particles had embedded onto and into the clear layer of paint causing corrosion to some degree. Seeing no color means no corrosion and that's a good thing because it means a longer lasting finish on the wheel. It's important to make sure though by periodically using a decontamination

product like Iron X.
After allowing Iron X to dwell 2-3 minutes, either re-wash the wheel and tire with the appropriate brushes to remove the residue or blast with a strong spray of water and then repeat to the rest of the wheels.

Wheel Safety
Use a wheel cleaner that's safe for your type of wheels so you don't cause damage. In order to choose the right wheel cleaner, you need to know what your wheels are made out of or the material they coated with. If you don't know what your wheels are made out of or coated with, contact the manufacturer.

For more information see: Identifying Wheel Type

■ Step 3. Wash and Rinse Car Body – Start at the top and work down

Next, wet the entire car down to start softening loose dirt. Saturate areas on the car that show excessive dirt to soften and loosen the dirt before running a wash mitt, sponge or brush against the paint. Start at the top and work down. Wash the roof, and if the vehicle is not too large, wash the windows, A-pillars and B-pillars. After washing a panel, immediately rinse off soap suds.

My comments...
I also continually rinse the wheels and tires as I work around the car so that any lingering residues that pool in low areas due to gravity are rinsed off.

Note the labels on the buckets? It's a simple idea but helpful because as you work around the car. Even though one bucket is the soap solution and the other is rinse water, they both end up with suds floating on top. The labels make it easy to quickly identify which bucket holds your fresh wash solution and which bucket holds your rinse water.

Moving quickly:

- I wash all the upper horizontal surfaces and the side windows too and then rinse these sections. I

follow this with washing the lower horizontal surfaces which include the hood and trunk lid and then rinse these sections.

- Next I wash one side of the car, tackling the vertical sides of the fenders and doors and then rinse. After the sides, I hit the front grille and bumper, then rinse. After rinsing a panel, I re-wet previously washed and rinsed sections to keep them wet and to prevent water from drying, which will prevent water spots.

- Next I wash the vertical panels on the back including tail lights, license plate and rear bumper then rinse.

- Lastly, I wash the very lowest portions of the vertical panels nearest the ground and rinse.

■ Step 4. Remove excess standing water off body panels, glass & plastic

After rising the car completely off, gently pat most of the water off the panels. It's not important to remove all the water just the majority of water pooling on any horizontal surfaces. This is to ensure more of the Iron X spray stays on the surface working instead of dripping off, it also keeps the standing water from diluting the active ingredients in the Iron X.

■ Step 5: Decontaminate car body with Iron X

Next, decontaminate the body panels by spraying Iron X onto each of the body panels and allow it to dwell for 2-3 minutes but don't allow the product to dry on the surface.

■ Step 6: Re-wash and rinse body panels to remove Iron X residues

After allowing the product to dwell for a few minutes gently re-wash the body panels and glass and then rinse off all residue.

Water sheeting technique
After rinsing with a spray nozzle, you can use what's called the water sheeting technique to remove the majority of standing water from the car. Remove the spray nozzle from the end of the hose and use a slow flow of water to flood the surface. This allows all standing water to combine with the flowing water, causing to run off in a single sheet or collection of water.

■ Step 7: Dry the car body panels and glass

After the final rinse, I use Guzzler Microfiber Waffle Weave Drying Towels to dry the car.

Wiping or Blotting
To dry a panel, you can either wipe or blot it dry. If you're work on a daily driver or getting ready to buff out the paint, wiping is sufficient. If you're doing a maintenance wash on a car with a finish in excellent to show car condition, you might consider the blotting technique followed by a light wipe with a spray detailer afterwards.

Optional: Blow excess water off car

Metro MasterBlaster Sidekick
Another cool tool that I really like is the Metro Blaster Sidekick because it completely blows all standing water out of all the cracks and crevices so you don't have to deal with trapped water as you're doing the next steps.

Metro MasterBlaster
With 8 Horsepower, the MasterBlaster blows filtered, warm air at 58,500 feet per minute to remove water from your car's body panels and out of all the nooks and crannies. Filtered air means no blowing any dirt, dust or other particles onto your freshly washed paint. By heating the air before blowing, drying is faster and more complete. Drying your car by blowing filtered, heated high volume air reduces the potential for inflicting any toweling marks. This is definitely a must-have tool for anyone striving to maintain a show car finish.

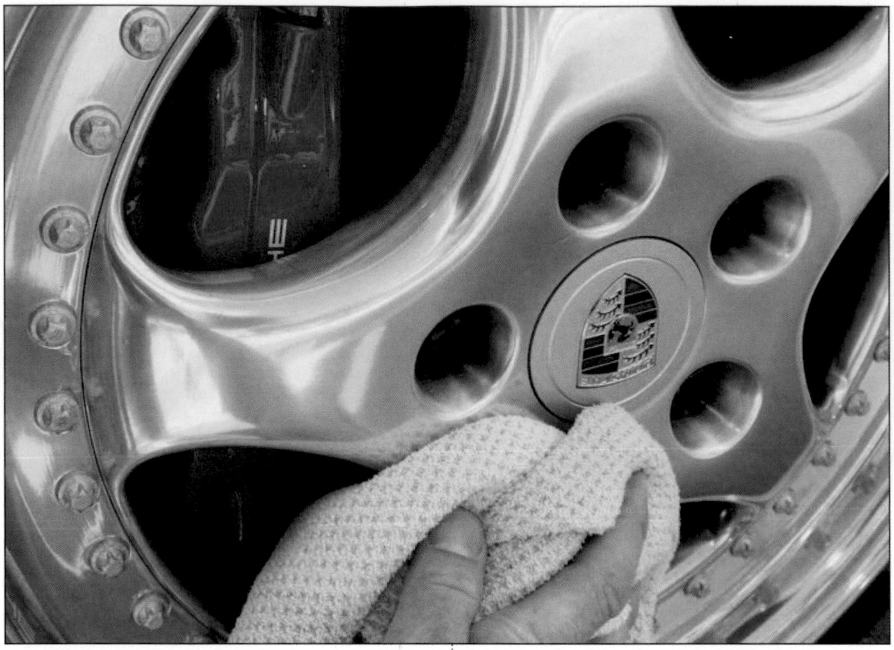

Dry Wheels and Tires – Use dedicated wheel towels
After drying the car body panels and glass, next dry the wheels and tires. For this you want to use drying towels that are dedicated just for use on wheels. The reason for this is that abrasive brake dust particles can become embedded into the towel and don't always wash out. You don't want to use wheel towels on body panels in the future. Mark dedicated wheel towels with a black sharpie marker. As an option you can get black microfiber towels. Many pro detailers use these just for wheels and tires and the black color is a visual identifier that the towels are only for use on wheels. http://www.autogeek.net/microfiber-wheel-towels.html

My comments…
After you have washed and dried the car, now is the time you want to inspect the paint both with your sense of touch and visually using bright overhead sunlight or with a Brinkmann Swirl Finder Light.

Car Wash Soap and Shampoos
In the best interest of your car, I recommend premium brand car shampoo. The days of using a dishwashing detergent to wash your car are long gone and detergent soaps are overkill for what you're trying to accomplish. Here are some features to look for in a premium quality car shampoo:

- **pH balanced** – pH is measured after the car wash soap is diluted with water, not as a concentrate in the bottle. After mixing your car wash solution, you want a pH neutral rating of 7. High levels of acidity or alkalinity can break the bond of some paint protection ingredients and remove them from the paint.

- **High lubricity** – You want a car wash solution that provides lubricity as this makes the surface slippery, allowing dirt and grime to glide off the surface instead of grinding into the paint causing swirls and scratches.

- **Long lasting suds** – Suds are bubbles at their core, which can help to cushion the contact between dirt and paint to reduce wash-induced scratching. Suds are also a visual indicator as to where you've already washed and also where you need to rinse in order to flush loosened dirt off the car.

- **Avoid detergents** – Avoid using detergent products like dish washing soaps, especially if you're working on any paint in excellent condition. While detergent washes work really well for cleaning and stripping your car's finish clean, they are overkill for the task at hand.

- **Exception** – If you're working on a car that has been neglected, some will argue that using a detergent wash won't hurt anything and will infact help to strip off any previously applied wax or paint sealant, thus preparing the paint for claying and correction work.

I would agree that any damage done by a detergent wash will be of little long term effect as long as you continue with the steps of claying, cleaning, polishing and sealing. If you choose to use a detergent soap for the initial, re-restoration wash, then after the finish is restored, switch back to only using non-detergent car wash shampoos.

Mike's Mixing Tip…
Always follow the manufacturer's directions for diluting car wash concentrate with water. The manufacturer knows their product best and has done their homework before writing any directions for correct dilution levels of car wash soap to water.

Mike's Method…
I always use a 5-gallon bucket filled with about 4 gallons of water. I add the water first, measure and pour in the car wash and then mix thoroughly with my hand or a long handle brush. This method creates a thoroughly mixed solution of car wash soap and water. After you mix the soap and water together, you can blast the solution with a strong spray of water to create mountains of suds.

■ The Caveman Method of Mixing Your Car Wash

The caveman method is to add your car wash soap to the bucket and then add the water. The problem with this method is that the blast of water hitting the concentrated car wash soap creates a bucket filled and overflowing with suds, but hardly any water. This wastes product and time and you don't have any soapy water solution to dip your wash mitt into.

Links: Car Washes and Shampoos

- Wolfgang Auto Bathe
- Pinnacle Bodywork Shampoo
- Pinnacle XMT Gel Shampoo & Conditioner
- Detailer's Pro Series Xtreme Foam Formula Auto Shampoo
- Prima Mistique Car Wash
- Prima Hydro Wash Shampoo
- Sonax Gloss Shampoo Concentrate
- Dodo Juice Sour Power Gloss Enhancing Shampoo
- Dodo Juice Basics of Bling Wax- Safe Shampoo
- Dodo Juice Supernatural Shampoo
- Sonus Gloss Shampoo
- P21S Bodywork Conditioning Shampoo
- Poorboy's World Super Slick & Suds Concentrated Car Wash
- Poorboy's Super Slick & Wax Car Shampoo
- Griot's Garage Car Wash
- Four Star Auto Wash Shampoo
- Mothers California Gold Car Wash
- Meguiar's Ultimate Wash & Wax
- Meguiar's Shampoo Plus
- Meguiar's #62 Carwash Shampoo & Conditioner
- Meguiar's Gold Class Shampoo & Conditioner
- Meguiar's NXT Car Wash
- Wurth Car Shampoo
- 1Z Einszett Perls Shampoo Premium Car Wash
- Optimum Car Wash
- Ultima Paint Guard Wash

■ 6 Reasons To Use A Waterless Wash, A Rinseless Wash Or A Spray Detailer

Now that we've walked through how to use a traditional car wash, let's take a look at some of your other options.

In a perfect world, everyone would have access to free flowing water, warm temperatures, and no restrictions on when and where they can wash their car. However, we don't live in a perfect world, so here are 6 reasons to use an alternative car wash method:

1. Areas with government enforced water restriction
There are many cities and even entire countries with government enforced water restriction. In these places, it's against the law and/or regulations to wash your car with a free flowing source of water.

2. Geographical areas of drought
In some places, there may be no official restrictions against water use, but the geographical area itself is experiencing severe drought. This prevents people from using a free flowing source of water to wash their vehicle.

3. People who live in apartments
If you live in a an apartment, a condo or a townhouse, there may be no place to wash your car with a free flowing source of clean water or there may be rules against it that you agreed to comply with.

4. Washing in cold winter months
In cold weather, extreme low temperatures can make washing a car with a free flowing source of water dangerous and difficult at best.

5. Mobile detailers
Rinseless washing enables mobile detailers to wash cars without having to depend upon a water source or the extra hassle of transporting hundreds of gallons of water. Besides that, some areas require mobile detailer to contain and capture their run-off water. This is an added expense and can be difficult and time consuming.

6. Anytime you're traveling
If you are doing any long distance traveling, you may not have access to a free flowing source of water. Using a waterless wash, rinseless wash or spray detailer enables you to get your car clean.

■ How To Use A Waterless Wash

Tools needed

- Waterless wash
- Wash mitts, sponge or microfiber towel for washing
- Microfiber towels for drying

Tips & Techniques
If you plan on using the Waterless Wash approach, here are two tips to help you:

1. Wash often
Clean your car often. Removing light amounts of accumulated dirt and road grime is much faster, easier and safer than putting the job off until the car is visibly dirty.

2. Maintain a good coat of wax, paint sealant or use a paint coating
Dirt and road grime will wipe off faster and easier if you wax your car often, because a coating of wax helps prevent dirt from forming a strong bond onto the paint.

Mike's Method – Step By Step How To Use A Waterless Wash
My method of using a waterless wash is pretty simple. Use a lot of product and only tackle a small section at a time. Use

premium quality microfiber towels with a fluffy nap, not a flat weave, so any dirt on the surface can bury into the fluffy nap.

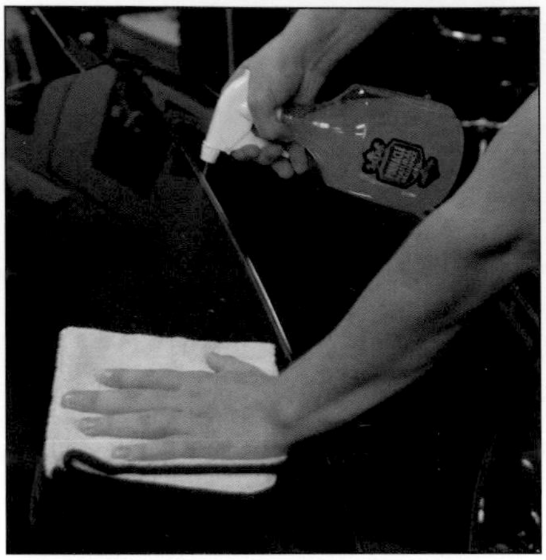

■ How-To Step By Step

1. Start at the top and work your way down
With a traditional car wash I recommend starting with the wheels and tires but when your water source is limited then you tackle wheels and tires last.

2. Set you spray nozzle for a wide fan spray and saturate an area of about 18" by 18". If your car is only lightly dirty, spray down a larger section of about 24" by 24", or even an entire panel as long as you have the ability to remove the product before it dries. The goal is to keep your work area manageable. The dirtier the car, the smaller the section you should wipe clean and the more microfiber towels you should use.

My Favorite Tool

The Double Action Kwazar Mercury Pro+ 1 Liter Spray Bottle
The Kwazar spray bottle sprays product both when you pull the squeeze lever AND when you release it. This double-action sprayer lays a lot of product down faster and with half the energy required by a normal spray head. Since the goal is to lay down plenty of waterless wash, the Kwazar spray bottle is the perfect choice. You can get these bottles in both 17 and 33 ounce sizes – for waterless washes, I prefer the 33 ounce bottle.

Have plenty of microfiber towels
A large collection of clean, premium quality microfiber towels is ideal when using a waterless wash.

Work clean
Because it's important to use a clean microfiber towel, dedicate a clean, accessible area on which to place your clean towels during the process. It doesn't do any good to maintain a collection of clean microfiber towels if you set them down on a dirty surface.

Use good wiping techniques
After wiping one or two sections, re-fold your microfiber towel to a clean, dry side. After using all 8 sides of your microfiber towel, switch to a clean, dry microfiber towel.

Links: Waterless Car Washes
- Detailer's Pro Series Waterless Auto Wash
- Detailer's Pro Series Waterless Auto Wash Concentrate
- Eco Touch Waterless Car Wash Ready To Use
- Poorboy's World Spray & Wipe Waterless Wash
- Griot's Garage Waterless Spray-On Car Wash
- Ultima Waterless Wash Plus+
- Ultima Waterless Wash Plus+ Concentrate
- Optimum No Rinse Wash & Shine
- Pinnacle Liquid Crystal Waterless Wash with Carnauba
- Pinnacle Liquid Crystal Waterless Wash with Carnauba Concentrate
- Blackfire Wet Diamond Waterless Wash
- Blackfire Wet Diamond Waterless Wash Concentrate
- Meguiar's Ultimate Wash & Wax Anywhere

■ How To Use A Rinseless Wash

Measuring your rinseless wash concentrate
Most rinseless car washes on the market are mixed at 1 ounce per 2 gallons of water.

Fast, easy way to measure 2 gallons of water
If you have a 5-gallon bucket like the ones that come with Autogeek's car wash bucket kits, here's a fast, simple way to measure two gallons of water.

Take any standard 12 inch ruler and fill the bucket until the water level reaches the 6 inch mark on the rule. This will be approximately two gallons of water. If you plan on using a rinseless car wash often, you can even use a permanent marker to mark the inside of the bucket for fast reference when adding water.

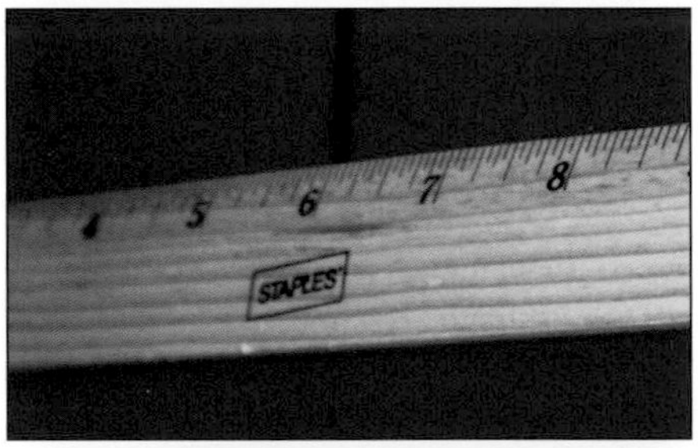

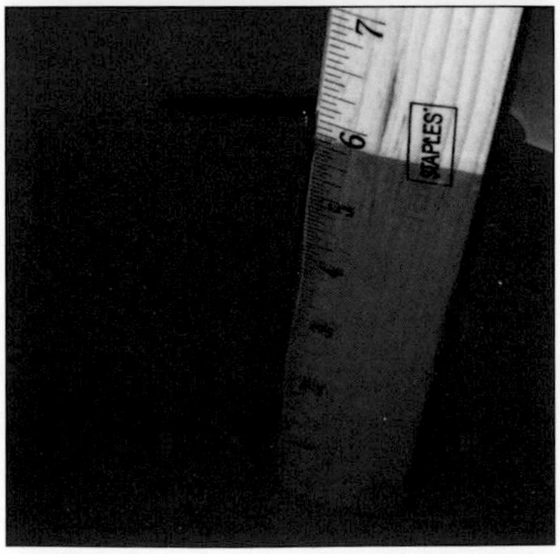

KISS – Keep It Simple Simon
Little techniques like this save time by making frequent procedures easy to repeat over and over again without having to measure or think about them.

Using a Grit Guard Insert In The Rinseless Wash Bucket
If you want to use Grit Guard Insert with either the one or two bucket method, add an extra gallon of water and an extra 1/2 to 1 ounce of rinseless wash concentrate to make up for the portion of water covered and protected by the Grit Guard Insert.

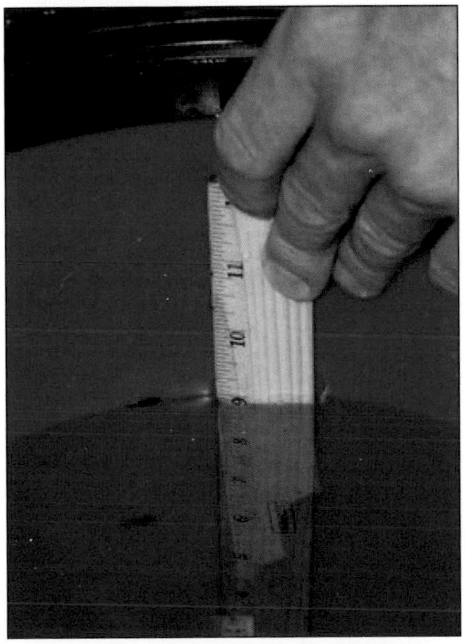

To measure an extra gallon of water when using a Grit Guard Insert, measure from the bottom of the bucket to about the 9" mark and then add water until it reaches this mark.

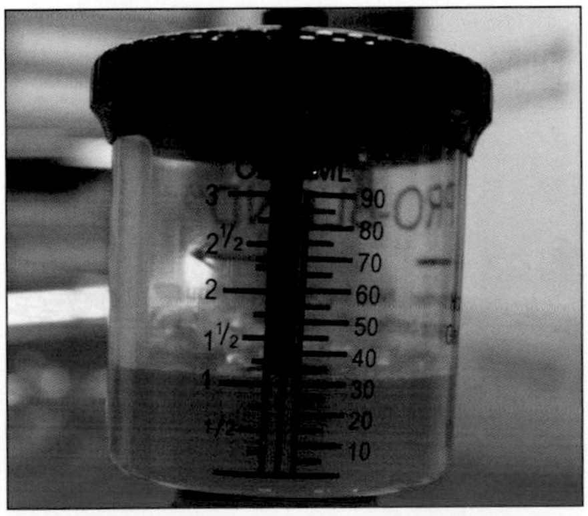

This will give you approximately 3 gallons of water with the protection of the Grit Guard Insert, so you'll want to add an extra 1 1/2 to 2 ounces of rinseless wash concentrate.

For more information on rinseless wash, check out these two articles:

- How to use a Pro Blend Bottle Proportioner
- How dirty is too dirty to safely use a rinseless wash

■ Step-by-Step How To Wash Your Car With A Rinseless Wash

Start at the top and work your way down
If you start washing the lower panels and move towards the roof, when you wash the roof, you'll likely have cleaning solution running down and re-wetting a dry panel. This means that you will have to dry the panel again or possibly wash and dry the panel a second time.

Wash one panel or section at a time
If you try to wash too large of an area before drying, the cleaning solution can dry onto the panel.

There are two factors that determine how large of a panel or section of a panel you tackle at one time:

- **Size of the panel**
  If you have a small panel to wash, such as the hood of a Mini Cooper, then it's small enough that you can wash the entire panel and dry it before the cleaning solution can dry. If, however, you're washing a vehicle with a large hood or other large panels, then you might find it easier to break it up into separate sections and wash and dry one section at a time.

  The goal is to wet the panel, loosen any dirt or road grime and then wipe or blot the panel or section dry. Again, if a panel is too large, you could risk having your cleaning solution dry before you have a chance to wipe or blot the panel or section of panel dry.

- **Temperature and air flow**
  On warm or hot days, or in areas where there's a strong wind, these two factors can cause your cleaning solution to dry faster than in lower temperatures or in a no-wind environment. Take this into consideration when deciding how large of a panel or section of a panel to tackle at one time.

Dividing your car into sections
When washing with a rinseless car wash I start at the top, but add a twist which goes like this:

- **Roof**
- **Side glass** –one side of the car at a time.
- **Horizontal panels** – The hood and trunk lid.
- **Vertical panels, upper portions only** – The upper portions tend to be cleaner than the lower portions.
- **Front bumpers and grilles**
- **Rear bumpers and rear vertical panels** – Found on SUV's and some passenger cars (for example, the tailgates on trucks). Keep in mind that air currents swirl around the rear of cars, trucks and SUVs as you're driving at highway speeds, sometimes depositing an oily road film onto these rear, vertical panels.
- **Vertical panels, lower portions** – Lower portions of the vertical panels are washed last, as these are the dirtiest section of the car.
- **Lastly, the wheels and tires** – For the wheels and tires you may choose to use a brush instead of a wash mitt. Admittedly, washing the wheels, tires and grilles is harder to do without a brush and source of free flowing water, so improvise and do the best you can.

For drying off wheels and tires see:
- The 4 minimum categories of wiping towels

Use a gentle touch
When using a rinseless car wash, the idea is to carefully move your wash mitt over the surface only enough to loosen the grip any dirt or road grime has on the paint and then STOP. It's pretty common to see people washing their cars without thinking about what they're doing. They push their wash mitt over the same section of paint for dozens of strokes. In reality, one or two passes would have been sufficient. Focus on the task at hand and only make as many gentle passes as you

deem necessary to loosen and dirt or road grime.

1. **Place wash mitt into your rinse water bucket**

2. **First things first - dry the paint**
   The first thing you want to do after washing a panel or section is to wipe or blot it dry.

3. **Rinse your wash mitt and re-gather fresh cleaning solution**
   After you wipe the panel dry and you're ready to wash another panel, that's when you'll clean your wash mitt or sponge by scrubbing it against the Grit Guard insert (this acts to extract dirt particles from your mitt or sponge) and then wring out the excess water before gathering fresh cleaning solution.

4. **Repeat the above process as you work your way around the car.**

■ How-To Use A Rinseless Wash To Clean Wheels And Tires

Wheels and tires tend to be dirtier than the body panels on your car and this is why you want to wash them last. Brake dust can contain small metal particles that can instill swirls and scratches, so always wash the wheels and tires last when using a rinseless wash.

1. Dip a wheel brush, microfiber towel or wash mitt into your remaining solution of rinseless wash and use this to clean your wheels and tires. Wash one wheel and tire at a time. Immediately after washing, wipe dry using microfiber or terry cloth towels that you have dedicated specifically for wheels and tires.

2. When washing wheels and tires using a rinseless wash, instead of using your high quality wash mitts and/or sponges that you use for paintwork, consider using ones that are dedicated for wheels and tires.

Links: Waterless Car Washes

- Detailer's Rinseless Wash & Gloss
- Optimum No Rinse Wash & Shine
- Pinnacle Liquid gloss Rinseless Wash

  with Carnauba
- Blackfire Wet Diamond Rinseless Wash
- Meguiar's Rinse Free Express Wash
- Duragloss Rinseless Wash with Aquawax

■ How To Use A Spray Detailer To Wash Your Car

The primary difference between using a spray detailer to maintain a finish or to wash a car is the amount of spray detailer you use.

Use product heavy or wet
In the detailing world, if someone recommends using a product heavy or wet that means use lots of the product. So if you're in a situation where the best option to clean your car is to use a spray detailer, use the product heavy or wet and have plenty of clean, microfiber towels on hand. As you're wiping sections of the car down, the dirt will be accumulating on the microfiber towel. To prevent scratching you want to be continually switching to a fresh, clean towel.

For more information see:
- How to use a spray detailer to maintain your car

■ Identifying Wheel Type

Before you can choose the right wheel cleaner to safely clean your wheels, you first need to determine what your car's wheels are either made out of or coated with.

Wheels come in 5 general categories

- Factory Painted
- Uncoated Metal
- Combination Coated and Uncoated
- Chrome
- Anodized

Factory Painted Wheels
Coated wheels have a layer of paint, but it's not the same as car paint. It is usually a much harder and corrosion resistant type of paint. Many new cars come with factory painted wheels.

- **How to check**
  If your car has painted wheels, chances are they have a clearcoat finish, although it's possible they could have a pigmented finish. To test, rub a light paint cleaner onto a small section of the wheel using a soft piece of cloth, like a piece of t-shirt, and then turn the applicator over. If your wheel is clearcoated, you shouldn't see any color change on the t-shirt. If the wheel is painted with a pigmented paint, you'll see the color of the wheel coming off and onto the cloth.

Machined aluminum wheels with a clearcoat finish can be deceiving as they can look like uncoated, polished aluminum wheels when in fact there is a clear layer of paint over the metal surface.

Uncoated metal wheels
Uncoated usually means aluminum or magnesium wheels. This means the exterior surface is bare metal and as such will oxidize and stain over time.

- **How to check**
  You can check to see if your wheel is uncoated aluminum or magnesium by rubbing a little metal polish onto the wheel with a white cloth like a piece of t-shirt. If it's uncoated aluminum or magnesium, your cloth will turn a dark grayish black color.

Magnesium wheel
Uncoated, magnesium tends to turn a dark gray if not constantly maintained or if an acid wheel cleaner is used on it.

Combination of coated and uncoated
Some modular or component wheels can be assembled using separate pieces to form the complete wheel, often for decorative purposes. Not all portions of the wheel have the same type of finish.

- **How to check**
  Because there are so many wheel companies and such a great variety of wheel types and fashions, if you have a modular wheel there are two things you can do.

1. **Safe approach**
   Use a wheel cleaner that's safe for uncoated polished aluminum. **Why?** Because uncoated polished aluminum is probably the most susceptible to dulling or staining by strong cleaning agents. Wheel cleaners formulated for uncoated aluminum are very safe and therefore generally safe for any type of wheel.

2. **Manufacturer's recommended approach**
   Contact the manufacturer of your brand of wheel and get their specific instructions for how to wash and maintain their wheels and their official recommendations for wheel cleaners.

Chrome wheels
The good news about chrome wheels is that when kept clean from dirt build-up, chrome coatings are incredibly corrosion resistant. It's only when dirt, road grime and brake dust are allowed to build up on the chrome coating, attracting and holding moisture over time, that the chrome will deteriorate. In extreme cases, the layer of chrome will peel and flake off the wheel. Since chrome is corrosion resistant, you can use strong wheel cleaners including wheel cleaners that use acid to dissolve and remove brake dust.

- **How to check**
  Real chrome has a mirror-like, reflective shine and is fairly easy to identify just by close examination. Rubbing a clearcoat safe paint cleaner should show no black or dark gray color on your cloth like you see when removing oxidation from uncoated aluminum wheels. Chrome is an electroplated layer of the element chromium; it is, in simple terms, grown onto the underlying metal substrate through an electroplating process. Because it is a type of metal, if you tap lightly on it with something metal, you will hear the sound of metal against metal.

Anodized Wheels
A process called anodizing is used by some wheel manufacturers to create a corrosion and oxidation resistant finish on aluminum wheels. Anodizing is not a coating "on" the aluminum; it is a process in which the surface is changed through an electrochemical process by which aluminum is converted into aluminum oxide. The aluminum oxide finish increases corrosion and wear resistance and can be tinted with dyes to a variety of colors. If you use the wrong wheel cleaner on anodized aluminum, it's possible to dull or stain the finish. The only way to undo the damage is to de-anodize the component, remove the stained portion of aluminum, and then re-anodize. The time, labor and expense is usually costlier than simply replacing with a new wheel.

- **How to check**
  In the early days of anodizing, you could usually see that the original aluminum finish was not a polished, but rather a brushed or matte finish. As anodizing technology has been improved, appearance quality has been increased to provide better gloss and shine in finished parts. Typically, the component will not impart color when rubbed on with some type of paint or metal polish. To be safe, check with the manufacturer of the wheel or check with a local custom wheel store as they should be able to determine if your wheel is anodized or not.

Wheel Cleaners

- Pinnacle Clearcoat Safe Wheel Cleaner
- Wolfgang Ubër Wheel Cleaner – Removes Iron Particles
- Wolfgang Tire & Wheel Cleaner
- Sonax Full Effect Wheel Cleaner – Removes Iron Particles
- P21S Wheel Cleaner
- Griot's Chrome Wheel Cleaner
- Mothers Foaming All Wheel & Tire Cleaner
- Mothers Polished Aluminum Wheel Cleaner
- Mothers Wheel Mist Chrome/Wire Pro Strength Cleaner
- Meguiar's Hot Rims Aluminum Wheel Cleaner
- Meguiar's Hot Rims All Wheel & Tire Cleaner
- Meguiar's D140 Wheel Brightener
- Detailer's Wheel Cleaner
- Griot's Garage Wheel Cleaner
- Griot's Garage Heavy Duty Wheel Cleaner
- Duragloss All Wheel Cleaner
- Dodo Juice Mellow Yellow Wheel Cleaner
- Dodo Juice Supernatural Wheel Cleaner
- Four Star Ultimate Wheel Cleaner Gel
- Poorboy's World Spray and Rinse Wheel Cleaner
- 1Z Einszett Wheel Cleaner
- S100 Wheel Cleaner
- 3M Tire and Wheel Cleaner
- Amazing Roll Off

Big picture

If you don't know what the wheels on your car are made from or coated with, before purchasing a wheel cleaner, contact the wheel manufacturer, the wheel store where you purchased your wheels, or the dealership where you purchased your car and find out to avoid making a costly mistake.

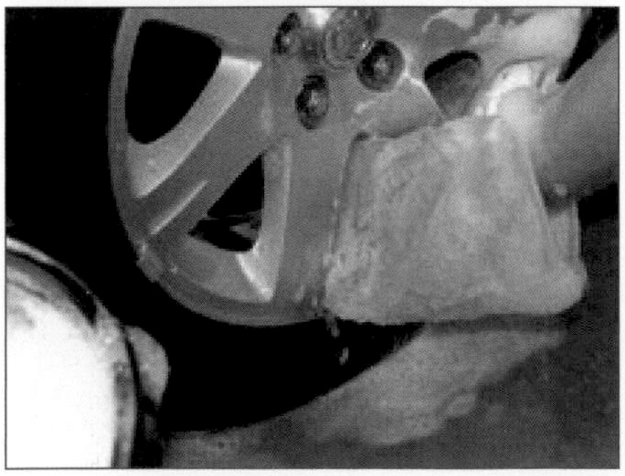

Car Wash Tools

- Foam Guns
- Foam Cannons
- Wash mitts
- Wash sponges
- Wash brushes
- Chamois and drying towels
- Buckets, dollies and car wash systems
- Grit Guard inserts
- Spray nozzles
- Brass quick connectors
- Air Blowers

My comment…
Quality tools help you to work more efficiently. In this chapter, you'll find tools I use and recommend.

There are two things to know about wash mitts, sponges and brushes:

1. **Use the best quality wash mitts, sponges and brushes you can obtain**
   Always use premium quality products that are soft and gentle to the paint, whether you choose a mitt, sponge, or brush. To judge the softness and gentleness of any tool, first let it soak in your wash solution for 10 to 20 minutes. Water has a softening effect and this must be taken into account. For example, a boar's hair brush should be allowed to soak for 20 to 30 minutes to allow water to soften the individual hairs. A natural sea sponge feels softer and is more gentle after it soaks in water; this is totally different than how it feels when it's right out of the package and still dry.

2. **Periodically switch to new wash mitts, sponges and brushes**
   Anytime your wash mitt, sponge, or brush appears worn, delegate it to work that doesn't include washing the major body panels. It's better to substitute a brand new wash mitt, sponge, or brush for carefully washing delicate, scratch-sensitive clearcoat paint than it is to try to squeeze every last use from your current wash mitt.

What's your time worth?
Simply think about how much time it takes to do a complete detail job to your car's finish. This includes washing, claying, removing swirls and scratches, polishing and sealing with wax or a paint sealant. I think you'll agree with me that the time and energy required to do the job right far outweigh the cost of a new wash mitt.

Wash Mitts, Sponges & Brushes

There are so many high quality options now available to carefully and safely wash your car that it would take up too much space to list them all here.

All the washing tools at Autogeek.net are top quality and best-in-class for their respective categories. They all work exceptionally well and when it comes to which one is best, that really comes down to personal preference. The best way to find out which one is best is to test out a few different types until you find the one that's best for you and for your car's unique shape and size.

Autogeek has a page dedicated specifically for all the available options, simply type the keywords into the Search AutoGeek box and check out the washing tools that interest you most.

- Wash Mitts, Sponges, Brushes & Tools

Below I'll try to share some of the more popular and unique car washing tools available…

Autogeek's Sheepskin Wash Mitt
Offers a one and a half inch thick pile made from the best all natural wool imported from Australia. This wash mitt provides a separate place for your fingers and thumb to help you wash the car and mold the wash mitt around

the various components on the car like contoured edges, rear view mirrors, spoilers, grilles, antennas.

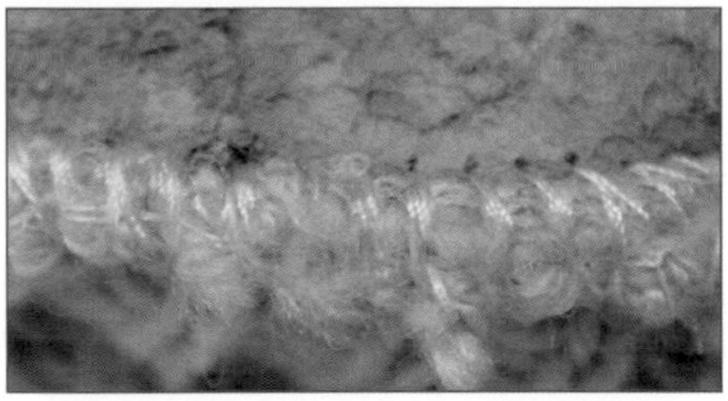

The real deal
This is a shot (shown above) of the inside of the mitt to show that this is real lambswool. This is how you can tell a fake or synthetic wash mitt from the real deal. Avoid fake or synthetic sheepskin wash mitts as the fibers quickly matte together and will scratch your car's paint.

Autogeek's Sheepskin Wash Mitt

My comments…
I really like real lambswool, also called sheepskin, wash mitts as long as they are in brand new condition. Once they become tatty stop using them and replace with a new one. When ordering online, order two at a time and when you switch to the second mitt you have time to re-order and you're never without a high quality mitt.

CarPro Wool Wash Mitt
This mitt is made from 100% Merino wool, which is a premium wool prized for its softness and length. This mitt has a mesh pocket on the back to slide over your hand while washing your car.

CarPro Wool Wash Mitt

CarPro 2Fingers Mini Wool Wash Mitt
This is a miniature version of the full-size CarPro Wool Wash Mitt specifically for washing hard to reach areas like under door handles, under wings and spoilers, under and around luggage and ski racks, and around rear view mirrors.

CarPro 2Fingers Mini Wool Wash Mitt

Dodo Juice Supernatural Wash Mitt "Wookie's Fist"
This is called the Wookie's Fist and it's probably the largest, fluffiest, furriest wool wash mitt you've ever seen. The wool used to make this wash mitt comes from the Merino sheep which is regarded as one of the finest, softest wools available from any sheep. Because of its large size, it is capable of holding lots of soapy water.

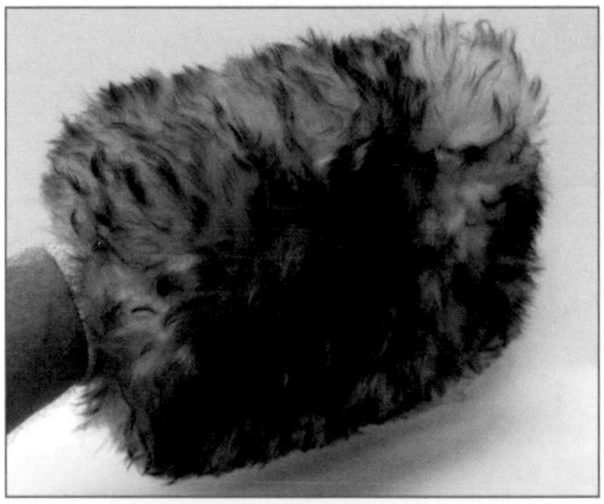

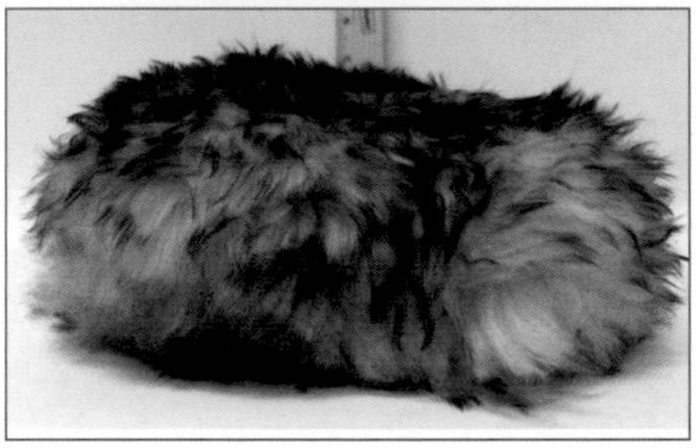

This is a very luxurious natural lambswool wash mitt made by Dodo Juice. Due to its long fiber strands, the manufacturer actually recommends you brush it with a pet brush to restore the fluffiness after it's dried. From my personal experience, this is an accurate recommendation.

Dodo Juice Supernatural Wash Mitt "Wookie's Fist"

My Comment…
I really like the long plush fibers of both the CarPro and Dodo Juice lambswool wash mitts. One thing I need to point out, however, is that if you plan on using one of these mitts, then do yourself a huge favor and get a Cat Brush at your local Pet Store to brush the fibers out after the mitts dry to separate the fibers and prevent them from matting together. It's normal for the long fibers for these styles of wash mitts to mat together. It's your job to brush them out before use.

Microfiber-Chenille Wash Mitt
This wash mitt always catches everyone's eye because it looks so strange. The word chenille is actually a French word meaning caterpillar, only these caterpillar-looking things are actually thin microfibers woven into plump caterpillar-like strands that are both absorbent and non-abrasive. This design gently removes dirt and road grime off clearcoat finishes and then releases any collected dirt easily when rubbed against the Grit Guard insert.

Microfiber-Chenille Wash Mitt - 3 pack

Foam Guns & Foam Cannons

Foam Guns and Foam Cannons lay down a thick layer of foam that clings and dwells on the surface of your car enabling the cleaning

agents in the car wash soap to go to work softening and loosening dirt to make washing faster and safer.

Marketing Yourself
If you detail cars as a business, the appearance of a car completely covered in foam creates a powerful image to your customers showing them you REALLY get their cars clean!

Foam Gun - Garden Hose

Autogeek Foam Guns are for attaching to garden hoses and work best with strong pressure from either city water or well water. Here's a Foam Gun being used at one of my recent Detailing Boot Camp Classes by Tyler, age 15.

Foam Cannon - Pressure Washer

Autogeek Foam Cannons are for use with gas or electric pressure washers and are available with your choice of fittings for your specific brand of pressure washer. This is me demonstrating a Foam Cannon at a recent Detailing Boot Camp Class.

Tornador Air Foamer – Air Compressor

The Autogeek Tornador Air Foamer HP turns your favorite car shampoo, or wheel and tire cleaner into super thick, long-lasting foam. This air-driven foam gun works with your air compressor to produce frothy, rich foam that has amazing cling. The Autogeek Tornador Air Foamer HP foam gun can be used for interior or exterior detailing. Use it with a carpet cleaner or with auto shampoo to spray a snow storm of foam!

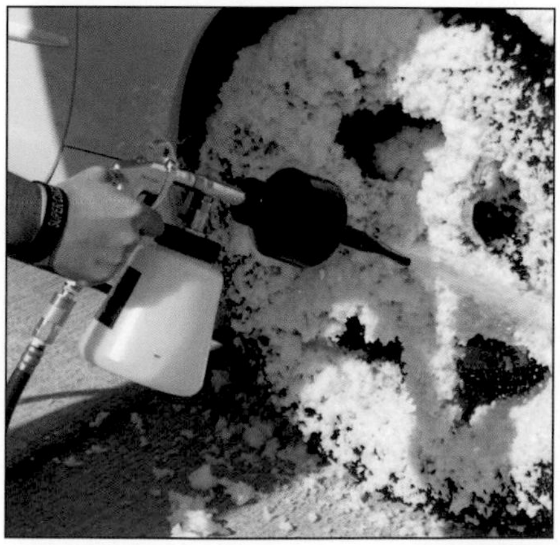

■ Buckets, Bucket Dollies & Grit Guard Inserts

Buckets
You really need a 5-gallon bucket no matter which method of washing you choose to use, and at Autogeek you can choose the color you like best and rest assured that Grit Guard Inserts fit in all the buckets we sell.

🖳 Buckets, Dollies and Car Wash Systems

To make washing your car easier, you can use dollies with wheels, allowing you to roll your bucket(s) as you work around the car. This prevents you from walking back and forth to the wash bucket and also dripping your wash solution all over the ground instead of using it to wash the body panels.

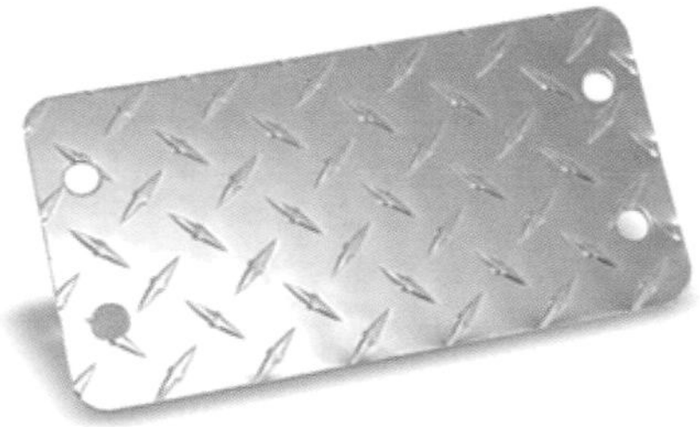

Diamond Plate Dolly Connector = Ultimate Two Bucket Wash System
Connects two Grit Guard Single Bucket Dollies together to form a two bucket dolly system.

🖳 Diamond Plate Dolly Connector

Grit Guard Inserts
The Grit Guard Insert is a plastic insert that fits into the bottom of a 5-gallon bucket that will trap the dirt that comes off your wash mitt on the bottom of the bucket. The design includes a plastic grille that dirt and other abrasive particles can fall past to rest at the bottom of the bucket. The grille is suspended off the bottom of the bucket by 4 vanes which also prevent the water at the bottom from swirling around, which prevents the trapped dirt from rising above the grille.

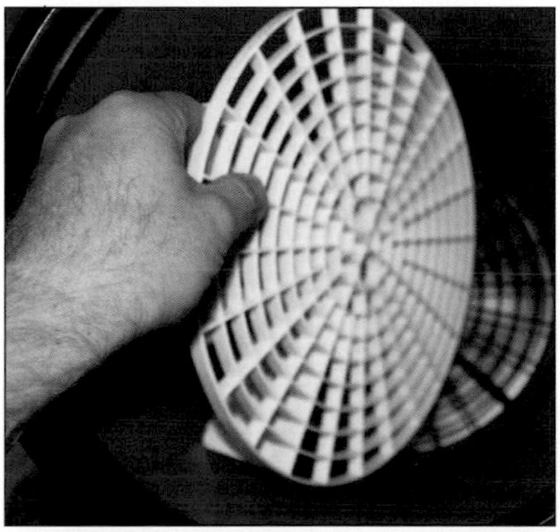

Once you use a Grit Guard Insert and see all the dirt it traps onto the bottom of the bucket, you'll never want to wash a car without one again. They fit into all the Autogeek 5-gallon buckets and most other conventional 5-gallon buckets.

🖳 Grit Guard Inserts

■ Spray Nozzles & Connectivity Tools

Connectors enable you to switch between tools quickly and easily. Shut-off valves enable you to turn the water off at the end of the hose instead of walking back to the spigot. This can be a huge time saver.

🖳 Fire Hose Nozzle

🖳 Industrial High Flow Fireman's Nozzle

🖳 Solid Brass Water Jet Nozzle

🖳 Brass Hose Connectors & Shut-Off Valves

Brushes

- Daytona Speed Master Wheel Brush
- Daytona Speed Master Wheel Brush Jr.

In my opinion, both of these brushes are indispensable if you really want to get your wheels clean and make the process easy at the same time. You can bend them to custom fit your wheel design to clean all the hard to reach areas quickly and efficiently.

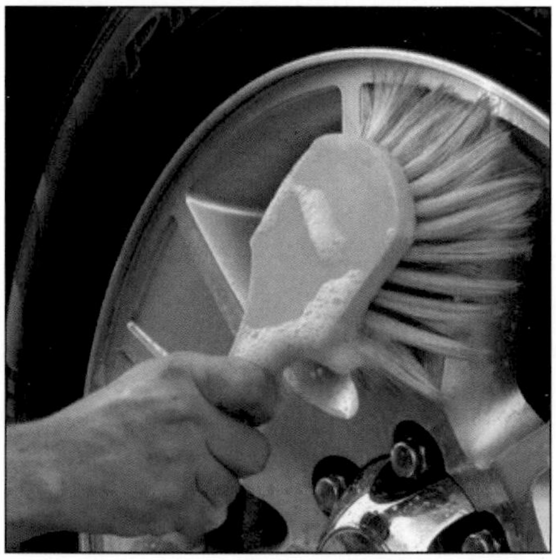

- 8" Montana Boar's Hair Wheel Brush

I really like this for safely cleaning the face of expensive scratch-sensitive wheels.

- Carrand Lug Nut Brush

This makes cleaning your lug nuts and

the barrel easy.

- Mothers Fender Well Brush

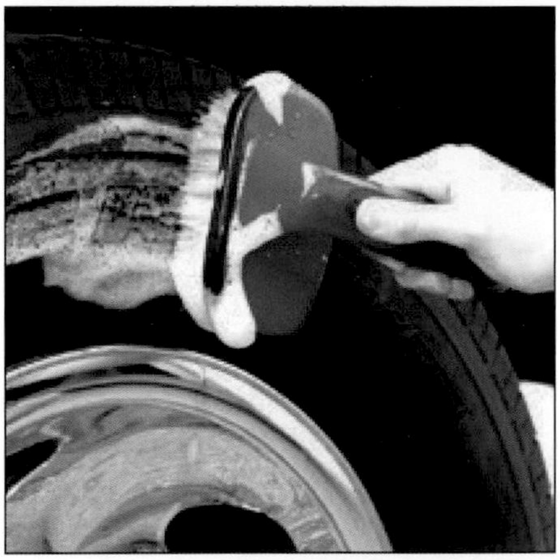

- Mothers Contoured Tire Brush

- Wheel Woolies 3-Piece Kit

The longest Large Wheel Woolie is 19 inches long and has a 3 inch diameter wool head. Use this long handled Wheel Woolie to reach deep into the wheels or clean the wheel wells of any vehicle, from cars to RVs. The Medium Wheel Woolie is over 12 inches long

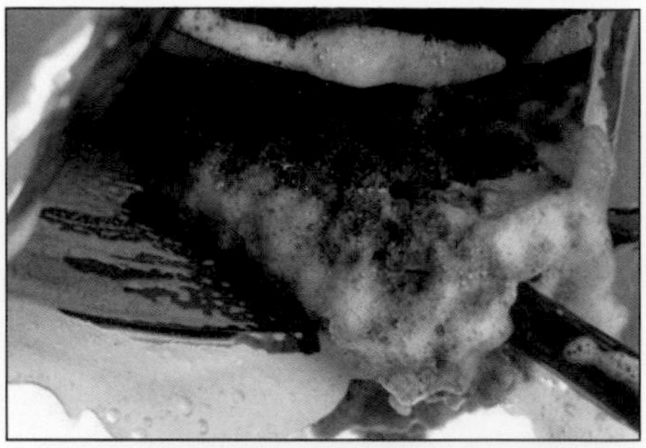

with a 2 inch diameter wool head. This one is ideal for smaller wheel gaps, air diffusers, door jams, engine areas, etc. Use the Small Wheel Woolie for small gaps, like grilles, and narrow spoke wheels. It is 8 inches long and 1 inch in diameter.

Microfiber Drying Towels and Chamois

Drying the paint without scratching is the goal and you can do this as long as you're using drying towels and chamois that are soft and gentle.

Blotting Method

Tip: Instead of wiping water off, try blotting. By blotting off the water, you will not be physically rubbing the towel or chamois against the paint. This is also known as the least evasive method of drying a car.

There are all kinds of high quality drying chamois and microfiber towels available. Like choosing a wash mitt, sometimes you need to test a product out in person to find the perfect match for your preferences. Below is a selection from the Autogeek store. To see everything that's available, click the link below.

- All Microfiber Products on Autogeek.net

- Guzzler Waffle Weave Drying Towels

These drying towels get their name because they simply guzzle up water. They make removing the water from your car's finish fast and easy.

- Cobra Guzzler Heavy Duty Waffle Weave Drying Towel - Inner Foam Core

This has an inner open cell foam core and works great for the blotting technique.

Mother's Microfiber Drying Towels
The Mothers Ultra Soft Drying Towel has an open cell foam core which acts like a sponge to soak up water. It's also easy to wring out so you can continue working your way around the car, gently wiping water off or using the blotting technique. The Wheel & Jamb Towel is a high quality waffle weave microfiber towel that dries and cleans the dirtiest parts of your vehicle, such as the wheels, grille and door jambs. Give this towel its own special place in the garage marked wheels only, because once it's used on them, it should never touch the paint again. Even after you've washed the wheels, some lingering brake dust can stick to the towel and be transferred to other parts of your vehicle. By designating Mothers Wheel & Jamb Towel for the work-horse parts of your vehicle, you can prevent cross-contamination.

- Mothers Ultra Soft Drying Towel - Waffle Weave Microfiber Towel
- Mothers Wheel & Jamb Towel
- The Meguiar's Water Magnet

The Meguiar's Water Magnet Drying Towel measures 22" x 30" and is a super soft and incredibly absorbent waffle weave microfiber towel perfect for any car, truck or SUV.

- Water Sprite Plus® Chamois 4 sq. Feet

This is a synthetic chamois that absorbs water like crazy. It is ultra-soft and safe for use clear coat finishes.

- P21S Drying Towel

Microfiber Towel Cleaning Detergents

There are detergents made specifically for cleaning and caring for microfiber drying towels to preserve their water absorbency while keeping the fibers soft and plush.

- Detailer's Pro Series Microfiber Cleaner
- Pinnacle Micro Rejuvenator Microfiber Detergent Concentrate
- Micro-Restore Microfiber Detergent Concentrate
- Sonus Der Wunder Microfiber and Pad Wasche

Traditional Leather Chamois
Genuine chamois are 100% natural leather and tanned using cod oil, which gives them softness and a pleasant leather smell. If you like the smell and feel of real leather, you won't be happy with a synthetic.

The Prince of Wales Chamois come in sizes of 2.5, 3.5, and 4.5 square feet of superb, high end leather. The 4.5 version is obviously the most popular for its size, sufficient for any job. Chamois are meant to be used without cleaning solutions or chemicals. If you use it for polishing and drying only and care for it correctly, your chamois may outlast you.

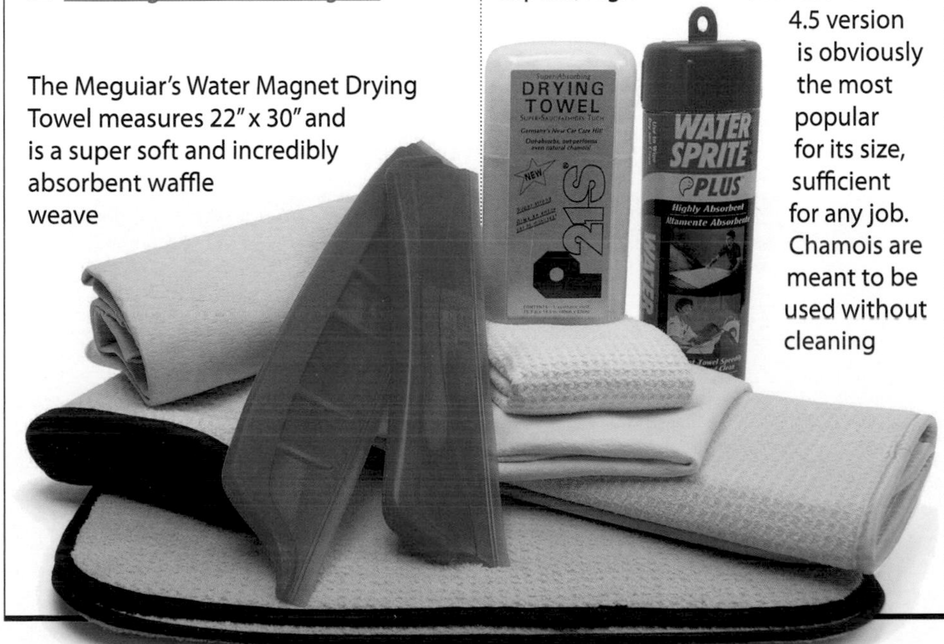

- Towel & Chamois Wringer

Save your hands for the other steps and wring your chamois out the easy way.

- The Original California Jelly Blade

- Metro MasterBlaster 8 Horsepower

Dry your car with filtered and pre-heated air and never touch the surface using the Metro MasterBlaster. Here I'm drying the water off the sunroof and out of the seams and gaskets using the MasterBlaster at a recent Detailing Boot Camp Class.

- Metro Blaster SideKick

The Metro Blaster Sidekick is a hand held powerful air dryer that works great and saves time. ■

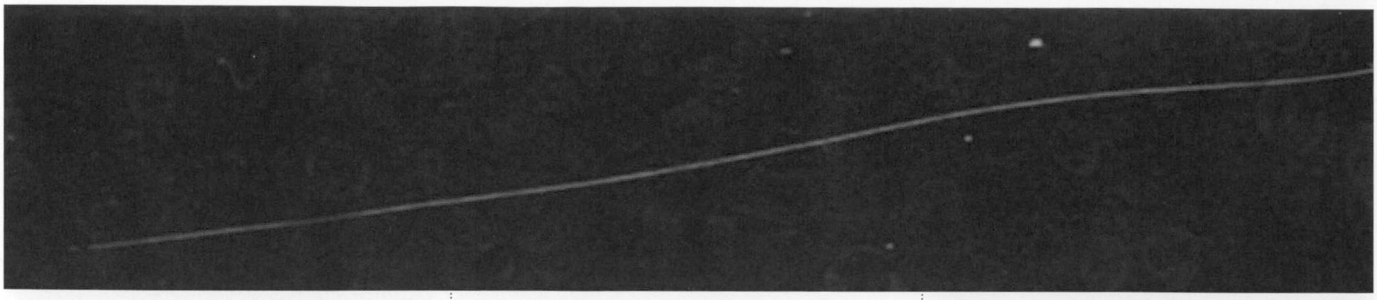

Inspecting your car's paint
Now that your car is clean and dry, you need to inspect the paint to determine what may be wrong. The results from your inspection will then guide you to which specific product you'll need to reach your goal. There are two ways to inspect your car's finish. One is with your sense of touch and other is visually.

■ Paint Condition Categories

As you inspect your car's paint, try to fit it into one of these 12 categories; most paint will fall into one of the first five groups:

1. Show Car Quality Condition
2. Excellent Condition
3. Good Condition
4. Mildly Neglected Condition
5. Severely Neglected Condition
6. Horrendous Swirls
7. Extreme Oxidation
8. Extreme Orange Peel
9. Unstable Condition
10. Beginning Clearcoat Failure
11. Clear Coat Failure
12. Past the Point of No Return

Two categories of paint defects

- Above-Surface Bonded Contaminants
- Below-Surface Defects

Paint defects can be placed into one of two categories. It's important to understand the two different types, because removing them requires different approaches. Let's take a look at the two different categories and how to inspect for paint defects.

■ Above-Surface Bonded Contaminants - Inspecting Using Your Sense of Touch

Using your clean hands, you can feel the above-surface bonded contaminants that you usually cannot see.

Types of above-surface Contaminants
Anytime your car is exposed to the environment, it is exposed to any and all the contaminants in the air and there are lots of them. These include:

- Overspray paint
- Tree sap mist
- Industrial fallout
- Airborne pollution
- Jet fuel exhaust
- Automobile and truck exhaust
- Brake dust
- Air blown dirt and dust

It's hard to see above-surface bonded contaminants because the particles are small. Your sense of touch, however, can easily feel the contaminants because they give the paint a rough,

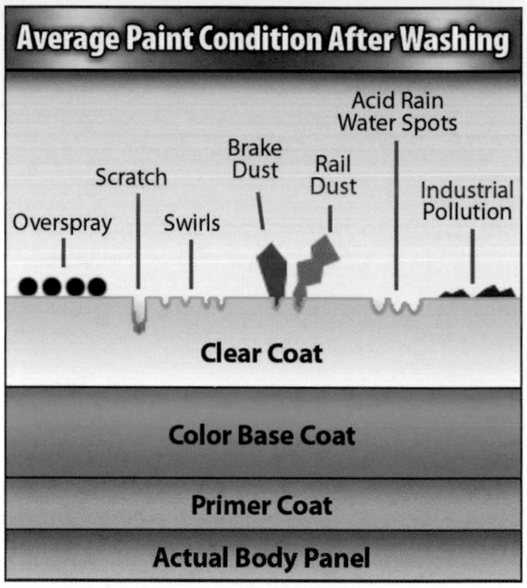

textured or pebbled feeling. In worst case scenarios, it can actually feel gritty or grainy.

If you really want to feel what's going on at the surface level of your car's paint, then use the baggie test when inspecting it for above-surface bonded contaminants. If working on a customer's car, let them also do the baggie test with you. The average car owner doesn't know how to test for above-surface bonded contaminants and doing so will reveal the true condition of the paint. Afterwards, letting them feel the smooth and slippery paint will solidify their trust in your expertise. This can help you to retain their business and potentially lead to referrals via word-of-mouth advertising.

In This Section:

- Paint Condition Categories:
- Above-Surface Bonded Contaminants - Inspecting Using Your Sense Of Touch
- Types Of Above-Surface Contaminants
- The Baggie Test
- Below-Surface Defects - Inspecting Your Paint Visually
- Scratches
- Cobweb/Spider Web Swirls
- Rotary Buffer Swirls/Holograms
- Water Spots
- Type I Water Spots
- Type II Water Spots
- Type III Water Spots
- Oxidation
- Rids = Random Isolated Deeper Scratches
- Tracers
- Pigtails
- Micromarring - Tick-Marks - DA Haze
- Paint Transfer
- Chemical Stains

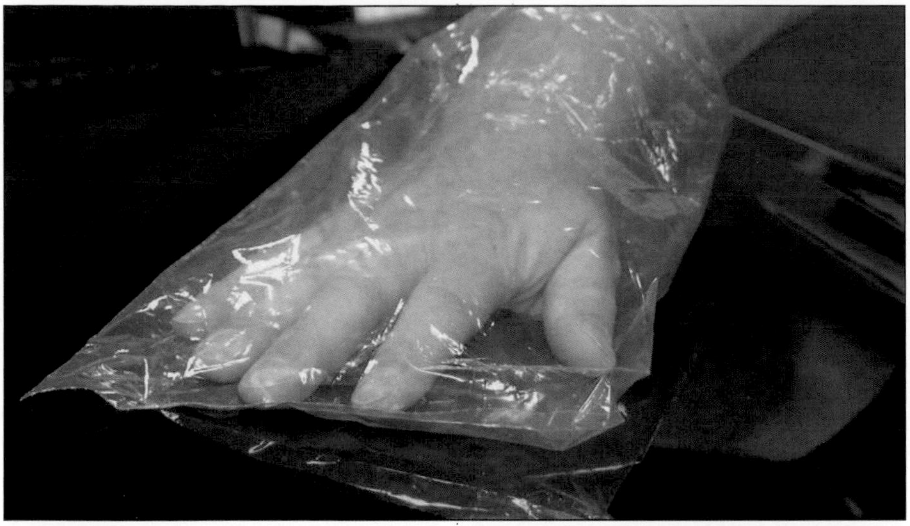

The Baggie Test
Simply place your hand inside a clean sandwich baggie and then feel the horizontal surfaces like the hood, roof and trunk lid. The thin film of plastic acts to intensify the surface texture created by contaminants bonded to the paint, making it more dramatic to your sense of touch.

Whichever way you want to inspect the paint, whether using just your hands or the baggie test, it's important to first wash and dry the car; this will prevent you from rubbing surface dirt over the paint.

What to do if your car's paint feels rough
This is an indicator that you need to use detailing clay or a Nano Pad Speedy Towel to safely remove the above-surface bonded contaminants.

■ Below-Surface Defects - Inspecting Your Paint Visually

After washing the car to remove loose dirt and then claying the paint to remove above-surface bonded contaminants, the next thing you want to do is inspect your car's paint for what we call "below-surface defects".

Below-surface paint defects describe any kind of defect that is "in" the paint or below the surface level.

Types of below-surface paint defects
- Water spots or water etchings (craters in the paint)
- Scratches and swirls
- Straight-line scratches

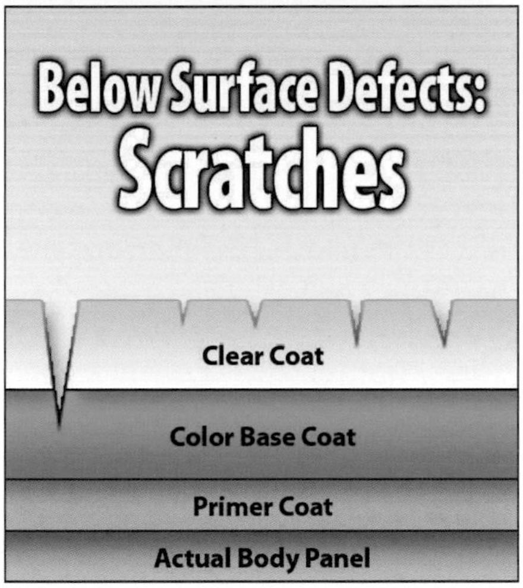

- Cobweb or spiderweb swirls
- Rotary buffer swirls, buffer trails or holograms
- Oxidation
- Sub-surface stains

It's important to know whether the defects are on the surface or in the paint. Knowing which type of defects you're trying to remove will determine how you remove them and which products you'll use.

Question: Which type of defect do you remove first?

Answer: Remove the above-surface bonded contaminants first and then go after the below-surface paint defects.

Why?
The above-surface bonded contaminants are on the top of the paint and should be removed first. Once they are out of the way, you can tackle everything that's below the surface.

Let's look at the different types of Below-Surface Paint Defects

■ Scratches

Most of us think of scratches as defects that are in straight-lines, like these.

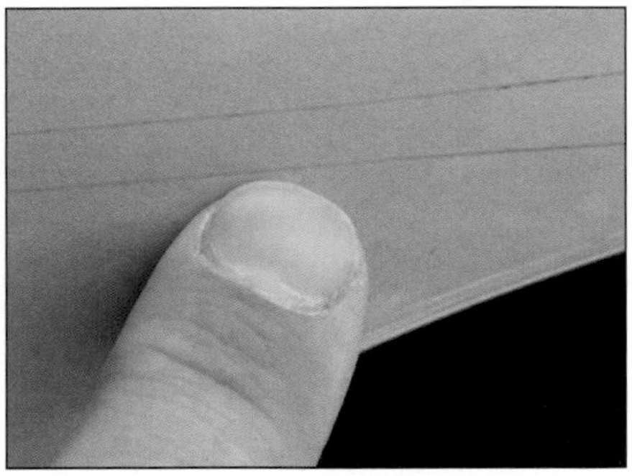

Straightline scratch

■ Cobweb (Spiderweb) Swirls

The terms cobweb and spiderweb swirls come from the appearance of swirls in the paint which can look like a spider's cobweb. The swirls have a circular or radial pattern to them when the paint is highlighted with a strong focused point of bright light, such as the reflection of the sun or a Brinkmann Swirl Finder Light.

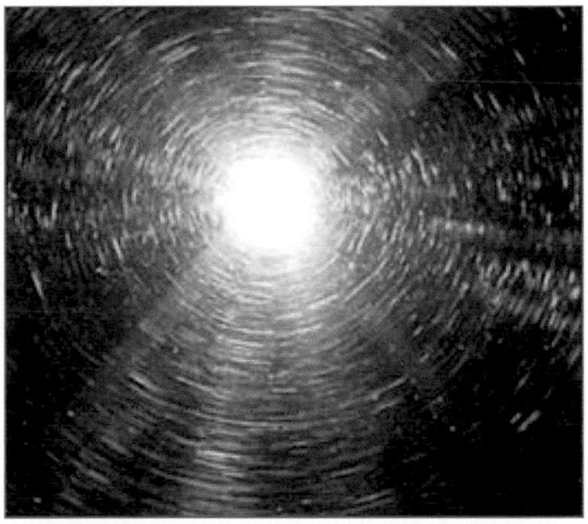

The scratches are not actually in circular patterns but are randomly inflicted throughout the entire finish. When you place a strong point of light on the surface, the edges of the scratches (no matter the length or shape) reflect back towards the point of light, creating the appearance of a circular pattern.

You can easily prove this to be the case by simply moving your body position in a way that moves the point of light around to a different place on a body panel. As you move positions and thus

Here you can see the rotary buffer was moved up and down the side of the door.

move where the light is shining onto the paint, it appears that wherever you place the point of light, there appears to be a circular or cobweb pattern of scratches. Cobweb scratches are instilled through normal wear and tear, improper washing and drying techniques, and use of worn-out wash mitts, sponges, brushes and drying towels or chamois. Automatic and hand car washes will also contribute to the cobweb effect.

Cobwebs swirls are not the same as Holograms
The cobweb swirl pattern is a different pattern than what you see with rotary buffer swirls. Rotary buffer swirls are not instilled randomly over time; they are instilled by a known source, usually in one detailing session.

How to remove
The only way to remove cobweb or spiderweb swirls is to use a compound or polish to abrade the paint.

For more information:

📖 How to Remove Swirls and Scratches: The Major Correction Step

■ Holograms or Rotary Buffer Swirls

These are circular scratches caused by a rotary buffer, usually by the individual fibers that make up a wool cutting or polishing pad. The abrasives used in most compounds and polishes can also inflict swirls into a car's finish. Any time you're using a wool buffing pad and a compound or polish, you now have two things potentially inflicting swirls into the paint.

Note how the swirls in the paint have an almost floating or 3D effect; this is where the term hologram comes from in the context of talking about swirls caused by the misuse of a rotary buffer.

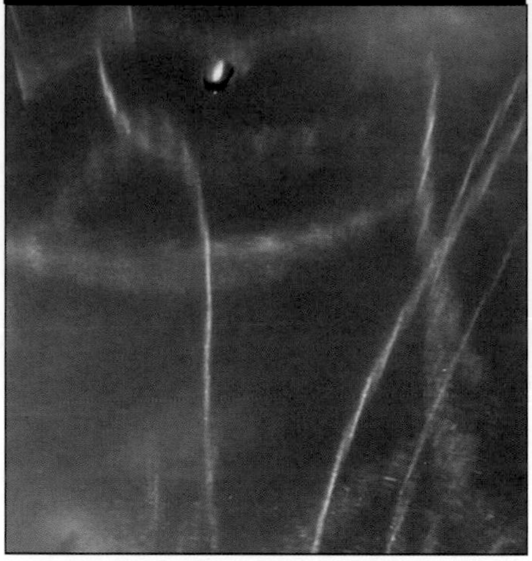

Foam pads can also inflict rotary buffer swirls into paint depending upon the aggressiveness of the foam formula and the product and tool used. It is the direct drive rotating action of a rotary buffer that instills the circular pattern of scratches into paint, usually in some type of zig-zag pattern that mimics that in which it was moved over the paint by the technician.

It's possible to use a rotary buffer and not instill swirls if the operator has a high skill level and uses quality pads and products. If swirls are instilled, a true professional will perform a follow-up procedure to remove them using less aggressive pads and products. For information on swirl removal, refer to this chapter:

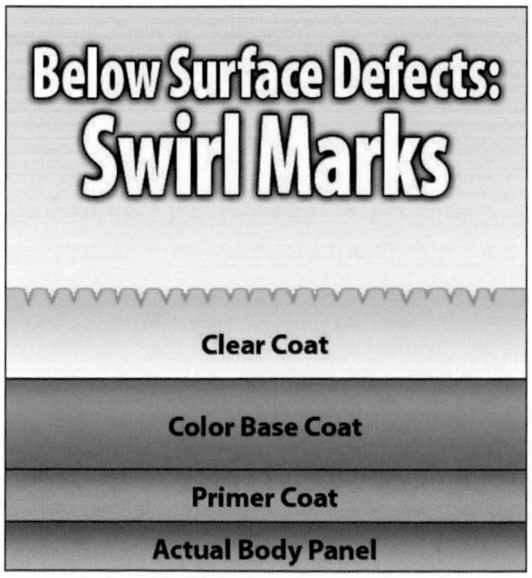

Here's the same hood under florescent lights. In this picture you can see the rotary buffer has left a pattern of trails which mimic how the rotary buffer was moved back and forth from the front of the hood towards the windshield.

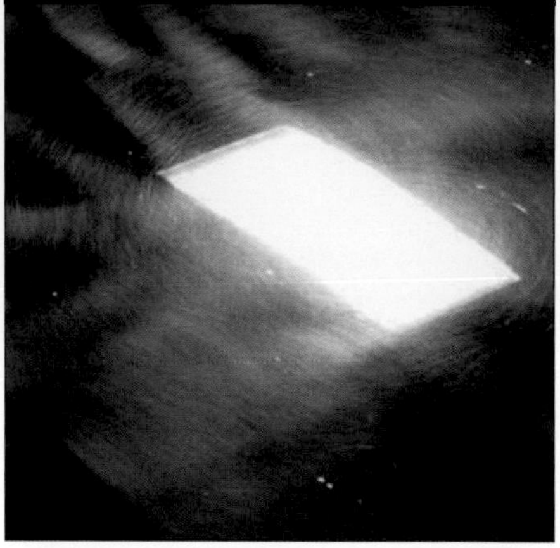

📖 How to Remove Swirls and Scratches: The Major Correction Step

■ Water Spots

Before you can remove water spots, you have to figure out which type you are dealing with.

Three Types of Water Spots - Type I, Type II and Type III

- **Type I Water Spots**
  Mineral deposits on the surface = Topical Defects
- **Type II Water Spots**
  Craters or etchings in the paint = Below Surface Defects
- **Type III Water Spots**
  Stains in the paint = Below Surface Defects

Type I Water Spots = Topical Defects
Type I Water Spots are mineral deposits or what people commonly call hard water spots. It's the minerals in water that people are referring to when they use the word hard in the term hard water spots.

Dirt Particles on paint after rain

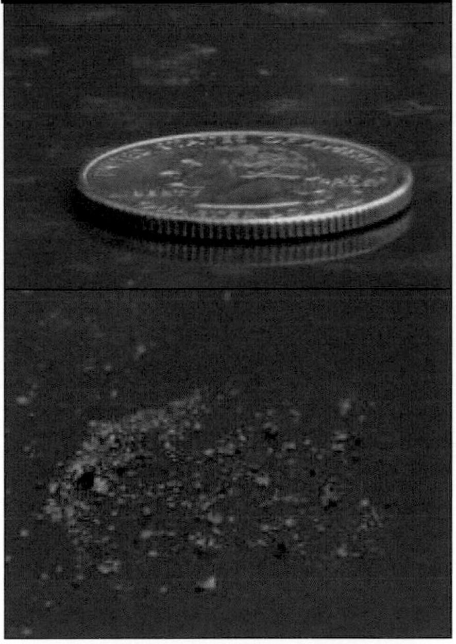

Type I Water Spots are primarily a mineral or dirt deposit laying on the surface of paint. Type I Water Spots can be the results of minerals suspended in city water or well water that are left behind after the water evaporates off the finish. This can happen by washing a car but not drying the water off the paint or if a sprinkler goes off next to the car covering the car with water drops that are not properly dried off the paint.

Type I Water Spots can also be dirt or pollution particles left behind after water from rain or inclement weather evaporates off the finish. Type I Water Spots can also be partially Type II Water Spots in that the water can leave both a deposit on the surface and an imprint ring or etching in the finish.

How To Remove

Type I Water Spots can usually be removed by washing or wiping the paint clean using a traditional car wash, rinseless wash, waterless wash or spray detailer. There are also specialty products just for this including:

- Duragloss 505 Water Spot Remover
- Meguiar's M47 Marine-RV Hard Water Spot Remover

About Meguiar's M47 Marine-RV Hard Water Spot Remover

The first sentence in the product description on the back of the Meguiar's label reads:

Specifically formulated to chemically break down and remove hard water Minerals off the surface.

When I worked for Meguiar's the common question about this product was can it be used on automotive paints? The company answer at that time was that all the field testing was done on Marine surfaces in Marine environments. My experienced guess is that it won't in and of itself harm a clear coat surface.

Two comments...

The average person doesn't know the difference between a topical mineral deposit, (Type I Water Spot), or a sub-surface etching, (Type II Water Spot). The average Joe Consumer buying this product to use on a modern clear coat to try to remove Type II Water Spots would be let down as they don't understand you would have to abrade the paint with a compound to remove Type II, thus they designate a product like this to the Marine market.

Type II Water Spots

These are actual etchings or craters in paint, caused by something corrosive in a water source landing on the finish without being removed before etching occurred.

Type II Water Spot - Crater Etching

If you look closely, you can see that the inner edges of the perimeter of the spot are angled downward. This is not a spot on the paint, it's a crater or etching.

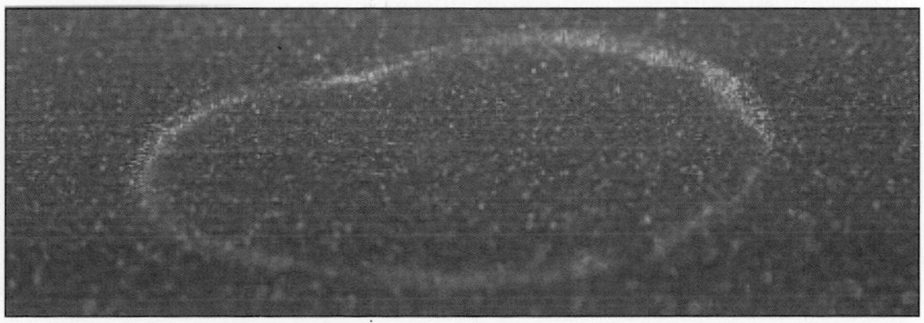

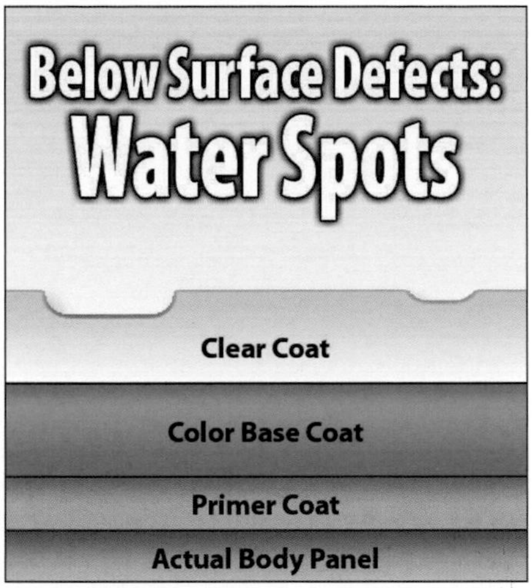

How to remove

You must remove enough paint to level the surface with the lowest depths of the craters you're trying to remove. The best and safest way to do this is by machine, but it can also be done by hand.

For more information:

- How to Machine Polish Paint to a High Gloss: The Polishing or Minor Correction Step
- How to Remove Swirls and Scratches: The Major Correction Step

Type I and Type II Water Spots

In some cases, a water spot can be both a Type I and a Type II. This means there are mineral deposits sitting on top of the surface and the water could be corrosive enough to leave an imprint ring marking the perimeter of the water spot or in worse case scenarios etching the paint, leaving a crater where the spot formed and dried.

Established Water Spots = Imprint Rings

If a vehicle is repeatedly exposed to rain, sprinklers or some other source of water drop, the water drops will form and pool in the same places and

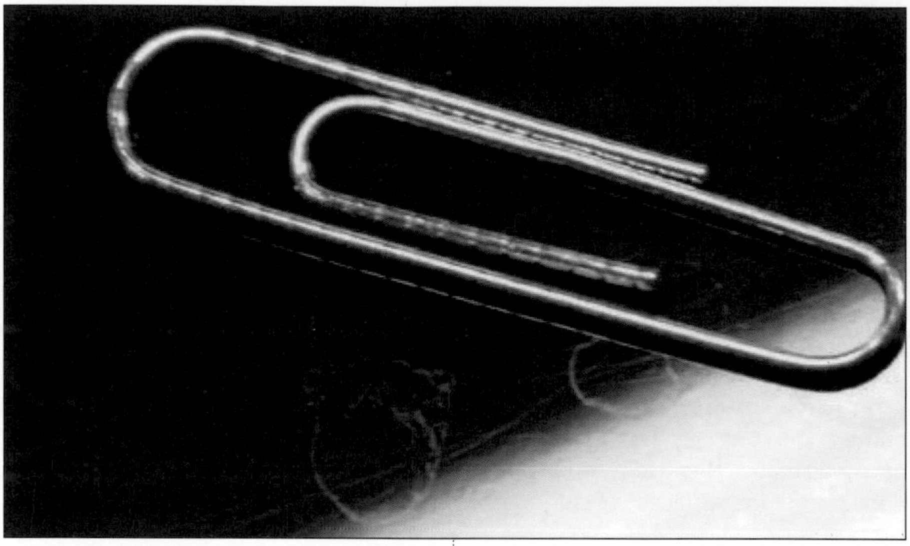

leave behind an imprint which usually outlines the perimeter where the water pooled and then dried. These imprints are actually where the border of the water drop etched into the paint and thus these are below the surface not outlines on the surface.

How to remove
If Imprint Rings remain after washing and drying you'll need to use a compound or polish to level the upper surface to the lowest depths of the imprints or craters left behind.

For more information:

- How to Machine Polish Paint to a High Gloss: The Polishing or Minor Correction Step
- How to Remove Swirls and Scratches: The Major Correction Step

Type III Water Spots
These are spots that look dull and faded and are found primarily on single stage paints. They are usually found after a water source pools on the paint and is allowed to dwell on the surface. Modern clearcoat paints tend to be harder and impermeable, so liquids don't penetrate easily. Therefore, stain spots tend to be topical, only affecting the very upper surface and are easier and safer to remove with a compound or polish. Older single stage paints tend to be soft and permeable or porous. It's common for liquids to penetrate into the paint and stain below the surface. Removing stains out of single stage paints can be risky because in order to remove the stains, you have to abrade the paint. If the stains penetrated too deep, then you risk removing too much paint in an effort to remove them completely.

How to remove
You'll need to use a compound or polish and abrade the surface until you see the stained portion of the paint has been removed.

For more information:

- How to Machine Polish Paint to a High Gloss: The Polishing or Minor Correction Step
- How to Remove Swirls and Scratches: The Major Correction Step

Type III Water Spots - Dull, faded spots

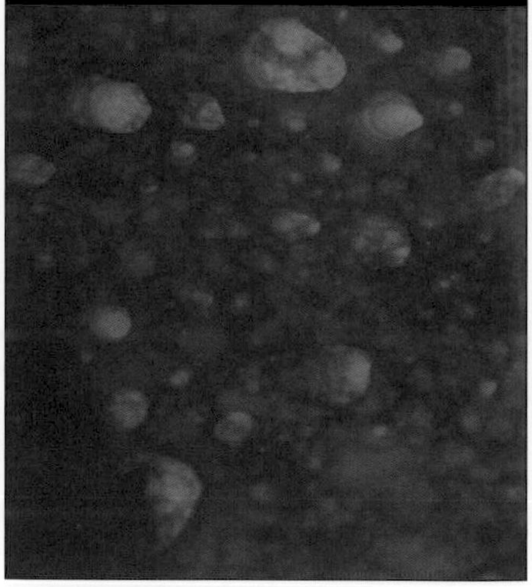

■ Oxidation

Oxidation is the loss of at least one electron when two or more substances interact. When your car's paint is exposed to oxygen and moisture, the oxygen molecules interact with the paint resin, causing free radicals to be eliminated.

Oxidation: Simple Explanation
A free radical is an organic molecule that is unstable, or lacking an even number of electrons. These free radicals attach to electrons from other

Oxidation Before (Above) **Oxidation After (Below)**

molecules, in this case referring to the oxygen molecules in the air or present in moisture/water. It is this process of losing electrons that eventually causes paint to appear dull, whitish, or chalky looking.

Oxidation is more common to old-school single stage paints, but it can and will happen to basecoat/clearcoat finishes if the paint is neglected long enough and exposed to outdoor climates for great lengths of time.

- Dodge Neon Extreme Makeover with Dodo Juice Need for Speed

How to remove
Oxidation can be removed by abrading the surface with some type of abrasive compound and/ or polish, which will remove the oxidized paint and expose a fresh layer of non-oxidized paint underneath. After the oxidized paint is removed, it's a good idea to use a finishing polish and then seal the paint with a wax, paint sealant or coating.

For more information:

- How to Remove Swirls and Scratches: The Major Correction Step

RIDS = Random Isolated Deeper Scratches

This type of scratch comes from normal wear and tear. RIDS are like tracers in that they are deeper scratches that show up after the shallow scratches have been removed through a machine or hand buffing process, usually with a compound or paint cleaner. After the shallow swirls and scratches have been removed, any deeper scratches that remain will now show up like a sore thumb to your eyes because there are no longer thousands of lighter, more shallow scratches camouflaging them.

After removing thousands of shallow swirls and scratches, this single, random, isolated deeper scratch remained in the paint on a 2011 Corvette.

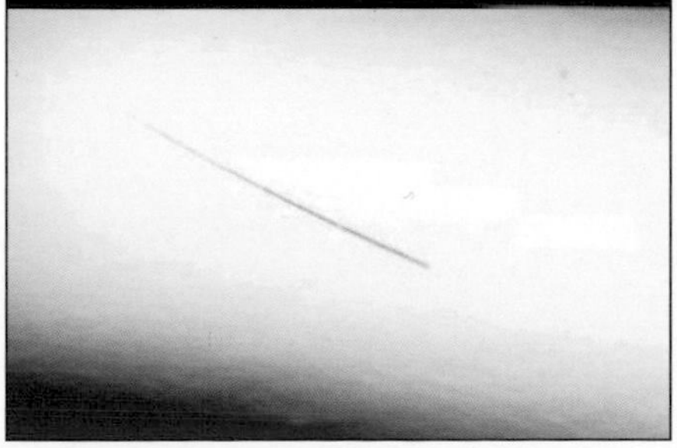

Tracers

Tracers are deeper scratches left by the hand sanding process, usually in straight lines because most people move their hand in a back and forth motion when wet sanding. Tracers show up after the paint is compounded and all shallow scratches have been removed. Remaining in the paint are the deeper sanding marks and these are called tracers.

This paint was sanded by hand and then the sanding marks were removed, but a few tracers remained.

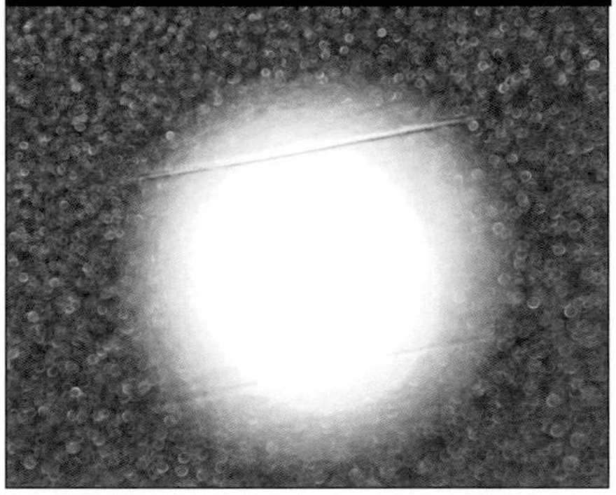

Tracers are usually difficult to remove because they are deeper and removing them means either re-sanding or re-compounding to level the surface. The problem with re-sanding is that you could remove one group of tracers, only to leave behind a new set of tracers, making this a catch-22 situation. This is why it's so important to use the highest quality finishing papers you can obtain.

Pigtails

When an abrasive particle gets trapped between the paint and the face of your oscillating sanding disc, it abrades the paint in a curly pattern that represents a pigtail, hence the name.

How to remove
Removing tracers and pigtails can be a little tricky. The safest way is to re-sand using a very fine grit finishing paper or foam backed finishing disc in the 3000 to 5000 grit range. You can use the Feathersanding Technique by hand using the techniques shared below.

- RIDS and Feathersanding - A Highly Specialized Technique by Mike Phillips

My personal favorite way to remove RIDS, tracers and pigtails is by using the Griot's Garage 3" Mini DA polisher with a 3000 grit Meguiar's Unigrit Finishing Disc or a 3M Trizact 5000 grit Disc.

The small 3" Griot's Garage Mini Polisher works great as a spot dampsander. After sanding the affected area, simply use a compound or a medium polish with the appropriate pad. Remember, if you're working on a daily driver, it's usually a good idea to improve a deeper defect than it is to try to completely remove it due to the risk of removing too much paint.

- Griot's Garage 3" Mini Polisher
- Meguiars Unigrit 3 Inch Foam Interface Pad
- Meguiars Unigrit 3000 3 Inch Finishing Discs, 15 per box
- 3M Trizact 3 Inch 5000 Grit Foam Discs

Pigtails

Extreme Micromarring - This micromarring was created using a compound that was too aggressive with a DA Polisher

Note: *Machine sanding paint to remove below-surface defects is an advanced skill and caution should be used.*

■ Micromarring - Tick-Marks - DA Haze

These three terms describe a scratch pattern caused by the oscillating and rotating action from compounding using a DA polisher. Unlike cobweb swirls or rotary buffer swirls, the scratch pattern instilled by a dual action polisher is made up of millions of tiny scratches. Some are curved or circular, but some are straight, like a small tick mark.

Tick marks are a sign that either the paint is easily scratched or the pad, compound or polish you're using is too aggressive to finish without leaving marring. In most cases, tick marks can be removed by re-polishing with a different pad and product combination.

How to remove
Micromarring is removed by re-polishing the area using a finer polish.

For more information:

How to Machine Polish Paint to a High Gloss: The Polishing or Minor Correction Step

■ Paint Transfer

This occurs when the paint from one object is transferred to another, usually the result of some kind of accident.

How to remove
Paint transfer is easier to remove by hand because you can exert a lot of force with a few finger tips to abrade

the offending paint from your car's paint. Then, after removing the paint transfer, finish with some machine polishing to perfect the paint. For more information on removing paint transfer, see my forum article.

How To Remove Paint Transfer

■ Chemical Stains

Chemical stains are more common with older single stage paints since they tend to be more porous, allowing liquids penetrate easily into the paint. It's much more difficult to chemically stain clearcoats because they are impermeable. Chances are that if some type of liquid chemical makes contact with your car's paint, it will attack and etch the very top surface of the clearcoat but not seep into the paint and stain it.

How to remove
To remove stains, you need to abrade the surface with some type of compound or polish until you remove enough paint to level the very upper surface with the lowest depths of the stain or etching. ■

For more information:

How to Remove Swirls and Scratches: The Major Correction Step

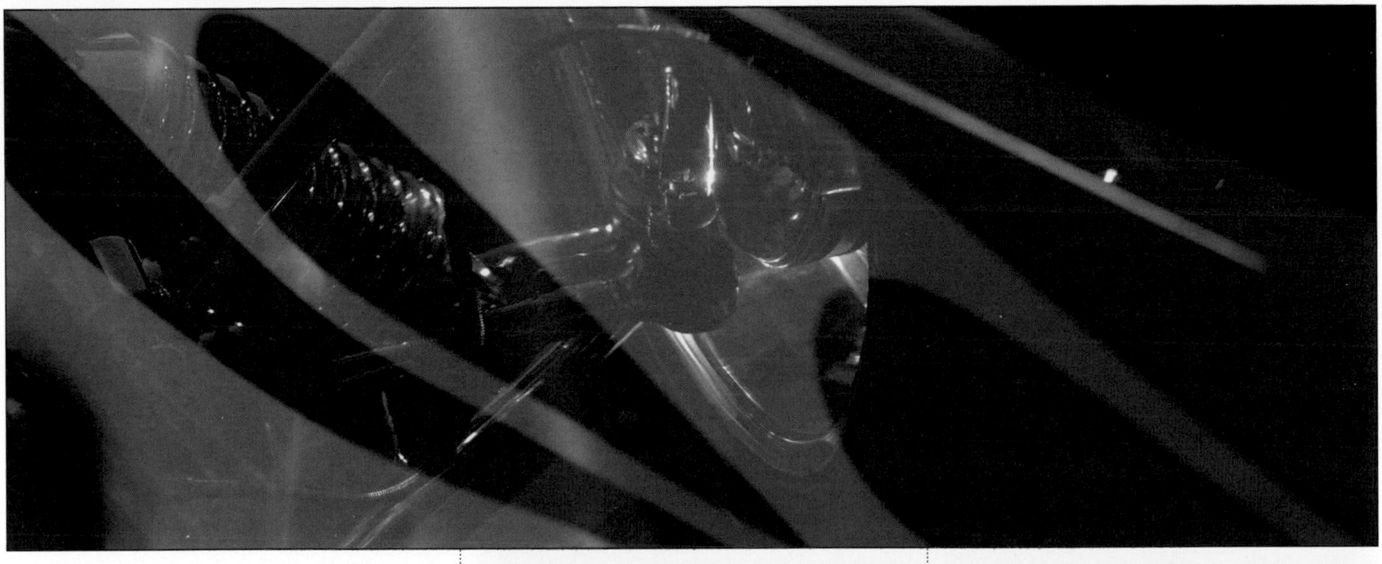

As you inspect your car's paint, try to fit it into one of the following 12 categories; most paint will fall into one of the first five groups:

1. **Show Car Quality**
2. **Excellent Condition**
3. **Good Condition**
4. **Mildly Neglected**
5. **Severely Neglected**
6. **Horrendous Swirls** - *Caused By The Misuse Of A Rotary Buffer*
7. **Extreme Oxidation**
8. **Extreme Orange Peel**
9. **Unstable**
10. **Beginning Clearcoat Failure**
11. **Clearcoat Failure**
12. **Past The Point Of No Return**

This is a 1934 Ford Pick-up with a Blown 426 Hemi Engine that we machine polished using the techniques in this how-to book and it has a finish in #1 Show Car Quality Condition.

1. Show Car Quality Condition

Paint in this condition is as perfect as it can be in any lighting condition. The only defects you should see are fingerprints, smudges or light dust on what otherwise appears to be a flawless show car finish. The finish on a car in this category can hold up to close scrutiny under bright lights by the most discerning eyes. The paint in this category has been put through a series of machine polishing procedures to maximize D.O.I. (distinction of image), gloss, clarity, depth, reflection, richness of color, shine and even slickness.

Blown 1934 Ford Pick-up - Show Car Makeover

If needed, the paint has been sanded, cut and buffed to remove orange peel and any other surface texture to create a 100% flat surface to maximize DOI. RIDS have been removed to the extent that it is safe to do so without compromising the top coat. Paint is meticulously cared for on an as-needed basis to ensure that it is always display-ready.

2. Excellent Condition

Paint in this category looks factory new or better. The paint looks like it has been professionally machine polished and sealed with a wax, paint sealant or coating and is regularly maintained. When viewed in bright sunlight, the paint looks excellent. There are few or no visible swirls or scratches, or so few that there are not enough of them to require machine polishing.

3. Good Condition

Paint in Good Condition has light swirls, scratches, water spots and oxidation,

In This Section:

- #1 - Show Car Quality
- #2 - Excellent Condition
- #3 - Good Condition
- #4 - Mildly Neglected
- #5 - Severely Neglected
- #6 - Horrendous Swirls
- #7 - Extreme Oxidation
- #8 - Extreme Orange Peel
- #9 - Unstable
- #10 - Beginning Clearcoat Failure
- #11 - Clearcoat Failure
- #12 - Past The Point Of No Return

This is a 2006 Mustang GT that was in #3 Good Condition and we brought it up to #1 Show Car Quality Condition.

when viewed in bright sunlight the paint should look pretty good overall with the exception that it has light or shallow looking cobweb swirls and scratches throughout the paint. Any water spot problems should be shallow imprint type stains common to Type I Water Spots, certainly not deep craters like Type II or Type III where the paint is physically stained. Paint in this condition would require one or two polishing steps before a finishing wax could be applied to bring the quality to #2 Excellent Condition or #1 Show Car Quality Condition.

Pictures & Videos: 2006 Mustang by Ford Show Car Shine by Autogeek!

4. Mildly Neglected Condition

Paint in mildly neglected condition encounters normal day-in, day-out

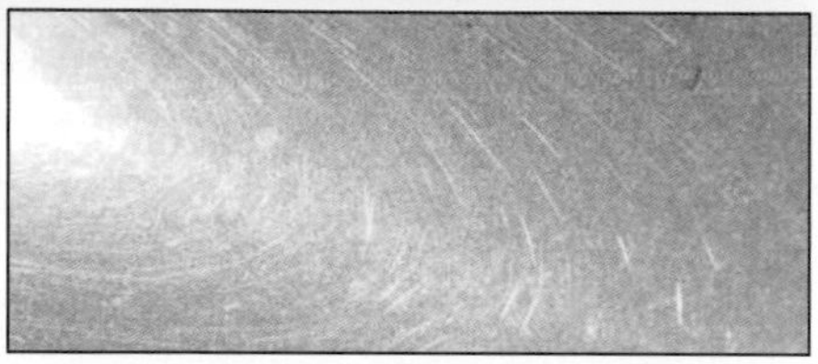

wear and tear and receives minimal appearance maintenance outside of the occasional wash. Paint in this condition has medium to light swirls, scratches, water spots and oxidation.

1939 Lincoln Zephyr - Swirls Removed

5. Severely Neglected Condition

Paint in this condition has deep swirls, scratches, water spots and oxidation. Paint in this condition has normal day-in, day-out wear and tear and recieves no real regular maintenance. Vehicles in this category are rarely washed on a regular basis and when they are washed, they are washed improperly or taken through an automatic car wash.

- Cobweb swirls and scratches Paint that is severely neglected, when

This is a 1939 Lincoln Zephyr that was in good condition and we brought it up to #1 Show Car Quality Condition at Autogeek.

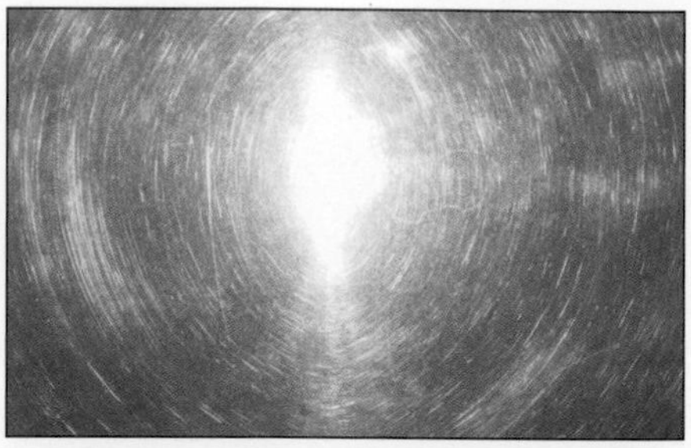

viewed in bright, overhead sunlight, will show many swirls and scratches with an overall hazy appearance.

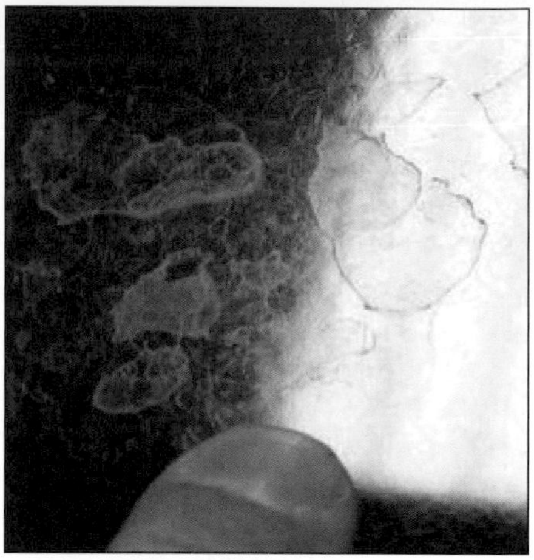

- Water spots Paint that is in the severely neglected category can have Type I, Type II and Type III water spots on all horizontal panels and even the vertical panels if caused by a sprinkler or some type of water spray.

- Severe oxidation Paint in this category has oxidized to the point where the surface has a uniform dull appearance to the horizontal surfaces, and to some extent, the vertical panels. Clearcoats do oxidize, but usually at a slower rate than single stage paints and clearcoats don't normally get the whitish, chalky appearance with a rough texture common to old, neglected single stage lacquers and enamels.

6. Horrendous Swirls

This category is primarily for cars that have been improperly polished using a rotary buffer, leaving the finish inflicted with horrendous rotary buffer swirls, also called holograms or buffer trails. The severity of the swirls can range from shallow to deep, depending upon

the pad and product used with the rotary buffer as well as technique, or lack thereof.

■ 7. Extreme Oxidation

Paint in this category is primarily associated with traditional single stage lacquer and enamel paints and normally found cars built before 1980. Extremely oxidized paint has deteriorated to the point that it has a chalky, whitish appearance.

Paint in this category is typically antique or original. Extreme oxidation can be corrected by carefully removing the dead, oxidized paint and rejuvenating the remaining paint with polishing oils. After polishing, the color is restored and remains even when exposed to sunlight. If the color fades away, this is an indicator that the paint has become unstable.

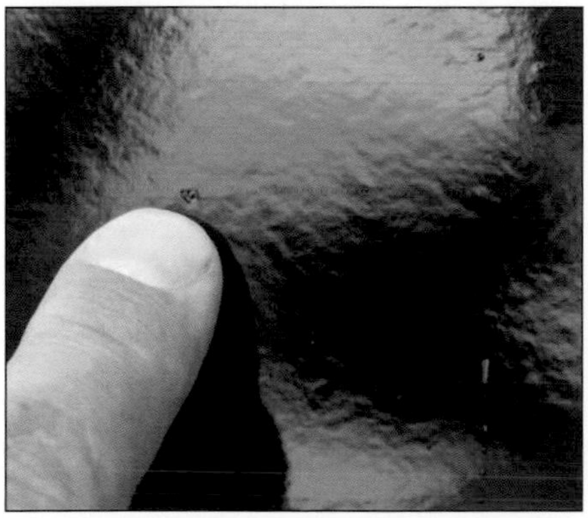

■ 8. Extreme Orange Peel

Paint in this category is primarily aftermarket. It doesn't normally include factory orange peel on a brand new car or truck. Due to how thin the top coat is on a factory paint job, there's a certain amount of risk you have to accept if you choose to remove the factory orange

Before and after example of removing oxidation

peel. Repaints will tend to have enough material that the problem can be safely corrected via sanding and buffing.

■ 9. Unstable Condtion

This category is for older, single stage paints that have been exposed to the sun for a long enough period of time that the pigments have become unstable. Even if you remove the oxidation and saturate the paint with some type of polishing oils, any original color that is restored is only a temporary fix. Therefore, when the paint is exposed to the sun or after a few days pass, the color fades back to where it was before you started.

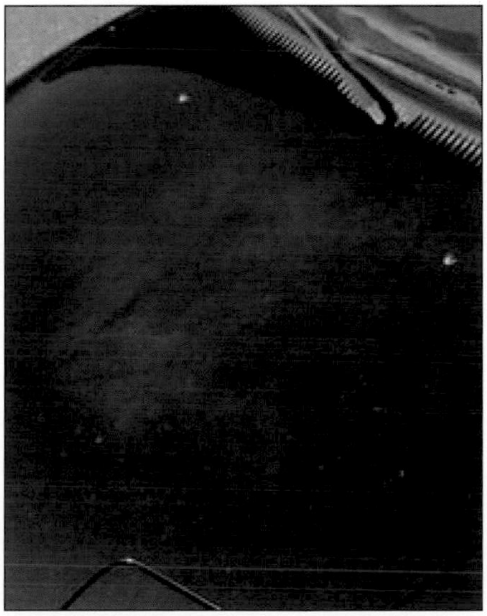

■ 10. Beginning Clearcoat Failure

This is when the clear layer is just starting to fail or deteriorate. On a darker colored car, the clear layer starts to have a cloudy or opaque look, which is a sign the clear coat is on its way to de-laminating and flaking off. There is nothing you can do at this point to stop the deterioration. The best thing you can do is keep the car out of the sun as much as possible. Avoid using any abrasive compounds or medium cut polishes. Wash with a non-detergent soap and keep the horizontal surfaces coated with a high UV protection wax like Optimum Polymer Technologies Car Wax.

■ 11. Clearcoat Failure

Clearcoat failure is the point in which the top clear layer of paint has either de-laminated from the basecoat and is peeling off or has deteriorated to the point in which it's turning a whitish color. Full blown deterioration occurs when it has turned white and is flaking off and the car looks like it has a severe rash. The only honest fix for clearcoat failure is to repaint the affected areas or the entire car.

■ 12. Past The Point Of No Return

Paint in this condition falls into one of the above categories, but it is so far gone that nothing you pour out of a bottle or scoop out of a can from any company will fix it. ■

Which products do you need?
After you wash and dry your car and inspect the paint both visually and with your sense of touch, it's time figure out which products you'll need to detail it.

Your goal will determine what products to use and the steps to follow

- *Do you want to create a true show car finish?*
- *Do you want to simply wash and wax your car?*

Simply washing and waxing your car is pretty straight forward. If you want to create a true show car finish, however, depending upon the condition of the paint, this could take a few hours or several days. The biggest time issue with creating a show car finish is what we call the major correction step. In this step, you'll be removing below-surface defects like swirls and scratches.

In order to remove below-surface defects, you need to use some type of abrasive product to gently and in a controlled manner remove a little paint from the surface until the upper surface is level with the lowest depths of the defects you're trying to remove.

The fastest way to remove swirls and scratches is by machine. Even if you work with a machine, it can still take hours because modern clearcoat paints tend to be harder than traditional single stage paints.

■ The 1-Step Approach

If you only want perform one step after washing and drying, but your paint is neglected, then you want to use a one-step cleaner wax.

1. **Wash and Dry**
2. **Inspect** - Inspect the paint both visually and with your sense of touch.
3. **Remove above-surface bonded contaminants** - Detailing Clay/Speed Prep Towel/Nano Autoscrub Pad.
4. **Apply Cleaner Wax**

As you can see, even a one step approach includes more than a single step as you have to wash and dry to remove loose dirt. If your inspection reveals a rough feeling texture to the horizontal surfaces of the paint, then it's best to use clay before applying any kind of wax. A cleaner wax will remove some above-surface bonded contaminants, but claying is the most effective way to remove all of them.

A cleaner wax will clean, polish and protect in one step:

- **Clean** - Cleaning undoes the damage done to the paint by neglecting regular maintenance and through normal wear and tear.
- **Polish** - Polishing will restore smoothness and clarity.
- **Protect** - Protection ingredients are left behind on the surface to protect the paint and lock in the shine created by the cleaning and polishing ingredients.

A one step approach does cut out two extra steps, but you're not going to remove any of the deeper below-surface defects like swirls, scratches and water spots. Cleaner waxes vary in that some are non-abrasive and rely on chemical cleaners, while others contain abrasives which will remove swirls and scratches. For show car results, you're going to want to perform a multiple-step process using a dedicated compound and polish. You cannot rely on a cleaner wax to tackle all the below surface paint defects.

My comments...
If you're detailing cars for money then you should be using a one-step approach and using a good quality cleaner/wax. The exception would be if you have educated your customer that removing more defects and creating a show car finish requires multiple dedicated steps and for this there is a higher charge for time, labor and materials.

For more information:
📖 *How To Apply Cleaner Waxes*

■ The Multi-Step Approach

If your goal is to create a like-new or show car finish and the paint needs to be clayed and/or have swirls, scratches and water spots removed, you'll need to do multiple steps to reach your goal.

How many steps you'll need to do will depend upon the condition of your car's paint. The worse the condition, the more steps you'll need to restore it to a like-new or show car quality. A multiple step process is usually as follows:

1. **Wash, Decontaminate and Dry.**
2. **Inspect** - Inspect the paint both with your sense of touch and visually.
3. **Remove above-surface bonded contaminants** - Detailing Clay/ Speed Prep Towel/Opti-Eraser/ Nanoskin Autoscrub
4. **Major Correction Step** - Use a compound or a swirl remover to remove swirls, scratches, oxidation, staining and water spot etchings.
5. **Polishing or Minor Correction Step** - Use a fine or less aggressive finishing polish to follow-up the more aggressive correction step. This will further refine any remaining shallow defects and maximize gloss, clarity and smoothness of the finish.
6. **Jewelling Step** - In this optional step, you will repeat the last step using your finest or least aggressive finishing polish and a soft foam finishing pad.
7. **Sealing or Protection Step** - Since you have already removed the defects and polished the paint to a high gloss, using a cleaner wax would be working backwards in the process. At this point, you would use either a finishing wax, a paint sealant or another coating that offers no cleaning, just pure protection. ■

In This Section:

- The 1-Step Approach
- The Multi-Step Approach

Introduction

In this chapter we'll take a look at multiple products you can use to remove above surface bonded contaminants.

Manufacturer's Recommendations
Most manufacturers of these products don't state that you must machine or hand polish the paint afterwards to remove any light or shallow scratching that may be induced from the process.

My recommendations
If your goal is a show car finish or even just to restore a good to excellent condition finish, then my recommendation is to plan on machine polishing after claying, even if all you use is a Light Cut Polish. The reason for this is simple: clearcoat paints are scratch-sensitive. That is, even though they are harder than traditional single stage paints, they still scratch easily. Rubbing a clay bar, a Speedy Prep Towel or any of the products listed in this chapter has the potential to leave fine scratches in the paint simply from the process. Softer paints are more prone to scratching than harder paints; even so it is my personal practice and recommendation to others to machine polish the paint after any process where you've removed above surface bonded contaminants.

In This Section:

- Introduction
  - Manufacturer's Recommendations
  - My recommendation
- Detailing Clay And How To Use It
- Clay Alternatives And How To Use Them
  - Ultima Elastrofoam Paint Cleaning System
  - Speedy Surface Prep Towels
  - Optimum Opti-Erasers
  - XENIT Natural Citrus Mold Cleaner
  - Nanoskin Autoscrub Pads

Detailing Clay And How To Use It

In This Section

- Claying - What, Where, Why & When
- 4 Benefits Of Claying Your Car's Paint
- How To Clay Your Car
- Frequently Asked Questions About Detailing Clay

When compared to most other car care products, detailing clay is a relatively new product on the market. It was introduced to the car detailing world sometime in the early 1990s and, relative to the history of the car which dates back to the late 1880s, it's only been around for a short time.

In that short time, it's gained popularity and has actually a staple in the professional detailing industry. Detailing Clay enables you to remove above-surface bonded contaminants without using a rubbing compound or sanding the paint. This key feature is invaluable when it comes to restoring and/or maintaining a high gloss finish because gloss comes from smoothness.

Any car that is driven daily is subject to a build-up of contaminants on the horizontal or flat panels, so claying is usually an important step for any detailing project. Most detailers use detailing clay as a normal procedure for every car they wash and wax - it's that important.

Claying - What, Where, Why & When

What is detailing clay?
Detailing clay is type of synthetic or man-made clay with a special type of abrasive in it.

What does detailing clay do?
Clay has the ability to remove contaminants that are bonded to your car's paint and won't come off when washing or wiping your car clean. In simple terms, it works to abrade off anything sticking to the paint above the surface level. It then glides over the surface of the paint - it does not sand or abrade the paint itself.

Where?
Any smooth surface, including glossy paint, glass, hard plastic, chrome, stainless steel, and gel coat.

Why use detailing clay?
By removing any contaminants from the paint, your choice of wax, coating or sealant can more easily bond or adhere, thus it can last and protect longer.

When to use detailing clay

Use detailing clay anytime you discover a rough or textured feel to your car's paint. It's a good practice to feel your car's paint after you wash and dry the vehicle to inspect for above-surface bonded contaminants. How often you need to clay depends upon what's in the air where you park your car. Normally, you would clay the paint after washing and drying and before any other paint-related procedure.

How to use detailing clay

Knead the clay into a round patty, like a pancake. It should be large enough to cover the palm of your hand or at least your 4 fingers. Spray a clay lubricant onto the clay patty and onto a section of paint and then rub the clay over the paint until it glides effortlessly. Wipe off the residue on this section of paint and move on to a new section, overlapping into the previous section.

Mist clay lubricant onto paint, then onto face of detailing clay and then rub clay over a section of a body panel until contaminants are removed.

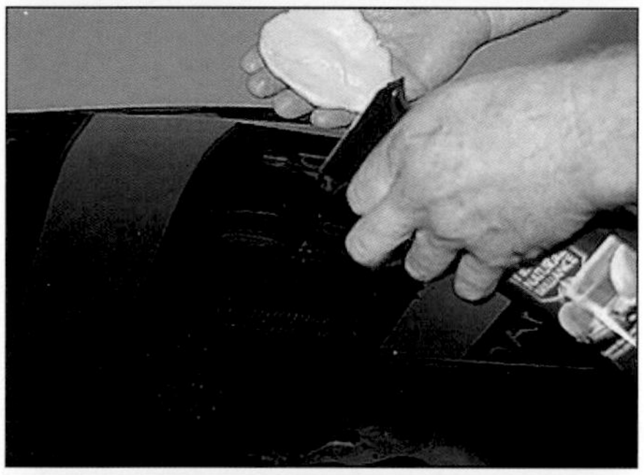

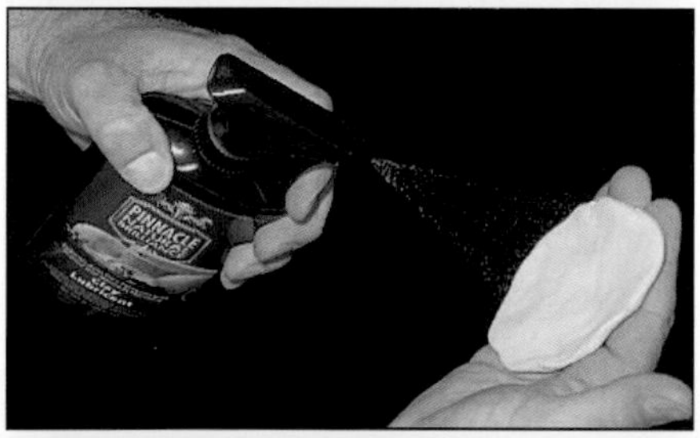

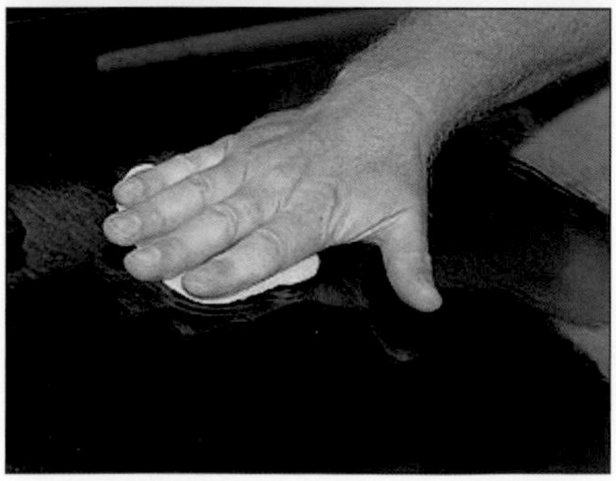

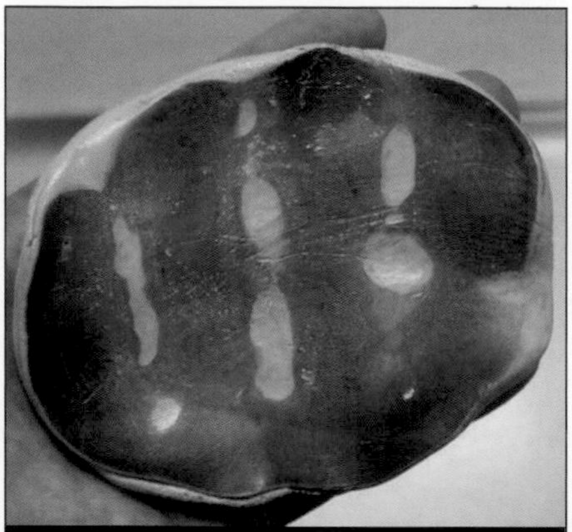

Fresh clay used on the hood of a 1973 Lincoln Continental that sits outside 24 hours a day, 7 days a week

4 Benefits Of Claying Your Car's Paint

Let's take a look at the four primary benefits to using detailing clay.

- Claying safely removes above-surface bonded contaminants
- Claying enables your choice of wax or paint sealant to better bond or adhere to the paint
- Claying restores a silky-smooth, clean surface
- Claying makes polishing easier, more effective and safer

1. Claying safely removes above-surface bonded contaminants

If your car is parked outside for any length of time, then any dirt or airborne contaminants that land on the paint will tend to bond if they are not removed in a timely manner. Once bonded, some of them won't come off with normal washing. This is where detailing clay comes into the picture.

Before detailing clay became popular, people would use coarse rubbing compounds to remove above-surface bonded contaminants and while these types of products would work, they would also,

- Instill scratches into the paint
- Remove perfectly good paint

These are two things you don't want to do to your car's precious and thin layer of paint.

2. Claying enables your choice of wax or paint sealant to better bond or adhere to the paint

Restoring a clean surface maximizes the bond between the paint and a wax, coating or sealant. One of the most common questions I am asked is, *"How long will brand X Car Wax last?"*

The correct answer is, *"It depends upon how well the surface is prepared to accept the wax"*

You see, a good chemist will create a car wax, coating or sealant formulation to bond or adhere to car paint, not a layer of dirt. When contaminants build up on the surface, they create a layer or film of gunk. The protection ingredients cannot reach the paint until this layer of contaminants is removed. If above-surface, airborne contaminants are on the paint when a wax or paint sealant is applied, it will not last very long because it won't be able to bond very well.

3. Claying paint restores a silky-smooth, clean surface

A build-up of contaminants on your car's finish creates an irregular surface or texture that feels rough or bumpy to

The paint on the 1949 Chevrolet Sedan Delivery is incredibly glossy and the results started with claying the paint to remove above-surface bonded contaminants.

the touch. This uneven, bumpy surface reduces gloss. Claying your car's paint will remove the contaminants, restoring a smooth, high gloss surface.

4. Claying paint makes polishing easier, more effective and safer
By removing any above-surface bonded contaminants, you enable your polish and pad to immediately work on the paint with nothing in the way. A smoother surface allows your pad to move over the surface more easily, with less potential for hopping or grabbing. You reduce the potential for accidental marring during the buffing process, since there are no contaminants that can come loose and become trapped between the pad and the paint.

■ How To Clay Your Car

Detailing clay can be purchased from a number of suppliers. In this example, I'm using Pinnacle Ultra Poly Clay, which is available as a single 4 ounce clay bar or two 4 ounce clay bars.

Four ounces is approximately 114 grams, which is very healthy chunk of clay that you can easily break into two pieces. Use one piece and save the rest for another project.

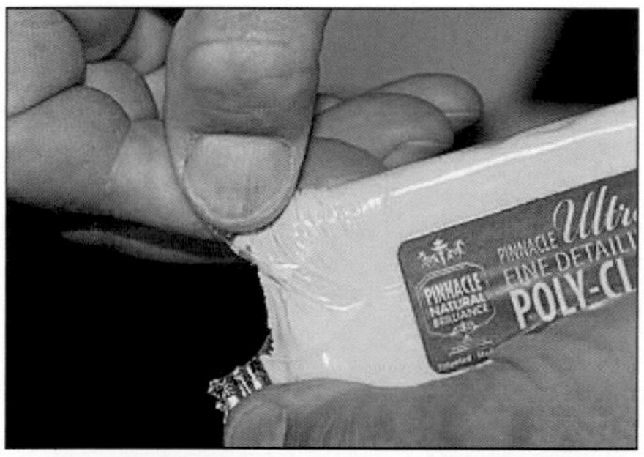

1. Remove the cellophane wrapper

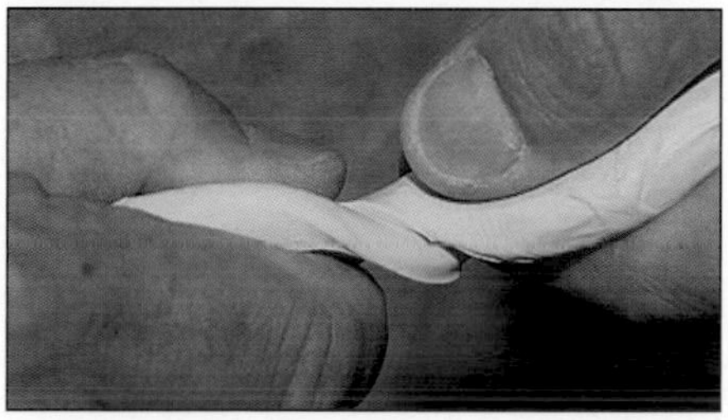

2. Tear the clay bar into two pieces You can store your clay in the plastic container it comes with or in a re-sealable sandwich baggie.

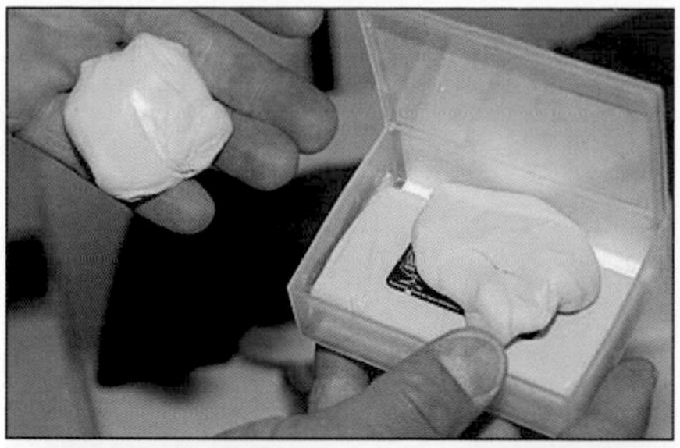

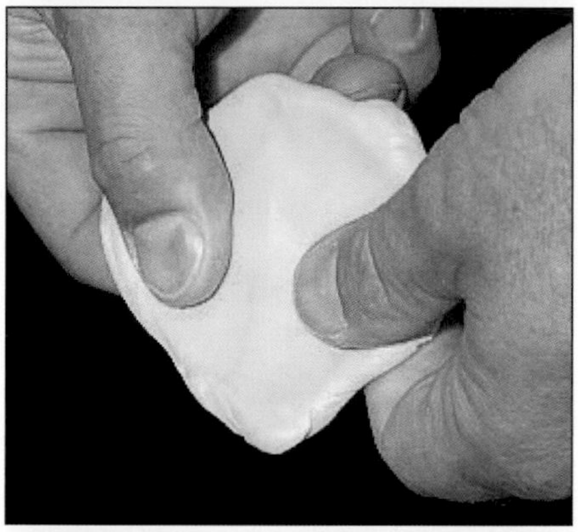

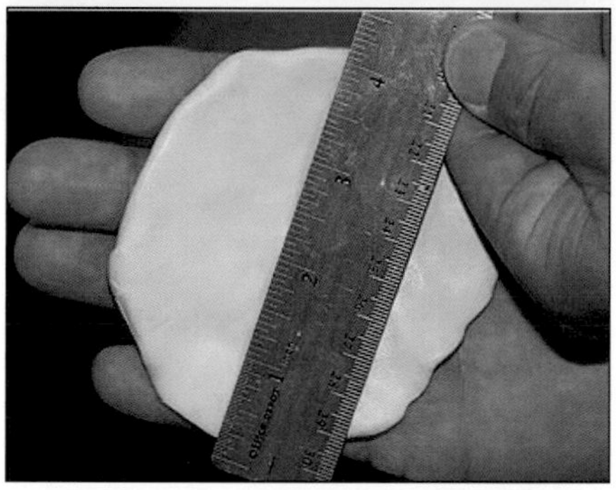

3. Knead the clay into a flat patty like a small pancake. A round patty of about 4 1/2 to 5 inches in diameter works well for most people.

4. When you're ready to start claying, mist your clay lubricant onto the face of the clay patty. In this example, we're using Pinnacle Clay Lubricant.

5. Next, spray the section you're going to clay. This is usually a section of approximately 16 to 20 square inches. You don't want to work on too large of an area at one time because you want to be thorough with your claying passes,

so stick with a manageably sized section.

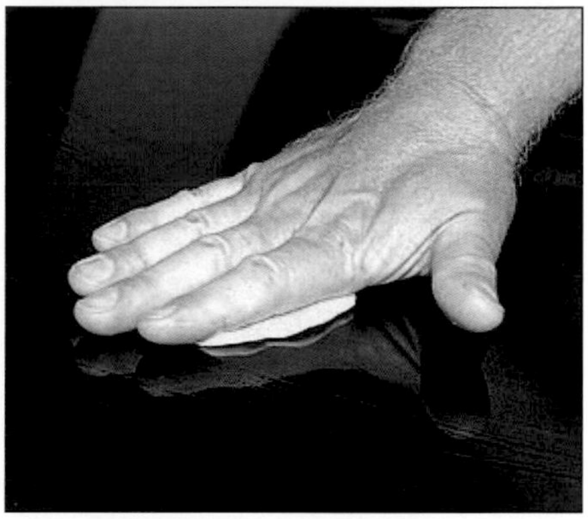

6. Begin moving the clay patty over the paint. Most people, including myself, use a simple back and forth motion, working the clay in straight lines over the paint. You can move your hand in straight lines, circles or a combination of both if you'd like. Because detailing clay is non-abrasive (except for aggressive grades), as long as everything is clean, it doesn't matter which way you move your hand because you shouldn't be instilling scratches into the paint.

In some cases, you will feel the clay try to drag as you move it over the surface. As the clay removes the bonded contaminants, you'll notice a decrease in drag and the clay will begin to glide effortlessly over the paint. This is an indicator that this section of paint is now clean and smooth.

After you're finished claying a section, wipe the excess residue from the surface before moving on to new territory. This means having an ample supply of clean microfiber towels on hand along with a clean and accessible area to store them.

7. After you wipe the section clean

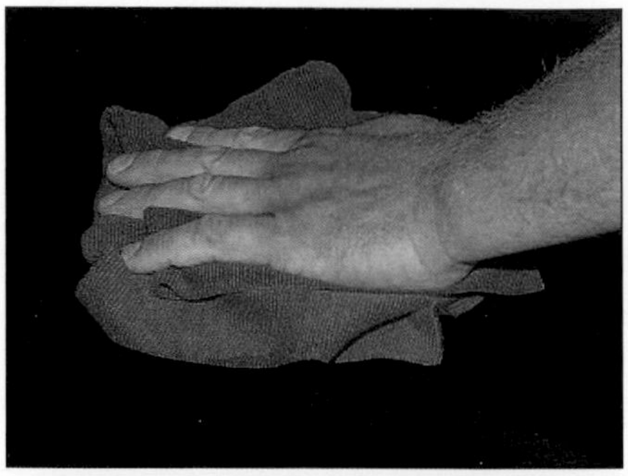

and dry, check the surface with your hand to ensure it is in fact smooth and glassy feeling.
If it is, try to remember how long you clayed the section or approximately how many strokes you used and then lock this into your memory and duplicate this on each new section you clay.
Keep in mind that some bonded contaminants are more stubborn than others and may take more effort or a more aggressive clay formula to remove.

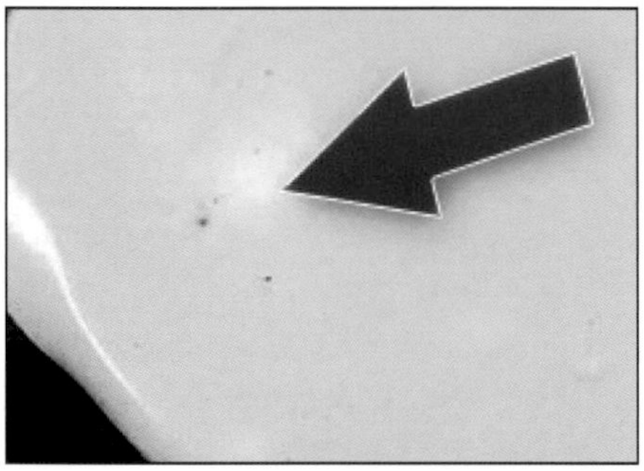

8. After claying each section, turn your clay patty over and inspect for contaminants.

If contaminants are discovered, remove any large dirt particles and then fold your clay in half and re-knead it to expose a fresh surface.

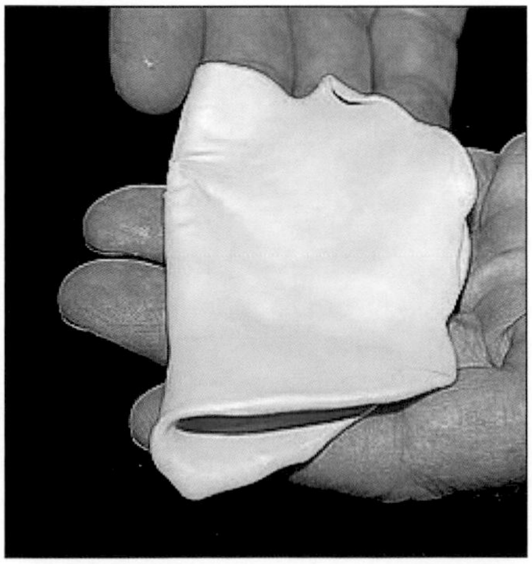

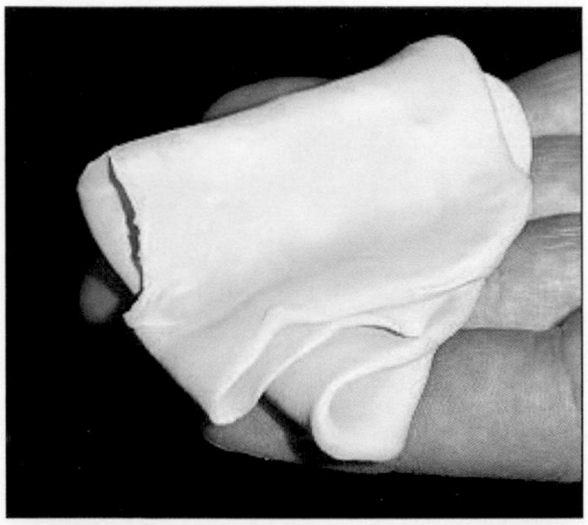

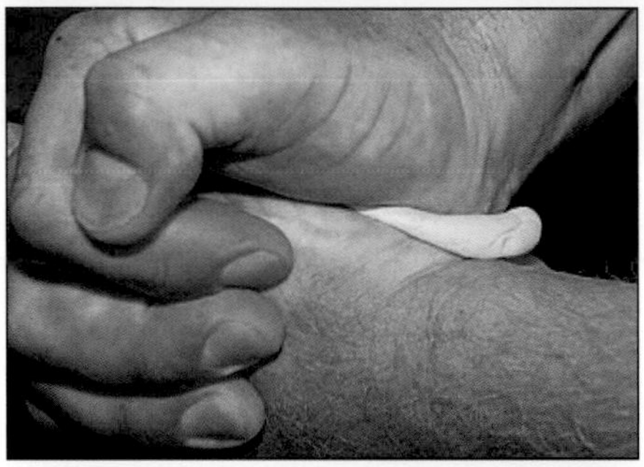

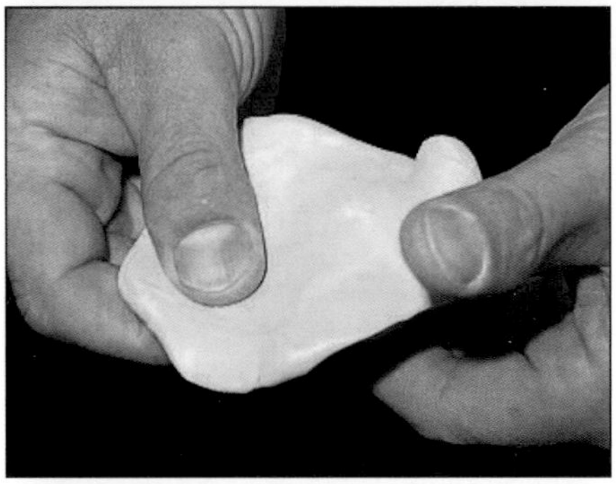

Now that I have the clay patty started, I will hold the small, thick patty between my fingers and thumbs and begin methodically kneading it to again create a round patty about 4 1/2 to 5 inches in diameter.

When your fingers are held closely next to one another, the patty should fit across the distance of your hand and

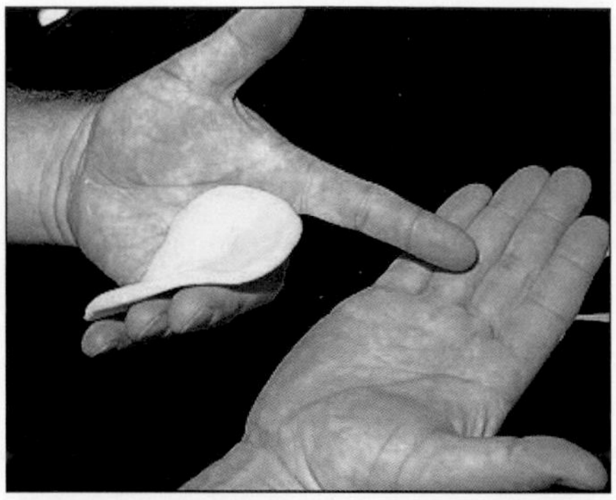

your fingertips should extend past the edge of the patty.

9. Repeat the above procedure until you've clayed all the contaminated panels, wiping the clay lube residue off after claying each section.

Here's why you should place the clay in your hand with your fingertips extended past the edge of the clay patty. If you position the clay like this, you'll apply

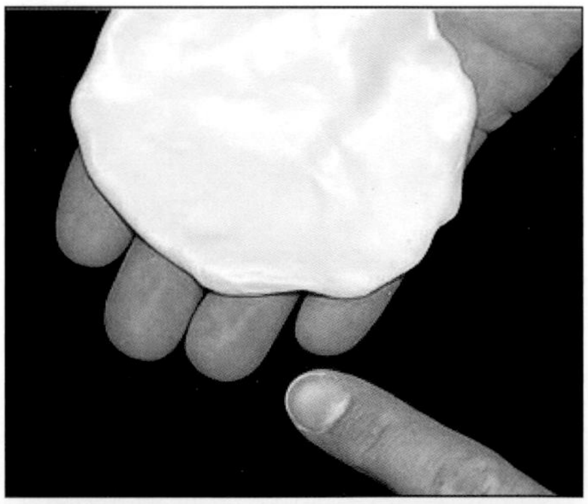

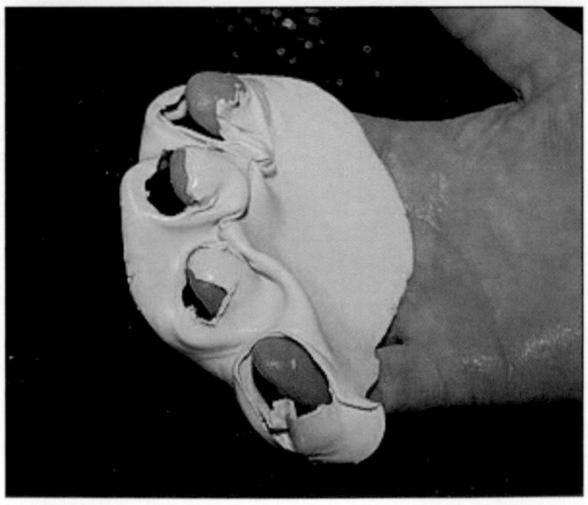

equal pressure over the entire surface of the face of your fingers without really thinking about it. This will help to place equal pressure over the surface of the clay patty. You can use the patty until you decide to stop, fold the clay over and re-knead it. In other words, you're in control. If you place your fingertips inside and on top of the clay patty, you tend to exert more pressure on your fingertips and you'll push holes through the clay patty. You now have to stop, fold the clay and re-knead it whether you were ready or not. Now, the clay is in control. It's just a little tip, but I like to be in control of each process; you can try this technique and then make up your own mind.

If the car you're working on has any kind of vinyl graphics, stickers or pinstripes, avoid claying over them as you can easily cause the edges to lift. Once the edges of any graphic have lifted, it's never going to lay flat against the surface again and usually will lift more and more. This also applies when working with paint care products.

Important

Claying your car's paint will tend to remove any previously applied wax or paint sealant. After you finish claying the paint, at a minimum, you'll want to apply a fresh coat of wax or a paint sealant.

If you don't re-apply a layer of protection, your car's paint will be exposed to the elements and subject to deterioration.

■ Frequently Asked Questions About Detailing Clay

What is detailing clay?

The website for the United States Patent and Trademark Office describes detailing clay as a plastic flexible grinding stone.

How long does clay last?

How long a piece of clay will last is completely determined by the amount of contaminants that have built-up on the paint of your car.

How much clay do I need?

You only need to use about 50 grams of clay to form a clay patty large enough to clay your car's paint. Clay normally comes in 50, 100 or 200 gram bars. If you have one of the larger versions, simply break it into smaller pieces and store the unused clay for a future detailing project.

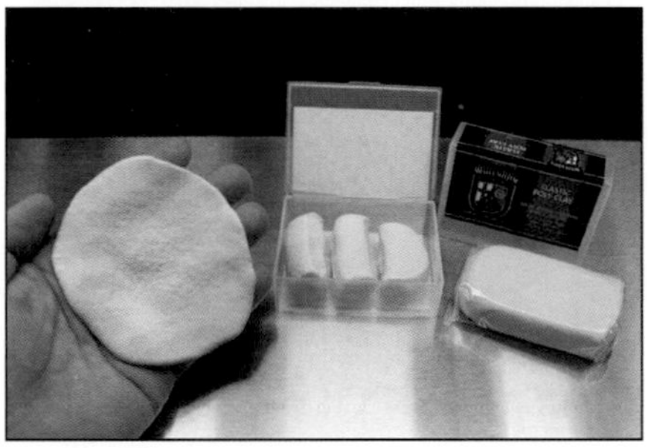

Example: Wolfgang Elastic Poly Clay bar is a hefty 200 gram bar of detailing clay that can easily be broken up into four 50-gram clay bars, or even 2-3 larger bars depending upon your personal preference. Form one chunk into a clay patty and store the other pieces for a future detailing session.

Will claying remove swirls and scratches?

No. Claying only removes above-surface bonded contaminants and does not remove below-surface defects like swirls and scratches and Type II Water Spot Etchings.

How often do I need to clay my car's paint?

Clay you vehicle's paint as often as needed as dictated by the results from your hands-on inspection.

For more information:

The Baggie Test

Do I use detailing clay before or after polishing?

First, remove the defects sitting on top of the surface (above-surface bonded contaminants) with detailing clay. Then, remove the defects that are in the paint (below surface defects) with a polish.

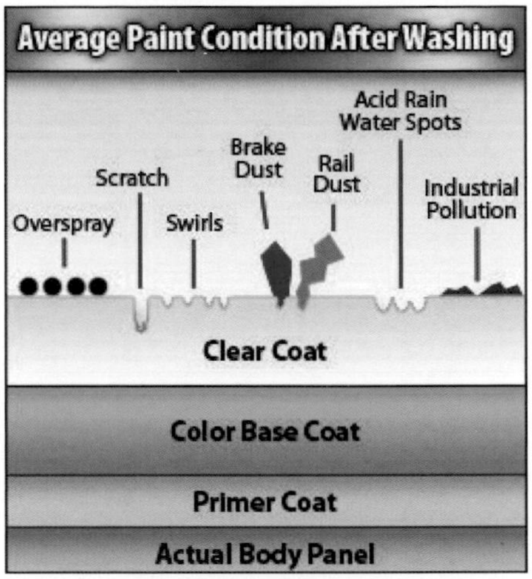

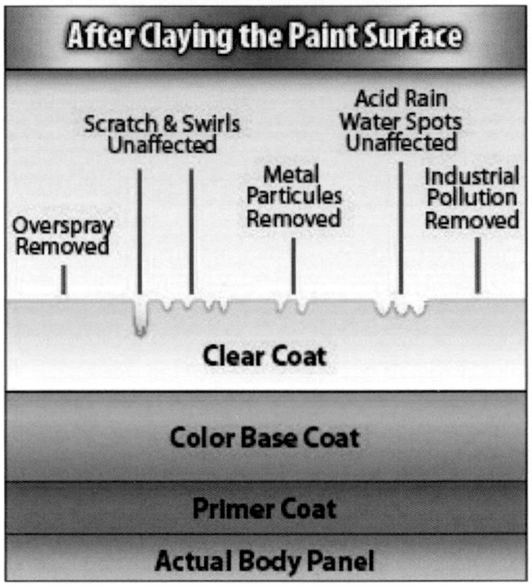

- **Above-surface bonded contaminant** = Tree sap, overspray paint, industrial fallout, rail dust, industrial fallout and airborne pollution.

- **Below-Surface Defects** = Swirls, Scratches, Type II Water Spots and Bird Dropping Etchings

Do I need to wash my car after I use detailing clay?

No. Simply clay a section and use a clean, microfiber towel to wipe off any clay lubricant residue and move onto a new section.

Read Full Article here:

Do I need to wash my car after I use detailing clay?

Do I need to use a dedicated clay lubricant or can I just use soapy water?

The goal of claying your car is to remove above-surface bonded contaminants safely, to do this you want and need to use a lubricant on

the surface of the paint so the clay will glide over the paint while it's abrading off the contaminants. Soapy water doesn't wipe off to reveal a "just detailed look". In fact, it usually looks streaky and this will worry people who are inexperienced. Of course, any follow-up steps like polishing and/or waxing will remove any smears or streaks, but again, inexperienced detailers tend to panic at the appearance of anything other than clean, shiny paint as they don't have the experience to understand the next steps will fix the problem.

My recommendation…
I recommend using a clay lube that is matched to the clay you use or a clay lube from a reputable company.

Will using detailing clay remove previously applied wax?
Yes. To what degree detailing clay will remove previously applied coats of wax or sealant is a great question. However, there is no simple definitive answer because there are too many variables involved, such as:

- Type of clay - level of aggressiveness or non-aggressiveness
- How many passes made over each square inch of paint
- Downward pressure used by the person using the clay
- Amount of lubricant used
- Skill level of person doing the claying
- Type of protection ingredients bonded to the surface

I bought a new car, do I still need to clay the paint?
Most people think that because the car they bought is brand new, it shouldn't need anything. However, from the time the car rolled off the assembly line and out of the manufacturing plant, it's been exposed to the air and any and all contaminants in the air.

This would include:
- Shipping by truck, train, ship
- Sitting parked in an unloading area
- Sitting parked at a VPC or Vehicle Processing Center
- Sitting parked outside at a dealership lot

Whether or not you need to clay your new vehicle can only be determined by the results of a hands-on inspection. For more information, refer back to the section covering Visual Inspection.

Here's the gunk I pulled off of a BRAND NEW 2012 CAMARO with only 2000 miles purchased off the dealership's lot.

Are there different types of clay?
Generally speaking, there are 4 different grades of clay:

- Ultra Fine Grade
- Fine Grade
- Medium Grade
- Aggressive Grade

There may other niche grades, but the above grades are the industry norm. The aggressive grades of detailing clay can be quite abrasive as they are intended to remove things like overspray paint, which can be very difficult. It's possible for aggressive clays to mar the paint during the claying process - this is called clay haze, which is another term for clay-induced scratching.

Keep in mind that the majority of the market that uses the aggressive clay is going to follow this with some type of machine compounding or polishing procedure.

Which type of clay should I use?
For most people working on their daily drivers, the Ultra Fine, Fine and Medium grades are normally considered safe for use by just about anyone and can be used for all general claying purposes. People that regularly wash and wax their cars will tend to stick with the Ultra Fine clays, because that's all that's needed to maintain a clean, smooth surface. Pinnacle Ultra Poly Clay is an ultra-fine clay and a good choice for frequent claying.

If I drop my clay on the ground, can I keep using it?
No. Detailing clay tends to be tacky and any sharp, abrasive particles on the ground will stick to it. Some of these particles will be invisible. If you attempt to use clay that has been dropped onto the ground, you risk instilling deeper scratches that will be difficult and time consuming to remove.

Cut your losses, discard the dropped clay and get some new or unused clay to finish the claying process. This is another good reason to cut larger clay bars up into smaller chunks.

Do you clay single stage paint the same way you clay a clearcoat finish?
This depends on whether or not the single stage paint is oxidized. If you're working on severely oxidized single stage paint, then it's a good idea to use a compound or a paint cleaner to remove the dead, oxidized paint. Otherwise, as you're claying, the dead, oxidized paint will load up onto your detailing clay.

The follow-up question I get to my answer on claying oxidized paint is: *"If I use a compound or paint cleaner to remove the dead, oxidized paint, can't I skip the claying step? Won't the compound remove the above-surface bonded contaminants?"*

The answer is, *"If you remove the dead, oxidized paint using an aggressive compound and wool cutting pad with a rotary buffer, then YES, you will likely remove any and all above-surface bonded contaminants".*

If you apply the compound any other way, like with a foam pad instead of a wool cutting pad, and with any other tool besides a rotary buffer, then here's what I know from personal experience: In the past, when I've removed heavy oxidation by hand or with a DA style polisher and then went back and clayed the cleaned paint, when I turned the clay over to inspect it, I've found above-surface bonded contaminants that were left even after compounding.

Foam pads tend to just glide over the contaminants, while a wool cutting pad will actually cut them off the paint. This has to do with both the type of material (foam vs. wool fibers), and the drive action of the tool, with the rotary buffer being the most aggressive tool.

Clay Alternatives And How To Use Them

- Ultima Elastrofoam Paint Cleaning System
- Speedy Surface Prep Towels
- Optimum Opti-Erasers
- Nanoskin AutoScrub Pads
- Nanoskin AutoScrub Wash Mitts
- XENIT Natural Citrus Mold Cleaner

There was a time when the way you removed above surface bonded contaminants like overspray paint, was to take an aggressive compound and either hand or machine apply it. This would remove the contaminants but the process would remove perfectly good paint and leave the finish looking scoured with swirls and scratches.

In the early 1990's detailing clay was introduced and this provided a way to remove above surface bonded contaminants without removing paint. The potential to mar or lightly scratch the paint still exists with clay depending upon the clay composition, the contaminants and even a person's technique.

Since the introduction of clay there are now even more tools and techniques for removing above surface bonded contaminants without using abrasive compounds.

Ultima Elastrofoam Paint Cleaning System

The Elastrofoam claying block is a rectangular foam block that measures 4 1/4" long by 2 1/2" wide and 1 1/2" thick. On one side of the foam is a rubbery surface that does the actual contamination removal. The foam backing is of medium density and this, along with its size, makes it very easy to hold while rubbing it over the paint. If the surface is mildly to severely contaminated you will hear an abrading sound that will go away as the contaminants are removed. There are several benefits to using the Ultima Elastofoam Paint Cleaning System:

- Outlasts normal clay
- Doesn't stick to your hands, leaves no smudges on the paint
- Ergonomically easy to use
- Can be used on glass and, unlike clay, it won't embed into pitted glass
- Can also be used on fiberglass Gel-coats and chrome

Directions for Use

To use the Ultima Elastrofoam claying block you simply mist the Ultima Cleaning Lubricant Gel onto the surface to be cleaned and onto the face of the rubber surface and then rub the block back and forth over the surface. Just like detailing clay you'll feel the Elastrofoam claying block grab at the beginning as it's removing contaminants and as the contaminants are removed the block will start to glide effortlessly over the surface. At this point you stop and wipe the residue off and move on to new territory.

One benefit to the Elastrofoam claying block is that if you drop it on the ground you can simply wash and rinse the rubbery surface off and continue using it.

The manufacturer recommends breaking-in a brand new Elastrofoam block by rubbing it over a glass window to flatten out the natural ridges in the polymerized rubber. The block comes in a plastic bag with a slip of wax paper against the rubber side; keep this piece of wax paper to store the rubberized side on when not in use. The manufacturer states it can be used to clean most cars up to twenty times and it won't remove or dull previously applied paint sealants.

My comments...

One of my friends active in the Mini Cooper world says they work great for removing contaminants off glossy vinyl graphics that you see on some Mini Coopers where as other products can mar or scratch.

Speedy Surface Prep Towels

These are a really ingenious invention in that they work like clay to remove above surface bonded contaminants

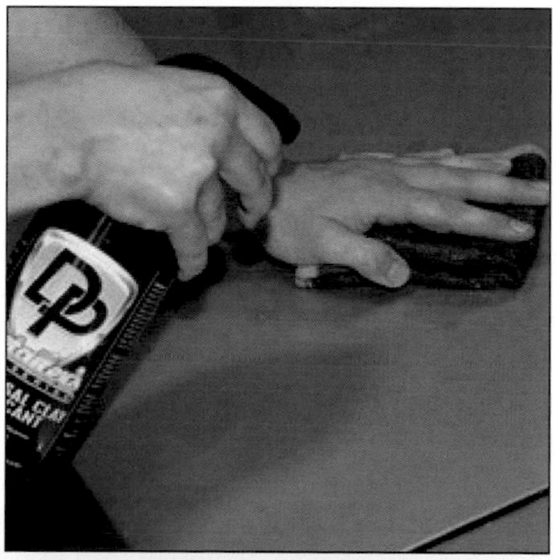

but use an advanced polymerized rubber that is coated over a flat weave cloth. This design works somewhat like a wash cloth when you bathe in that you hold the cloth side of the towel in your hand and rub the polymerized rubber side over the surface. You can use any quality clay lubricant or spray detailer but it is recommended to avoid using soap and water.

Unlike clay, the Speedy Prep Towel does not need to be kneaded and formed into a patty and can be used as is, right out of the package. If you drop the Speedy Prep Towel you don't have to worry about contamination, simply wash and rinse the towel and it's ready to use again. The Speedy Prep Towels are available in Fine and Medium Grades can be re-used for up to 50 cars, depending upon how contaminated they are.

Fine Grade & Medium Grade
The practical difference between a fine and a medium grade Speedy Prep Towel is that the Medium Grade towel will remove contaminants a lot faster and with fewer passes than the Fine Grade. The trade-off is that this extra aggressiveness can mar and haze the surface. The words mar and haze are a kinder and more gentle way of saying that these towels can inflict shallow swirls and scratches but here's the deal, these are professional grade tools for professional use. In most cases if the finish quality of a car has been neglected enough to require using the Medium Grade Speedy Prep Towel it also needs to be machine buffed to remove the results of neglect anyways.

The manufacturer recommends using the Fine Grade for darker colored cars and using the Medium Grade on lighter colors. As long as you plan on machine polishing the vehicle after using either of the Speedy Prep Towels, this isn't an issue. I always recommend planning doing some type of machine polishing after any method of removing above surface contaminants.

My comments…
I really like the Speedy Prep Towels and recommend them to anyone that already knows how to machine buff paint or is willing to learn as a part of restoring any car with a neglected finish.

Directions for Use

- The Speedy Surface Prep Towel comes with a protective coating from the factory. Before using the towel, you must break it in. Saturate the towel with a clay lubricant and using no pressure, wipe the towel back and forth and then up and down on clean, lubricated glass, such as your windshield. After several passes, the protective coating will be removed and the Speedy Surface Prep Towel will be ready for use.
- Use on clean, cool surface in the shade.
- Fold the towel 4-ways and use one side at a time. You can use the towel laid out flat but by folding it you'll find it easier to hold, it will conform over curves better and you'll get more use out of it. (See my tip)
- Mist a section of paint about 2' by 2' using your favorite clay lubricant or spray detailer and then rub the towel over the surface. If the surface is mildly to severely contaminated, you will hear a sound as the contaminants are being removed. As the contaminants are removed and the surface becomes smooth the sound will disappear.
- Wipe residues off and move onto new territory.

Note: *Best performance is seen when used between temperature ranges between 50° F and 99° F. Do not store or use on surfaces over 144° or polymerized rubber surface can melt. Black and dark colored paint can easily exceed 140° when exposed to direct sunlight. To clean simply wash in warm water, do not use soap.*

My tip for the Speedy Prep Towel
Take your Speedy Prep Towel and place it on a clean table with the cloth side up. Write the numbers 1 through 4 in each quadrant of the towel. Now when you fold the towel 4-ways, lift the edge of the side you're going to use and remember the number. Fold and use this side till you see performance falling off and then switch to an unused quadrant until you've used all 4 quadrants to their fullest service life. With this simple system you can monitor how many cars or how much you've used each quadrant.

■ Opti-Eraser

The Opti-Eraser uses an elastic polymer media over two sides of a foam block to safely remove above surface bonded contaminants. The unique thing about Optimum's elastic polymer media is it is incredibly soft and pliable and together with a spray lube, it is probably the least abrasive product in this category. It was purposefully designed for the average person to use to remove above surface bonded contaminants off their car's paint without having to machine polish to remove any marring, dulling or scratching afterwards.

The Opti-Eraser comes in two grades, the pink Opti-Eraser is the light grade version and the white Opti-Eraser is a heavy grade version.

The Opti-Eraser can be used with Optimum's No Rinse diluted at 2 ounces per gallon as a lubricant. The manufacturer states that the Opti-Eraser is very gentle to painted surfaces and while designed primarily for enthusiasts to maintain a car in good condition, it can also be used by professionals on neglected vehicles.

The Opti-Eraser is easy to grip and hold while rubbing over the surface and if dropped, the surface can be rinsed clean and used again. One thing I like about the white working surface is that you can see the contaminants building up on the surface to indicate when you need to rinse the face clean. The white color also reveals the color of the bonded contaminants and this can sometimes help to discover the source of the contaminants. For example a blue color could indicate blue overspray paint while a yellow/brownish color can indicate tree sap mist.

Directions for use
Wash and rinse vehicle first to remove loose dirt and use on clean, cool surface in the shade. Mist a small section of the vehicle with Optimum No Rinse diluted for use as a clay lubricant and then gently rub the Opti-Eraser over the surface. If contaminants are present you will feel the Opti-Eraser drag and as the contaminants are removed it will begin gliding effortlessly, meaning the surface is now clean and smooth. Wipe any excess residue off and move onto a new section.

■ XENIT Natural Citrus Mold Cleaner

Xenit is pronounced zee-nit. This product can be a real time saver in some instances of overspray paint removal. I've used this myself and been amazed at how well it's worked. Here's what the manufacturer states:

Unique Cleaning Power
XENIT's proprietary formulation does NOT contain soap OR water. XENIT contains more than five high performance ingredients such as Citrus 66, an all natural, highly refined extract of citrus fruit. Unlike most water-based cleaning agents that are designed to lift and carry dirt, XENIT is specially formulated to break down the complex molecules found in sticky materials. This unique micro-active cleaning action gives XENIT unequaled abilities to loosen and dissolve difficult grime like tar, grease, gum even adhesives. It even removes dried latex paint if accidentally dripped on carpet, flooring, or furniture.

It also works great to clean and shine brushed stainless steel like that used in kitchens and even disinfects at the same time while leaving a fresh, citrus scent. I use this product to clean the stainless steel counter on the workbench you see in the Autogeek Show Car Garage Studio.

■ Nanoskin Autoscrub Pads

Most people that know me know I like to do as much work as possible by machine, even machine applying waxes and paint sealants because working by machine is faster and produces better and more consistent results.
The Nanoskin Autoscrub Pads are round pads with a textured rubber surface on one side and a hook-n-loop interface on the other side and sandwiched between this is a half inch pliable foam core. The way you use these is to attach them the backing plate of a DA Polisher and then let the machine do the work for powering the pad over a painted surface to remove above surface bonded contaminants. You want to use plenty of lubrication and the manufacturer warns against just trying to use water as best results are achieved using a true lubricating clay lube or spray detailer.

Recommend Tools the Nanoskin Autoscrub Pads can be used with:

- Porter Cable 7424XP
- Meguiar's G110v2
- Griot's 6" ROP
- Shurhold DA Polisher
- Cyclo Polisher
- Makita BO6040
- Flex 3401

Note: *Not for use with rotary buffers*

The Nanoskin Autoscrub Pads, available in 3", 4" and 6" with the larger 6" being perfect for large flat panels and the smaller pads for thinner body panels for working between edges, body lines or trim. The 4" pads work perfect on the Cyclo Polisher and turns the Cyclo Polisher into a well balanced, low vibration decontaminating polisher.

According to the manufacturer, Autoscrub Pads use and advanced rubber technology that won't mar or scratch paint but from experience I recommend that if you're going to use this type of tool that you should plan on also doing at least one machine polishing step to ensure a clear, defect-free finish perfect for sealing with a wax, paint sealant or coating. ■

The DA Polisher – Porter Cable, Meguiar's, Griot's, & Shurhold polishers

DA polishers Overview

All five of the below tools are of the same type. They are all single head, random orbital polishers that use a free floating spindle assembly for a drive mechanism.

Porter Cable 7424XP

- 4.5 AMP
- 500 Watt Motor
- 5 pounds
- 3 Year Limited Warranty
- 1 Year Free Service

Meguiar's G110v2

- 4.2 AMP
- 430 Watt Motor
- 5 pounds
- 1 Year Limited Warranty

Griot's Garage Random Orbital polisher

- 7.0 AMP
- 850 Watt Motor
- 5.5 pounds
- Griot's Lifetime Warranty

- **Griot's Garage 3" Mini polisher**
- 2.0 AMP
- 240 Watt Motor
- Griot's Lifetime Warranty

Shurhold Dual Action polisher

- 4.2 Amps
- 500 Watt Motor
- 5 pounds
- 1 Year Limited Warranty

The Basics

- Lightweight, compact in size and easy to hold while buffing.
- Very easy to learn how to use and master like a professional.
- Always enable you to create better results faster on clearcoat paints as compared to working by hand.
- Variable speed polishers - you can pick and set the speed setting from a very low speed of 1 to a very high speed setting of 6 for removing swirls and scratches.
- Offers more than enough power to remove swirls and scratches out of

In This Section:

your car's clearcoat finish.

- Very versatile in that they can all be used to remove swirls, polish paint to a high gloss, and apply or remove wax or paint sealant.
- Can safely be used on cars, trucks, SUVs, boats, motorcycles, RVs, trailers and pretty much anything with paint, plastic, or gel-coat.
- Easiest tool to learn how to use if you are new to machine polishing.
- Very safe and when used correctly, they will neither instill swirls into your car's paint nor burn through it.

To show just how safe these types of tools are to use, here is my son (shown above) at age 9 using a Meguiar's G110v2 Dual Action polisher to apply wax to the front of a 1966 Batmobile recreation owned by my good friend Nate Truman in Southern California.

■ Safest tool to learn how to use

A lot of people are apprehensive about letting anyone work on their car's paint with a machine let alone learning to do it themselves. This is because of all the horror stories associated with machine buffers.

Here are the two common fears people have about machine polishing.

1. Burning through the paint, also called strike-through.

To burn through the paint means to buff so long on a section of a car that enough paint is removed to abrade through the clear layer of paint, exposing the colored layer of paint. If by chance you're working on a single stage paint and burn through the colored coat, then you'll expose the primer.

The problem with burning through the clear layer of paint and exposing the colored layer is that the colored layer is dull or matte in appearance. No amount of buffing with any kind of polish or wax will restore a glossy appearance to the exposed color coat. When this happens, the only way to fix the problem is to have the area repainted.

The problem of burn-through is normally a problem associated with the misuse of rotary buffers, which are direct drive tools. DA polishers, on the other hand, use a free Floating Spindle Bearing Assembly, which makes this a non-issue.

2. Swirls

Swirls are scratches that appear to us as being in some type of circular pattern instead of straight lines. They can be the result of improper maintenance techniques as well as improper use of a rotary buffer.

For more information:

📖 Paint Condition Categories

DA Polishers Are Very Safe!

When used correctly, you can safely buff out your car's paint without burning through or instilling swirls. DA polishers are the easiest and safest polishers to learn how to use.

I have personally taught thousands of people how to successfully use DA polishers and the techniques taught in this how-to book will ensure that you don't experience either of these two problems.

■ Free Floating Spindle Bearing Assembly

The reason why DA polishers, including the Porter Cable 7424XP, Meguiar's G110v2, Griot's Garage 6" ROP and Shurhold polishers are so safe to use for beginners and pros alike is because

they all use what's referred to as a free floating spindle bearing assembly.

With this drive mechanism, if you apply too much downward pressure to the face of the buffing pad or hold the tool so that more pressure is applied to just an edge of the buffing pad, it will simply stop spinning. Therefore, you cannot burn through the paint nor instill swirls.

Rotary buffers are direct drive tools. With this drive mechanism, the pad will continuously rotate and there is no mechanism or design feature that will stop it. This gives the rotary buffer a lot of power for correction work, but with that power comes a certain level of risk.

It is the free floating spindle bearing assembly that takes the risk or danger out of machine polishing. This has cleared the path to introduce machine polishing to the masses enabling anyone to machine polish and truly create professional, show car results without having to learn how to use a rotary buffer.

■ Handle Or No Handle

The topic of handles on DA polishers comes up from time to time. In all my classes, I show how to use these tools with and without the handles. I leave it up to each person to decide which approach works best. Regardless of which approach you prefer, the handle can affect pad rotation, so check out the information below and then do some experimenting with your DA polisher and see which approach works best for you.

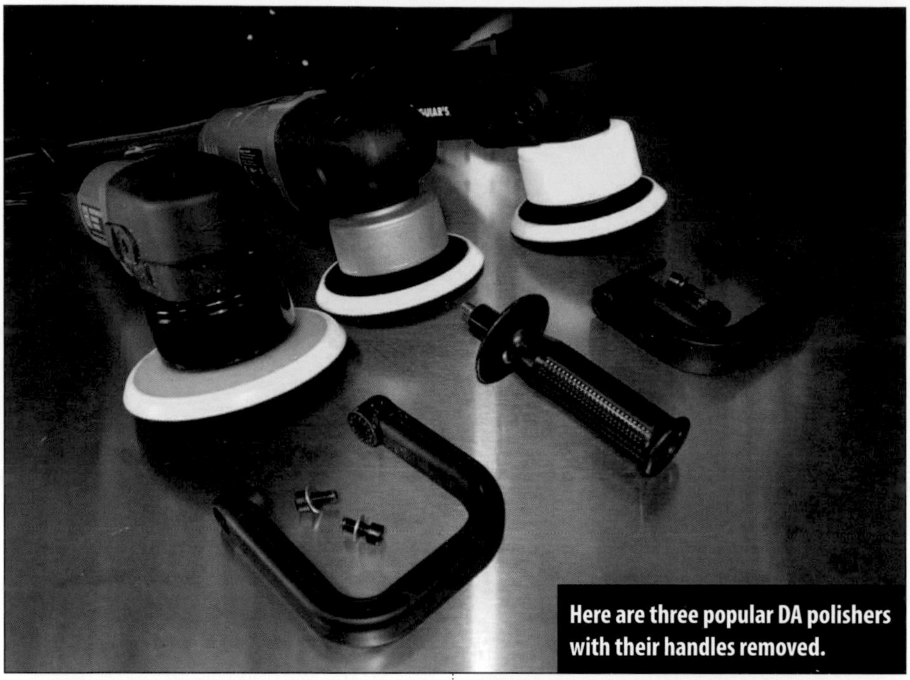

Here are three popular DA polishers with their handles removed.

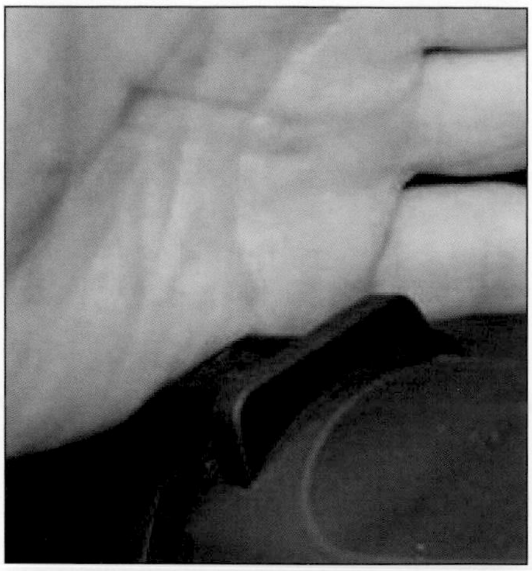

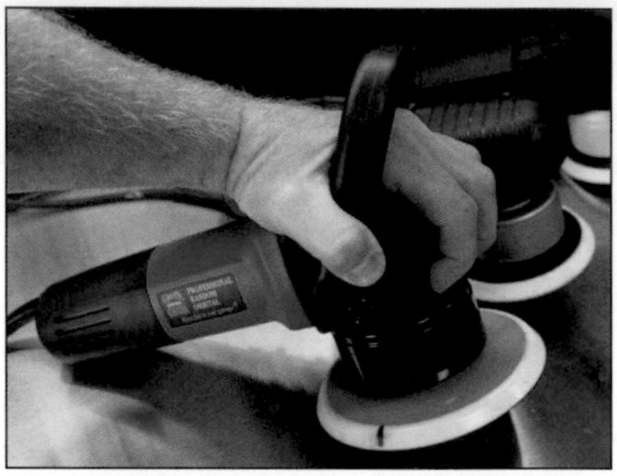

- Reduced fatigue Without a handle, you will have better control over the polisher and pad with less overall energy required for operation. Reducing fatigue is important because buffing out an entire car requires anywhere from an average of 4 to 12 hours, depending upon the size of the vehicle, condition of the paint and the goal for the end results.

- Keeping the pad flat to the surface When using a DA polisher, it's important to keep the pad flat to the surface. This helps to maintain pad rotation, which is essential in the defect removal process. Without the use of a handle, even downward pressure can be applied over the head of the polisher. If you apply uneven pressure to the head of the polisher, you can stop the pad from rotating and at this point you will no longer be removing swirls and scratches.

Stick handle - Porter Cable
The stick handle enables you to easily control directional movement of the polisher. The drawback to the stick handle is that if you're not paying attention, you can easily apply too much pressure to the handle side of the polisher. This causes you to hold the pad crooked or on edge, which can and will slow down or even stop pad rotation.

Personal preference My preference is to remove any handle and simply place my hand on the head of the polisher to guide and control it. This is especially helpful when using the polisher with one hand.

Bail handle - Meguiar's, Griot's and Shurhold polishers
Like using a polisher without a handle, the bail handle enables you to apply pressure directly over the head of the polisher, which helps you to keep the pad completely flat against the surface. The drawback to a bail handle is that it extends your hand away from the head of the polisher. This can cause you to expend more energy and tire the muscles in your forearm that control the polisher. It also reduces your control over the movement of the polisher.

With the handle removed from your DA polisher, your hand fits comfortably over the plastic housing covering the head of the polisher.

With the bail handle removed from the Meguiar's G110v2, there's a built-in tool rest (pictured top right). This keeps the polisher from tipping over if you place it on its back with the bail handle removed or adjusted to the extreme forward position. While this does provide a benefit, this tool rest gets pressed into your hand. This might bother some people buffing without the bail handle.

Griot's Garage = Locking Tab

Meguiar's G110v2 = Locking Tab

Of course, there's enough room inside the bail handle on both the Meguiar's and the Griot's polishers to place your hand on the head of the unit while leaving the bail handle in place.

With their handles removed, the Griot's and Meguiar's units have built-in, plastic locking tabs to prevent the plastic housing from sliding off. You can pry it off, but it won't slide off. The plastic housing on the Porter Cable polisher, however, doesn't have a built-in plastic locking tab. If you remove the handle, the plastic housing can easily slide off. If you're buffing out a car and this happens, it may startle you.

■ How To Bolt The Plastic Cover Onto A Porter Cable 7424Xp

The above photo shows the inside of the plastic housing on the Porter Cable polisher. As you can see, there is no plastic locking tab. For this reason, if you want to use the Porter Cable polisher without a handle, you should go to your local hardware store and pick up two metric M8 x1.25 socket cap bolts for new PCs or two 5/16" x 1/2" socket cap bolts and matching washers for older models.

Porter Cable recently switched the thread type over to metric. Below are the dates of the change from the Porter Cable website.

- **U.S. Threads = 5/16-18 Threads** Date Code 2009-10 and earlier
- **Metric Threads = M8x1.25 Threads** Date Code 2009-11 and newer

■ DA Backing plates

DA Backing plates are very important components that can have a huge effect on the performance of a DA polisher. The right backing plate will ensure your buffing pad and choice of compound or polish are being worked to their fullest potential. The wrong backing plate can negatively affect the transfer of power from the tool to the face of the buffing pad. This loss of efficiency means any job involving correction work will take longer.

■ Mark your backing plates

Mark your backing plate with a line like you see here. This will make it easy to see if the buffing pad is rotating versus just vibrating against the paint.

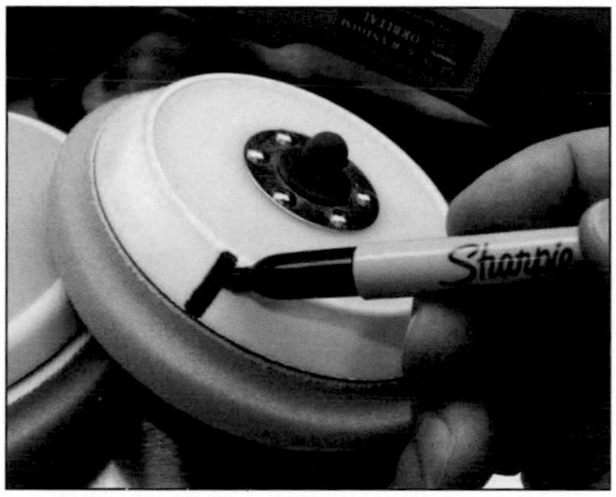

For more information:

Marking your backing plate

■ Design features of a backing plate

Here are the primary design features that make up a good backing plate.

Well Built And Reinforced
Firm, downward pressure to the head of a DA polisher puts more stress on everything. This includes the foam used to make the foam pad, the adhesive used to attach the hook and loop to the foam pad and backing plate, the hook and loop material, the backing plate and also the tool itself. Every component of the DA buffing process is subjected to more stress and this leads to more failures of the various components.

One common component known to fail is the backing plate, because it is subjected to the oscillating action of the tool where it's attached to the free floating spindle bearing assembly. The oscillating actions at low speeds are fairly non-violent and don't build up a lot of heat at the center of the backing plate. Bump the speed up to the 5 or 6 speed setting and the oscillating action becomes a lot more violent and powerful. With time and pressure added to this violent oscillating action, backing plate designs begin to fail in two ways:

1. The attachment of the 5/16" threaded arbor to the inner hard plate material breaks at some place and renders the backing plate unusable.

2. The adhesive that holds the hook and loop material breaks down and loses its bond.

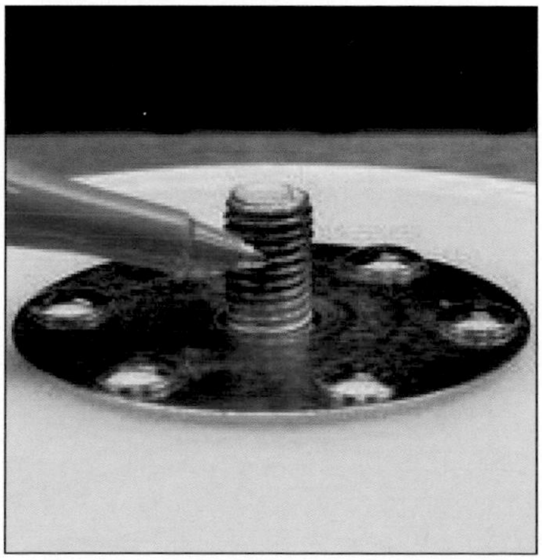

5/16" arbor

The spacer must be in place for proper clearance and operation of the backing plate.

The hook portion of a hook and loop interface

Not holding the pad flat

When you hold a DA polisher at an angle so that more pressure is applied to just one edge of a buffing pad, you create more force against the arbor where it mounts into the backing plate and against the spindle where the 5/16" arbor attaches to the DA polisher. The results are more broken backing plates and DA polishers. Today's high quality, long lasting backing plates are well-manufactured in all aspects. This includes overall design, materials, adhesives, rivets, hook and loop and even the arbors.

Correct Hook And Loop Design

There are different types of hook and loop designs. The most important part is that the hook on the backing plate matches the loop material on the buffing pad for best attachment strength and longevity of the hook and loop material.

KISS = Keep it Simple Simon

One simple thing you can do is to purchase backing plates and foam pads from the same manufacturer. Most of the time, this will prevent any mismatch issues as most reputable companies do their homework and ensure they are using the correct hook and loop materials for both their backing plates and their pads. You can run into trouble when purchasing lesser quality and cheaper backing plates that don't belong to a line of pads. There is a difference, so invest in a quality backing plate.

Hook and loop material - three general grades of quality

Hook and loop material is available in three general grades: consumer-grade, industrial strength and mil-spec. Leading manufacturers of backing plates use industrial strength materials.

3 important characteristics:

1. **Pull-apart strength**
   Pull-apart strength is a measure of how much force is required to separate two pieces straight apart from each other.
2. **Shear strength**
   Shear strength is a measure of how much force is required to slide the opposing hook and loop pieces apart.
3. **Cycle life**
   Cycle life is the measure of how many times two apposing pieces of hook and loop material can be pulled apart before the attachment strength degrades to 50% of its original value.

Hook and loop wears out

The more you use your backing plate, the faster the hook and loop will wear out. At some point, you'll want to replace a worn backing plate with a new one.

3 Types of hooks

- J-hooks
- Barb or Mushroom Hooks
- Micro-Hooks

All three styles will work and are being used in the industry.

1. J-hooks

J-hooks come in varying lengths. Shorter J-hooks work well, but longer

J-hooks are too long for use with DA backing plates and buffing pads. Long J-hooks create a measurable distance or gap between the pad and the backing plate, even though the J-hook does mesh into the loop material.

This gap leads to grinding between the J-hook and loop material, which leads to friction when the tool is operated at high speeds. Over time, this friction generates excessive heat.

2. Barb or mushroom hook

Barb style hooks are not good for DA polishers as they offer high engagement, which means the two types of material form a very strong attachment to one another. This strong attachment is ideal in situations of low frequency of engaging and disengaging the hook and loop. When engaged and disengaged frequently, these hooks wear out quickly, which decreases their pull-apart strength and cycle life.

3. Micro-hooks

There are 3 different types of designs of micro-hooks, but they all offer sufficient attachment strength and long cycle life. The short distance of the hook also helps to keep temperatures low, which helps all aspects of backing plate performance.

4. Flexible Backing Material With Tapered Edge
Early backing plates were basically hard plastic with a hook and loop interface on one side and a 5/16" arbor on the other side. New designs incorporate both rigid and flexible materials, each serving their own purpose. The centers of quality backing plates are made using a rigid fiberglass and glass cloth material to provide a strong and stable support for attaching the 5/16" arbor. Fiberglass offers superior heat resistance and can be heated to higher temperatures than plastics while retaining its shape and strength. The rigidity also works best to transfer power from the tool to the pad without absorbing or dissipating any power. The outer edges are usually made from a flexible urethane material and are tapered. The flexibility comes from both the urethane material and its tapered edge. These are both features that help to maintain flat pad contact and provide flexibility when changes in pressure occur due to curves and contours of body panels.

5. Thin Versus Thick
The thinner the backing plate, the more successfully the energy and the oscillating pattern from the tool will be transferred to the buffing pad. This is what you want anytime you're trying to remove below surface defects like swirls, scratches and water spots. A thick backing plate will dissipate energy and interfere with the oscillating pattern provided from the tool. This could be ideal when machine sanding and a less aggressive sanding action is needed. Backing plates for machine polishing trend towards being thin for the important reasons listed above and also to help in flexibility of the backing plate as well as to reduce heat retention by simply reducing mass. Less material also usually means lower manufacturing cost.

6. Correct Diameter
It's important to match the correct sized backing plate to the size of the buffing pad you are using. You want this to fit as close as possible. This will ensure maximum surface area for contact between the hook and loop interface. This maximizes potential grip strength between your backing plate and your buffing pad.

Too big
If you use a backing plate that is too large, there will be little to no safety margin between the edge of your buffing pad and the edge of the backing plate. This presents the potential for the backing plate to make contact with a painted surface, possibly marring the paint.

Too small
If you use a backing plate that is too small, there won't be enough support to ensure even pressure over the face of the buffing pad. This can reduce the effectiveness of any mechanical abrading taking place. It could also mean not properly breaking down any product that uses diminishing abrasives, which can lead to swirls or micromarring. A backing plate that is too small can also lead to a muffin or mushroom effect. When this occurs, the foam tries to deform and curl up over and around the backing plate, reducing pad life.

The Cyclo Polisher

Video: How to use the Cyclo Polisher to remove swirls and scratches

The Cyclo Polisher is available in a number of different configurations including,

- Model 5 – 110 volt
- Model 5 Pro – 110 volt – Variable Speed Adjustment
- Model 5C – 230 volt
- Model 5CE 230 volt
- Model 12A – Pneumatic

All Cyclo polishers come with the Vibration Elimination System the key is to get the correct weighted inserts to match the right weights to either the backing plates being used or in instances where brushes are being used. The result is a virtually vibration free tool that reduces fatigue while using your Cyclo Tool.

The Cyclo Polisher was introduced in 1953 and has a very interesting history, the below is from the CycloToolMakers.com website,

Cyclo Toolmakers, Inc.
In the early 1950s, two former US army pilots flew home to Colorado from the Middle East. Their twin engine airplane had been badly battered by the wind, sand, and sun of the harsh Arabian desert. The plane needed extensive bodywork but the men became frustrated with the swirl marks left on the fuselage by rotary polishers. They wanted a "hand-rubbed" quality finish. So, together, they worked to developed a unique design and after several revisions, the first orbital polisher, called the Cyclo, was manufactured in 1952 in Denver, Colorado.

As early as 1953, the United States Government had approved the polisher for routine use on its military aircraft and missiles. It was, (and continues today) to be the polisher used by the President's Air Force One fleet and Smithsonian museums. Soon thereafter, consumers quickly expanded its use beyond the aircraft industry to include auto, boat, and RV detailing as well as hockey rink maintenance, carpet and tile cleaning, woodworking, industrial metal polishing, and even casket making.

Interestingly, the Cyclo tool that was initially manufactured as an aircraft polisher, also became known as the "slenderizer", a massager that was used not only to relieve tension but also to stimulate circulation and trim one's figure.

The massager's use soon expanded to horse stables. Trainers and owners alike discovered that the animals were calmed and healed by the relaxing motion of the hand-like movements. Even Roy Roger's famous horse, Trigger, routinely benefitted from its use!

In late 1954, the small Colorado company signed a deal with Sear-Roebuck to produce the Cyclo under the Craftsman brand, and by mid-1955, the Craftsman version of the tool was on the shelves in Sears stores nationwide. Ultimately, Sears tried to buy the company but was unsuccessful in its bid.

For many years thereafter, the original company continued to manufacture and distribute the polisher, whose design has virtually remained unchanged since the fifties (a tribute to its creators ingenuity) and to great industrial engineering. It is not uncommon for us to hear from owners of 40-50 year old tools that are still in use today!

Specifications:

- 115 Volts
- 60 Hertz
- 220 Watts
- Motor: alternating current, semi-enclosed 24-bar commutator
- Speed: 650-3000orbits/minute
- Variable Speed Controller
- Output: 1/3 H.P. (.25 Kw)
- Weight:6.5 lb. (2.9 kg)
- Head Rotation/ Diameter:clockwise/4"
- Electric Cord: 10' length
- Housing: heavy-duty cast aluminum, double insulated.
- Three year warranty
- Complete VES System

Box includes: 2 ProGuard Orbital Backing Plates, VES Yellow, Silver and Blue Weighted Inserts, L Hex-Key Wrench, Flat Wrench.

The Cyclo Polisher is the only dual head orbital polisher on the market. Cyclo polishers are risk free, even for first time users. With their dual, counter-rotating, and oscillating buffing heads, you cannot burn the paint or instill swirls. Cyclo polishers are the easiest polishers to control, even with one hand. They are vibration-free and lightweight. No other tool even comes close. Cyclo Polishers are versatile in that you can polish paint, scrub carpets, and even clean leather seats. All you need to do is match the right pad or brush to the job and let your Cyclo Polisher do the work. The really cool thing about the Cyclo polisher, besides all its design features, is the abundant selection of pads and brushes available for it.

Including:

4 Inch Premium Foam Pads (Hook-n-Loop Attachment)

- **White Finishing Pad:** The white pad is Cyclo's softest pad. It is intended for final buffing and wax application. It will render a glossy shine without polishing. This pad has no cut.
- **Blue Polishing Pad:** The blue foam pad is the perfect pad for light polishing on any surface. Use it to apply wax for a fine gloss finish, or use it with a light finishing polish or pre-wax cleaner. The blue pad has slightly more texture than the white pad.
- **Green Polishing Pad:** The green pad is more aggressive than the white pad. It has a mild cut for gentle polishing. Use your favorite polish or pre-wax cleaner to remove light oxidation and bring out a bright, glossy shine.
- **Orange Compounding & Polishing Pad:** The orange pad is the all-around swirl remover, polisher, and paint deoxidizer. Made of high density foam, this pad will correct most mild to moderate paint imperfections and polish metal and chrome.
- **Yellow Cutting Pad:** The yellow cutting pad is intended for more aggressive swirl and scratch removal. It is made of dense foam and will work well with compounds and advanced swirl removers. This pad is comparable to our Wolfgang™ yellow cutting pad.
- **Yellow Scrubbing Pad:** The yellow scrubber is the most aggressive pad. It is the highest density foam and will take care of your most stubborn surface problems. Use this pad to remove bugs, tar, sap, and as an aggressive paint deoxidizer.

4 Inch Wool/Acrylic Blend Pads – One sided

These pads can be used for aggressive correction work on paint or for restoring neglected aluminum and polishing to a mirror shine.

- **Yellow Medium Cut – 50% Wool, 50% Wool Acrylic Pad:** The yellow wool pad is moderately aggressive.
- **Blue Finishing – 70% Acrylic, 30% Wool Pad:** Use the blue pad for general polishing and gloss-enhancement.

4 Inch Wool/Acrylic Blend Pads – Double sided

- **Blue Finishing – 70% Acrylic, 30% Wool Pad:** Use the blue pad for general polishing and gloss-enhancement. The blue pad can be used with any finishing polish to bring out a fine luster on any finish.

- **Yellow Medium Cut – 50% Wool, 50% Wool Acrylic Pad:** The yellow wool pad is moderately aggressive. It removes swirls and moderate scratches, and reduces significant pits and deeper scratches. Use a swirl remover with the yellow pad when aggressive cutting is not needed.

4 Inch Cyclo Double Precision™ Foam Pads

- **Yellow Double-sided Cutting Pad:** The yellow cutting pad is intended for more aggressive swirl and scratch removal. It is made of dense foam and will work well with compounds and advanced swirl removers. This pad is comparable to our Wolfgang™ yellow cutting pad.

- **Orange Double-sided Light Cutting Pad:** The orange pad is the all-around swirl remover, polisher, and paint deoxidizer. Made of high density foam, this pad will correct most mild to moderate paint imperfections and polish metal and chrome.

- **Green Double-sided Polishing Pad:** The green pad is more aggressive than the white pad. It has a mild cut for gentle polishing. Use your favorite polish or pre-wax cleaner to remove light oxidation and bring out a bright, glossy shine.

- **White Double-sided Finishing Pad:** The white pad is Cyclo's softest pad. It is intended for final buffing and wax application. It will render a glossy shine without polishing. This pad has no cut.

4 inch Light Cutting Wool Pads

Cyclo Wool Pads each measure 4 inches in diameter and feature hook & loop backing. Cyclo calls these Light Cutting in the aggressiveness level and can be used for leveling severely oxidized paint and deep scratches. You will need to do at least one follow-up step to remove any buffing haze after using wool buffing pads.

4 Inch Fastcut 600 Grit Disc

These are a tough nylon sanding or grinding disc you can use to remove paint and rust for restoration projects. They can also be used to resurface tile and grout.

Cyclo Pad Covers (Bonnets)

- **Microfiber Suede:** This is the softest fabric of the two pad covers. The microfiber is manufactured to mimic the softness of suede. Use this pad cover for final buffing after you have removed the wax residue. It will pick up any remaining dust and gently buff your paint to a glossy shine.

- **Cotton Terry:** The 100% cotton pad cover is ideal for removing dried polishes and waxes, and gentle polishing. The hooked fibers are excellent at removing residue and gently polishing the paint surface. Cyclo also says it can be used to clean interior surfaces.

4" Premium Terry Bonnets

4" Premium Microfiber Bonnets

■ How to use a Cyclo Polisher to Remove Swirls

You use the Cyclo Polisher in much the same way you would use dual action polisher. Match the aggressiveness level of the pad and product to the condition of the paint you're trying to restore.

Buffing Pads
For deep swirls, scratches and severe oxidation you're going to want to use either a wool pad or one of the aggressive foam cutting pads. The yellow, blue or white wool cutting pads are the most aggressive pads for working on paint and with a quality compound they will remove defects fast. Follow-up with either the green or blue foam polishing pads for swirl-free and haze-free results. Switch over to the white finishing pad to machine apply wax or a paint sealant for a show car finish.

Compounds and Polishes
For deep swirls, scratches and severe oxidation you're going to want to use a true compound approved for use with an oscillating tool. Optimum Compound II and Blackfire SRC Compound are good choices and work well with the Cyclo polisher. For polishes, any of the Medium Cut to Fine Cut Menzerna Polishes work well as does the Optimum Polish II. Wolfgang Total Swirl Remover and Finishing Glaze as well as Pinnacle Advanced Swirl Remover and Advanced Finishing Polish all remove defects well and polish out nicely.

Divide large panels into smaller sections
Most car hoods can be divided into 4 quarter sections. Larger hoods should be divided into 6 sections. When you're finished with one section, move on to the next section of paint but be sure to overlap a little into the previous section for uniform defect removal.

Use the high speed setting for both correction and polishing steps.
For the Mark 5 you simply turn the tool on as it's a fixed speed model. For the Mark 5-Pro you set the variable speed indicator on the 6 setting.

Machine Applying Wax
For machine applying a wax or paint sealant you don't need or want the highest speed setting so use either the 4 or 5 speed setting.

Machine Removal of Wax
There are a number of bonnet options available for the Cyclo Polisher the key to using one of the bonnets is to use a the orange or green foam pads. This gives you a firm backing to enable the bonnet to grab and remove the wax but with enough pliable cushion to contour to curves and body lines.
Carpet, fabric and upholstery cleaning
There are 4 different brushes available for use with the Cyclo Polisher.

Cyclo Polisher Brushes

- **Grey Ultra Soft Upholstery Brush:** This brush is for your most delicate carpet and upholstery. Each bristle is flagged, meaning they are split in to multiple fine tips. This brush is ideal for headliners, leather upholstery, natural fibers, and more fragile upholstery and carpets.

- **Aqua Soft Carpet Brush:** This brush is an all-around carpet scrubber. It has medium crimped bristles for gentle but thorough cleaning. It loosens and removes spots and stains from most types of carpet.

- **White Standard Carpet Brush:** This brush is meant for rigorous scrubbing of durable carpets. The bristles are stiff enough to dislodge old stains and they will hold up better than the Soft Carpet Brush on heavy duty carpet. You can also use this brush on tile, grout, and floor pads.

- **Black Stiff Scrub Brush:** The black brush has very stiff bristles and is meant for intense scrubbing of hard surfaces. Use it on tile, grout, stone floors, and truck bed liners.

The key to cleaning with the brush options is to use the correct brush for the material you're cleaning. It's better to err on the side of caution and start out with a brush that uses softer bristles because if you find it's not aggressive enough you can always substitute a more aggressive brush.

** CE marking on a product is a manufacturer's declaration that the product complies with the essential requirements of the relevant European health, safety and environmental protection legislation in CE marking countries*

The Flex XC3401

The Flex 3401 is ready to use right out of the box except for adding a few drops of light machine oil to the felt ring. The forward Bale Handle works really well and makes the tool easy to control.

■ Overview

The components that make up the Flex 3401

- Handle Cover
- Bail Handle
- Spindle Lock
- Gear Head
- Locking Button
- Switch
- 4.0 m power cord with plug
- Speed Dial
- Velcro Pad

■ Optional Flex Grip Side Handle

Flex offers as an option, their Flex Grip Side Handle which is also called a stick handle in the detailing world. The Flex Grip Side Handle can be used in place of the Bale Handle and can be attached to either side of the polisher. The side without the Flex Grip Handle should have one of the included slotted screws attached to firmly hold the handle cover in correct placement during use.

■ Unique Features

Designed specifically for polishing paint

Flex paint polishing tools are specifically made for machine polishing paint. Most tools used in the body shop and detailing industries are manufactured using what's called a Global Manufacturing Process, which means the tool are designed for multiple applications, such as,

- Steel grinding, sanding and cutting
- Concrete grinding and cutting
- Polishing paint

The Global Manufacturing Process is a one-size fits all approach so that one tool design can be marketed into multiple industries. Flex engineers and designs their paint polishers specifically for the needs of compounding, polishing and machine waxing automotive paints.

Forced Rotation Dual Action Buffing Head

The key feature that separates the Flex 3401 paint polisher from all other tools is the unique forced rotation, dual action design of the drive mechanism.

Video: All about the FLEX-3401 Forced Rotation Dual Action Polisher

Drive Mechanism for Flex 3401

Seven Function Microprocessor

Each Flex 3401 comes with a seven-function microprocessor to control and protect the electronics and mechanical drive system of the tool. The seven function microprocessor controls these seven aspects of the Flex 3401,

1. Provides constant speed control via the Tachometer Generator
2. Provides a soft or gradual start of the rotation of the electric motor that powers the drive mechanism.
3. Controls the accelerator Trigger Switch
4. Provides restart protection after a power interruption
5. Provides overload protection
6. Monitors the temperature of the coil windings and turns the polisher off before damage can occur
7. Controls speed set by the variable speed dial

Mike's comments…

Low Vibration

The Flex 3401 is a low vibration tool. This has to do with the precision machined gears, quality German bearings and gear-driven, dual action forced rotation plus oscillating action of the drive mechanism.

9' Rubber Cord

In order to cut costs, most power tools come with a vinyl covered power cord; the problem with this is the vinyl cover is prone to kinking and coiling anytime it's wound around the tool. Most people wrap their cords around their tools when not in use for storage purposes. Vinyl cords retain the curves and bends you put into them so that when you go to use the tool the electrical cords are difficult to un-coil and a pain to work with.

Natural Rubber
Flex tools are designed to be user-friendly and because the cord is a major component of any electrical tool, Flex has chosen to use natural rubber for a cover for the electrical wires. Rubber is more flexible and doesn't have a memory so when you unwind the cord it won't kink or coil.

Quality Manufacturing
In 2011 Flex invited me and my co-worker Nick to visit the Flex Corporate Offices and Manufacturing Plant in Stuttgart, Germany. I created a thread about our visit to the manufacturing plant with lots of pictures in the link below.

Germany Flex Plant Tour Pictures

The copper wire that is used for the windings is powder coated which keeps the wires clean and provides long term protection from corrosion and deterioration. This is a unique feature to all Flex electric motors that you don't find on similar tools in the industry. It adds extra time, labor and cost to the part but the end-result is a component that will outlast the competition.

Here's a finished Armature that has been balanced and give an individual part number for future quality control identification.

From left to right: 4", 4 3/8", 5 1/2", 6"

Backing Plate Options

- Factory backing plate = 5 1/2"
- Optional Factory 4 3/8" backing plate
- Lake Country = 4" backing plate
- Lake Country = 6" backing plate

Pad Options

There are so many pad options for the Flex 3401 that to do the topic justice would require a chapter all on its own. Instead, here's the nutshell version and for specific information on which pads for which backing plates for your specific project the best thing to do would be to call me, call Autogeek or join the AutogeekOnline.net discussion forum and start a thread with your questions that myself and our forum community will be glad to lend a cyber-hand in answering.

Foam Pads

- **4" Backing Plates**
  - 5" Hybrid Pads
  - 4" CCS
  - 4" Hydro-Tech
  - 4" Purple Foamed Wool Pad

- **4 3/8" Backing Plates**
  - 5.5" CCS
  - 5.5" Hydro-Tech
  - 5.5" Flat Pads
  - 6.0" Kompressor

- **5 1/2" Backing Plates**
  - 6.5" CCS
  - 6.5" Hydro-Tech
  - 6.5" Flat Pads
  - 6.5" Hybrid Pads
  - 6.5" Kompressor
  - 6.5 Purple Foamed Wool
  - 6.5 Blue Foamed Wool Hybrid

- **6" Backing Plates**
  - 6.5" CCS
  - 6.5" Hydro-Tech
  - 6.5" Flat Pads
  - 7.0" Kompressor
  - 6.5 Purple Foamed Wool
  - 6.5 Blue Foamed Wool Hybrid

Lake Country Foamed Wool Pads

- 6.5" Purple Foamed Wool Pad
- 6.5" Blue Hybrid Foamed Wool Pad

Lake Country's Foamed Wool Pads combine the polishing ability of foam with the cutting ability of a wool pad. The wool fibers help to cut or abrade the paint to remove defects fast while polyfoam particles encapsulate the base of the foam fibers providing a dense, base to support the outer portion of the wool fibers.

These pads are not as aggressive as a traditional wool cutting pad but are more aggressive than foam cutting pads and able to withstand dramatically more punishment than foam by itself. Foamed wool pads last a long time and like wool pads are pretty much indestructible. These pads leave a nicer looking finish that can easily be maximized by following with a foam polishing pad and suitable polish.

Foamed Wool Pads work great on the Flex 3401 for restoring neglected paint where you want to remove below surface defects quickly so you can move on to the polishing step using only foam for a show car finish.

Mike's comments...
If you own a Flex 3401 and use it for correction work, (removing swirls, scratches, oxidation and water spots), then you should really have at least one of the foamed wool pads in your arsenal.

Microfiber and Surbuf Pads
All of the Microfiber pads and Surbuf MicroFinger pads can be used on the Flex 3401. Microfiber pads with a thicker foam backing buff smoother versus microfiber pads with thin, dense backing. Also, compounds and polishes with good lubricity make buffing a lot easier. Compounds that tend to flash or dry during the buffing cycle can make the Flex 3401 feel, what I call, grabby. This is even more noticeable when using microfiber pads with thin, dense foam backing. So if you're going to use microfiber pads with the Flex 3401 then stick to the microfiber pads with the thick, softer foam backing and/or Surbuf MicroFinger pads.

■ How to use the Flex 3401

Crosshatch Pattern
The way you use the Flex 3401 is basically the same way you would use any of the Porter Cable style DA polishers in that you move the polisher using a crisscross or crosshatch pattern while overlapping your passes by about 50%

Divide Body Panels Into Smaller Sections
Look at each panel of the vehicle you're buffing out and divide the panel up into smaller sections.

Buff Larger Sections
With more power you can tackle larger sections of paint for your section passes. You can easily tackle a 2' by 2' section when using a Flex 3401 and effectively remove swirls and scratches while with the PC style DA Polishers you're more effective if you tackle smaller section.

Work One Section At A Time Making Section Passes
There are two definitions of the word "pass" as it relates to machine polishing.

- **Single pass:** A single pass is when you move the polisher from one side of the section you're buffing to the other side of the section one time.

- **Section pass:** A section pass is when you move the polisher back and forth with enough single overlapping passes to cover the entire section

For more information:
📖 *Time To Start Buffing*

More Power
Because the Flex 3401 is a direct drive tool the pad is going to rotate and oscillate when you pull the trigger no matter how much downward pressure you apply or if you're buffing out curved panels.

Faster Correction
The direct drive feature enables you to buff out a car faster than the Porter Cable style DA Polishers. The reason for this is because buffing pads on the PC style DA Polishers will stop rotating when too much downward pressure is applied or when the pad is not flat to the surface. (That's also a safety feature of the PC style tools in that you really can't cause any damage).

💻 *Variable Speed Power Options*

■ The Variable Speed Dial on the Flex 3401

The Flex 3401 has an advertised OPM range from 3200 OPMs to 9600 OPMs with a variable speed dial that ranges from 1, (low speed), to 6, (high speed). The variable speed dial is located perfectly to allow you to quickly and easily adjust the power using your thumb while operating the tool.

Below are the recommended ranges

for using the Flex 3401 Forced Rotation Dual Action Polisher. The tool is actually easier to control and move over the paint at higher speed settings versus lower speed settings. Keep this in mind if you're brand new to using the Flex 3401 and you turn it on for the first time using a slow speed setting.

Get a feel for the tool when you first turn it on using a slow speed setting and then use your thumb to turn up the speed as your comfort level increases.

When first starting out, practice on a large, flat horizontal panel like the hood or trunk lid of a car.

■ Two approaches, Show Car Detailing & Production Detailing

Show Car Detailing
Multiple Step Procedures using Dedicated Products & Pads

- **5-6 Speed Setting - Heavy Correction Work**
  The Flex 3401 is actually easiest to use at higher speeds when doing any type of correction work. For any cutting or correction work use the 5-6 Speed setting.

  You can spread your product out using the low speed settings but once you get the product spread out, use your thumb to move the dial up to the high settings.

- **4-6 Speed Setting - Polishing Work**
  For polishing work you can bump the speed down to the 4-5 speed setting or if you're using a polishing pad for correction work then use the 5-6 speed setting.

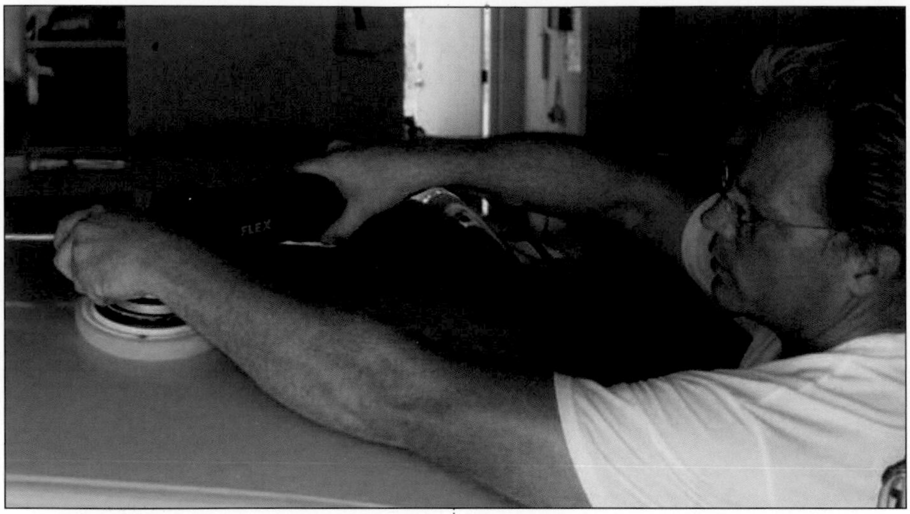

- **2-4 Speed Setting - Final or Finish Polishing/Machine Applying Wax**
  Any time you're doing any final polishing or you're machine applying a finishing wax or paint sealant then you want to be on the 2-4 setting.

Of course there's a little personal preference to all of this but the above are good general ranges for using this tool.

Production Detailing Work
Single step procedure using one product and one type of pad

Try to use a foam polishing pad
No matter which brand of cleaner/wax you choose to use, try to apply it using a foam polishing pad and not a foam cutting, finishing or fiber pad. A cutting pad may remove defects faster, but the goal is to only do one buffing step to the vehicle and, too often, the aggressive nature of a cutting pad can leave micromarring. Just the opposite is true for a finishing pad; it will always finish better but it might not offer enough cleaning power to utilize the cleaners and/or abrasives in your choice of cleaner/wax to do a good job. A polishing pad is a good happy medium.

Perfect tool for the job
The Flex 3401 is the perfect tool for doing high quality production detail work. Notice I said high quality. Most production work is hack work and detailers misuse a rotary buffer and the end result is a swirled-out finish. With the power provided by the Flex 3401 you can do high quality work in one step and avoid leaving swirls in the finish or burning through the paint.

- **4-6 Speed Setting**
  If you're doing production work and using a one-step cleaner/wax or AIO (All-in-One) type product, you should be in the 4-6 speed range and you'll want the speed and power to aid in doing any correction work.

There's nothing wrong with doing a one-step procedure to a car. In fact, if you're buffing out cars for money you should be using a one-step product unless you've sold and charged for a multiple-step procedure

Large Projects
Anytime you're buffing out large projects like Boats, RV's, Motorhomes, etc. you should be using a one-step cleaner/wax and only going around the project one time. A large project like a 40' Motor home will take a long time to buff out the entire thing. You certainly don't want to be doing a three-step procedure unless your customer really wants show car results and is willing to pay for your time, labor and materials.

Knock out the highest point first
Like any detailing project, when using the Flex 3401 I will tend to knock out the roof first, all they way through to the waxing or protection step and then tackle the rest of the car working downward.

Doing the Major Correction Step to the roof of a 1957 Chevrolet

Tips & Techniques

I have two primary tips for anyone wanting to learn to use and master this tool.

1. Hold the pad flat – Avoid Walking Around
This is what I call a "Self-Teaching" tool. The reason why is because if you don't hold the body of the tool in a way to keep the pad flat to the surface the tool will feel like it's trying to walk around on the panel as you're buffing.

That is, If you hold the body of the tool at any type of angle so the pad is not flat you will feel the buffing pad trying to,

- Walk away from you
- Walk towards you
- Walk to the right
- Walk to the left

This is easy to overcome if you simply focus on the task at hand. If you feel the polisher trying to walk in any direction that's a message to you that you're not holding the pad flat to the surface.

2. Use Smaller Pads
The larger the pad the more leverage it has over the tool. That's not a good thing or a bad thing, just a fact. Here's another fact, smaller pads on any tool are easier to control than larger pads and this is especially true for the Flex 3401.

My recommendation
The Flex 3401 is a wonderful tool for enthusiasts, pro detailers and even body shops wanting to turn out swirl-free finishes. The dual action of rotating and oscillating with the direct gear driven design gives this tool plenty of power but also helps to prevent you from instilling swirls or burning through the paint.

If you want to step-up to the Flex 3401 then here's my recommendation: invest in the Lake Country FLEX XC3401 Changeable Backing Plate System and then invest in the Lake Country 5" Hybrid Pads.

From left to right: 4", 4 3/8", 5 1/2", 6"

[4" and 6" Backing Plates for Flex 3401]

Pictured abve: On the left is the 6" backing plate, center is the 4" backing plate and on the right is the interface plate that enables you to switch between either the 6" or the 4" backing plate.

[5 inch pads for the 4" Backing Plate on Flex 3401]

- **5 inch Hybrid Orange Heavy Cutting Pad:** This hybrid foam pad provides the level of cut expected from a foam cutting pad, but finishes like a foam finishing pad! It removes most paint imperfections and leaves a finish that is nearly wax ready.

- **5 inch Hybrid Blue Light Cutting Pad:** This light cutting pad features super dense construction which enables it to remove defects quickly without compressing, like softer pads can.

- **5 inch Hybrid White Polishing Pad:** The white hybrid pad features very dense foam. Use this pad to remove light imperfections, apply a light polish, cleaner wax, and any jobs for which you'd use the standard Lake Country white polishing pad.

- **5 inch Hybrid Black Finishing Pad:** This pad provides no mechanical cutting ability but thanks to its dense foam, it provides superior control while polishing. It features super soft foam, which makes it ideal for finishing polishes, waxes, sealants, and glazes.

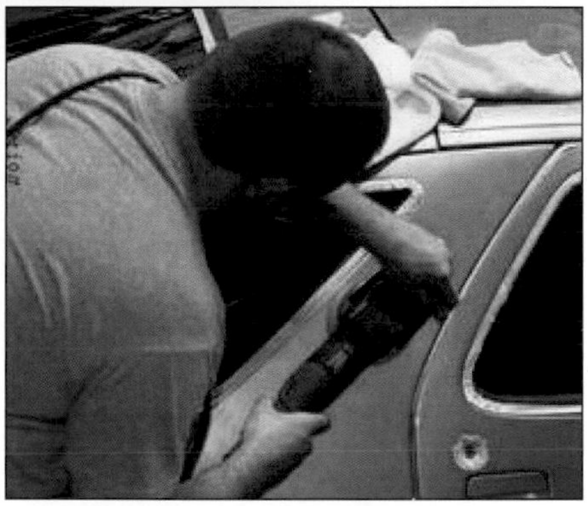

Here's my friend Kyle using a 5 inch Hybrid Blue Light Cutting Pad on the B-Pillar of a 1986 Porsche 928 to remove swirls.

Here's my friend Justin using a 5 inch Hybrid Orange Heavy Cutting Pad on a 1965 Valiant

For some real detailed tips and techniques on how to use the Flex 3401 get a copy of my DVD on this tool.

[How To Properly Use Flex Polishers DVD]

Rotary buffers

Rotary Buffers
A lot has changed when it comes to the design of modern rotary buffers. Gone are the days of heavy and large sized tools that require a lot of muscle and energy to use when buffing out entire cars. The two best features I like about modern rotary buffers are:

- Low RPM Speeds
- Lightweight designs

■ Flex PE14-2-150 Rotary Polisher

This is one of my favorite rotary polishers. It weighs in at 5 pounds has a compact size and a low RPM range of 400 RPM off-lock and 600 RPM in the locked position. I really like the low RPM range for the polisher because there are a lot of times when I want to buff at low RPMs. Fact is, you don't have to use high RPMs just because you're using a rotary buffer. 2100 RPM is the max for the Flex PE14 which is perfectly fine for clear coat paints as you never really need to buff over 1500 RPM. I prefer to use this polisher for all the complex surgical buffing of intricate or tight areas. Flex states you can use up to an 8" pad on this tool for heavy duty buffing on large panels.

Flex PE14-2-150 Rotary Polisher

■ DeWALT DWP849X

The DeWalt 849X is also one of my favorite rotary buffers. A few years ago a DeWALT Rep by the name of Eric asked for feedback from both pro and enthusiasts detailers as to what features they would like to see in a DA Polisher and the results from his research are the features and benefits you see in the 849X. With a low range of 600 RPM and a high of 3500 RPM plus a rubber molded grip on the head of the tool and vent guards to keep wool fibers out of the motor make this is a very well-built full size rotary buffer.

DeWALT DWP849X

■ Makita 9227C

My first rotary buffer was a Makita SPC 9277 which was the precursor model to the current 9227C. The 9227C offers an RPM range from 600 to 3000 this new model is also a great choice for buffing out clearcoat paints as well as just about anything else you want to detail.

Makita 9227C

Powerful Tool
The rotary buffer is a powerful tool for primarily buffing out paint but it's also used to work on boats with gel-coat finishes, RVs & Motorhomes, polyester and epoxy molds, plastics, glass and metals like aluminum planes and Air Stream Travel Trailers.

Direct Drive Tool
The rotary buffer is what we call a direct drive tool that rotates a buffing pad in a single circular direction. This single rotating action when used with an aggressive wool pad and a compound will quickly remove below surface defects like swirls, scratches, severe oxidation, and wet sanding marks. It does this by forcing the abrasives over the surface causing them to abrade and remove material quickly.

Power with risk
Out of all the tools commonly used to polish paint, the rotary buffer is the most powerful. This power comes with risk however because if you buff in one area too long you can heat up the paint and twist it or abrade so much material off that you burn through the paint. If you're working on a basecoat/clearcoat finish you'll burn through, (or abrade through), the clear layer and expose the basecoat. If you're working on a single stage paint you'll burn through and expose the primer coat or even shiny metal. You can also burn-through high points like raised body lines or edges and corners, where paint tends to be thinner.

Can impart holograms
Rotary buffers also tend to impart their own scratch pattern into the surface called, holograms, rotary buffer swirls or buffer trails. This is caused by a number of things, the first being the singular, rotating action of the drive mechanism that turns a buffing pad in a single direction against the surface. So the action of the tool is one factor that causes swirls. Other things that contribute to swirls are the type of buffing pad and type of product.

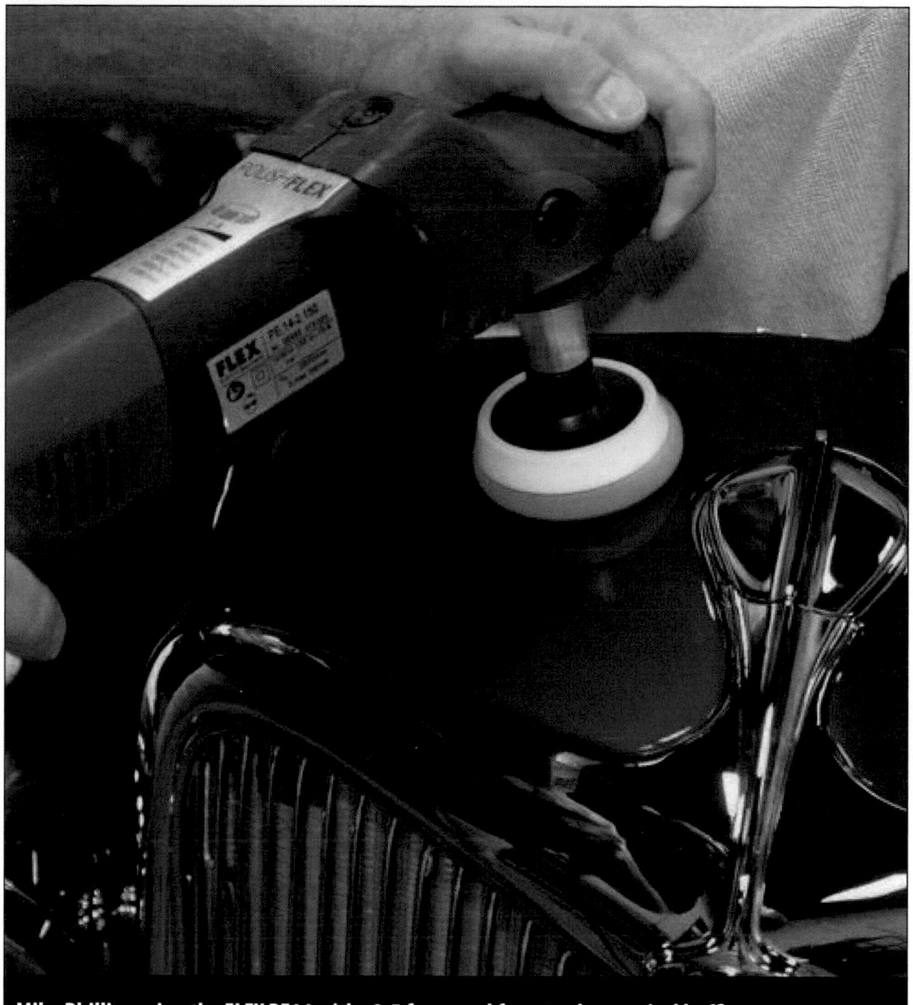

Mike Phillips using the FLEX PE14 witha 3.5 foam pad for complex surgical buffing.

Buffing Pads

- **Fiber pads:** this can be any type of fiber pad including aggressive wool cutting pads, soft sheepskin polishing pads and even microfiber pads. Fiber pads are made of millions of individual fibers and when you press these fibers against the surface under pressure the fibers themselves can cut or abrade the paint leaving swirl marks.
- **Foam pads:** These can also leave swirls depending upon the foam type. Aggressive foam pads like foam cutting pads can easily leave a hologram pattern when used with a rotary buffer.

Compounds, Polishes & Cleaner/ Waxes
When applied with a rotary buffer, the abrasives used in compounds, polishes and some cleaner/waxes can also impart scratching that shows up as holograms. More aggressive and larger abrasives will leave deeper holograms or rotary buffer swirls but even fine, smaller abrasives will leave holograms behind when used with a rotary buffer.

The sum of all three...
The single rotating action of the rotary buffer, the pad material and the abrasives used (aggressive or non-aggressive), all join together to instill circular scratches into the paint that we see as holograms or rotary buffer swirls. It is the sum of these three things that imparts swirls and this needs to be recognized not just a single item when discussing swirls.

Not a bad thing...
The fact that a rotary buffer will instill swirls isn't a bad thing as long as you're aware of this characteristic and perform the appropriate follow-up steps to remove the swirls. It's nice to have a rotary buffer for removing deeper paint defects like scratches, swirls, bird dropping etchings, Type II Water Spots or severe oxidation because it will get the job done quickly. It's also historically been the fastest way to remove sanding marks after wetsanding a car to remove orange

peel (think custom paint job for a show car).

Swirls are a people problem, not a tool problem
The rotary buffer gets a bad rap for leaving swirls in paint but it's actually not the tool's fault but rather the person behind the tool. If you're using a rotary buffer it's your responsibility to first understand that this type of tool has the potential to leave swirls in the paint. It is your responsibility to do the necessary follow-up steps to ensure a swirl-free finish. These could include two options:

- **Option A:** Using an high quality, ultra fine cut polish with a soft foam finishing pad for the last rotary buffer step.
- **Option B:** Switching to an orbital polisher for the last machine polishing step. This would include switching to a Porter Cable style DA Polisher, Flex 3401 DA Polisher or a Cyclo Polisher.

Out of the above two options, option B is the safe bet. Simply switch to some type of dual action polisher for the last machine polishing step. By changing the action of the tool you will effectively work-out the swirls left by a rotary buffer leaving you with a swirl free finish.

Option A can be used too but the thing I like to point out is that some paint systems are harder to polish swirl-free using only a rotary buffer. Unless you chemically strip the paint and then inspect the true and accurate results under bright overhead light the polishing oils will mask the swirls you're leaving behind. You won't know the true condition of the paint until these polishing oils are removed, which is usually after a few car washes.

If you want to finish out only using a rotary buffer then you must also be sure to use the a clean, soft premium quality foam finishing pad together with a premium quality Fine Cut Polish. For this step, there are a number of really good foam finishing pads you can use made by companies like Lake Country or Meguiar's. The key thing with your choice of pad is to continually clean it as you work around the car or switch to a clean, fresh pad after a panel or two. As for fine cut polishes, to date, the best polish I've used that consistently finishes out swirl-free is either the Optimum Finish, which is a Fine Cut Polish or the Menzerna SF 4500.

Even with these pads and fine cut polishes you still have to use expert technique and work surgically clean. Thus it's easier and even fool-proof to simply put the rotary buffer down and switch to a polisher that offers both rotating and oscillating action, like a Porter Cable 7424xp or FLEX XC3401.

I have a very in-depth article on the topic of finishing out hologram-free here:

Hologram Free with a Rotary Buffer

Now that we've talked about the hologram issue related to using a rotary buffer let's take a look at using a rotary buffer.

How To Use A Rotary Buffer

Free advice – No Black Vipers your first time out…
If you're new to the rotary buffer, don't learn on something that's important to you, like a Black Viper, (or whatever your pride and joy is). Instead, work on an older car that no one cares about or get a practice hood from a body shop or out of a salvage yard.

Dark Colored Hood
Hoods work best as they offer a lot of room to practice on. Compared to a door or fender they are easier to set-up on some type of stand, table or on sawhorses to hold them steady while you're buffing. Doors can be heavy and thick and fenders don't offer a lot of practice real-estate. Body shops are constantly replacing hoods on wrecked cars and even if the hood is bent a little it's still perfectly fine for practicing on and you can usually get it for free. You can also go to a salvage yard to find a straight hood but you'll have to pay for it since it has value as a usable replacement part. Try to get a hood painted a dark color like black because this will make it easier for your eyes to inspect and see your results. Like the saying goes, if you can make black paint look good you can make any color look good.

Tip: *If you get a panel from a salvage yard, keep in mind parts of high end cars will command a higher price than lower priced entry level cars. Just ask the folks that work at the salvage yard what they charge for a hood so you have an idea. Be sure to take plenty of U.S. Standard and Metric sockets and wrenches and a buddy to help you un-bolt and hold the hood so you don't get hurt in the process nor damage the part you're about to purchase. I routinely obtain hoods and trunk lids to use as demo panels for my wetsanding classes so I speak from experience. Watch out for snakes, rats, spiders etc., as well as sharp steel, broken glass and other accidents waiting to happen. Salvage yards are fun to go into but they are no picnic in the park.*

Practicing on a car
When you're first learning how to use a rotary buffer, it's a good idea to only tackle a single panel your first time. The reason for this is that going

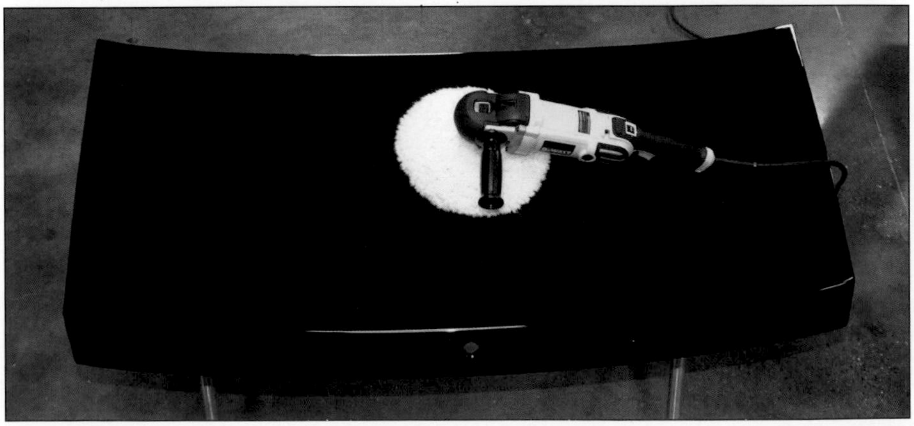

from the first step where you typically compound the paint and working all the way through to applying a wax, sealant or coating, will easily take you a few hours. By only tackling a panel you can complete each step and monitor your progress by inspecting your results and make tweaks to your technique until you get to the last step without tiring or burning-out. If you try to do an entire car your first time, it will take you 4-6 hours just to do the first step of buffing the car out with compound. You still have to rebuff the entire car with at least one more step to remove the swirls either with the rotary buffer or a dual action polisher of some sort and then you still have to apply a wax, synthetic paint sealant or coating. Buffing out an entire car using a rotary buffer and doing a good job will take you the entire day. So consider just tackling a panel when learning how to use a rotary buffer. Spread this type of project out over a few weekends and as you get better you'll improve your technique and thus get faster. As you gain experience, skill and confidence, you'll be tackling entire cars in no time.

Here's what you do,

Gather your supplies
Get yourself a collection of wool and foam buffing pads. You'll also need some compounds and polishes formulated for use with rotary buffers. These are "tools" for your tool chest. You'll need plenty of clean, soft microfiber polishing cloths and a bonnet or two if you want to remove the wax by machine.

If you're new to using a rotary buffer, here are my recommendations for starting out. With these products you can tackle everything that comes into your garage, whether you're wetsanding, cutting and buffing a brand new custom paint job or removing water spots off glass or paint. Because I'm a systems guy I'm listing a number of brands that offer a complete line of products for use with rotary buffers that are also Pro Grade; by this I mean they are formulated for use in body shops after wetsanding steps.

The ultimate achievement for a detailer is to be able to take a car fresh out of the paint booth and then sand it down and buff it out swirl free. If you can do this, you are at the top of your game and a member of an elite group of people. Most people that do this do it in a production shop environment and their end result has holograms. That doesn't cut it. If you want to run with the big dogs you need to do whatever it takes to finish out swirl-free, otherwise you're putting out hack work.

Meguiar's System

Meguiar's M105 Ultra Cut Compound – Super Micro Abrasive Technology can remove down to 1200 grit sanding marks and finish out like a polish. It's versatile in that it can be used with a rotary buffer, DA Polisher and even by hand - which comes in handy for removing sanding marks and other defects close to edges and raised body lines where it's too risky to buff by machine.

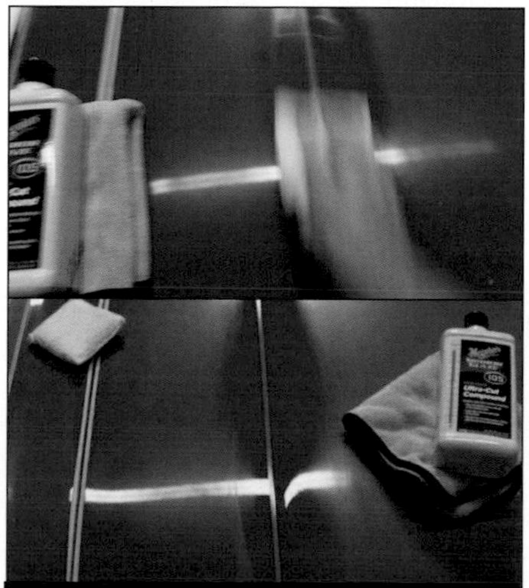

Removing sanding marks by a raised body line by hand using M105

M105 Ultra Cut Compound

Meguiar's M205 Ultra Finishing Polish – Super Micro Abrasive Technology will remove any swirls or haze left by the M105 for an almost perfect finish. This polish has an incredibly long buffing cycle with easy wipe-off and low dusting characteristics. Like M105 it can also be used with DA Polishers and/or by hand.

M205 Ultra Finishing Polish

Optimum System

Optimum Compound – Optimum Compound is a fast cutting compound with a long buffing cycle and incredibly easy wipe-off with minimal to no dusting. Fast cutting is important but when you're buffing out cars all day long you really want a product that buffs easy and wipes-off easy as these two aspects can really tire you out fast. Optimum Compound II can be used with a rotary buffer, DA Polisher or by hand.

Optimum Compound

Optimum Polish II – Like Optimum Compound, Optimum Polish II has an incredibly long buffing cycle and wipes-off effortlessly leaving behind a high gloss, clear shine. Optimum Polish II can be used with a rotary buffer, DA Polisher or by hand.

Optimum Polish II

Optimum Finish – Optimum Finishing Polish is an Ultra Fine Cut Polish and works as an option to use instead of the Polish II depending upon how hard the paint you're working on is. If the paint you're buffing on is fairly hard you might need Optimum Polish II to remove any swirls or haze left after the compounding step, (remember wool pads leave their own swirl marks). In some cases however you can go right to Optimum Finish Polish cutting your process down to two steps with the same show car results. Optimum Finish can be used with a rotary buffer, DA Polisher or by hand.

Optimum Finish

■ 2 more complete lines with a "system approach"

There are a lot of really good professional grade "systems" on the market that I can't include in this chapter due to space limitations but I would also include both Mothers' Professional Line as well as 3M's Professional Line. So if you're a 3M guy or a Mothers fan, be sure to check these system approaches out too.

Mothers' Professional Line – A lot of people know Mothers for their popular consumer line of car care products and have no idea Mothers also offers a complete Professional Line for use in body shops and detail shops. This includes to very aggressive compounds, two machine applied polishes and a hand glaze.

Mothers' Professional Line

3M's Professional Line – 3M pretty much dominates the industrial side of the compounding industry with their popularity and strong presence in body shops world wide. Their compounds cut as fast as or faster than anything on the market and their polishes work really well too.

3M's Professional Line

Menzerna USA – Everyone should have SF 4500 in their detailing arsenal. This is one of the best Ultra Fine Cut polishes I've ever used. Meguiar's and Optimum mentioned above make great compounds and polishes like I stated, so this is not to take anything away from them but there is something about the SF 4500 that is hard to beat for a final machine applied polish or a jewelling polish. I have not come across a single paint system that this polish didn't squeeze every last bit of shine out of for a true, show car finish. It can be used with any machine polisher or by hand and it's truly what I would call "Bubba-Proof" as far as getting professional results the first time and every time.

Menzerna SF 4500

Misc Tools

Because rotary buffers tend to throw splatter and can quickly burn through paint on an edge, you'll want to use painters tape to tape off risky areas. You'll also want to cover and protect some areas like plastic, vinyl or rubber components or trim or convertible tops, etc. So gather some painters tape, tinfoil, beach towels, bed sheets, newspaper, plastic drop cloths, plastic bags and even old gym socks. With a little creativity you can use all of these things to quickly cover and protect just about anything on any car that you don't want to get compound or polish spatter on.

Work Clean

Always work clean, this means a clean car and a clean work environment. You don't want any dirt getting into any of the machine buffing processes as you will risk instilling swirls into the paint. Sweep the floor, this will prevent dirt and dust from being kicked into the air from foot traffic as you work around the car. You should at least start out clean; you're going to get dirty in the process.

Dress for success

Put some work clothes on including a soft cotton t-shirt that covers your waist line and you won't care if it gets splatter on it. Sometimes you'll find yourself leaning over a fender or door with your body touching the paint. Having a soft cotton t-shirt to cover your pants will prevent things like belt loops, snaps etc., from coming into contact with the paint. The bigger the car, the bigger the panel and the better the odds are that you might have to "touch" the paint somewhere when you're leaning out to buff the hard to reach areas. You can wear an apron but most of the time it's hard to find an apron that's as soft as an old cotton t-shirt.

Safety Glasses

Safety glasses are a good idea if you don't wear glasses. The rotary buffer does have a spinning head/pad on it and it could throw something into your eyeball.

Good shoes
Using the rotary buffer involves you legs, back, arms, shoulders, etc. You'll find that you'll use your legs/feet to anchor your stance while you control the machine. Again it's not that big of a deal if you're just working on just a singe panel but when the day comes and you start tackling entire cars, especially larger vehicles in bad condition where you're going to go around the vehicle 2-3 times with just the rotary buffer, if you don't have good shoes your feet, legs and even the rest of your body are going to pay a price as you work through the day. Something that encases your ankles like high-top tennis shoes work really well, (at least for me).

Prepare the car
Choose a car, wash it and then clay it if it needs it and only tackle one panel on one day to start with. Choose a horizontal panel like either the hood or the deck-lid.

Tip: *Wash the day before*
If possible, wash the vehicle the day before, that way it will be dry when you go to work on it. Rotary buffers can create an air current and pull water in body seams, cracks and crevices onto the panel as you're buffing.

Always be able to look across from the panel you're buffing
Unless you or your customer has a floor lift, then you can't bring the car up to you and you're going to need to lower yourself to the car in order to properly buff out the lower panels. You should be looking across from the panel as you buff on it. That means for the lower panels sitting your butt on the floor of the garage. It's a bad idea to try to buff out lower panels by bending over; this will stress your lower back. You can drop to one knee, or both knees, (have knee pads on), or use rolling stools, milk crates, or foam cushion pads. Use whatever works for you but avoid bending over while running a rotary buffer.

Evaluate the condition of the finish
Before you choose your compounds, polishes and pads you want to inspect the paint to get an idea of the type of defects you're going to remove. I divide these into two categories,

- **#1 Normal wear-n-tear, neglect and abuse**
  Normal wear-n-tear, neglect and abuse includes deeper defects like swirls, scratches, water spots and oxidation. These types of defects come from owner neglect. This category also includes deep scratches from a brush style automatic car wash and/or shoddy wash techniques by the owner, and severe oxidation caused by neglect and constant exposure to the elements. Boat detailers commonly remove severe oxidation from gel-coat finish and for this they use a rotary buffer with a wool pad and compound. Holograms can be inflicted from the misuse of a rotary buffer at a body shop, dealership or even a detail shop.

- **#2 Sanding Marks**
  In the body shop industry, the goal is to have a painter and a paint system so good that all the paint jobs come out looking perfect with little to no orange peel or surface imperfections. Some body shops will wetsand the paint after it's cured and dried for a few days. Then, after the sanding process, rotary buffers are used to remove the sanding scratches or sanding marks. If you're new to wetsanding my best advice for you is to invest in the highest quality sanding papers and/or sanding discs you can obtain. After sanding you'll need to compound each panel to remove 100% of the sanding marks.

Sandpaper
When it comes to sandpaper, Meguiar's has been offering the Nikken brand of "Finishing Papers" since the late 1970s. These are an electronics grade paper and offer both Unigrit particle size and Uniform particle placement over 100% of the face of the paper. The benefit to these two features is a paper that cuts faster while leaving behind a uniform sanding mark pattern that buffs out faster and more completely with fewer tracers. When hand sanding, try to finish out with the Nikken 2000, 2500 or 3000 grit. The higher the grit level paper you finish out with, the faster and easier it will be to remove your sanding marks.

Use two kinds of light
It's a good idea to inspect the paint in at least two kinds of light. Sunlight is very good at revealing swirls while florescent lights, like those found in garages, are very good at revealing water spots, etchings, isolated deeper scratches and orange peel. Halogen lights on work stands work great for lighting up and revealing paint defects

on the vertical panels. The Brinkmann Swirl Finder Light is also a great option because it is hand held and easy to keep by your side as you're working a panel to inspect your work.

Use the least aggressive product to get the job done
With experience you can make a judgment call based upon the visual inspection of the paint you're about to work on to choose the appropriate product.

Paint Thickness
If you have a paint thickness gauge, before tackling any project, first take some measurements to make sure the paint is not already too thin to work on. See my chapter, Paint Thickness Gauge

Synergistic Chemical Compatibility
In simple words, I tend to be a system approach guy, that is I will tend to use all products from a single manufacturer using a system approach. Here's how this works:

The chemists that formulates the first step products are better able to formulate the follow-up, or second step products so there's a synergistic chemical compatibility. Using a product designed to be used after the results of the previous product is a system approach.

If you're getting into using rotary buffers, then consider getting a collection of products from a single manufacturer designed as a system approach for use with rotary buffers. This usually means products manufactured for the professional side of this industry which includes products for body shops or the detailing industry. Here's a list of companies that offer system approaches for use with rotary buffers.

- Meguiar's
- Menzerna
- Optimum
- Mothers
- 3M

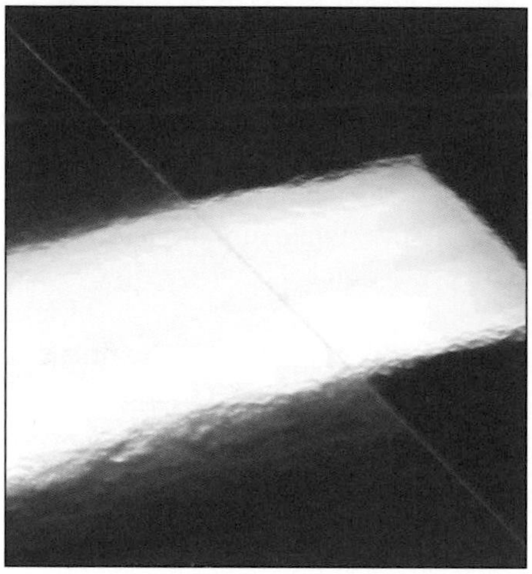

Prove it first
Dial-in your system via the Test Spot approach until you prove a pad and product combination that works. The last thing you want to do is spend hours running a rotary buffer around a car only to find out you're not getting the results you expected. If you run into problems, start a new thread on the AutogeekOnline.net discussion forum and we'll do our best to tweak your technique and see you through to success.

See test spot section

Tape-off and cover up
Once you dial in a process and prove it works, it's time to tape-off and cover anything you don't want to get compound or polish splatter onto.

Rotary buffers spin buffing pads in a circular motion and compounds and polishes, (liquids), will tend to sling outward due to centrifugal force getting splatter onto nearby panels. When using foam pads, as they become

more saturated with product they can sling more splatter than wool pads. Even seasoned professionals can throw splatter, and that includes me. Cleaning your pad often helps but won't entirely prevent splatter.

You need to make a judgment call as to whether you want to tape-off and cover up trim, emblems, cracks and crevices, raised body lines, edges and corners or try to clean-up these areas at the end of the project.

I tape-off everything!
If you've ever seen any pictures of

cars I've buffed out you'll see I always tape-off and cover up ANYTHING I don't want to clean-up at the end of the project. I'm not a lazy person but I hate trying to get compound and polish spatter off plastic trim or out of cracks and crevices. I also don't want my customers to use my name as a cuss word every time they look at their car so I tape-off and cover-up EVERYTHING! At the end of this chapter I include a list of resources that will show you how to tape-off a car before taking a rotary buffer to it.

Knock out the top horizontal panels first

Here's a tip, if you think you're going to have to lean against a vertical panel in order to safely reach one of the horizontal panels like the roof, hood or trunk lid, then knock out these areas first.

When I say knock these areas out, I mean do all the steps from beginning to end and then tackle the vertical side panels. This way you won't re-instill scuffs or scratches into panels that you've previously buffed because you leaned against a fender while buffing out the center of the hood. This is really important if you buff out classic cars with large hoods.

Roof First

I always knock out the roof on cars, truck and SUVs first. Not only does this keep me from wasting time by repeating wiping steps, (wiping spatter off lower panels), I can also use this to market myself to anyone that's stops by to ask questions or check out my work.

For example, if the car is trashed and I buff out the entire roof including compounding, polishing and then waxing, and then someone stops and asks about having me detail their car, I can show them a panel I have not worked on to show them how the paint looked before I started and then show them the roof to show them how the entire car will look when I'm finished. In the past, this type of before and after presentation has worked really well to earn a new customer and please the current customer. ■

Types of Foam Pads

There are a lot of foam pads on the market to choose from and it can be overwhelming to pick an appropriate type and style of pad if you're new to machine polishing. The truth is that as long as you're using premium quality paint care products and good technique, then any top quality pads from reputable pad companies will get the job done. Let's talk about the types of foam formulas used to make foam buffing pads as this is an important factor that affects how a foam buffing pad performs.

Reticulated = Open Cell

Open Cell Foam means the cell wall structure is open, leaving only the framework in place. Reticulation is created by exploding the foam, which blows out the membranes, leaving behind an open pore skeletal structure which fluids and gasses can easily pass through. Think of a window frame without the glass.

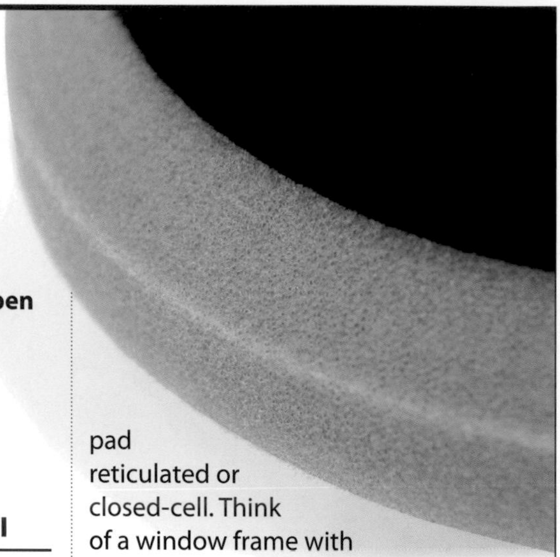

Pictured bottom left is a close-up of the cell wall structure of open cell foam. There are no membranes walling-off the cell structures, just a porous skeletal structure in which liquids or air can easily pass through.

Compared to closed cell foam, open cell foam is:

- More absorbent
- More porous
- Less dense
- More elastic

Non-Reticulated = Closed Cell

Closed Cell Foam means the cell wall structure is closed with the membranes intact. This makes the foam non-porous, and while it's not impossible for air and liquids to flow through it, it is more difficult.

Below is a close-up of the cell wall structure of closed cell foam. If you look closely, you can see the membranes intact and this is what makes a foam pad reticulated or closed-cell. Think of a window frame with the glass in place.

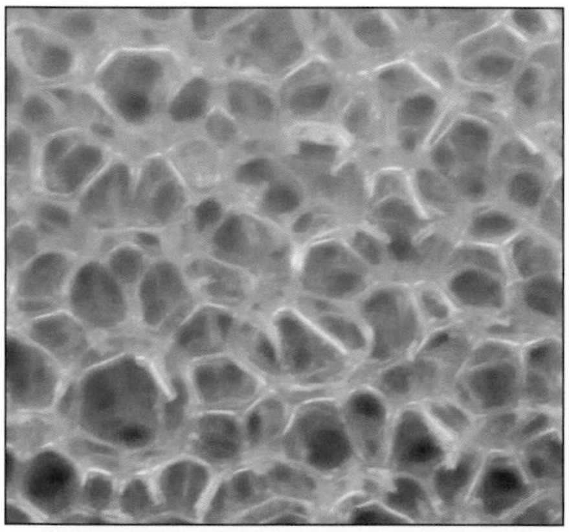

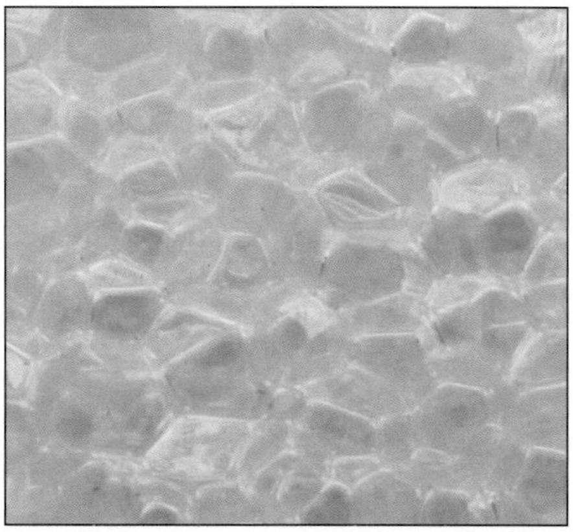

Compared to open cell foam, closed cell foam is:

- Less absorbent
- Less porous
- More dense
- Less elastic

The Practical Difference

Open Cell Foam
With an open cell wall structure, both air and liquids can pass through the foam easily.

- **Air** – In an open cell foam composition, air can flow through and this aids in heat transfer. The pad will buff cooler as heat from the pad transfers to the air passing through the foam. Increased air flow allows liquids to evaporate, causing the product being used to dry up.

In This Section:

- **Liquids** - Because liquids can easily flow through the open cell wall structure of the foam, it is more easily penetrated by and saturated with any chemical you're applying.

■ Closed Cell Foam

With a closed cell foam structure, air and liquids cannot easily pass through the foam.

- **Air** - Because air cannot flow through the closed cell membranes easily, heat will tend to build up faster. This will decrease the evaporation rate of any liquids.

- **Liquids** - Because liquids cannot easily penetrate into the foam, they will be trapped on the surface of the pad and remain between the surfaces of the pad and paint. As you use closed cell pads, liquids will tend to migrate into the inside of the pad.

Closed cell foam formulas like to retain liquids, so this can make cleaning a tad more difficult and time consuming.

PPI or Pores Per Square Inch
The term PPI is often used when differentiating between types of foam pads. However, there are many other factors that affect the benefits and features of a foam pad in addition to PPI. PPI becomes an extreme generality as far as it relates to any specific comparison between types of foam. For this reason, it's better to focus on the other factors discussed in-depth in this chapter.

Density of foam
In simple terms, density refers to how stiff or soft the foam is. The stiffer the foam, the more aggressive it will tend to be, while the softer the foam, the more gentle it will be. Foam cutting pads tend to be denser than polishing pads, and polishing pads tend to be denser than finishing pads.

Density changes with use
As polishing and cutting pads become saturated with liquids and warm from use, density drops off and the stiffness of the foam decreases. This reduces the mechanical ability of the foam's performance. This is why a clean, dry foam cutting pad will be more aggressive than the same pad after it's been used to buff a panel or two.

If you're going to rely on foam cutting pads to remove below-surface defects, a good rule of thumb is to have one pad per panel to maximize efficiency. More pads are always better. As soon as a pad becomes broken-in, or saturated with product, remove it and switch to a clean, dry pad.

Elasticity - tensile strength
Elasticity is another way of referring to the tensile strength of foam. Tensile strength is a measurement of how far foam will stretch before it will tear. Open cell foam pads tend to have higher tensile strengths than closed cell foam.

Example: *Hydro-Tech pads (closed cell foam) have lower tensile strength and will tear and wear more easily than CCS pads (open cell foam).*

Aggressiveness or gentleness
How aggressive or how gentle a foam pad is can be controlled and tailored to specific tasks by the addition or subtraction of different chemical agents added to the foam. Like car wax companies, foam companies are very secretive about their formulas and this kind of information is proprietary. Reputable suppliers of foam pads will state whether a foam pad is aggressive or gentle.

Two tests you can do to gauge aggressiveness or gentleness:

- Compress a pad between your two palms. A stiff or dense pad will offer more mechanical ability than a soft or less dense pad.
- Draw your clean fingertips over a clean pad. An aggressive foam pad will have a coarse feel to it, while a non-aggressive pad will feel soft and gentle.

■ Foam Pad Face Design

Foam buffing pads come in a variety of different face designs in which the working face of the pad has a distinct pattern cut or formed into it. Manufacturers state that the different designs offer specific benefits to the buffing process, the user or both.

Comment *- When buffing with a DA polisher, as long as you're using good quality foam pads, the best type often comes down to personal preference. More important than the choice in type of pad is the product you choose to use and your technique. If you're using great products (compounds, polishes and waxes) and perfect technique, the design of the pad is the least of your worries.*

More important
Matching the correct aggressiveness or

gentleness of the foam for the product and process is more important than the design on the face of the pad. Simply put, you can get great results from any of the below pads as long as you choose and use the right product and technique.

■ Lake Country CCS Pads Reticulated/ Open Cell Foam

CCS stands for Collapsed Cell Structure. This means the face of the pad has little pockets formed into the foam through a heat process in which the cells are melted and closed to make these pockets more dense and less porous. This will prevent the product you're using from penetrating inside the foam, allowing it to remain on the surface between the pad and the paint. CCS pads help create a smoother buffing experience. Product in the pockets is released as you buff, maintaining a well lubricated surface.

Other benefits include longer buffing cycle for the product and a decrease in pad saturation. Pad saturation is a common problem with all foam pads due to the fact that foam absorbs liquids. The more wet or saturated your pad becomes with product, the more it will absorb and dissipate the energy and oscillating pattern provided by a DA polisher.

■ Lake Country Constant Pressure CCS Pads (referred to as CP Pads)

These pads include a layer of soft foam as a cushioning interface between the backing plate and the actual foam formula used for the working face of the pad. The design allows the foam to flex and conform to curved body panels. These are available in both CCS and Flat pad designs.

■ Lake Country Kompressor Pads Reticulated = Open Cell

Slotted tabs
Kompressor pads have a slotted or tabbed face. They are cut in a criss-cross pattern to create flexible, rectangular tabs instead of a solid foam interface. The benefits include incredible flexibility which means they easily conform to curved panels.

Compressed sweet spot
These pads are arched in a way that when you place them onto your backing pate, the center compresses into itself, making the foam stiffer or denser in this area. You still get plenty of flex for buffing curved panels, but polishing products will tend to remain in the center of the pad versus slinging outwards.

Recessed back - (7″ versions)
The Kompressor pads come in both 6″ and 7″ sizes. The 7″ versions have a recessed backing that makes centering a 6″ backing plate quick, easy and accurate for smooth buffing operation. It also provides a safety margin of foam surrounding the lip of the backing plate in case you accidentally run the edge of the pad into any portion of a car's painted panels. This prevents the actual backing plate from contacting and harming the paint.

Easy to clean
The slotted tabs make cleaning the pad easy as you can spread the tabs apart with your fingers to allow product residue to escape. If you use a Grit Guard Universal Pad Washer, the tabs spread apart as you push the face of the pad against the Grit Guard insert. Built-up product residue is easily removed from the face and sides of the slotted tabs.

■ Lake Country Hydro-Tech Kompressor Pads - Closed Cell

Same closed-cell foam formula as the Lake Country Hydro-Tech flat pads, with the Kompressor slotted design. These pads are excellent for buffing contours and curved body panels.

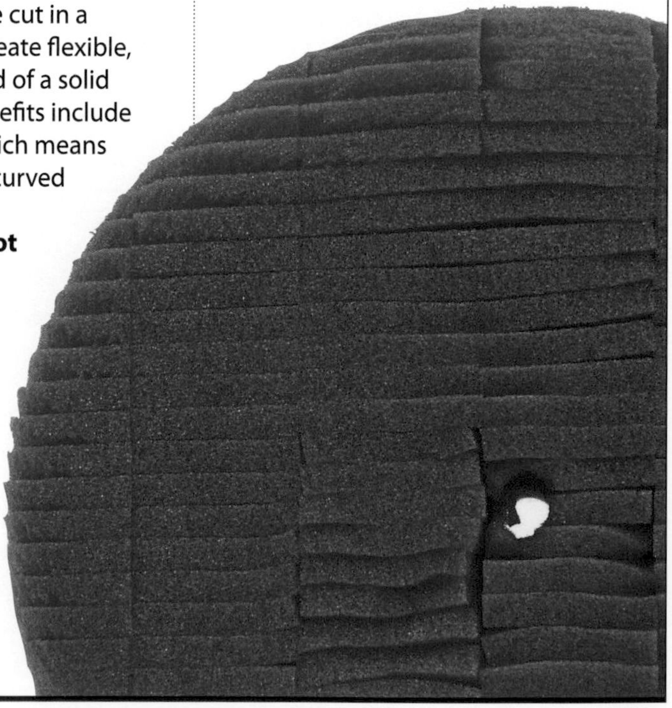

■ **Cobra Cross Groove DA Pads**
Reticulated = Open Cell

Reduces surface tension
The Cross Groove name comes from the way the face of the foam pad is cut in a criss-cross pattern. This design reduces tension by reducing the total surface area of foam in contact with the paint for a smoother buffing experience.

Reduces product waste
The grooves also trap and hold product inside themselves, releasing throughout the buffing cycle.

Beveled edges
A soft curve to the edge provides gentle polishing action when buffing inside or around curves.

Reduces heat build-up
The cross-cut grooves allow air to flow through the pad as you're buffing, capturing heat and then releasing it to maintain low surface temperatures.

■ **Flat Pads**

The flat-faced foam buffing pad was introduced to the car detailing world by a man named Larry Meguiar, son of Floyd Meguiar of Finish Kare. Larry dropped the foam pad project and it was revived by Water Cotton. This first foam buffing pad was introduced to the market back in 1965, about the time the Ford Mustang was introduced and Gilligan's Island debuted.

The introduction of the foam buffing pad was a pinnacle moment for car detailing perfectionists. It enabled them to turn out a dramatically nicer looking finish than could be obtained using wool pads. Wool buffing pads are great for when you need an aggressive pad to remove below-surface defects, but when it comes time for the finishing work, foam, with its uniform surface texture will always leave a nicer finish.

Here are three companies that offer a flat-faced foam buffing pad. While the colors and sizes between the different brands will vary, they all have a few things in common.

- Lake country = Reticulated/ Open Cell
- Meguiar's Pads = Reticulated/ Open Cell
- Griot's Garage Pads = Reticulated/Open Cell

100% contact
With a flat pad design, you get maximum engagement of the foam to paint which means maximum efficiency when working product against the paint.

Easy to clean
Any contaminants or particulates will be on the face of the pad, not lodged into any of the subsurface sections of the pad. Inspecting the face of the pad is faster and easier.

Optimized for diminishing abrasives
Any time you're using a product that uses diminishing abrasives to correct paint, the goal is to work them until they have completely broken down. If you stop buffing before the abrasives have completely broken down, it's possible to have left swirls or micromarring in the paint as the abrasives were still actively cutting or abrading.

■ **Lake Country Flat Pads**
Reticulated = Open Cell

The 5 1/2" Lake Country Flat Pads are pretty much the simplest and easiest pads for people new to machine polishing to use. Their small size makes them perfect for modern cars with long, thin panels. They are easy to control, easy to clean, and work with any DA-approved compound, polish, paint cleaner, glaze, cleaner/ wax or finishing wax.

■ **Lake Country Hydro-Tech Pads**
Non-Reticulated = Closed Cell

To use any of these on a DA polisher, you'll need either a 6", 5" or 3.5" backing plate. Lake Country Backing Plates are shown here. When you purchase backing plates and buffing pads from the same manufacturer, you can

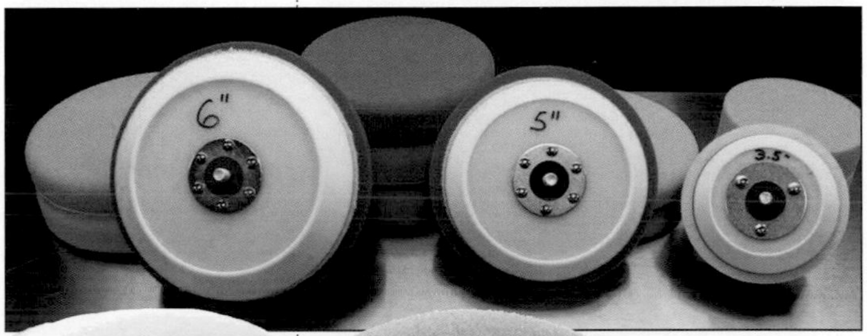

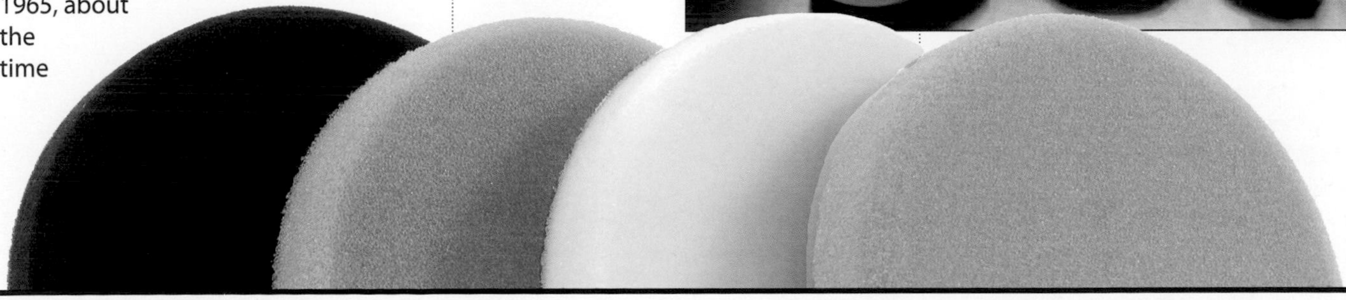

trust the hook and loop materials will match for maximum attaching strength and longevity.

Hydro-Tech Pads are a flat-faced pad, but what makes them unique is they are made using closed cell foam. They'll retain their density longer and absorb liquids more slowly.

■ Meguiar's 4", 6 1/2" and 7" Soft Buff Flat Pads, Reticulated = Open Cell Exception: W7207 Foam Cutting Pad = Non-Reticulated = Closed Cell

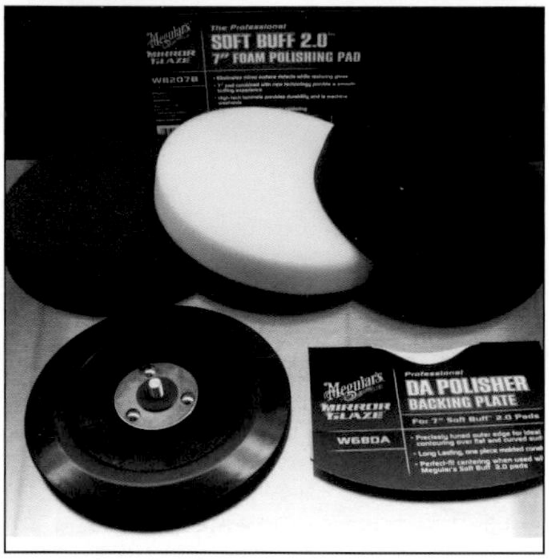

All of these pads from Meguiar's are flat pad designs. All of the pads in the 4" and 6 1/2" group are open cell. In the 7" size group, the yellow polishing and black finishing pads are open cell while the maroon cutting pad is closed cell (the 4" and 6 1/2" maroon cutting pads are open cell).

4" Soft Buff Pads - At this time, Meguiar's does not offer a 3 1/2" backing plate for use with DA Polishers, but the one from Lake Country works well.

Note: *Meguiar's does not recommend using their maroon foam cutting pad with DA polishers. This is because the foam is very aggressive and it can cause micromarring to some automotive paints.*

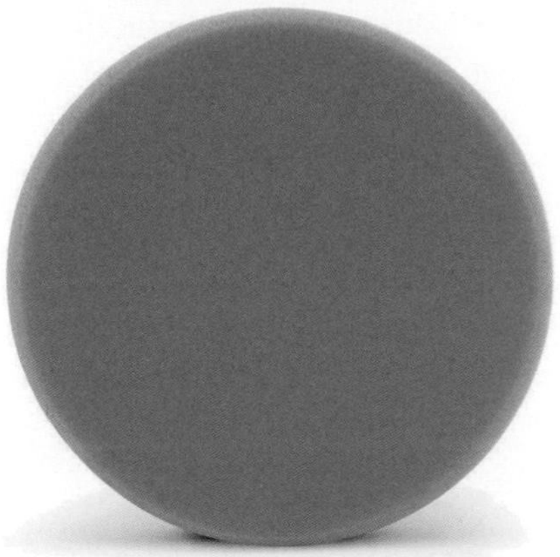

■ Griot's Garage Foam Buffing Pads Reticulated = Open Cell

Griot's offers a really simple flat pad system that will take care of most people's machine polishing needs. Use the polishing pad with either an aggressive compound or polish, or for less cut, use it with a light or ultra light polish. After the paint is corrected to your expectations, use the red wax pad to apply your choice of wax or paint sealant.

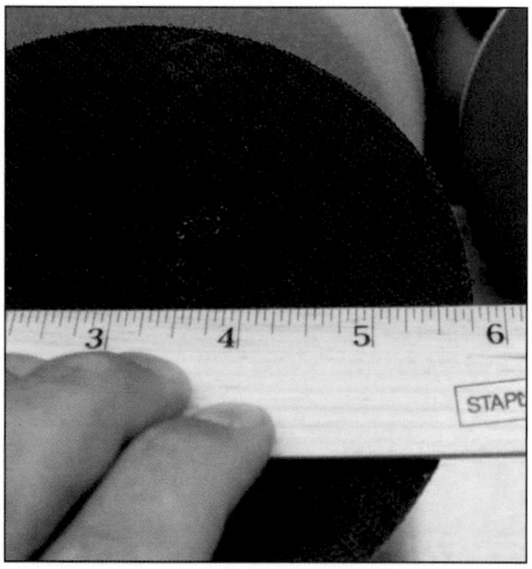

The factory 6" backing plate that comes with the tool measures in at 5 3/4". Like most 6" backing plates, the actual diameter is a little smaller to provide some safety margin around the outside of the pad while buffing.

■ Foam Pad Thickness and Diameter

Foam buffing pads come in a variety of thickness levels, and while foam pads have traditionally been on the thick side, the trend now is for thinner pads.

The first foam pads were made for use on rotary buffers. For this application, a thick foam pad works well as it provides plenty of cushion to conform to the curves of car body panels. Thick foam pads can also help to reduce swirls due to the fact that thick foam offers more cushion. Additionally, a rotary buffer is a direct drive tool that, by design, has more than enough power to rotate pads regardless of how thick they are. Originally, foam pads were simply configured to attach to air powered orbital DA sanders used in body shops. Not much thought was given to the design requirements, like the diameter and thickness of a pad, for use on a DA polisher as compared to a rotary buffer.

<u>The history of the DA Foam Pad</u>

Thin is in
The trend today is for thinner, smaller buffing pads for use with DA polishers.

Why?
Because thinner pads rotate better than thicker pads due to less friction and rotating mass.

Surface area for different pads sizes
3.0" pad = 7.1 Square Inches
4.0" pad = 12.6 Square Inches
5.5" pad = 23.7 Square Inches
6.0" pad = 28.2 Square Inches
6.5" pad = 33.1 Square Inches
7.0" pad = 38.5 Square Inches
8.0" pad = 50.2 Square Inches

The difference between buffing with a 5 1/2" pad and a 6 1/2" pad means an increase of 9.4 square inches of

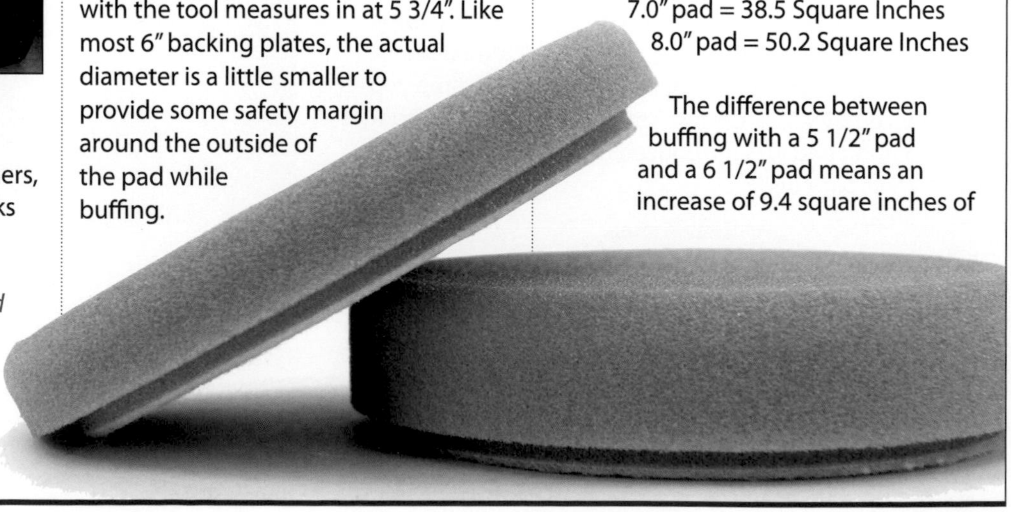

foam for the DA polisher to rotate and oscillate.

If you think in terms of diameter, to go from a 5 1/2" to a 6 1/2" pad looks like a very small change of only 1", and while this is true, it's not an accurate representation of what's really taking place on the surface.

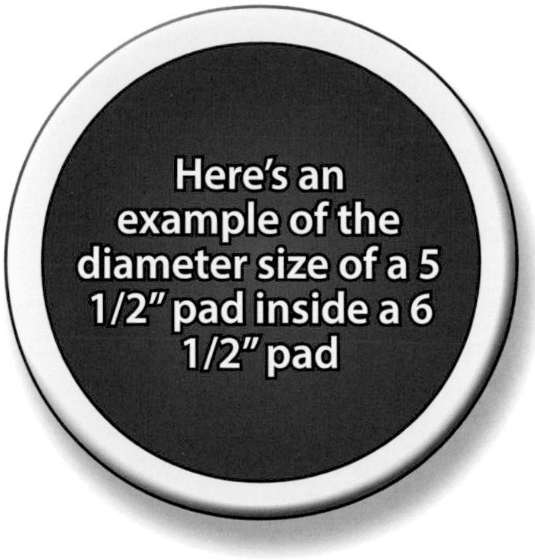

Here's an example of the diameter size of a 5 1/2" pad inside a 6 1/2" pad

Leverage
A pad with a larger diameter has a larger circumference and this gives the pad leverage over the tool's ability to rotate it. The further outward a pad extends from the center, the more power it will require to overcome the friction between the pad and the paint. For this reason, smaller diameter pads rotate more easily on DA polishers and are more effective at removing below-surface defects.

■ Foam Pad Attachment Systems Hook and loop Interface

The majority of all pads are attached using a simple hook and loop material, with the loop material being used on one side of a buffing pad and the hook side being used on the backing plate.

Hooks

Loops

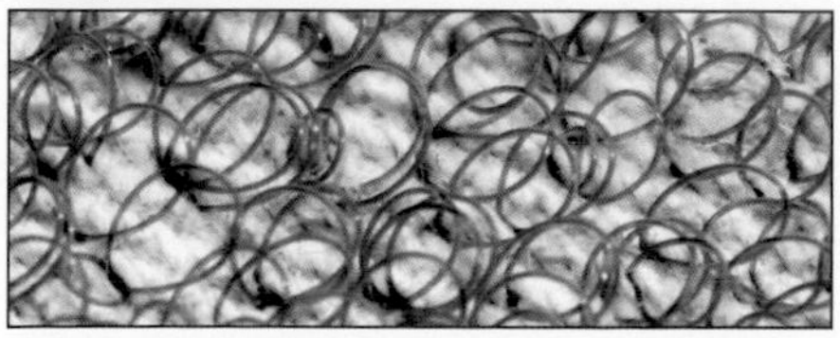

Center pad onto backing plate
When attaching a pad to a backing plate, the goal is to center the pad onto the backing plate as close as you can. This will reduce vibration.

■ How To Prime And Apply Product To A Clean, Dry Pad

Priming the pad
Priming a clean, dry pad is considered the best approach for using a DA polisher. This ensures that 100% of the working surface of the pad is wet with product and working at maximum efficiency when you turn the polisher on. I originally learned of this technique from my friend Kevin Brown.

Priming the pad also ensures that you don't have any dry, un-lubricated portions of the pad working over the paint.

Start with a clean, dry pad and add some fresh product to the face of the pad. Using your finger, spread the

product over the pad and work it into the pores. Don't saturate the pad - use just enough product to make sure that 100% of the working face of the pad has product coverage.

Any extra product can be taken and applied to the outer edge until 100% of the working face of the pad is primed with product. This helps if you're buffing panels that the edge of your buffing pad may come into contact with.

Adding "working product"
Some people will recommend 3 to 4 pea-sized drops of product. This can be correct for concentrated products or working small sections, but if you follow this advice, make sure you are not under-lubricating the surface. For

some products and paint conditions, you may want more product on the surface working for you. Here's an example of dime-sized drops of product.

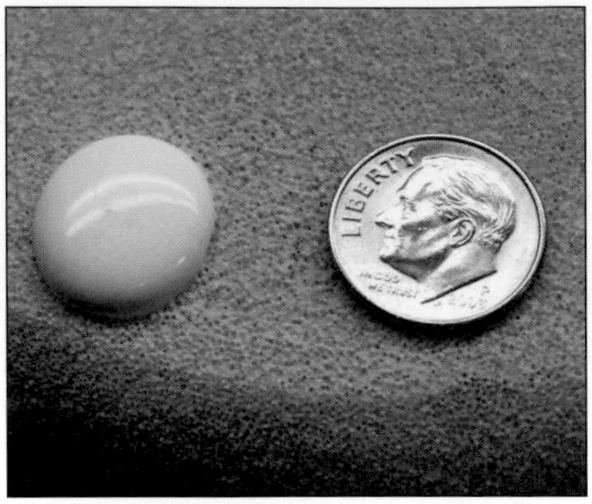

■ The Circle-Pattern And X-Pattern Method Of Applying Products

The circle pattern
As you work around the car, you'll find that your product will migrate to the center of the pad on its own, leading to saturation. This can cause problems because wet foam will retain heat better than dry foam. Over time, this can accelerate delamination between the hook and loop material and the surface it is attached to. For these reasons, I prefer applying product to the outer edge of the pad, also known as the circle pattern.

If you're placing pea or dime-sized amounts of product to the face of your pad, then it's also a good idea to avoid placing the product directly in the center of the pad.

Circle Pattern

The X-pattern Applying product using an X-pattern is a fast and simple way to get product out of the bottle and onto the pad in a measured way. This method is easy to teach others and is easy to duplicate.

X-pattern

Cut down on product after your first section pass
After making a thorough section pass, the pad is now equally primed with residual product. At this point, you could clean your pad or add fresh product. In this example, I used half an X-pattern, or a single strip of product since the pad is already primed.

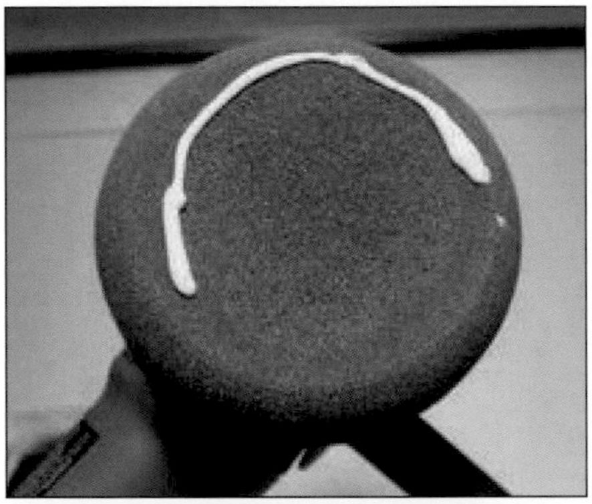

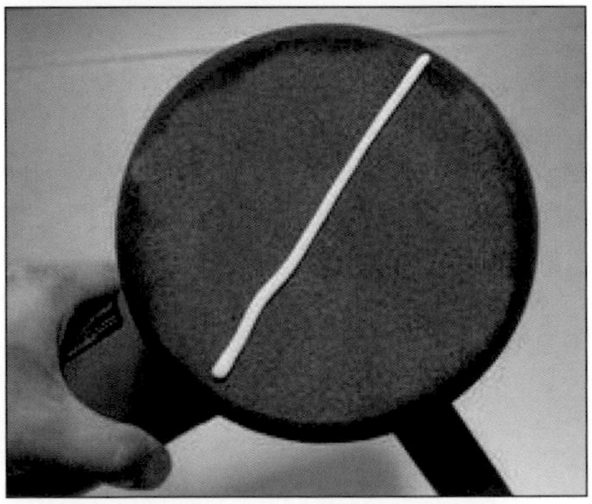

■ How Much Product Do I Use?

Use an "ample" amount of product. This means not too much and too little product.

- **am·ple** - adjective - Fully sufficient to meet a need or purpose: They had ample food for the party.

Using too much product
This will over-lubricate the pad and paint. Excess liquid will interfere with the abrasives' ability to abrade the paint and they will tend to glide over instead of biting into the surface.

Using too little product
Under-using product reduces lubricity and will make it more difficult for your pad to rotate efficiently. You need the pad to rotate so that it will engage or force the abrasives against and into the paint. The question then becomes:

How much is an ample amount?
In this chapter, Priming and Prepping Pads Before Use, I showed three ways to prime and apply product to a clean, dry pad. After you have broken-in a clean, dry pad by making your first section pass, it's time to clean the pad and then apply fresh product.

Pea, dime or nickel-sized portions of product
In some applications, a pea-sized amount of product will be sufficient. This depends upon the condition of the paint, what you're trying to accomplish and how concentrated the products are that you're using. If this doesn't give you a long enough buffing cycle, increase the size of the portion from a pea-sized drop to a dime or even nickel-sized portion.

■ Pad Conditioners & Wetting Agents

Another option to prep a clean, dry pad before first use is to use a pad conditioner to lubricate and condition the surface. This will improve the buffing cycle and provide protection to the paint surface. Pad conditioners are wetting agents that contain ingredients that will moisten and soften the surface of the pad.

They also provide some lubricating agents to ensure the face of the pad is lubricated.

How To Use
Mist a spray or two onto the face of the pad. Using your clean gloved hand, work the spray over the face of the pad and into the foam. You're now ready to apply your choice of product to the pad.

Note: *Pad conditioners are primarily for use with wool and foam cutting and polishing pads when using compounds and polishes. You don't need to condition soft waxing pads before applying waxes and paint sealants.*

Why? *Because most waxes and paint sealants are not water soluble. Adding a wetting agent will adulterate the formula. It might not harm anything, but the idea is to use the wax, paint sealant or coating in its virgin form.*

■ Cleaning Foam Buffing Pads

There are four general ways to clean foam buffing pads.

- Washing by hand
- Cleaning on the fly
- Using a Pad washer
- Using a pad conditioning brush

■ Washing By Hand

You can generally use buffing pads multiple times before they need to be replaced. However, during and after use, you need to clean them and remove any built-up compound, polish or wax residue. The way most people do this is by washing and rinsing their pads in either a sink or a bucket. This actually works pretty well since you can stand up as you clean the pads because most sinks are at waist level. Plus, you have running water to flush residue out of the pad.

Because there are all kinds of chemicals involved (compounds, polishes, waxes, paint sealants and the soap, cleaner, degreaser or detergent) and there's no way of knowing the safety of factor of all these different chemicals on their own or mixed together, I recommend wearing some type of chemical resistant gloves.

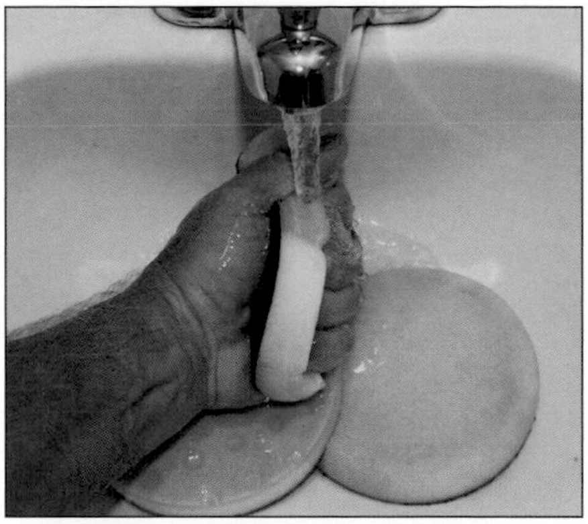

- Place a few pads into the sink and then add your choice of cleaning product. Agitate the foam pads, squeezing and kneading them to work both the cleaning solution into the foam and the built-up residue out of the foam.

- As you work the cleaning solution into the foam, the cleaning agents will break down, dissolve, and emulsify whatever products are in and on the pad. Once the products are liquefied and embodied together with the cleaning agents, you should rinse the pad by placing it under running water and continuing to squeeze, knead and work the pliable foam into itself.

- Once you see clear water coming out of the foam as you rinse and you're satisfied with the level of cleanliness, you can then set the pad aside to dry and move onto the next one.

■ Washing By Hand In A Bucket

This is pretty easy to do and it keeps all the different residue from your paint care products out of your sink.

- Start by placing a Grit Guard insert into your wash bucket to help trap any dirt or abrasive particles on the bottom of the bucket. Then, add water and some pad cleaning soap and mix thoroughly.

- Use the same approach listed above for washing pads in a sink.

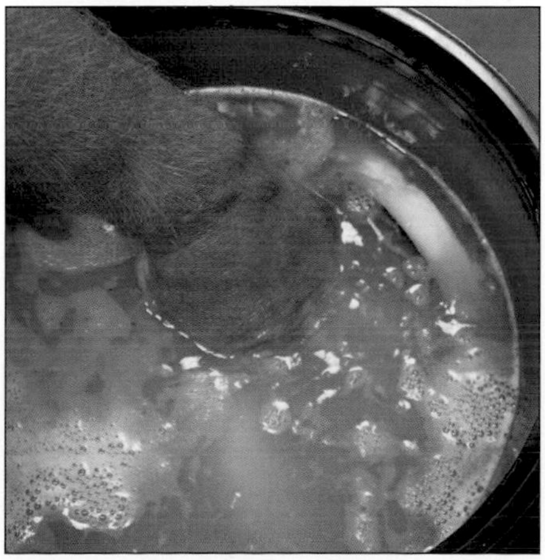

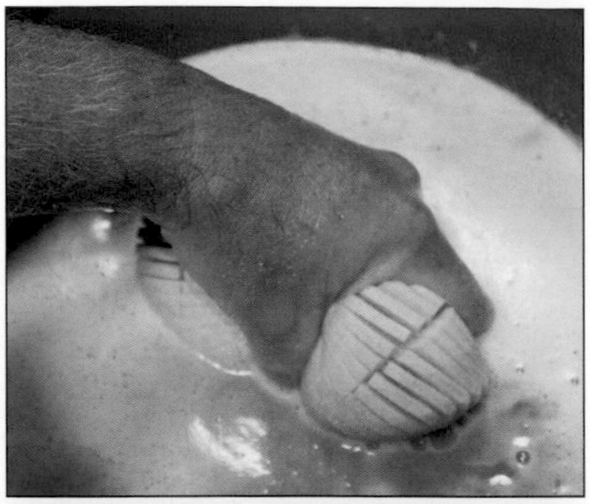

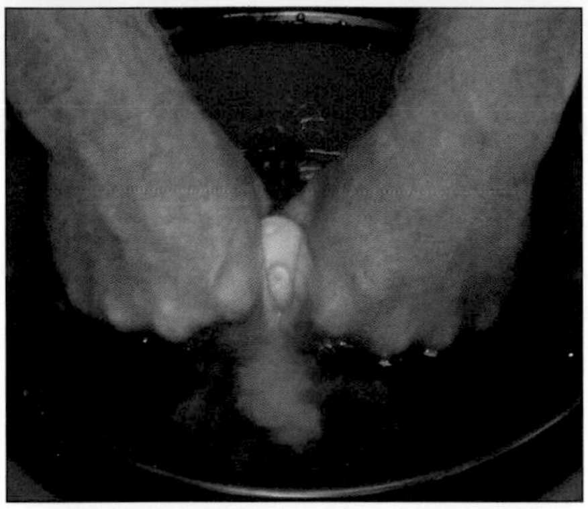

Rinsing your pads
The benefit to washing in a sink is you have running water right at the sink. With the bucket method, you can tackle this issue a few different ways.

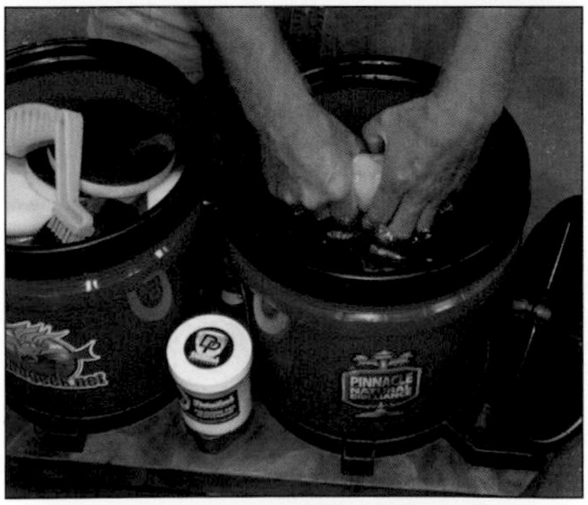

Secondary rinse bucket
Have a separate bucket with clean rinse water. Once you're satisfied with how clean you've gotten the pad, hold it above the bucket and squeeze out as much of the cleaning solution and product residue as possible. Then, place the pad into your rinse bucket.

Keep your bucket near a source of running water
If you use a hose, attach either a sprayer or a brass quick-change valve to make controlling the water easier. Simply rinse your pads by squeezing them at the same time you're flushing them with water.

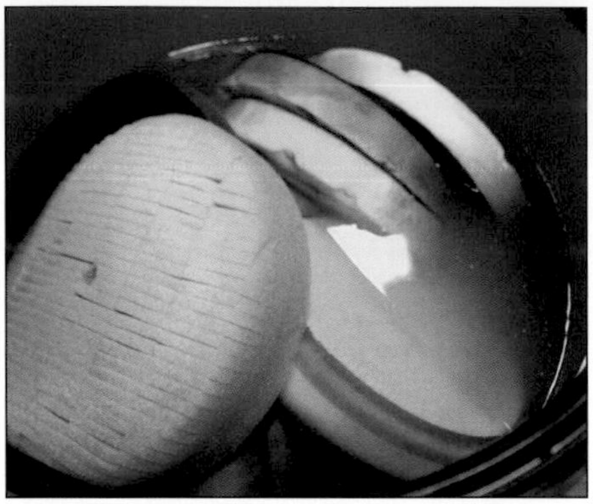

Time Saving Tip *- Soak pads after use regardless of whether you're going to wash your pads in a sink or in a bucket. Before you begin buffing your car, mix up a bucket of pad cleaning solution. When you're finished using a buffing pad, place it into the bucket of pad cleaner.*

Soaking your pads after use but before washing them enables the cleaning agents to dissolve and emulsify any compound, polish or wax residue. This will make washing your pads faster and easier. Another benefit to this technique is the polish residue won't have a chance to dry and harden on and in the pad.

Don't cross-contaminate
If you're washing pads in a bucket or sink, wash your compound and polishing pads first. Then, wash any pads with waxes and paint sealants. This will keep your wash water cleaner and will make cleaning multiple compounding and polishing pads easier.

- **Compounds and polishes = water soluble**
  Because most compounds and polishes are water-soluble, they are fairly easy to clean and rinse from buffing pads.
- **Waxes and paint sealants = water insoluble**
  Waxes and paint sealants, on the other hand, are not water soluble. They will not easily dissolve when agitated in a solution of water with a pad cleaning soap. You can clean pads used for applying waxes and paint sealants, but it will take a little more time and effort.

■ Cleaning On The Fly

Products needed: *Clean, medium-sized terry cloth towel*

When using a dual action polisher to remove below-surface defects with any type of abrasive product, you're going to have two things building up on the face of the foam pad that you need to clean off:

- Spent residue
- Removed paint

You can't see clear paint
If you're working on a clearcoat finish, you won't see the paint residue building up on the pad because the paint is clear.

You can see colored paint
If you're working on a single stage paint, then you'll see the color of the paint building up on the face of your foam pad. For example, if you're working on single stage blue paint, you'll see blue paint on the face of your foam pad.

The important thing to understand is that as you work on any paint system, whether it's a basecoat/clearcoat, single stage or a tinted clearcoat, you're going

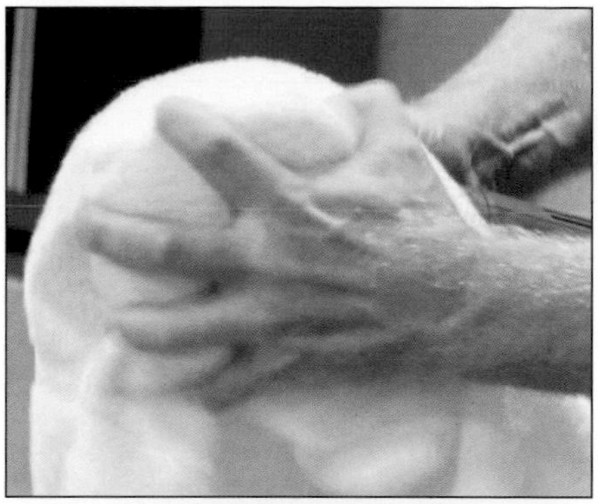

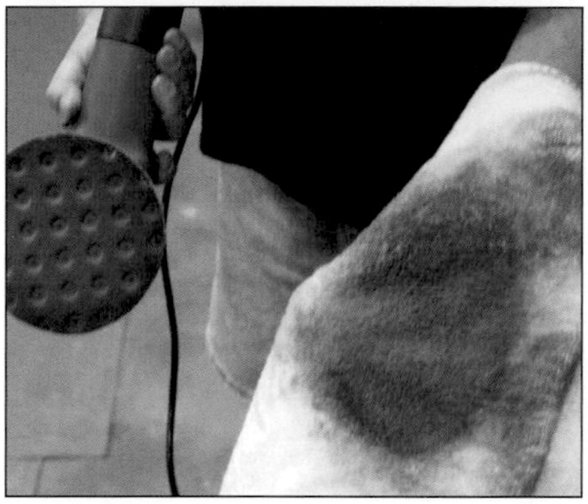

to be removing a little paint. Both the paint you've removed and the spent residue from the compound or polish you're using are going to be building up on the face of the foam pad. It's important to clean this gunk off your pad often.

How to clean the pad on the fly
The whole idea and success behind the "cleaning your pad on the fly" technique is that it allows you to quickly clean your pad and quickly get back to work.

How to clean your pad on the fly

How to do it...
In this technique, you hold a terry cloth towel against the face of the pad with one hand and holding the polisher in the other hand, turn the polisher on and press the towel into the face of the pad.

Smaller towels, like hand towels are easier to manage and my preference. You also need to make sure your towels are clean, as a dirty towel can contaminate your buffing pad.
The speed setting should be the same as when doing your correction work, which is usually the 5 to 6 speed setting. You don't want to continually adjust the speed setting in-between buffing sections of paint just to clean the pad. Plus, the higher speed setting actually helps to do a better job of cleaning the pad.

Tip: *I will tend to use my extended fingers to grip around the pad and grab the backing plate and actually pull the face of my hand (against the towel) against the pad as this will help to blot out or astringe any excess liquid from the pad.*

Question: *Why use terry cloth instead of microfiber?*

Answer: *Great question!*

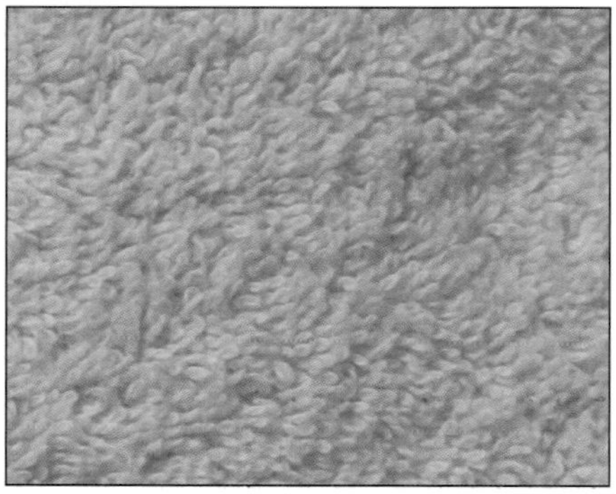

Terry cloth is very good at absorbing liquid, so when you push the terry cloth into the foam, the liquid in the foam will transfer into the terry cloth fibers through capillary action. The nap of terry cloth will help to slice into the caked-up and gummy residue, which will loosen its hold so the residue will transfer from the pad to the towel. Compared to most microfiber polishing cloths, the terry cloth is more stout, allowing it to work better to break up the residue on the pad.

How to use a Pad Washer

How to use a pad washer

A pad washer is a device used to clean or remove built-up residue from the face of a buffing pad quickly, efficiently and painlessly.

How it works
There's a Grit Guard insert resting on top of four spring loaded plastic cups (water pumps) that ride on what is called the Vortex Base. This sits inside a 5-gallon bucket that you fill to a specific volume with water or pad cleaning solution.

Step 1: With the buffing pad attached to your DA polisher, insert the pad into the Grit Guard Pad Washer with the face of the pad against the Grit Guard insert.

Step 2: Close the Splash Guard Lid; this prevents splatter from escaping the bucket as you clean pads.

Step 3: Turn the polisher on. Use a medium speed setting (around the 4 setting) and as the pad is rotating, push it against the Grit Guard insert and pump the polisher up and down.

Step 4: After you've cleaned the pad for about a minute or so, slowly lift the pad away from the Grit Guard insert and allow the it to spin freely while still inside the bucket and under the Splash Guard Lid. Adjust the speed setting to ensure the pad is rotating. Don't simply use

the highest speed setting as this is too fast for proper cleaning and will also splatter and sling cleaning solution out of the bucket.

What's happening inside the pad washer?
When you pump the polisher up and down against the Grit Guard insert, the spring loaded water pumps squirt or inject the pad with water and/or cleaning solution. The cleaning solution penetrates the face of the pad as it mixes with and dissolves the built-up compound. As the pad rotates against the components of the pad washer, excess water is squeezed out of the pad.

How the Grit Guard Universal Pad Washer Works - Here's a cutaway view of the internal components of the Grit Guard Universal Pad Washer.

1. Splash Guard Lid
2. Grit Guard insert with blank insert on center top
3. Spring Loaded Water Pump Cups
4. Stainless Steel Springs
5. Vortex Base
6. Rubber Grip Boots on Feet of Vortex Base
7. Housed inside a 5-Gallon Bucket

Drying towel
Take any clean, dry absorbent towel, press it into the buffing pad and hold it for a few moments. This will extract most of the excess cleaning solution. At this point, you can return to work using your clean pad or place the pad aside to dry in a dust and dirt-free environment.

Clean pad washer - replace water
The more you use the pad washer, the more often you should replace the water and cleaning solution. If you're doing heavy compounding work, then your pad washer is going to load up with compound residue and paint solids faster than if you're lightly polishing a car in good condition. For this reason, you'll want to clean out the pad washer more often. The same goes for buffing either an oxidized gel-coat boat or single stage paint finish. Projects like these remove a lot of dead, oxidized material and you also generate a lot of compounding residue. Monitor your pad washer and clean and refresh the water as needed.

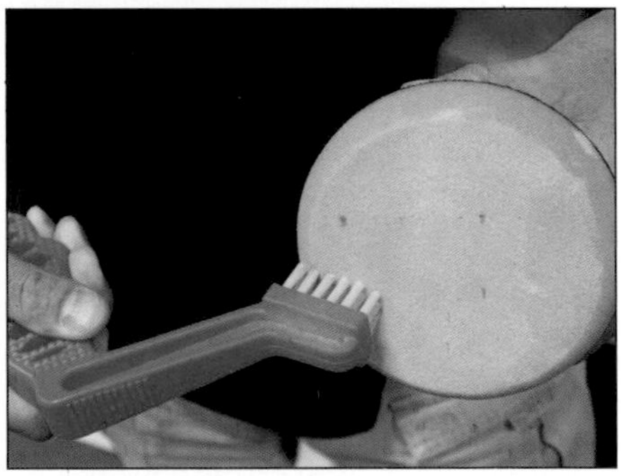

■ Cleaning Dry Pads Using A Pad Conditioning Brush

The fastest way to clean residue from a dry pad is to simply take a nylon pad conditioning brush and carefully scrub the dried product from the face of the pad. When using a pad conditioning brush, you must do so with the polisher in the off position. Hold the polisher while gripping the back of the backing plate to keep it from spinning and then draw the bristles of the brush over the face of the pad.

■ Pad Cleaners And Soaps

Pad cleaning soaps are important because water by itself is not very

good at dissolving and removing all compounds and polishes quickly and easily from buffing pads. A good quality pad cleaning solution or soap will dramatically help get your buffing pads clean and ready to go back to work. There are two options when it comes to pad cleaning solutions:

1. Spray-on pad cleaners
- Pinnacle XMT Polishing Pad Cleaner
- Grit Guard Pad Renewing Solution
- Wolfgang Pad Werks Polishing Pad Cleaner
- Wolfgang Pad Werks Pad Cleaner & Extender
- BLACKFIRE Advanced Pad Cleaner

This type of pad cleaner comes in a spray bottle and is sprayed directly onto the face of the pad.

- **Benefits**
  Concentrated cleaning solution instantly dissolves and loosens built-up product residue from the buffing pad.

For extremely dirty pads, you can agitate and work the cleaner with your hand before placing the pad into a pad washer. Because there is no cleaning solution in the water, you get a cleaner rinse initially. Cleaning several pads introduces more cleaning solution and product residue into the water. At some point, what was once clean rinse water will now be similar to a cleaning solution similar to that in option 2.

2. Powdered pad cleaning soaps
These citrus-based cleaning soaps work really well for dissolving and emulsifying compound and polish residue.

- Detailer's Pro Series Pad Rejuvenator
- Wolfgang Polishing Pad Rejuvenator
- Snappy Clean Pad Cleaning Powder

This type of pad cleaner normally comes in a concentrated powder form. Mix a measured amount of the powdered cleaning solution into your bucket of water before installing the Vortex Base. Then, mix the pad cleaning soap and water until you have a uniform cleaning solution. Then, re-insert the Vortex Base and the Grit Guard insert. Add or remove water until the level of cleaning solution in the bucket measures about 1/4" above the Grit Guard insert with it depressed against the spring loaded water pumps until they bottom out.

- **Benefits**
  Cleaning solution floods the pad with cleaning agents as it's being pumped and rotated against the Grit Guard insert.

- **Drawbacks**
  Some people have concerns that not enough of the cleaning solution will be removed from the pad. If put back into service, the cleaning solution could interfere with or affect the compound or polish being used.

The benefit of being able to clean your pads quickly and easily far outweighs any potential drawbacks. I've never seen any of my own work suffer due to residual cleaning solution being left behind on the pad. Given the choice, I will choose a pad washer over all the other options every time.

Recommendation
If you routinely use a machine polisher, invest in a pad washer.

Note: *The Grit Guard Universal Pad Washer works with all modern and popular polishers, including:*

- DA polishers: Porter Cable 7424XP, Griot's Garage DA polisher, Meguiar's G110v2 and the Shurhold Polisher
- All Rotary Buffers
- Cyclo Polisher
- Flex 3401
- Even a drill with a pad attached in some fashion.

How Often Do I Need To Clean My Pads?

- **Option 1: After each section pass**
  In a perfect world, you would clean your pad after each section pass. Each time you buff a new section of paint, you'll be removing some level of paint from the surface if you're using any type of abrasive product (even a cleaner/wax), along with other substances like stains, road grime, impurities and anything that your detailing clay didn't remove. Plus, you'll have the spent product residue on the face of the pad. If you are a perfectionist, you'll want to clean your pad on the fly after each section pass.

- **Option 2: After every other section pass**
  While perfection is a nice achievement, not everyone is trying to perform this type of work. For most people that are trying to balance doing great quality work in a timely manner, then cleaning your pad on the fly after every other section pass is a faster and still very effective approach.

- **Option 3: After each panel**
  Cleaning your pads after buffing an entire panel will get you by. If your pad is not rotating very well, this is an indicator of built-up residue and removed paint on the face of the pad and a sign you need to clean it.

Problems Caused By Not Cleaning Your Pad Often

Compounds and polishes become less effective during application. If you don't remove the spent product, then it will act to dilute the strength or power of any fresh product you apply.

Product Becomes More Difficult To Wipe Off

After buffing a section, the residue will become more and more gummy as it's continually becoming a mixture of product residue, removed paint and any contaminants that were on or in the paint. Add to this a little heat and evaporation of any carrying agents and you're left with a gummy residue that's going to be hard to wipe off.

Harder For The Tool To Rotate The Pad

A build-up of gunk on the face of the foam pad makes it more difficult for the tool to rotate it.

Increased Risk For Instilling Swirls Back Into Paint

As product residue and removed paint builds on the face of the pad, the potential for abrasive particles to accumulate and embed into this mixture of gunk increases and the potential to instill swirls as you're buffing increases.

Pad cleaning products

There are all kinds of products that can be used to clean residues from buffing pads, but for the context of this how-to book, the only ones I'm going to list are products that specifically state on the label they are formulated for this type of job.

- Detailer's Pro Series Polishing Pad Rejuvenator
- Wolfgang Polishing Pad Rejuvenator
- Wolfgang Pad Werks Polishing Pad Cleaner
- Wolfgang Pad Werks Pad Cleaner & Extender
- BLACKFIRE Advanced Pad Cleaner
- Pinnacle XMT Polishing Pad Cleaner
- Snappy Clean Pad Cleaning Powder
- Grit Guard Pad Renewing Solution

Pad cleaning tools

Here are some pad cleaning tools specifically made to help you clean foam buffing pads.

- Foam Pad Conditioning Brush
- Duo Spur Wool & Foam Pad Cleaning Tool

How to clean pads on the fly using a rotary buffer

Wool Pads = Steel Spur

When using a wool pad for any type of cutting work and ESPECIALLY removing heavy oxidation, use a steel pad cleaning spur. The steel spur rotates on an axis and the teeth on the spur act to both remove caked-up residues and re-fluff the fibers.

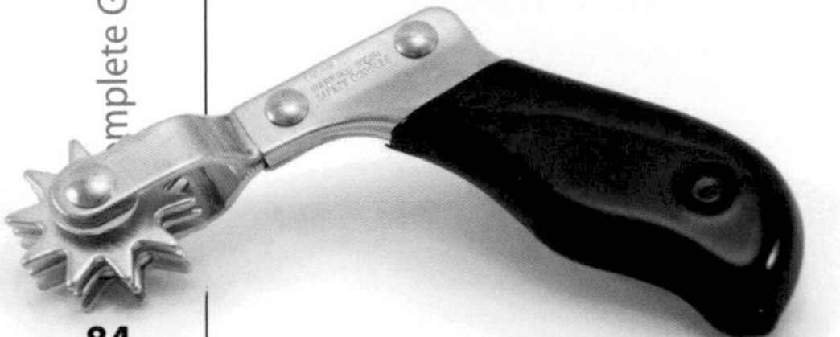

Cleaning wool pads often with a steel spur makes controlling the rotary buffer easier and it helps prevent the product you're using from becoming gummy on the surface you're buffing. Both of these are HUGE factors for making using a rotary buffer easier and making the project faster and less tiring. Don't be a Caveman and use a screwdriver or other sharp instrument. Not only can it be dangerous but sharp edges being ground into the face of the buffing pad can tear up and fray the fibers.

They way I use a spur is I hold the rotary buffer against my left leg and use my right hand to draw the spur from the center of the pad outward. If you're left handed you can improvise your own version of this technique. Try to avoid having the spur being drawn against the pad in a way that could throw the spur at your face in case you lose control or lose your grip.

Foam Pads = Pad Conditioning Brush

To clean foam pads on a rotary buffer you want to use a brush with nylon bristles. A stiff or hard bristled toothbrush will work but what works better is an actual tool made just for cleaning pads called a Pad Conditioning Brush. Unlike a tooth brush, the Pad Conditioning Brush offers a larger footprint of stiff, nylon bristles and this acts to clean the pad better while reducing the potential of damaging the foam.

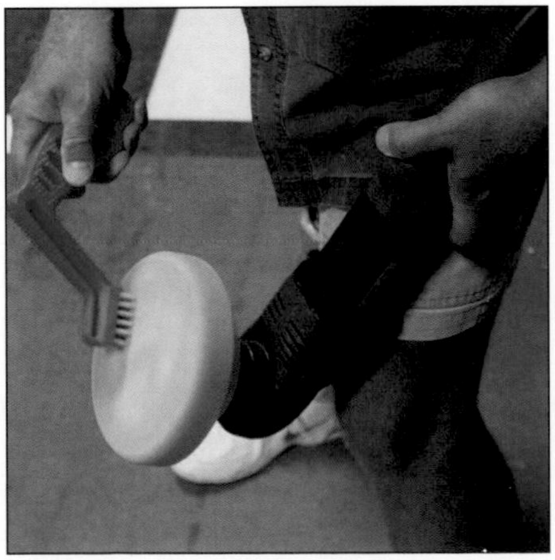

The Terry Cloth Towel Technique

This technique is for foam pads only and works really well when you're getting a build up of excess liquid in the pad plus built up oxidation, paint residue and spent product residue. It's kind of dangerous so use at your own risk.

How to use terry cloth towel to clean your pads on the fly with a rotary buffer.

Take a clean terry cloth hand towel and hold it around your hand in a way that you can gather some material around your index finger.

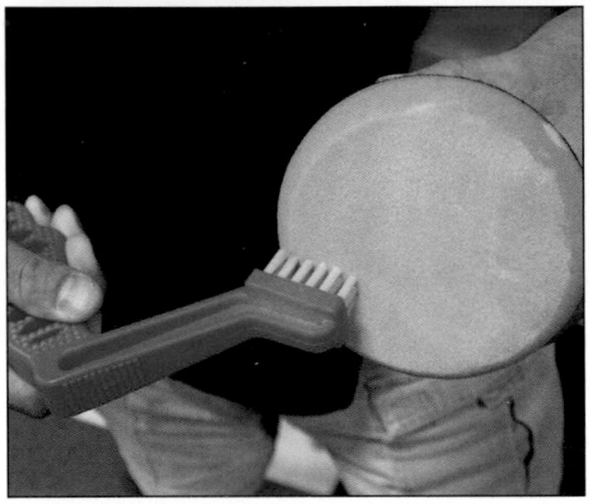

With the rotary buffer turned on a medium speed, (not locked for safety purposes), press your finger flat into the spinning foam pad and then rotate your finger/hand upward or clockwise. You'll see excess gunk plus excess liquid come off the pad and onto the terry cloth towel. Move your finger to a clean section of the towel and repeat until you feel the pad is ready to put back to work.

Pad Washers

Another great way to clean both wool and foam pads when using a rotary buffer is to use a Pad Washer like the Grit Guard Universal Pad Washer. See the DA Polisher section on cleaning pads to learn how the pad washer works.

Tip for cleaning pads with a pad washer

Because you need to pump the buffing pad up and down against the Grit Guard Insert in order to inject the pad with water and cleaning solution here's a little tip and a tool to make the cleaning process faster and more efficient.

Get an adapter for use with Double Sided Buffing Pads line one of these,

- Lake Country Double-Sided Pad Rotary Buffer Adapter
- Optimum Double-Sided Pad Rotary Buffer Adapter

Then attach the adapter to the spindle on your rotary buffer and attach your backing plate to the adapter. What this does is moves the backing plate and pad further away from the body of the rotary buffer. This provides you with more room to move the body of the rotary buffer up and down with the pad inside the pad washer.

How To Dry Foam Pads After Washing

After you've washed your pads, you need to dry them in a clean, dust-free area. Then, store them in a way they will remain clean until you need them for your next detailing project.

Here are some tips...

Upside down or right side up?
Dry your pads with the hook and loop material facing upwards so any water can drain out through the foam unhindered. This way, you won't have water or any remaining residue pooling between the foam and the hook and loop material, potentially affecting the adhesive.

Hang drying pads
Here's a creative way to hang your pads up in the air to dry that uses the hook and loop interface. This method was submitted by John aka Swimmer on the AutogeekOnline.net Detailing Discussion Forum.

Cut a strip of hook material about 6"' in length so you can attach it in a loop fashion to the loop material on the back of your buffing pad. Then, run a clothesline on which you can hang your pads to dry. This positions them out of the way, where air can flow around them but airborne dust cannot land and settle on the face of the pads.

Drying with Grit Guard inserts
If you own a Grit Guard insert, here's a tip from Tad aka DarkHorse on the AutogeekOnline.net Detailing Discussion Forum.

Towel drying
Using a clean, dry terry or microfiber towel, roll your washed and rinsed pad inside the towel.

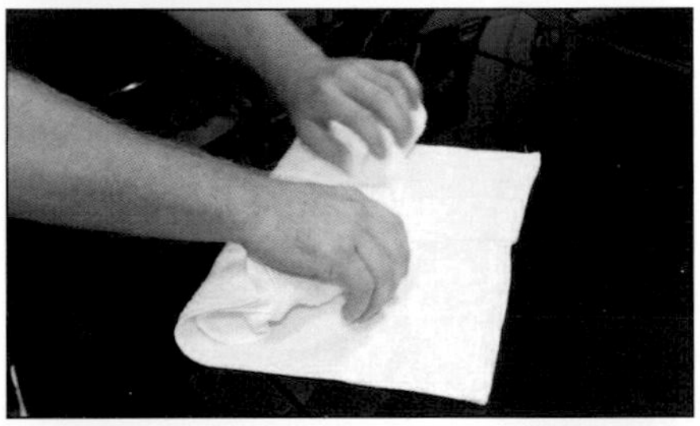

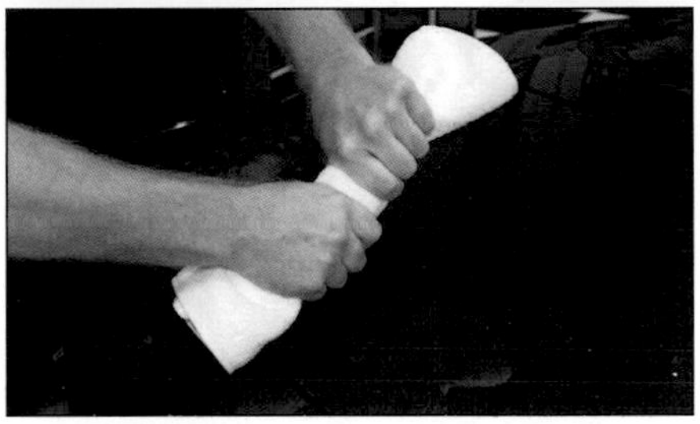

Press the towel into the foam as you're folding and rolling the pad into it. Then, squeeze and wring the pad inside the towel, forcing any excess water out of the foam and into the absorbent towel.

Afterwards, place your foam buffing pads where they will stay clean and air can circulate around them so that moisture can evaporate.

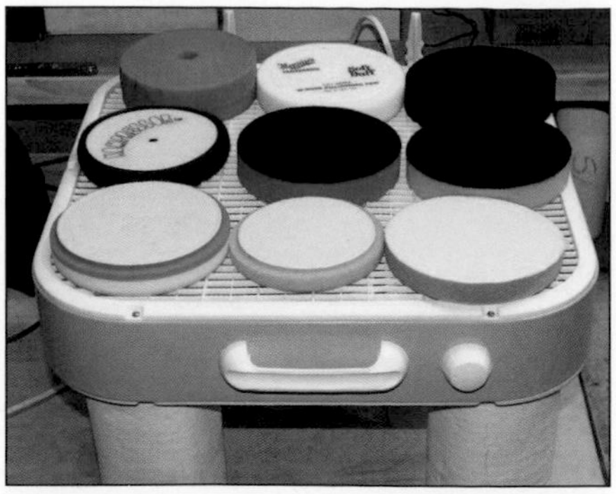

Box fan pad dryer
From Truitt aka Bill - Position and suspend a box fan from a clean, flat surface and then place your foam pads onto it face-down. Because your pads are face-down, dirt particles won't land and lodge into the pores and the air being drawn past them will dramatically increase drying time.

■ How To Store Clean, Dry Buffing Pads

Clean cupboard - enclosed shelves
If you have an empty cupboard in your laundry room, utility room, or garage, this will make an ideal place to store your clean, dry pads.

Plastic Storage Containers
These containers work great not only for storing your foam buffing pads, but also microfiber towels and other detailing tools you want to keep clean like wash mitts, sponges, brushes, etc.

Tip: Mold and Mildew *- If you're going to store foam pads in any kind of air-tight container or bag, be sure the pad is 100% dry to prevent the potential for mold and mildew forming. If it does form, you can simply wash the pad again.*

Original packaging bags
Some pads come with a re-closable plastic bag. Keep the bag and use it for storage.

Large sealable plastic bags
These work great for storing clean buffing pads. Just make sure your pads are 100% dry if you choose to seal the bag shut.

■ Foam Pad Color Coding

Each pad manufacturer uses a different color coding system for the pads they manufacture. Even inside a single company's pad lines, there can be confusion. Since pad options are continually changing, the best thing to do is to post any questions you have to the AutogeekOnline.net discussion forum.

■ Surbuf MicroFingers

Surbuf MicroFingers Buffing pads were originally developed in the woodworking industry for applying stains to wood by machine. In the woodworking industry, wood stain is applied to the center of the pad. When worked at a low speed, and with very light pressure, the MicroFingers work the stain into the grain of the wood. While Surbuf pads are used to apply stain in the woodworking industry, in the detailing world, they are used on DA polishers for correction work.

- **Benefits**
  Generally speaking, the fibers of this type of pad work as a type of abrasive to compliment the abrasives in the compound or polish. When used with a DA polisher, you will in effect have two types of abrasives (the mechanical abrasives in the compound and the MicroFingers) working for you to level the surface.

- **Drawbacks**
  The MicroFinger fibers tend to leave micromarring in the paint, also called DA haze. This isn't a big deal because an aggressive foam cutting pad on a DA polisher will also leave micromarring or haze. Anytime you use a Surbuf pad, just keep in mind that after using this pad for your correction step, you need to follow it by re-polishing the paint using a softer pad and a less aggressive polish to remove the micromarring and create a clear, defect free finish.

Sizes Available
- 4 inch
- 5 1/2 inch
- 6 1/2 inch
- 7 inch

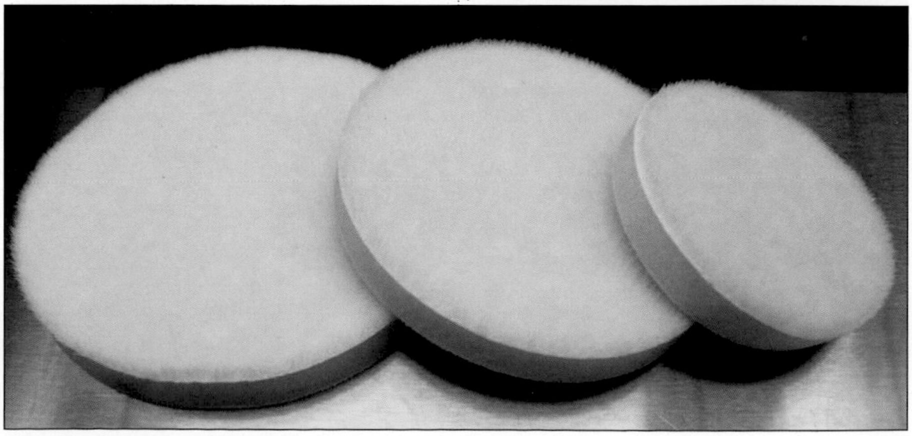

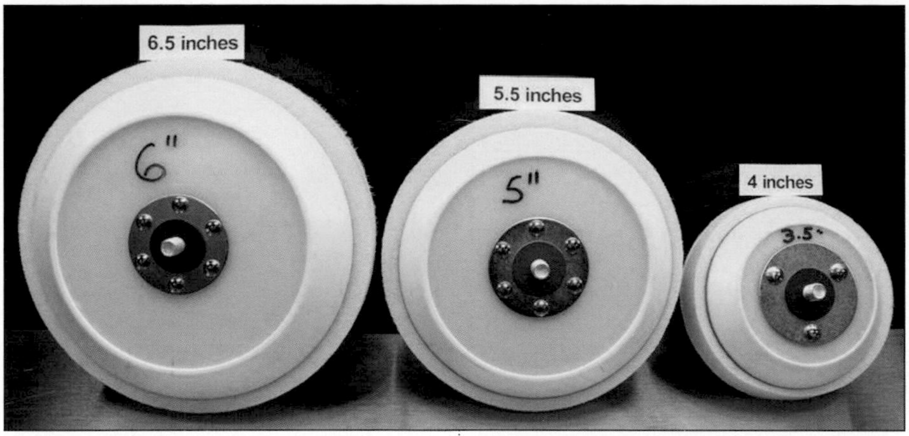

Tips For Using Surbuf Pads

Match the pad to the correct sized backing plate and center the pad onto the hook and loop interface. Always hold the pad flat to the surface and use light to moderate pressure, letting the combination of the MicroFingers, abrasives and oscillating/rotating action do the abrading work.

- 4 inch = 3.5" Backing Plate
- 5 1/2 inch = 5" Backing Plate
- 6 1/2 inch = 6" Backing Plate
- 7 inch = 6" Backing Plate

Use firm pressure and slow arm speed When removing swirls and scratches, you want to use firm pressure and slow arm speed. Some people recommend using light pressure so you don't flatten down the MicroFingers. While that sounds good, the truth is, after you make a few passes with any pressure, the MicroFingers naturally lie down and flatten out. You can't stop this from happening and the pads still cut well. If you try to only use light pressure in an attempt to keep the MicroFingers from lying down, you won't engage the abrasives with the paint.

When to clean
Clean your Surbuf pads after each section pass. As the MicroFingers lie down, your product and any paint you're removing will build up on the surface of the pad. You want to remove this residue before adding fresh product. You should always be wiping any product residue from the paint after doing a section pass. Compound and polishes shouldn't be allowed to dry. There's no benefit to this and normally it makes wiping this type of residue from the paint more difficult.

How To Clean Surbuf Microfiber Pads

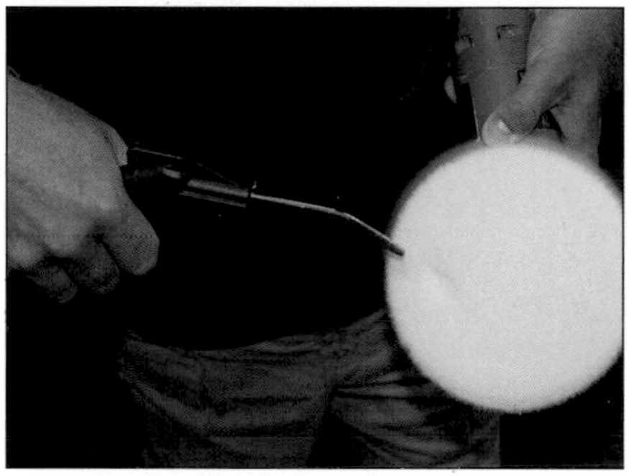

Compressed air
The best way is using an air squirter with an air compressor. Always use safety glasses when using compressed air.

Pad conditioning brush
If you don't have an air compressor, you can use the nylon bristles of a pad conditioning brush to agitate the working face of the Surbuf pads. Hold the polisher in such a way that you can keep the backing plate from spinning freely, and then draw the brush against the MicroFingers. This will remove caked-up product and re-fluff the fibers. What I do is brace the pad from

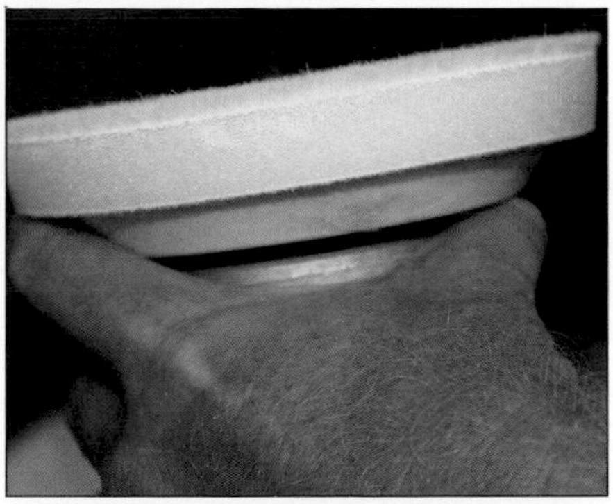

behind by holding my thumb and index finger against the backing plate. This keeps the assembly from spinning while I run the brush over the face of the pad to remove built-up residue.

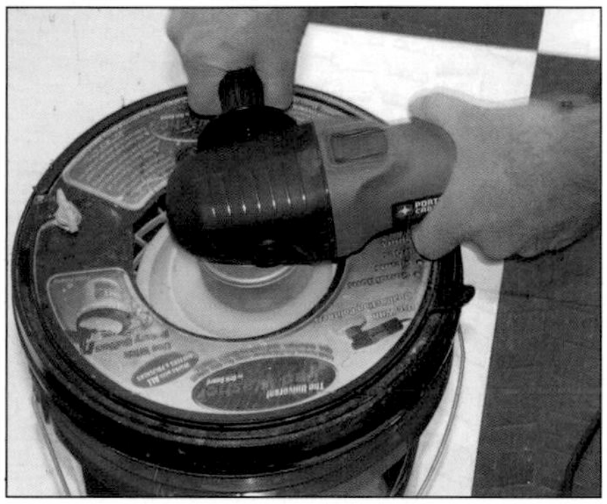

Pad Washer
The Grit Guard Universal Pad Washer works excellent for cleaning Surbuf pads. Use the same technique shared in this chapter.

For more information:
Cleaning Pads using a Pad Washer

Wash by hand
You can also wash your Surbuf pads by hand in either a sink or a bucket in the same way you would wash a foam buffing pad by hand.

Note: *It's not recommended to wash Surbuf pads in a washing machine or to dry them in a clothes dryer.*

Microfiber Pads

- *Meguiar's Microfiber Pads*
- *Lake Country Ultra-Fiber Pads*
- *Optimum Microfiber Pads*

Microfiber pads were first introduced and used at the OEM level for spot repair on the assembly line. The technology has since been improved

and introduced to the detailing industry for reconditioning the paint on used cars.

What is a Microfiber DA pad?
Microfiber polishing pads use a specific type of open-ended microfiber material that is extremely soft to the touch when new, clean and dry. The microfiber material is attached to a foam backing interface with a hook and loop backing to attach them to DA Backing Plates.

Meguiar's Microfiber Pads
Meguiar's microfiber pads are available in 3 different sizes - 3", 5" and 6". The actual exact size for pads and backing plates varies as is the norm for all buffing pads and backing plates. Normally, you want the backing plate to be a little undersized so there's a safety margin around the pad preventing you from gouging the paint with the edge of the backing plate. At the same time, it's important to have equal and uniform pressure applied over the entire working face of the pad to maximize efficiency.

Cutting Discs

- **Foam backing**
  These pads feature maroon foam backing that is approximately 1/4" thick with a medium density cushion to it.
- **Microfiber pile**
  The face of these pads uses an open-ended microfiber material that is very soft, yet different when compared to the microfiber used for the finishing disc. The fibers appear to be longer in length and slightly larger in diameter. The microfiber pile is also more dense than the finishing pad with more fibers per square inch.

Finishing Discs

- **Foam backing**
  The black foam backing is approximately 3/8" with a soft cushioned feel to it that's slightly softer than the maroon foam backing of the cutting disc.
- **Microfiber pile**
  This soft, open-ended microfiber material is even softer than the microfiber pile used for the cutting pad. The fibers themselves are both shorter in length and smaller in diameter than the microfiber pile used to make the cutting disc. The microfiber pile also appears to be less dense with fewer fibers per square inch as compared to the microfiber cutting discs.

■ The Meguiar's Microfiber DA Correction System

Video: Meguiars Microfiber DA Correction System

Meguiar's DA Microfiber discs are part of a multi-component system designed and optimized specifically for use with DA polishers. These pads are used with their matching D300 Compound and D301 Finishing Wax providing a 2-step approach for removing swirls and scratches and restoring a swirl-free, high gloss finish on FACTORY paint - not repaints.

First Step - Remove Swirls And Scratches
The microfiber cutting discs, when used with the matching compound, will remove most swirls and scratches in one step with a residue that wipes off easily. Deeper swirls and scratches would require more applications or more aggressive products, pads and tools. This system is targeted toward high volume detailing, not show car detailing. In high volume detailing, the goal is not to remove 100% of all defects - it's to remove the majority of medium to shallow swirls and scratches and do it without instilling any additional swirls.

First, prime a clean, dry pad.

Once it is primed, apply your working product using 3-4 pea-sized to dime-sized drops of product to the face of the pad.

Second Step - Refine Results, Create Gloss And Seal Paint
The microfiber finishing disc, when used with the matching polish/wax, has the ability to lightly abrade the paint to remove any haze left by the aggressive first step and refine the results to create a high gloss finish.

Official product recommendations
Use the Microfiber Cutting Disc with D300 Correction Compound and use the Microfiber Finishing Discs with D301 Finishing Wax. There are no official recommendations for using these types of pads outside of the matching compound and polish/ wax that makes up the DA Microfiber System. When used as intended, they work very well and reduce the overall time it takes to restore the finish on cars with factory paint.

Using with non-system products
I've included these two discs in this how-to book because they are an option for DA polishers outside of conventional foam buffing pads and other fiber-type pads like the Surbuf pads. They should be used as intended with their matching compound and polish/ wax. If you choose to use them with any product outside the system, I would strongly recommend doing a test spot to a small section of paint and checking your results. Make sure you're getting the results you want before attempting to buff out the rest of the car.

■ Optimum Microfiber Pads

Optimum Polymer Technologies introduced two new microfiber pads which can be used with either dual action polishers or rotary buffers. Optimum microfiber pads use an advanced laminating system to help prevent delamination under heavy correction use. All Optimum Microfiber pads are machine washable.

Optimum DA Microfiber Correction System
An important key to good performance when it comes to microfiber pads on rotary buffers and/or the Flex 3401 are compounds and polishes with excellent lubricating characteristics and long buffing cycles. This is where Optimum Polymer Technologies excels. Dr. David Ghodoussi, PhD is an Organic Chemist and a personal friend of mine known for manufacturing some of the best car care products available. His sprayable Hyper-Compound and Hyper Polish as well as his Compound II, Polish II and Finish all work great with these new microfiber pads as well as traditional wool and foam pads.

- **Optimum Microfiber Cutting Pad**
  These pads are available in 3 ¼", 4 ¼" 5 ¼" and 6 ¼" sizes. The cutting pads have a semi-dense yellow foam core that measures ½" thick.

- **Optimum Microfiber Polishing Pads**
  The polishing pads are available in 3 ¼", 4 ¼" 5 ¼" and 6 ¼" sizes. The polishing pads have a soft white foam core that measures 5/8" thick.

My comment: *Having a thicker foam backing dramatically helps provide smooth buffing action when used with a rotary buffer or the Flex 3401.*

■ Lake Country Ultra-Fiber Dual Action Microfiber Pads

Lake Country, a leader in pad technology has introduced a new microfiber pad for both DA Polishers and Rotary buffers. The Lake Country design uses different types of adhesives designed specifically for the materials they bond together to ensure the pads don't delaminate, even after countless uses. Lake country Ultra-Fiber pads use microfiber material that is super plush and denser than other microfiber pads. This allows for a microfiber pad that cuts fast when compounding and finishes to a high gloss when polishing.

LC Ultra-Fiber pads are available in 2-packs in four sizes, 3 1/4", 4 1/4", 5 1/4" and 6 1/4". The DA pads have a firm foam core that measures 1/4" thick with a hook and loop backing. Thin, firm foam cores like this maximize power transfer from the tool to the face of the pad.

Product Recommendations
Lake Country's Microfiber pads are universal pad that should be used with premium quality compounds and polishes.

■ How To Clean Microfiber Pads

- **Compressed air**
  The best way is using an air squirter with an air compressor. Always use safety glasses when using compressed air.

- **Bug scrubbing sponge**
  Interestingly enough, this simple bug scrubbing sponge works really well to remove caked-on product residue while also re-fluffing the microfibers.

Pad conditioning brush

If you don't have an air compressor, you can use the nylon bristles of a pad conditioning brush to agitate the working face of microfiber pads. Hold the polisher in one hand in such a way that you can keep the backing plate from spinning freely, and then draw the brush against the microfibers. This will remove caked-on product and re-fluff the fibers.

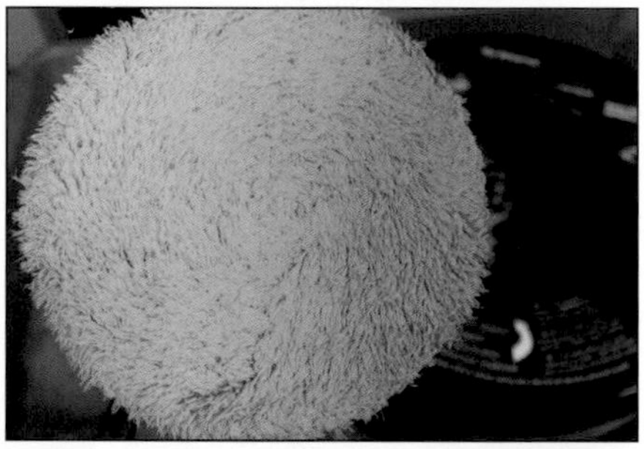

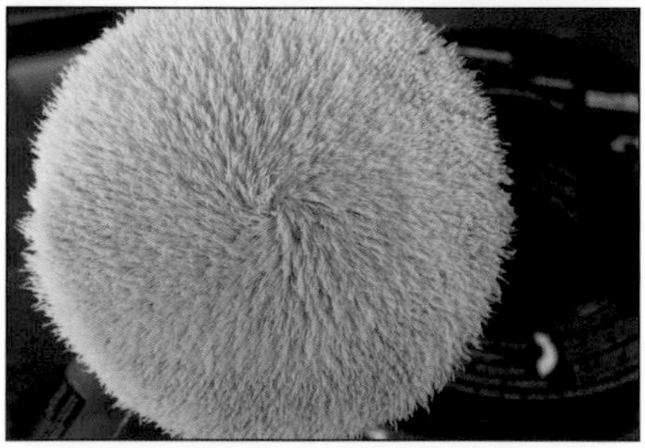

- **Pad Washer**
  The Grit Guard Universal Pad Washer works excellent for cleaning microfiber pads. Use the same technique shared in this chapter.

For more information:

📖 Cleaning Pads using a Pad Washer

■ Machine washing and drying

All of the listed manufacturers of microfiber pads state that their pads can be machine washed and dried. I personally think that your pads will last longer if you hand wash them or use a Grit Guard Universal Pad Washer. Machine washing is somewhat hard on pads and generally decreases their life expectancy. Use the same techniques shared in this chapter.

Wash by hand

All microfiber pads can be washed by hand in either a sink or a bucket in the same way you would wash a foam buffing pad by hand as previously shown.

Drying and storage

Dry and store your microfiber pads in the same way that you would your foam pads.

■ How To Choose The Right Pad For The Job

Any time you're buffing out a car for the first time, it's a good idea to do what's called a test spot to one of the horizontal panels. Dial in a system approach that removes the defects to your satisfaction and creates the quality of finish appearance that you're looking for before buffing out the entire car.

- If you can make one small section of paint look great, then duplicate the same process to the rest of the car, you will get the same uniform results throughout.
- If you run into any kind of problems or issues working on your test spot, then you'll be glad you didn't just start buffing out the entire car only to find out towards the end of the project you're not getting the results you wanted.

- If you have already worked on the paint for your current detailing project, then you probably already have an idea as to which pad to start out with. If not, then hopefully the information below will help to guide you to pick the right pad.

Why test?

The hardness of the paint you're buffing is a huge variable. Paint manufacturers are continually introducing new paint lines and modifying existing ones. This means the paint on a 2011 Ford manufactured in January can buff differently than the paint on a 2011 Ford manufactured in March. It all depends upon the paint system being used at the time.

So don't rely on past experiences to base future product choices upon for your next detailing project. If you're working on a car you've never worked on before, new or old, before buffing out the entire car, do a little testing and dial-in a system that works great in one location. Theoretically, this same process will work perfectly over the rest of the car. Always do a test spot.

- *"Use the least aggressive product to get the job done"*

Some people read the above quote and think it applies to the liquid paint care products used to buff out a car. While this is true, it's not limited to just the liquid products. It actually includes everything that is going to touch the paint, including your choice of pads.

There are 3 basic categories of buffing pads:

- **Cutting**
- **Polishing**
- **Finishing**

Inside these 3 groups are sub-groups:

- **Cutting**
  - Aggressive
  - Medium
  - Light

- **Polishing**
  - Medium Polishing
  - Light Polishing

- **Finishing**
  - Finishing pads
  - Jewelling pads

In most cases, the differences are subtle. But, because modern clearcoat paints are thin and scratch-sensitive, little differences can have huge effects, thus the variety of different types of pads and levels of aggressiveness.

■ Paint Conditions And Pad Recommendations

Here are the basics of choosing the right pad for the job. The first step is to evaluate your car's finish as explained in the Visual and Physical Inspection chapter. After reading that chapter, you should be able to inspect your car's paint and determine where it falls into one of these 11 categories:

- **Show Car Quality**
  Foam Polishing Pad, Finishing Pad or Jewelling Pad

- **Excellent Condition**
  Foam Polishing Pad, Finishing Pad or Jewelling Pad

- **Good Condition**
  Foam Polishing pad

- **Mildly Neglected**
  Foam Polishing or Cutting Pad

- **Severely Neglected**
  Aggressive Foam or Fiber Cutting Pad

- **Horrendous Swirls**
  Aggressive Foam or Fiber Cutting Pad

- **Extreme Oxidation**
  Aggressive Foam or Fiber Cutting Pad

- **Extreme Orange Peel**
  Remove by sanding and compounding

- **Unstable**
  Correction not possible - repaint

- **Clearcoat Failure**
  Correction not possible - repaint

- **Past the point of no return**
  Correction not possible - repaint

Which type of foam pad to use
All of the foam pads listed in this book work great - CCS pads, Flat Pads, Kompressor Pads, Cobra Pads, Hydro-Tech Pads, etc.

Which pads are best
Personal preference is a huge factor when it comes to what's best. Flat pads have been around the longest and have a long track record of success. CCS pads have been around for close to 20 years and have a large and loyal following. Here's the deal, I get asked all the time which pads are best and I understand that people new to machine polishing want to get the right pads and the best pads when making an investment into their arsenal of detailing tools.

So here's what I think, buffing pads are important but as long as you're using a good quality, clean pads with a quality product, technique becomes more important than the pad or the products.

That said, if you need to do some heavy correction, that is remove swirls and scratches, a fiber pad will always cut faster than a foam pad because the fibers themselves can be a type of abrasive. It's for this same reason that a fiber pad will never finish out as nice as a foam pad. So for aggressive cutting when using a DA Polisher look at any of the microfiber cutting pads or the Surbuf pads.

For foam pads, I'm a fan of flat pads for a number of reasons. Flat foam pads are in 100% contact with the surface meaning the abrasives in your product are being equally worked at all times. These pads are also easier to clean because the surface is flat and there is no place for abrasives or contaminants to build up. With a flat pad, you get a uniform, flat surface working against a uniform flat surface. But, that's just me. I like the 5.5" Lake Country Flat Pads and also the 5.5" Hydro-Tech Pads. The LC Flat pads are open cell and thus will last longer and are easier to clean. The Hydro-Tech pads are closed cell so they won't last as long and are harder to clean but each of the three types - cutting, polishing and finishing - work really well. ■

Compounds, Polishes And Waxes Overview

There's always a lot of confusion when it comes to words and terms used in the car detailing industry.

Part of the reason for this is because there's no organization in the auto appearance industry that regulates or has oversight over the language used to describe and market car appearance products. Manufacturers, marketers and distributors of car care appearance products can and do name their products using whatever terms they like, regardless of the confusion it may cause or any historical precedents.

In This Section:

- Compounds, Polishes And Waxes Overview
- Factors That Affect How Aggressive Or Non-Aggressive A Product Is
- Use The Least Aggressive Product To Get The Job Done
- The Graphic Equalizer Analogy To Polishing Paint

Judge a product by the function it performs, not the name on the label

Because there's no universal standard definitions for words and terms used in the car care appearance world, my practice and recommendation to others is to judge a product not by the name on the label, but by what function the product serves.

For example, if a product is referred to as a polish but acts as a paint sealant, then the product is in fact a paint sealant and not an abrasive polish in the historical use of the word.

If a product is referred to as a glaze but acts to seal the paint, then the product is a wax or paint sealant and not a glaze in the historical use of the word.

Here's a list of commonly used words in our industry and my attempt at creating some type of standardized definition for each word.

- Aggressive Cut Compound
- Medium Cut Polish
- Fine Cut Polish
- Ultra Fine Cut Polish
- Non-Abrasive Glaze or Pure Polish
- Pre-Wax Cleaner
- Paint Cleaner
- Carnauba Wax
- Synthetic Paint Sealant
- Hybrid Sealant/Wax
- Paint Coating
- Cleaner wax or AIO

Aggressive Cut Compound

This is a very aggressive liquid or paste that uses some type of abrasive technology to cut or abrade paint quickly. In the body shop world, compounds are used to remove sanding marks. In the detailing world, compounds are used to remove deep below-surface defects like swirls, scratches and water spot etchings. Depending upon the abrasive technology and the application method and material, some automotive compounds can remove down to 1000 grit sanding marks. Of course, topcoat hardness is an important factor that determines effectiveness.

Historically, the more aggressive the compound, the more follow-up polishing will be required to restore a defect-free finish. Due to major advancements in abrasive technology, the trend is for very aggressive compounds that finish out like medium and even fine polishes.

In most cases, an aggressive compound should be followed with either a medium or fine polish to refine the surface to a higher degree than the results produced by only the compound. Most compounds are dedicated products in that their function is primarily to abrade the paint. For this reason, after the compounding step, further polishing and sealing steps are required. Most compounds are water-soluble, so that they can be washed off body panels and out of cracks and crevices.

Medium Cut Polish

A medium cut polish is a liquid or paste that uses some type of abrasive technology to cut or abrade the paint, but is less aggressive than a true cutting compound. Depending upon the abrasive technology, the application method and material,

some medium polishes can remove down to 2000 grit sanding marks and finish Last Step Product (LSP) ready. Topcoat hardness is an important factor that determines a medium polish's effectiveness at removing below-surface defects.

Most medium polishes are dedicated products in that their function is primarily to abrade the paint. For this reason, after the polishing step, further steps are required. This may include another final polishing step depending upon the results after using the medium polish. At a minimum, the paint should be sealed with a wax, paint sealant or coating.

Fine Cut Polish

A fine cut polish is a liquid or paste that uses some type of abrasive technology to cut or abrade the paint, but is less aggressive than a true medium polish. Depending upon the abrasive technology, the application method and material, some fine polishes can remove down to 2500 grit sanding marks while still finishing out LSP ready. Topcoat hardness is an important factor that determines a fine polish's effectiveness at removing below-surface defects.

Most fine polishes are dedicated products in that their function is primarily to abrade the paint. For this reason, after the fine polishing step, further steps may be required. This could include another final polishing step depending upon the results after using the fine polish. At a minimum, the paint should be sealed with a wax, paint sealant or coating.

Ultra Fine Cut Polish

This is a liquid or paste that uses some type of abrasive technology to cut or abrade the paint, but is less aggressive than a true fine polish. Depending upon the abrasive technology, the application method and material, some ultra fine polishes can remove down to 2500 grit sanding marks while still finishing out LSP ready. Topcoat hardness is an important factor that determines an ultra fine polish's effectiveness at removing below-surface defects.

Most ultra fine polishes are dedicated products in that their function is primarily to abrade the paint. For this reason, after the ultra fine polishing step, at a minimum, the paint should be sealed with a wax, paint sealant or coating.

Non-Abrasive Glaze or Pure Polish

Historically, the term glaze is used to describe a bodyshop safe, hand-applied liquid used to fill-in and mask fine swirls while creating a deep, wet shine on fresh paint. It's a category of products used on fresh paint in body shop environments, which will not seal the paint surface.

A body shop safe glaze is used in place of a wax, sealant or coating because it won't interfere with the normal out-gassing process of fresh paint for the first 30 days of curing. The function of a bodyshop glaze is to hide rotary buffer swirls while giving the paint a uniform, just waxed appearance to ensure customer satisfaction. After 30 days cure time, it's normal to the seal the paint using a wax, paint sealant or coating.

• Hiding swirls

There's a number of reasons why body shops use a glaze on fresh paint to hide swirls. Most body shops are production oriented and perform a limited number of machine buffing steps due to time restrictions and profitability. This would include machine compounding with a wool pad and polishing with either a wool finishing pad or a foam polishing or finishing pad, both steps using rotary buffers.

The end result is normally an excellent shine, but with rotary buffer swirls in the paint that can be seen in bright light. The glaze is normally hand-applied to fill in and hide the swirls as hand application is fast and relatively effective as long as the swirls are shallow. This glazing procedure produces a finish that customers will

accept at the time of vehicle pick-up. The results are somewhat misleading, however, because body shop glazes are water soluble. As such, they will wash off after a few car washes or repeated exposure to rainy weather, making the swirls visible again. This is the standard and accepted practice in the body shop industry.

Note: *Because there are no rules or regulations governing the definition or the use of the word "glaze", manufacturers and sellers of paint care products use it as a name for all types of products that are not true glazes in the historical sense of the word. Most common is the use of the word glaze in the name of a car wax or paint sealant.*

■ Paint cleaner

A liquid, paste or cream that relies primarily on chemical cleaning agents to remove any light topical contamination or surface impurities to restore a clean, smooth surface as part of a process to prepare a painted finish for application of a wax, paint sealant or coating. Paint cleaners are for very light cleaning and not normally intended to be used like an abrasive polish to remove below-surface defects.

■ Pre-Wax Cleaner

These are similar or the same as a paint cleaner. Most pre-wax cleaners are complimentary products in that they are part of a specific brand's system in which the pre-wax cleaner is matched to a wax or paint sealant. There's a chemical synergistic compatibility to ensure maximum performance between products that might not be achieved using products from outside the brand.

■ Carnauba Car Wax

A carnauba wax is generally defined as a product that contains some type of naturally occurring waxy substance intended to protect the paint while creating a clear, glossy finish. Carnauba wax is the most commonly used naturally occurring wax found in car wax formulations. This category of traditional waxes will wear off under normal wear and tear, repeated washings and exposure to the environment and should be reapplied on a regular basis to maintain a protective coating on the surface of the paint.

■ Synthetic Paint Sealant

A synthetic paint sealant is generally defined as a product that contains some type of man-made or synthetic protection ingredients to protect the paint while creating a clear, glossy finish. Perception on the part of the public is that a paint sealant is made from synthetic polymers with no naturally occurring wax type substances or other naturally occurring protection ingredients.

The general consensus among car enthusiasts is that because the protection ingredients are synthetic, a paint sealant will protect better and last longer than a traditional car wax made using naturally occurring waxes. Paint sealants will wear off under normal wear and tear, repeated washings and exposure to the environment and should be reapplied on a regular basis to maintain a protective coating on the surface of the paint.

■ Hybrid Sealant/Wax

The term "car wax" refers to a category of products that uses naturally occurring wax ingredients for protection and beauty, while the term "paint sealant" refers to a category of products that uses synthetic polymers. The fact is, most products are a blend of both natural and synthetic ingredients and are thus hybrid sealant waxes.

■ Paint Coatings

A paint coating is generally defined as any paint protection product that contains man-made or synthetic protection ingredients that are intended to permanently bond to the paint to both provide a barrier-coating of protection as well as create a clear, high gloss finish. The products available in this category are considered permanent coatings because like your car's paint, they cannot be removed unless you purposefully remove or neglect them.

■ Cleaner Wax or AIO

A cleaner wax, or what is also referred to as an All-In-One (AIO), is a one-step product. These formulations use a blend of chemical cleaners and often some type of abrasives, plus some type of protection ingredients that will remain on the surface after the cleaning action is finished and the residue is wiped from the paint. The combination of chemical cleaners and abrasives will remove topical defects like oxidation and road grime from the surface, which will restore clarity to the clearcoat.

At the same time, the product will leave behind a layer of protection using some type of protection ingredients to help lock in the shine and protect the surface from the elements.

Abrasive cleaner waxes
Some cleaner waxes have the ability to remove below-surface defects like swirls and scratches. To what degree depends upon how aggressive the abrasives are in the formula. There are some fairly aggressive cleaner waxes available and these are normally marketed at the production detailing industry.

Retail car waxes = cleaner waxes
When you go to your local auto parts store, most of the retail waxes on the shelves do in fact fall into the cleaner wax category. They are targeted at the average person, driving what we refer to as a daily driver. Over time, the finish quality deteriorates and in order to restore it with just a single product, it must offer some level of cleaning ability or abrasive action.

Production detailing
Cleaner waxes are the norm for production detailing. The goal in this industry is to restore shine to the paint on a car as fast as possible to maximize the profits for the detailer or detail shop. For this reason, multiple step procedures are not ideal - you want to clean, polish and protect in one step.

Maintenance wax
Some cleaner waxes are formulated to be very light in their cleaning ability. As such, they make great one-step maintenance products for cars that are in good to excellent condition. Because they will clean, polish and protect in one step, a lot of people prefer to use a light cleaner wax to maintain their car's finish.

■ Factors That Affect How Aggressive Or Non-aggressive A Product Is

When working on automotive paints, it's important to remember that it's not just the compounds and polishes that determine total correction ability, it's anything that touches the paint and even the way the paint is touched.

Here are some factors:

Application Materials
Wool cutting pads are more aggressive than soft foam finishing pads. Applying any product with a more aggressive pad will make the process more aggressive overall, while applying any product with soft foam will tend to make the process less aggressive.

Buffing Pads
Most Aggressive to Least Aggressive
- Fiber cutting pads
- Foam cutting pads
- Foam polishing pads
- Foam finishing pads

Application Process
The application process is how you apply your compounds, polishes and waxes, whether it's by hand or machine.

Listed in order of most to least powerful:

Rotary buffer
Out of all the common tools used to polish paint, the rotary buffer is the most powerful and has the ability and potential to make any product and/or any application material more aggressive than other tools simply by its power.

Forced rotation dual action polishers
The Flex XC-3401VRG and the Makita BO6040 both offer a forced rotation dual polishing action. While neither have the same ability for powerful correction work like a rotary buffer, they do offer more correction power than any of the Porter Cable style DA Polishers.

DA polishers
DA polishers use a free floating spindle bearing assembly, which means if you push too hard on the head of the unit or hold the tool so that pad is on edge, you will stop the pad from rotating. This is the feature that makes the DA very safe and user friendly for people new to machine polishing. However, this also means it doesn't have the same power for correction work as either the forced rotation dual action or rotary buffers.

Cyclo polishers
The dual counter rotating heads of a Cyclo polisher use a combination of a direct drive and a free floating spindle bearing assembly. This dual drive feature provides a lot of power while

being safe at the same time. The Cyclo is about equal to a DA polisher in terms of correction power.

The human hand
The human hand is actually very powerful in terms of correction power. Using your 4 fingers, you can exert a lot of pressure to a small area and when using a quality compound and applicator, you can remove a lot of paint fast. However, your finger, hand, arm and shoulder muscles get tired whereas the all the above mentioned tools offer consistent power output.

Big picture
No matter which tool you're working with or if you're working by hand, you can increase or reduce how aggressive any procedure is by changing the type of application material you're using.

Size of work area
To increase the aggressiveness of a process, you can shrink the size of your work area. This will concentrate more product to the process. To decrease the aggressiveness of a process, you can increase the size of the work area. This will act to dilute the strength of the product being used.

Product amount
Normally, you want to use an ample amount of product for the procedure you're doing. Using too much product can hyper-lubricate the surface, making it more difficult for abrasives to work. Using too little product means not having enough product on the surface to actually get the job done.

When it comes to using cleaner/waxes on neglected surfaces, you should lean towards using the product heavy or wet so that you err on the side of caution and have plenty of chemical cleaning agents and abrasives working for you. Not using enough product will result in less overall cleaning ability.

Number of applications
Applying a product multiple times can affect how aggressive it is after the first application. The first application will tend to do the initial grunt work, removing all the topical impurities, enabling second and third applications to go right to work on freshly cleaned paint.

Technique
Using proper technique is vitally important. For example, moving a DA polisher too quickly over the surface will decrease a product's aggressiveness because you don't give the combination of the product, the pad material and the machine's dual action rotation and oscillation time to affect the paint in one area before moving the polisher further along the paint. In essence when you move any tool over the surface too fast the pad ends up just skimming over the paint, not forcing the abrasives to bite into the paint. Sounds ironic but by slowing down the speed at which you move a polisher over the surface, you can actually do a better job and do it faster.

Summary
When working with a DA polisher, for more powerful and aggressive cutting or correction power, use foam cutting pads, Surbuf pads or microfiber cutting pads. To reduce the aggressiveness of a DA polisher, switch to foam polishing and finishing pads or microfiber finishing pads.

■ Use The Least Aggressive Product To Get The Job Done

I'm a strong advocate of giving credit where it is due, for both professional and personal reasons. To this point, I want to give credit to Meguiar's for this quote and philosophy towards working on automotive paints. I learned this when I worked for them in 1988 as an Outside Sales Rep and Trainer for Oregon, Washington and Idaho.

"Use the least aggressive product to get the job done"

The logic behind this statement and approach towards working on car paint is valid for two reasons.

- **Reason 1 - Automotive paints are thin**
  Factory applied paint, whether it came on a Model T or a brand new Ford Mustang, is thinner than most of us prefer. It's thin because it costs more, in materials and time, to apply more paint.

- **Reason 2 - Removing below-surface defects means removing a little paint**

Below-surface paint defects are things like swirls, scratches, and etchings like Type II Water Spots. Because these types of defects are below the surface level, the only way to remove them is to level the paint.

Now, let's tie the two concepts together. Paint is thin, and removing defects means removing paint, but there's not a lot of paint available to remove. This is why the "use the least aggressive product to get the job done" philosophy is so important.

Here's the "why" part
The reason why you want to use the least aggressive product to get the job done is so that you'll leave the most amount of paint on the car to last over its service life.

- **Digging deeper**
  In order to use the least aggressive product to get the job done, you need to do some testing. This means you have to have more than one product in your arsenal of detailing supplies.

- **Tool time**
  Products are like tools. They enable you to perform a specific procedure or task that you couldn't do otherwise. Just like a screwdriver enables you to either remove or install a screw, a quality compound or polish enables you to remove defects and restore a show car finish.

  In the context of detailing, this means you don't know if you can remove the swirls with a fine polish and a soft polishing pad until you try.

  Sure, you can remove them with an aggressive compound and cutting pad, but if your goal is to preserve your car's precious, thin coat of beauty, then start each project by doing some testing. Try to find the least aggressive product in your detailing arsenal that will enable you to get the job done.

- **You need some tools in your tool box!**
  If you haven't already, consider adding a few tools to your tool box. That way you'll already have the tools you need to do some testing and then tackle the job.

  A well rounded inventory would include:

  - Aggressive compound for serious paint defects
  - Medium cut polish
  - Fine cut polish
  - Ultra fine cut polish
  - Hand applied paint cleaner
  - Non-abrasive glaze or pure polish
  - Cleaner/Wax
  - Finishing Wax, Sealant or Coating

■ The Graphic Equalizer Analogy To Polishing Paint

Mike Pennington, the Director of Training for Meguiar's, gave me this analogy a long time ago so I want to give him credit for it. You can adjust your pad, product, tool and technique just like you can adjust music using a graphic equalizer. When everything is dialed-in perfect for the paint you're working on, you'll get the results you're looking for. It does mean sometimes playing around a little to find the perfect combination of products and procedures, kind of like adjusting a graphic equalizer for a single song so it sounds perfect to your ears. When everything is right, you'll make beautiful music, or in this case, you'll create a show car finish. ■

****IMPORTANT****

This section and the next are purposefully placed in this how to book at this point in time because you need to know how to carefully wipe compounds, polishes and waxes off paint so you don't put scratches back in during the wipe-off process.

You're going to need to wipe off compound or polish residue when you do your first test spot and you don't want to skew your results by inflicting toweling marks. Learn how to properly use a microfiber towel to carefully wipe compound and polish residues off.

People watching
I often try to observe people and the techniques they use for any and all aspects of detailing cars. The goal is to help them tweak their technique if anything they're doing could use some improvement. Most pros would agree, when it comes to taking a car's finish to its maximum potential, that even more important than pad, product and tool selection is technique. That includes all techniques, not just how you move the polisher.

"Technique is everything"

A basic technique that's vitally important
One common procedure that is as basic as you can get is also one of the most important procedures involved in creating a true show car shine, and that's correctly folding and using a microfiber towel to remove a coating of polish, wax, paint sealant, spray-on-wax or spray detailer.

In This Section:

- How To Correctly Fold And Use A Microfiber Towel
- How To Carefully Wipe Off Compounds, Polishes And Waxes By Hand
- Washing Microfiber Towels
- The 4 Minimum Categories Of Wiping Towels

Good technique - Used correctly, your hand and a microfiber towel will create an eye-dazzling finish that that will hold up under the intense scrutiny of bright light conditions, like full overhead sunlight or while on display at an indoor car show.

Wrong technique - Used incorrectly, you can easily instill swirls and scratches into the paint, requiring machine polishing to remove them. You're then back to wiping the polish off without instilling swirls all over again. Are you starting to get the idea of how important it is to carefully wipe anything off paint?

■ How To Correctly Fold And Use A Microfiber Towel

Here are the basics of how to correctly use a microfiber towel.

■ Correct Technique

1. Start with a clean, microfiber towel. If the towel has been washed and dried, I will usually inspect each side to make sure there are no contaminants stuck onto the fibers of the towel. Microfiber acts like a magnet and can easily attract and hold all kinds of things that you don't want to rub against your car's paint, so take a moment to visually inspect your microfiber polishing towels.

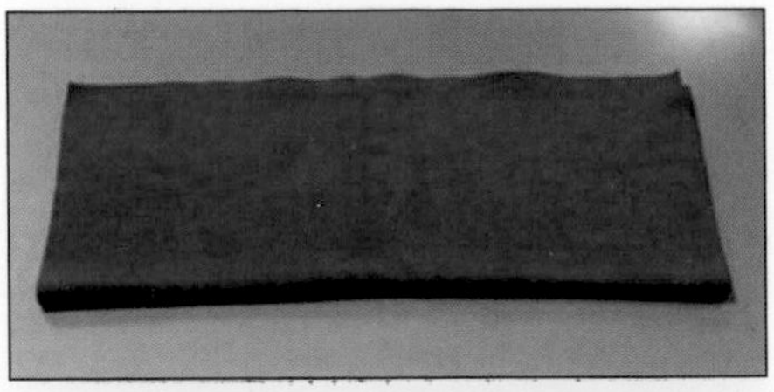

2. Fold the microfiber towel in half and then in half again...

Control over the towel
By folding your microfiber towels into quarters, you will now have 8 dedicated sides to wipe with and you have control over all 8 sides. When you simply lay a microfiber towel flat or scrunch it up into a wad, you don't have any control over it because it's too hard to gauge and remember how much of the towel has already been used. This is what I mean by having control over the towel - it's being able to monitor how much of the towel has already been used. You can only do this if you have a repeatable system in place like folding your towels.

Cushion to spread out the pressure from your hand
Folding your microfiber towel also provides cushion to spread out the pressure from your hand. This provides two benefits:

1. Helps reduce the potential for fingermarks, caused by excess pressure from your fingertips.

2. Helps to maintain even contact between the working face of the folded microfiber towel and the surface of the paint. This is important at all times, but especially whenever you're working on any panel that is not flat.

Incorrect Techniques

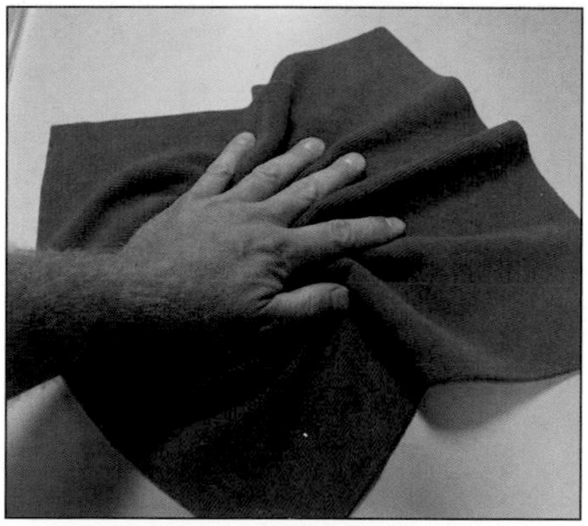

Unfolded Microfiber Towel
Simply laying the towel flat against the paint increases the potential for swirls and scratches due to pressure points against the towel. Using a towel flat and unfolded offers little to no cushion and reduces even pressure between the cloth and the paint. I cringe when I see someone wiping a nice finish by simply placing the towel down flat on the paint and then placing their hand flat on the towel.

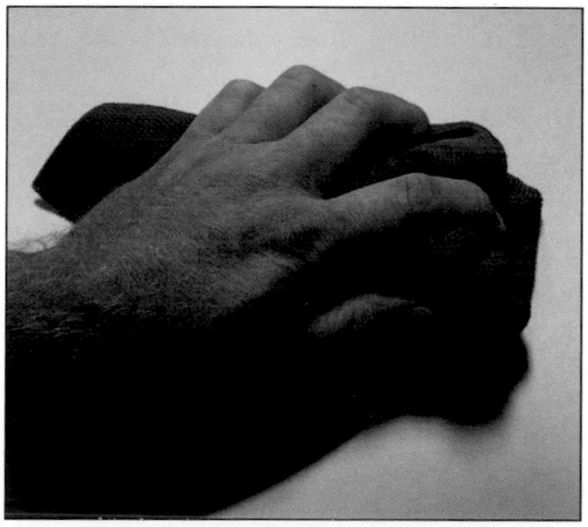

Scrunched-up Microfiber Towel
Just as bad as the unfolded microfiber towel is the scrunched-up Microfiber towel, that's where a person basically scrunches the towel into a wad and then uses this waded up towel to wipe their car's paint. This technique leads to rubbing the edges of the towel over the paint and this can lead to swirls and scratches.

How To Carefully Wipe Off Compounds, Polishes And Waxes By Hand

Now that you know how to correctly fold and use a microfiber towel, let's take a look at how to correctly wipe compound, polish and wax residues without harming the paint.

• Waxes and paint sealants
Applying a thin, uniform coating of any wax or paint sealant will ensure easy removal.

• Compounds and polishes
Compounds and polishes should be wiped off immediately after polishing when the residue is still a wet film. If you do this, the wetness acts to lubricate the surface during wipe-off.

When using the wet buffing technique, immediately after you buff a section, turn your polisher off, allow the pad to stop spinning and then set the polisher aside. You should have a clean, dry microfiber towel nearby so you can quickly start wiping the leftover compound or polish residue off the paint.

Big picture
When it's time to wipe any product off the paint, your job is to remove it without struggling and without inflicting toweling marks back into the paint. The words "toweling marks" are a nice way of saying light or shallow swirls and scratches from pushing too hard with your wiping towel. In other words, you're struggling as you're trying to remove something that's not coming off easily.

Let me share with you the technique I call, "breaking open a coat of wax and then creeping out". This technique also works with any film on a painted surface. First, let me share the problem.

Trying to wipe off too much product at a time
Most people try to wipe off huge sections of product with each wipe. For some products, this works well because the product is incredibly easy to wipe off in the first place. But for a lot of other products, wipe-off requires a little more work and effort.

If a product is difficult to wipe off, trying to take huge chunks of it off in a single stroke doesn't work very well. When you try to remove huge amounts of product in a single wiping pass, the surface tension between the layer of product and the paint is greater by the shear volume of surface area compared to what your hand and a wiping cloth can pull away from the paint and onto the cloth.

Solution: Take little bites
Instead of trying to wipe off huge sections at a time, just wipe little bites of product off using an overlapping, circular motion with your hand and microfiber polishing towel. When you only try to take off little bites of product at a time using overlapping circular wiping passes, taking off any product is easy.

You need a starting point
Before you can remove any type of residue, you need a clean starting point. After you remove the product from one small area, you will uncover the paint you have just compounded, polished or waxed and thus you'll have a shiny spot.

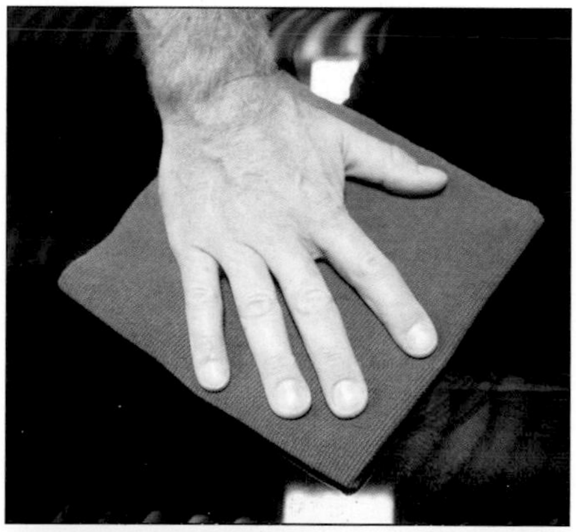

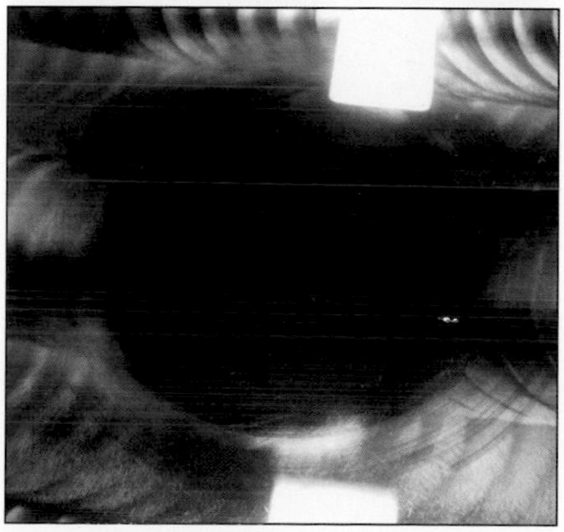

You can do this anyway you'd like, but here's how I usually do it: Place a clean microfiber towel folded 4-ways flat on a panel, and then gently but with firm pressure, twist the microfiber in a circle. This will usually remove most of the wax in that area and create a shiny spot. This is called "breaking open a coating of wax".

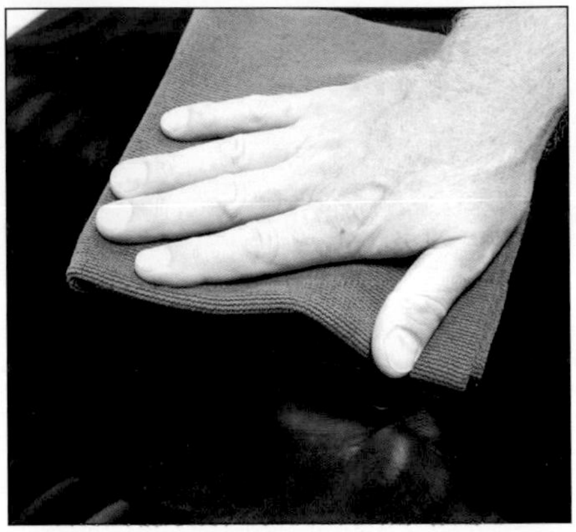

Now, you can start taking small bites of wax off the paint by making small overlapping circular swipes with your microfiber towel and then creeping outward from the shiny spot.

Washing Microfiber Towels

It is very important not to overload the washing basin. Your microfiber towels need room to swish around during the washing and agitating cycle. If you overload the machine, you'll reduce the machine's ability to properly clean your microfiber towels.

Most important: Add soap and fill wash basin first
The idea is to create a uniform mixture of soapy water before placing microfiber towels into the washing machine.

1. To do this, set the water level to low or medium. Then, add your cleaning solution and allow the washing machine to fill to set level and begin its agitation cycle. This will thoroughly mix the water with the cleaning solution for a uniform mixture.

2. Place your microfiber towels into the washing machine.

3. Reset the switch/timer for it to run through the entire washing cycle.

This technique will maximize the time the microfiber towels are being agitated because from the very start of the cycle, your microfiber towels are saturated with a uniform mixture of water and cleaning solution. If you wash your microfiber towels by adding them to the washing machine first and then adding soap, part of the washing or agitating cycle will be wasted while the cleaning soap uses valuable time to mix throughout the water.

Second rinse cycle
If your washing machine has the option for a second rinse cycle, use this to ensure all laundry detergent as well as any other residues are completely rinsed from your microfiber towels.

Microfiber Cleaning Detergents
When it comes to cleaning your microfiber towels, you want to use a good quality detergent soap to emulsify and remove any compound, polish or wax residues.

- *Pinnacle Micro Rejuvenator Microfiber Detergent Concentrate*
- *Detailer's Pro Series Microfiber Cleaner*
- *Sonus Der Wunder Microfiber and Pad Wasche*
- *BLACKFIRE Microfiber Cleaner & Restorer*
- *Chemical Guys Microfiber Wash + Microfiber Cleaning Detergent*

Pre-wash Maintenance
One of the best things you can do to maintain the quality of your microfiber towels is to sort them as you use them into dedicated laundry bins.

- **Bin 1** - Water-soluble residues - compounds, polishes, glazes, paint cleaners
- **Bin 2** - Waxes, paint sealants
- **Bin 3** - Everything else - Don't use these to wipe polished paint.

By separating your microfiber towels by the type of product they are used with, you can avoid any chemical cross-contamination. You can pick up laundry bins like the one you see here to help keep your laundry organized and clean.

The 4 Minimum Categories Of Wiping Towels

Just as important as any product or tool in your detailing arsenal are your wiping towels. You can use the best compound, polish, LSP and buffing pads and top of the line polishers, but if you're using wiping towels that are in some way, shape or form contaminated, then you risk putting swirls and scratches into your car's finish.

4 categories minimum
Everyone should have at least 4 types of wiping towels. These are the minimum, so feel free to separate your wiping towels more if you'd like.

- **Good Microfiber Towels**
  You can "touch" paint with microfiber polishing towels from

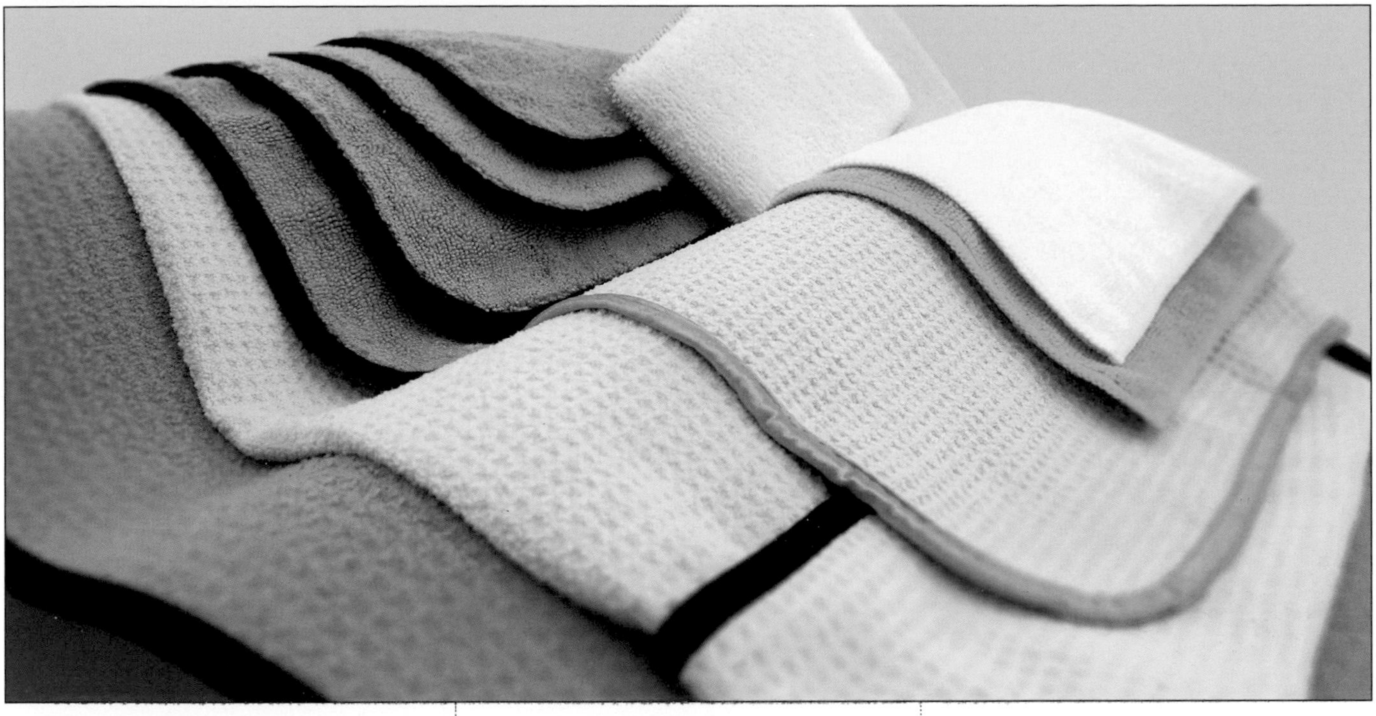

this collection. These are the microfiber towels in your collection that are new or you have washed and dried and you trust them to be safe on a high gloss, polished finish.

- **Tatty Microfiber Towels**
  These are washed, dried and clean, but their quality has fallen to a level that you have deemed them not worthy of touching a high gloss, polished finish. You don't throw them away because they still have value for wiping spray detailers or cleaner/waxes out places like door jambs, chrome wheels or bumpers, and some components in the engine compartment. The point is they are still great at removing residue, just not off a swirl-free, scratch-free, high gloss surface.

- **Good Cotton Towels**
  While microfiber towels are superior for removing products from smooth, high gloss finishes, there's still a place for good quality cotton towels. For example, cotton towels are a great choice for cleaning your pad on the fly. Cotton towels with a large nap work better than microfiber towels. Some people prefer a cotton towel with a large nap to remove compounds because they offer a more aggressive bite, but then switch over to microfiber for removing polishes and LSP's.
  Your good cotton towels should be clean and soft and worthy of working on paint in good condition or better.

- **Tatty cotton towels**
  Secondary Cotton Towels are washed and dried, but for whatever reason, their quality is fallen off too far from what's acceptable to touch paint in good condition or better. They still have value, however, for mundane tasks like wiping excess tire dressing from the face of a tire, applying or wiping cleaners and dressings in the fender well area, applying or removing cleaners, dressings or cleaner/waxes in the trunk area or door jambs and engine compartments. They have value because they are absorbent, clean, ready to use and paid for. After some projects you might be better off discarding them versus trying to clean them well enough that they can be used again. ■

Work Clean, Get Organized & Dress Casual

Before you begin buffing out any car, you should also have a clean and well-lit work environment.

Work clean
Do the simple things like sweep the garage or shop floor. You don't want any dirt or dust to get on the paint as you're working through your paint polishing procedures via foot traffic and air circulation in your work environment.

Get organized
If you have a workbench or any kind of table, clean it off and make a place for all your detailing tools.

Microfiber towel supply
Not only do your microfiber towels need to be clean, but you need a clean area to place them where they're readily accessible.

After using microfiber towels, it is a good idea to store them in a clean container so they don't end up on the garage floor. When you're done using a microfiber towel, you still need to prevent it from becoming contaminated before you wash and dry.

Paint care products
Have all your compounds, polishes and waxes in one place for easy access.

Buffing pads
You're going to need a clean area to place your buffing pads so they're readily available, but won't get dirty as you're working around the car. You'll also need a place for dirty pads as you go through them until you can clean them and put them away.

Miscellaneous tools and supplies
It's a good idea to have some painter's tape, wheel maskers, plastic drop cloths, beach towels, etc.

More light is better
Good lighting is important because you need to see the paint as you're working on it. Turn all garage or shop lights on, and if needed, replace worn out bulbs. Some people go to great extents to increase the light in their garage by mounting fluorescent lights on the sides of the walls to light up the vertical panels.

Power-up
Have heavy duty extension cords ready and accessible for all sides of the vehicle. A heavy duty 14 to 12 gauge extension cord is recommended with a 12 gauge recommended for any extension cord over 25 feet in length.

Get comfortable
Wear comfortable clothing. Avoid wearing things like belts, watches, ties and jewelry. Also avoid wearing hot or uncomfortable clothes as well as shoes or sandals that don't provide good ankle support.

Miscellaneous Items
- Cold drinks
- Snacks
- Music for when you're not running the polisher
- Ear protection
- Eye protection
- Camera
- Assortment of nylon detailing brushes for removing residue from cracks and crevices
- Fan to blow air on hot days

Having a clean, well organized work environment will speed things up and make the project a lot more enjoyable. After each step, take a moment to do a little clean up and organization. ■

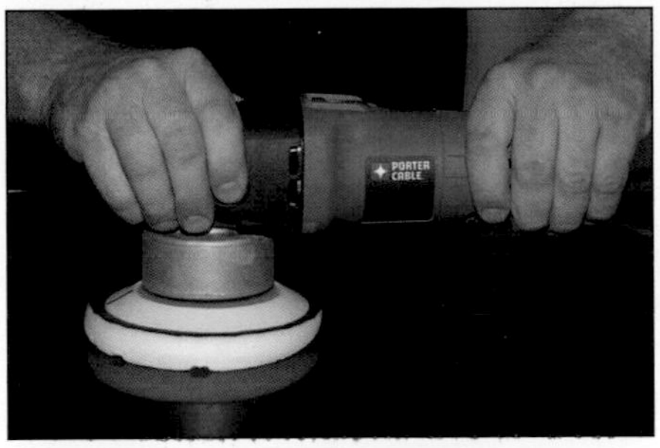

■ What Is A Section Pass?

When talking about machine polishing on discussion forums and in detailing classes, we talk about "making passes" with the polisher. During these discussions, people that are new to machine polishing always have one or all of the below questions:

- What's a pass?
- How many passes do I make?
- What's a section pass?

■ The Definition Of A Section - The Size Of An Area To Work At One Time

To understand what a section is, you first need to know what a panel is.

- **Vehicle** - Body shell with panels
- **Panels** - A door, hood, roof, etc. - the major portions of the vehicle
- **Section** - A portion of a panel

In order to buff out a vehicle, you need to divide or slice the various panels into smaller sections. In most cases, the size of a section should be in the 16" x 16" to 20" x 20" size.

In This Section:

- What Is A Section Pass
- The Definition Of A Section - The Size Of An Area To Work At One Time
- The Definition Of A Single Pass And A Section Pass
- Buffing Cycle
- The Wet Buffing Technique
- Wet Film Behind Your Path-Of-Travel
- Dry Buffing
- The Remedy To Dry Buffing

Here's a trunk lid that is divided into sections for the correction step.

The tape is only to give you a reference point as to how to divide up a panel into sections. You would not use tape to create sections and then try to remove swirls and scratches. The section you see would be larger without the tape because in the real world, when you're buffing out the different sections, you'll be overlapping each new section into the previous section.

This tends to naturally increase the size of the section you picture in your imagination when sizing up a panel and dividing it into a manageable section.

Because modern vehicles come in all different shapes, you can't always create perfectly squared-up sections of paint to buff out. What I teach people is to let the panel be your guide.

■ Avoid Buffing On Raised Body Lines

It's a good practice to avoid buffing on raised body lines. Knowing and practicing this will help you to divide a car's panels. You won't always be working on a perfectly square, flat hood. There are many places where you'll be buffing thin panels of paint, like around the top portion of a fender, the A-pillars and B-pillars, and other complex panels. In these cases, you need to let the panel be your guide and this may mean buffing very small areas or areas that are longer than they are wide.

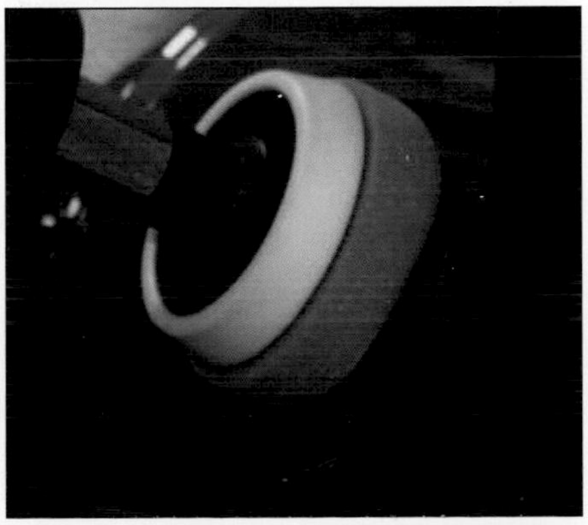

Maximize Buffing Cycle

If you try to tackle too large of a panel at one time, you'll shorten the buffing cycle of your product. While you're polishing one section, the product not being worked will be drying. By working a smaller section, you'll be actively engaging the wet, working film of product, keeping it in liquid form. The longer any film of product sets undisturbed, the more quickly it will tend to dry and you'll decrease the buffing cycle.

Maintain Equal Downward Pressure

The farther away from your body you move your hand, the more likely you are to exert less pressure. The longer your arm stroke, the more likely it is that you'll remove less paint. This makes for uneven material removal. It can also lead to removing too much material in the area closer to your body. By keeping your buffing area to a manageable size, you'll improve the likelihood that you'll only remove the necessary amount of material to get the job done. You'll also remove material equally over the section you're buffing.

Here is a single pass with a polisher.

The first set of overlapping passes in a side to side direction is one section pass.

Next, make your overlapping passes in the opposite direction, which would be your second section pass.

Each time you go over the entire section that would be a section pass. For correction work you will make 6 to 8 section passes to each section to remove defects.

The Definition Of A Single Pass And A Section Pass

There are two definitions of the word "pass" as it relates to machine polishing.

- **Single pass** - A single pass is when you move the polisher from one side of the section you're buffing to the other.
- **Section pass** - A section pass is when you move the polisher back and forth with enough single overlapping passes to cover the entire section one time.

Question: *Which directions do I move the polisher when doing section passes?*

Answer: *Use a repeatable pattern.*

Successfully removing all the swirls out of the entire car means removing all the swirls out of each section you work. In order to do this, you need a method that you can control and duplicate as you buff out each section. For most people, following a back and forth, side-to-side pattern works because it's easy to remember, easy to do and easy to duplicate. If you run a detailing business, it's an easy pattern to teach your employees to ensure they are successful.

Question: *How many section passes do I do?*

Answer: *6 to 8 section passes minimum.*

In most cases, if you're removing any substantial below-surface defects, you're going to make at least 6-8 section passes before you either feel comfortable you've removed the defects or you're at the end of the buffing cycle for the product you're using.

When doing your test spot, remember how many section passes you make and the results you obtain. This will give you an idea as to how many section passes you'll need to be doing for each section as you move around the car. The deeper the defects and the harder the paint, the more section passes you'll need to do.

Arm Speed

Arm speed is the term for how fast you move the polisher over the paint.

Major Correction Work = Slow Arm Speed
For any major correction work, you want to use a slow arm speed.

Polishing Work = Slow/Medium Arm Speed
For polishing work, you still want the combination the abrasives in the product, the aggressiveness of the pad, and the oscillating/ rotating action to further abrade the paint to maximize gloss and clarity. For this reason, you don't want to move the polisher too quickly, but slightly faster than you would if you were removing swirls and scratches.

Waxing or Sealing the paint = Medium/Fast Speed
When it comes to applying a wax, you're no longer limited to a small area. You can work as large of an area as you can reach as long as you have enough wax to spread out. You can move the polisher fairly quickly, because you're no longer trying to abrade the paint. My recommendation is to always make 2-3 passes over each square inch of paint.

Downward Pressure

Removing swirls and scratches = firm pressure
I recommend about 15 to 20 pounds of downward pressure, but you must be able to see the pad rotating. Swirls and scratches are best removed when the pad is rotating, not just jiggling or vibrating against the paint.

Polishing to a high gloss = medium pressure
I usually make my first two section passes with firm pressure. This ensures any haze left by the correction step is cut out by the abrasives while they are at maximum abrading ability. For the remaining passes, I reduce pressure and increase arm speed slightly. At this point, polishing paint becomes an art form due to the level of care used during the final 3-5 section passes.

Machine waxing = light pressure
When applying a finishing wax or paint sealant, you only need to apply light pressure - just enough to keep the pad flat against the surface.

Note: *If you were using a one-step cleaner wax, then you would be using firm pressure because you would be trying to restore neglected paint.*

Tool Speed Setting

Here is a general range of speed setting used for most procedures. Specific speed settings can be subjective and vary based on numerous circumstances. Always follow the manufacturer's recommendations for specific products being used.

Typical speeds for most procedures using most DA polishers
- 5 to 6 speed setting for removing swirls
- 5 to 6 speed setting for polishing after swirls are removed
- 4 to 5 speed setting for applying wax.

How To Hold The Polisher

When doing your section passes, you want to hold the body of the polisher in a way that the face of the pad is flat against the paint. Buffing pads rotate best when equal pressure is applied over the entire face of the pad. If you hold the body of the polisher so that more pressure is applied to just the edge of a pad, this increased pressure will cause the pad to slow down and even stop rotating in some situations.

How Much Product To Use

See the following chapters:
- *Priming your pad*
- *How much product to use*

Clean Your Pad Often

See the following chapter:
- *Cleaning Buffing Pad*

Remove Spent Residue

See the following chapter:
- *How to carefully wipe off compounds, polishes and waxes by hand*

Buffing Cycle

The buffing cycle is the amount of time you are able to work the product before the abrasives have broken down and/or the product begins to dry. With most diminishing abrasive products, the diminishing abrasives will have broken down after around 6 passes using good technique, with firm downward pressure and slow arm movement.

Different products have different buffing cycles, depending upon the type of abrasives used in the formula and the different lubricating ingredients as well as carrying agents used to suspend the abrasives and provide lubrication.

Note: *With SMAT (Super Micro Abrasive Technology) products, you can stop anytime during the buffing cycle if the defects are removed. The only limitation when using SMAT products is to make sure you always have a wet film of product on the surface.*

Factors that affect the buffing cycle:
- Ambient temperature
- Surface temperature
- Size of work area
- Type of machine
- Type of pad material
- Humidity
- Wind or air flow surrounding the car
- Amount of product used
- Technique

The Wet Buffing Technique

Most compounds and polishes should be used so that there is enough product on the surface to maintain a wet film while the product is being worked. The wetness of the product provides lubrication so the abrasives don't simply scour the finish leaving behind swirls and scratches.

Wet Film Behind Your Path- Of-Travel

As you're making a single pass with the polisher, the path of travel should have a visible wet film behind it. If the paint behind the pad is dry and shiny, you've run out of lubrication and you're dry buffing. Turn the polisher off. Wipe

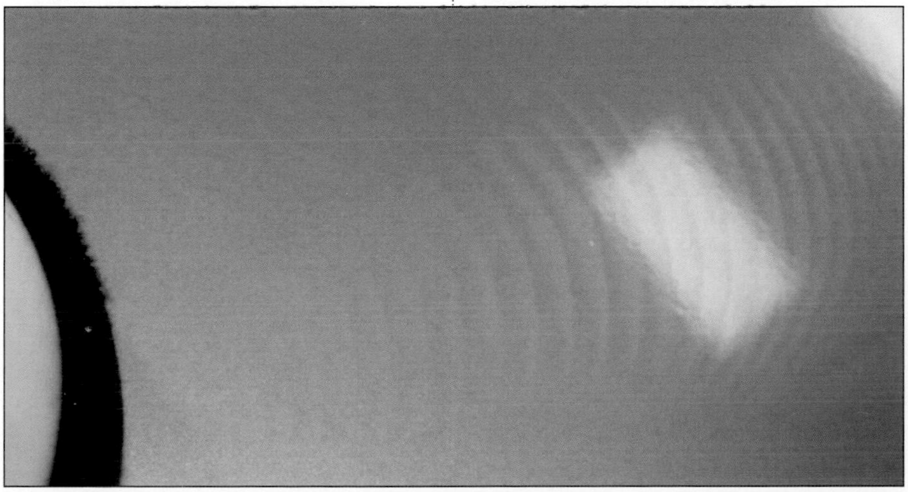

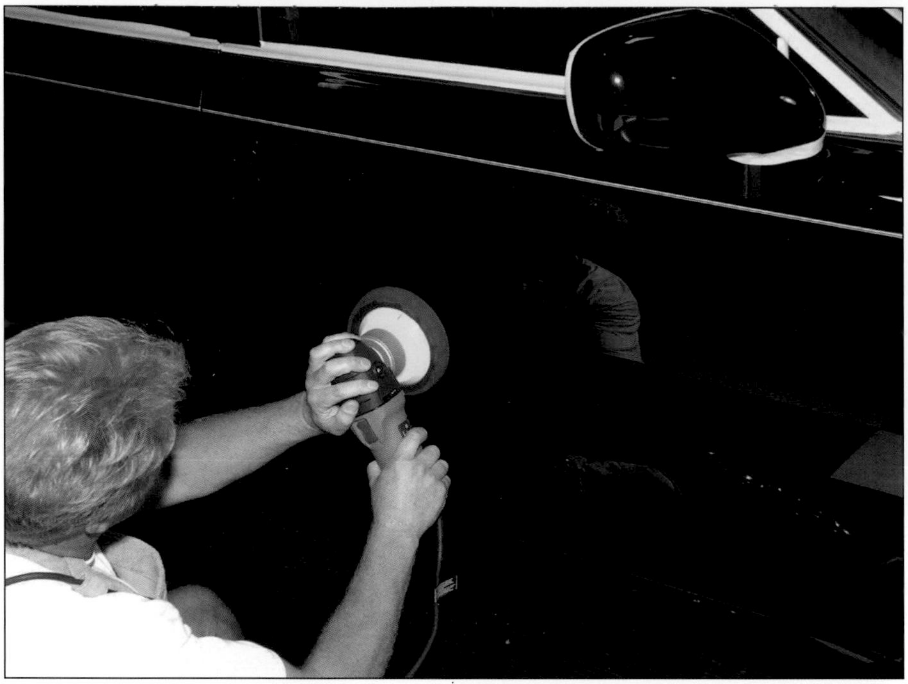

the residue off and inspect the paint. It's pretty rare to actually cause any harm, but pay attention when you're running the polisher and try to avoid dry buffing.

■ Dry Buffing

There are some products on the market in which the manufacturer recommends buffing the product until it dries. As the product dries, you'll tend to see some dusting as the product residue becomes a powder and the paint will have a hard, dry shine to it.

Although some manufacturers recommend this, it's important to understand what's taking place at the surface level. As the product dries, lubricating features are lost. As this happens, friction heat and the risk of micro-marring the paint will increase.

■ The Remedy To Dry Buffing

If you accidently dry buff, don't panic. You can quickly re-polish that section by cleaning your pad and adding fresh product and making a few new section passes.

IMPORTANT: *Read this before doing your test spot. You need to nail the test spot so your process is dialed-in and proven before you attempt buffing out the entire car.*

Here's a list of the most common problems:

- Trying to work too large of an area at one time.
- Moving the polisher too fast over the surface.
- Using too low of a speed setting for removing swirls.
- Using too little or too much downward pressure on the head of the polisher.
- Not holding the polisher in a way to keep the pad flat while working your compound or polish.
- Using too much or too little product.
- Not cleaning the pad often enough.

Here are the solutions:

Trying to work too large of an area at one time.
Shrink the size of your work area down. You can't effectively tackle too large of an area at one time. The average size work area should be around 20" by 20". Most generic recommendations say to work an area 2' by 2', but for the correction step, that's too large. You have to do some experimenting to find out how easy or how hard the defects are to get out of your car's paint system and then adjust your work area to the results of your test spot. The harder the paint, the smaller the area you want to work.

Moving the polisher too fast over the surface

For removing defects, you want to use slow arm speed. It's easy and actually natural for most people new to machine polishing to move the polisher quickly over the paint, but that's the wrong technique. One reason I think people move the polisher too quickly over the paint is because they hear the sound of the motor spinning fast and this has psychological effect, which causes them to match their arm movement to the perceived fast speed of the polisher's motor.

Another reason people move the polisher too quickly over the paint is because they think like this,

"If I move the polisher quickly, I'll get done faster"

But it doesn't work that way. Anytime you're trying to remove swirls, scratches, water spots or oxidation using a DA polisher, you need to move the polisher s-l-o-w-l-y over the paint.

Using too low of a speed setting for removing swirls.
When first starting out, many people are scared of burning or swirling their paint. They take the safe route of running the polisher at too low of a speed setting, but this won't work. You need the speed, oscillation, and rotation of the pad, along with the combination of slow arm speed, product abrasives, pad aggressiveness, and downward pressure to level the paint.

Using too little downward pressure on the head of the polisher.
For the same reason as stated in #3, people are apprehensive about applying too much downward pressure to the polisher. The result of too little pressure is that no paint is removed, thus no swirls are removed.

Using too much downward pressure on the head of the polisher
If you push too hard, you will slow down the rotating movement of the pad and the abrasives won't be effectively worked against the paint. You need to apply firm pressure to engage the abrasives against the

paint, but not so much that the pad is barely rotating. This is where it's a good idea to use a permanent black marker to make a mark on the back of your backing plate so your eyes can easily see if the pad is rotating or not. This will help you to adjust your downward pressure accordingly.

Not holding the polisher in a way to keep the pad flat while working your compound or polish.
Applying excess pressure to one side of the pad will cause it to stop rotating and thus decrease abrading ability.

Using too much or too little product.
Too much product hyper-lubricates the surface. The abrasives won't effectively bite into the paint, but instead will tend to skim over the surface. Overusing product will also accelerate pad saturation as well increasing the potential for slinging splatter onto adjacent panels. Too little product means too little lubrication and this can interfere with pad rotation.

Not cleaning the pad often enough.
Most people simply don't clean their pad often enough to maximize the effectiveness of their DA polisher. Any time you're abrading the paint, you have two things building up on the face of your buffing pad:

- Removed paint
- Spent product

As these two things build up on the face of the pad, they become gummy. This has a negative effect on pad rotation and makes wiping the leftover residue from the paint more difficult. To maintain good pad rotation, you want to clean your pad often and always wipe off any leftover product residue from the paint after working a section. Never add fresh product to your pad and work a section that still has leftover product residue on it. ■

For more information on cleaning your pad see this chapter:
📖 *Cleaning your pad on the fly technique*

A test spot is simply an area of paint in which four things are tested simultaneously:

- Products
- Pads
- Tool of choice
- Skills and abilities

The idea is to test out the products, pads and process you're thinking of using over the entire car to just one small section and make sure you can make it look great!

Good results
If you can make one small section look great, then you'll have proven your system approach and this will give you the confidence to duplicate the process over the rest of the car.

Bad results
If you run into any kinds of problems, you'll be glad you only worked on this one small section of your car. It's easier and faster to undo any issues and fix a small area of paint versus having to redo the entire car.

Where to do a test spot
The best place to do a test spot is on a horizontal panel that you can look down on, like a hood or trunk lid. You normally want to inspect the paint using bright light like the sun or a Brinkmann Swirl Finder Light. The sun works best, but using it to inspect your results works best when it is directly overhead, thus a horizontal surface works best.

Before you start

- Wash and dry car - Paint must be clean before you do any testing.
- Inspect paint visually for swirls - this tells you whether or not you need to machine polish.
- Inspect paint physically with your sense of touch for above surface bonded contaminants. This tells you if you need to use detailing clay or not.

Option - clay only the test spot
If there's any question or doubt that the paint is so far gone that it cannot be saved, before claying the entire vehicle, you can just clay the area you're going to test on. Wait to clay the entire car after your test results confirm the paint can be saved.

Save your clay
Sometimes, a finish can be past the point of no return. This means no amount of work and nothing you pour out of a bottle or scoop out of a can will undo the damage and restore an acceptable finish. For extreme detailing projects like this, you might as well save your clay until you confirm the paint can be successfully corrected and you're going to commit to buffing out the rest of the car.

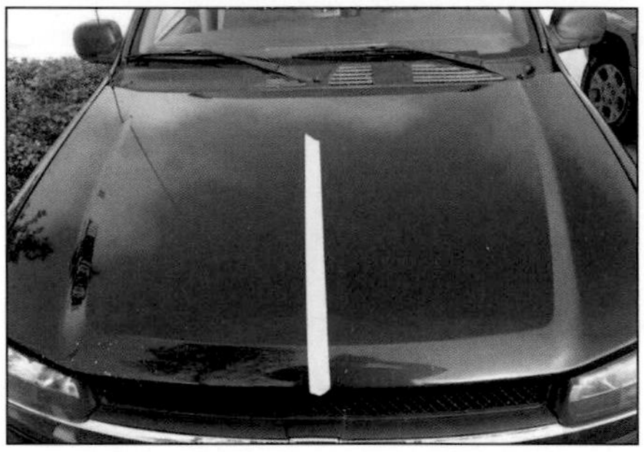

Use a tape-line
I'm a big fan of using a tape-line on the paint when doing a test spot because it makes it really easy for your eyes to see and gauge the before and after differences. This will make it easier for you to tell if you're making progress or if something's not working right. The idea is to place some painter's tape onto the paint and only do your testing to one side of the tape. After applying, working and then wiping off each product, you can compare the side you're working on with the "before" condition of the paint. The goal, of course, is to remove the defects from the paint and restore it to like-new condition.

Caution: *Be careful not to buff to aggressively right on the tape-line or you'll create a line in the paint that you'll then have to remove. Just buff up to the line.*

Use the least aggressive product to get the job done
If you've never worked on the vehicle you're planning on detailing, you should start your testing with the least aggressive products in your collection

In This Section:

and check to see if the safest approach will work. If the first product you test doesn't work quickly or effectively enough, you can always substitute a more aggressive product. Through some simple trial and error testing, you should be able to figure out which pad and product combinations work best. By testing first, you'll already know and have the confidence that you're going to get excellent results over the entire car.

For more information:

📖 Use the least aggressive product to get the job done

RIDS = Random, Isolated Deeper Scratches

When you do your testing, the goal is to find a product and pad combination that removes the majority of the defects, not each and every scratch. Because you're using a DA polisher, chances are you cannot remove 100% of all the deeper swirls and scratches.

Chances are very good that you'll remove a majority of the shallow swirls and leave the deeper RIDS behind. Make sure as you're testing that your expectations are realistic.

If you're aiming for a show car finish, then you should be working on an actual show car or a garage queen, not a daily driver. If you're working on a daily driver that has swirls and scratches now, even if you're careful, you'll likely get a few more swirls and scratches in the future just from normal, day-in, day-out, wear and tear. For this reason, you don't want to try to remove 100% of all swirls and scratches out of a daily driver as it sacrifices too much paint.

For more information:

📖 RIDS = Random Isolated Deeper Scratches

New test spot = new section of paint

If you don't get the results you're looking for from your first test spot and want to be as accurate as possible, then each time you start a new/different test spot, try to use a fresh section of paint that has not been buffed yet. This is why a hood or a trunk lid works well for doing test spots. More often than not, they are large enough to allow you to easily do 2 to 5 test spots, but normally you'll dial in a process that works with the first one or two tests. If and when you move to a fresh section of paint to perform a new test spot, continue using painter's tape to make a tape-line so you can quickly and easily check your results and confirm that you're making progress.

Chemically stripping the test spot

The lubricating agents used in all high quality compounds and polishes will tend to remain on the surface and fill or mask any defects still remaining in the paint. If you want to make 100% sure your process is working, you can chemically strip the paint used for your test spot and then inspect the results. This is normally done after the polishing steps and before any wax, paint sealant or coating is applied.

Isopropyl alcohol is the most common solvent used to chemically strip paint. Mineral spirits is another option and there are a few products on the market formulated just for removing any polishing residues. Another option is to wash the test area using a detergent soap with a water rinse. For more information on how to chemically strip the paint in order to accurately inspect and view the results, read the below article and pay attention to the warnings.

For more information:

📖 How to Mix IPA for Inspecting Correction Results

■ Step By Step How To Do A Test Spot Using A DA Polisher

I'm going to show how to perform a test spot. This process will work with any collection of quality paint correction products.

Pad selection

For the following example, I'll use a specific pad system to walk you through the process. You can use any pad line or design you'd like. The key point is to use clean, high quality pads so you don't hinder the performance of the products being used.

■ First Test Spot

Process:

1. ***Finishing polish w/polishing pad***

To demonstrate "using the least aggressive product to get the job done", I'll start my first test spot using a fine or finishing polish and then progressively test with more aggressive pad and/or product combinations until an approach is dialed in.

- **Step 1** - Prime a clean, foam polishing pad with a finishing polish, and then apply 3 dime sized drops of working product.
- **Step 2** - Turn polisher on using a slow speed setting (3 or 4), then spread the product out over an area of about 16" x 16".
- **Step 3** - Turn the speed setting of your DA polisher up to 5 or 6 and start making your overlapping section passes. Do anywhere from 5 to 8 section passes to your test spot.
- **Step 4** - After you finish making your final section pass, turn the polisher off and carefully use a microfiber towel, folded 4-ways to wipe the leftover residue from the paint.
- **Step 5** - Inspect the paint - Depending upon how bad the paint was before you started, you should be able to see a noticeable difference between the "before" and "after" sides divided by the tape-line. When inspecting, use a Brinkmann Swirl Finder Light or move the car into bright, overhead sunlight.

- **Step 6 - Optional** - Chemically strip paint before inspecting. If you want to make sure you're seeing the true results and that no polishing oils or other fillers are masking defects, then chemically strip the paint and inspect the results.

Questions after the first test spot

- A: Does the paint look better?
- B: Are the defects removed to your satisfaction?

Answers:

- A: Yes
- B: Yes

If the answer to both questions is "yes", then this combination of pad and product are aggressive enough to remove the defects. Theoretically, if you duplicate the same process over the rest of the car, you should get the same results. If the defects are not removed to your satisfaction, then do a second test spot.

Second Test Spot

Process:
1. ***Medium polish w/polishing pad***
2. ***Finishing polish w/finishing pad***

For this second test, you're going to be doing two steps since you were unable to remove the defects with one step.

Inspect after the polishing step
Keep in mind the first step, also known as the correction step, will be followed by the polishing step. The true results are gauged after both steps are completed.

As you become more aggressive in your choice of products and pads, it's possible that while the more aggressive pad and polish will remove the defects faster and more effectively, you could also leave behind what we call micro-marring, DA haze or tick marks. It just depends upon how polishable the paint is and how aggressive your pads and products are.

Questions after the second test spot

- A: Does the paint look better?
- B: Are the defects removed to your satisfaction?

After the second test spot, if you answered "no" to both questions, then perform a third test spot.

Third Test Spot

Process:

1. ***Medium polish w/cutting pad***
2. ***Finishing polish w/finishing pad***

If you're still not removing the defects fast enough using a medium polish with a polishing pad, try the same product but substitute a more aggressive foam cutting pad. With the combination of a quality medium polish, a foam cutting pad and good technique, you should be able to remove the majority of swirls and scratches. Then, you'll refine the results during the polishing step. After performing both steps, inspect your results. If you still cannot remove the defects to your expectations, it may have more to do with your technique than it has to do with the pad and product.

At this point, you may want to re-read these two chapters.

- *What is a section pass and how to do one*
- *The DA Polisher Troubleshooting Guide*

Sealing the test spot - optional
After you remove the finishing polish, the paint should look awesome!
It should be clear, with no defects blocking or clouding your view of the color coat under the clear layer of paint. What you have done is perfectly prepared the paint for application of a coat of wax, paint sealant or a coating. At this time, if you really want to see how the entire car is going to look after you've completed the entire process, then apply a quality wax, sealant or coating. You should see a show car finish if you've done everything right. What you see in your test spot is how the entire car is going to look and this should get you motivated.

Step-by-Step How To Do A Test Spot using a Rotary Buffer

Just like using any other tool, before you buff out the ENTIRE car, first do a Test Spot to get a feel for how hard or soft the paint is and to dial-in a system approach that remove the defects to your satisfaction. I cannot stress this step enough especially when you're about to take a rotary buffer to any car you've never worked on before.

Do all steps
When doing your Test Spot you want to test your compound and pad combination, followed by your polish and pad combination. There are a lot of compounds and polishes on the market as well as a lot of buffing pads including wool, microfiber and foam. You want to test both the cutting and the polishing step on your test section and make sure your choice of products is producing results that meet your expectations.

Compounds & Cutting Pads
Most quality brand name compounds do what they're supposed to do and that's cut the paint to remove defects quickly. The type of pad you use can affect how aggressive or non-aggressive your compound is. For the most aggressive cut, choose a 100% twisted wool cutting pad. I tend to like wool pads with a longer length to their pile versus a shorter length. A longer pile length makes buffing easier, provides plenty of cut and also makes cleaning your pad easier and more thorough. One pad I like is the Lake Country 41-125A 4-ply, 100% twisted wool 6 1/2" pad. This pad has a 1 1/2 pile or fiber length and works great on all rotary buffers for compounding and polishing.

Polishes and Foam Pads
Choosing the right polish requires you do a really good job of inspecting the results. The goal is to use the least aggressive polish and pad combination that offers enough cutting ability to completely remove any swirls or haze left by the abrasives in the compound and the wool fibers of the pad. The determining factor for just how fine a cut polish you can get away with is paint hardness. Harder paints will require a Medium Cut to Fine Cut Polish with a foam polishing pad. Softer paints can be perfected using either a Fine Cut or Ultra Fine Cut Polish with either a foam polishing pad or finishing pad.

Performing a Test Spot - Rotary

- **Step 1: Map out a section of paint on a horizontal panel like the hood**
  This section should be about 20" square or so to give you plenty of real-estate to work both the pads and the products in order to get an accurate example of how they work. You want a flat panel that's easy to buff and easy to inspect so you can quickly do your testing and inspecting and dial in a system approach that works on the paint system in front of you.

- **Step 2: Test your compound and cutting pad**
  Apply a bead of product about 8" long and pick up your bead using the 10 @ 10 Technique.

- **Step 3: Spread the product out over the area you're going to work**
  As soon as you move the polisher past the last portion of the bead of product instantly move the raised portion of the buffing pad so that the entire pad is now flat against the paint and proceed to spread the product out over the area you're going to work.

- **Step 4: Start with firm pressure for the first few passes**
  After the product is spread out, start working the product against the paint with slow overlapping passes with firm downward pressure to start with. Firm pressure will engage the abrasives with the paint to force them to cut into the paint and scoop out small bites of it.

  Note: **Buff in two directions – Crosshatch Pattern**
  Like using a DA Polisher, you can make overlapping passes and go in two different directions to Ensure UMR, Uniform Material Removal. Work the buffer long enough to make six to eight passes in two directions over this section. Don't buff to a dry buff. Then wipe of the excess residue and inspect.

- **Step 5: Reduce pressure for the last passes**
  After abrading the paint with firm downward pressure you'll need to reduce your downward pressure for the remaining few passes. Reduce pressure until just a little more than the weight of the machine is being used while maintaining the pad flat to the surface. This applies to both SMAT products and DAT products and the reason for this is to reduce the pressure being applied to everything touching the paint. This includes what's left of the abrasives. The carrying agents the abrasives are suspended in either the fibers or the foam that makes up the pad.

  Why?
  Polishing paint is an art form Buffing out paint isn't a grinding process; it's a craft or skill used to create beauty.

- **Step 6: Inspect your results**
  Are the majority or all of the swirls and scratches gone? If yes you now know the pad and product combination you chose is working and you also have an idea for how long and how many passes you

need to work a section of paint to remove the defects. As you gain experience, you can judge whether or not to start out with a wool cutting pad and an aggressive compound or a foam cutting or polishing pad and a polish.

Defects still remain
If you inspect the finish and most of the swirls and scratches are still there, then you can try one of two approaches.

1. Buff a second time
Rebuff the area a second time using the same pad and product and see if a second application gets the job done

2. Substitute a more aggressive pad and product combination
If the first pad and product combination isn't removing the defects fast enough or effectively enough, then do a second Test Spot to a new area of paint using a more aggressive product and pad combination.

- **Step 7: Test your polish and polishing pad**
Basically repeat steps 2-6 to the same section of paint. Your goal is to use the least aggressive polish to remove any haze or swirls left by the first step and finish out to a show car finish.

What To Do Next?

The next step is to get busy!

Claying
If you only clayed the hood or the test-spot area, then the first thing you want to do is finish claying the rest of the car.

How To Tape Off A Car before Machine Buffing

I love detailing cars, specifically the paint polishing aspect where I take a diamond in the rough and turn it into a glistening gemstone. I hate trying to get the wax out of the cracks afterwards using an old toothbrush. So instead, I will spend my time up front taping and covering everything up instead of trying to get the wax off trim and out of the cracks at the end of the job when I'm tired and worn out. First let's talk about tape…

The difference between Painter's Tape and Detailing Masking Tape

There are two kinds of masking tape used in the car industry; there is "Painter's Tape" and there is "Detailing Masking Tape". I asked Mike Pennington, the Director of Training at Meguiar's to share what makes the Meguiar's tape different than normal tape and wrote this article with the information he provided.

Meguiar's Professional Masking Tape
Meguiar's Masking Tape is really designed to be a great general purpose tape which lends itself well to use in the detailing world.

Product Attributes:
- Excellent handling
- Instant adhesion and good holding power
- Resists curling and lifting
- Solvent and moisture resistant
- Ideal for automotive detail application

Normal painter's tape, usually the blue or green tape we commonly see and use when taping-off a car, is a fantastic tape, however it is really overkill from a design perspective for the detailing market.

Normal painter's tape is purposefully constructed for application where a wet edge (critical edge) is present, that is where fresh paint is being applied and for this reason one of its main features is designed to prevent bleed-through. That is to say that painter's tape is designed so that wet paint won't leak under it at the edges. This is an important feature when applying fresh paint.

When detailing cars, this is an unnecessary feature that affects price. The Meguiar's masking tape is more specific to the needs of detailing, it is safe enough to protect what you want to cover and protect from product residue but not over-designed for its intended use. In addition, the Meguiar's tape has greater adhesion performance over traditional painters tape when exposed to situations where water is present (for example, wet sanding).

Note that because Meguiar's masking tape is not designed for use where a critical edge is a factor, it is not recommended for use as an actual "Painter's Tape". Painter's Tape and Detailing Masking Tape offer different designs for different applications.

My comments…
While I understand the differences, I tend to use whichever one is either:

- closest to my hand at the time I'm taping off a car
or
- a color that will contrast best with the color of the car I'm taping-off, especially if I'm taking pictures for educational purposes.

Video: How to tape-off car trim before machine polishing

It's a lot easier to show someone how to tape-off a car with a video then to try to explain it. Here's a very complete video on how-to tape-off and cover up all the areas you want to avoid getting splatter onto.

On the forum
On YouTube

The most important tip…
When using painter's tape to tape-off

trim on a car, pull the tape out about 2-3 feet holding the roll of tape in one hand while using your other hand to guide the placement of the tape.

Besides that, be sure to have a selection of tape-widths to make taping off thin or wide areas or larger components off easier and faster.

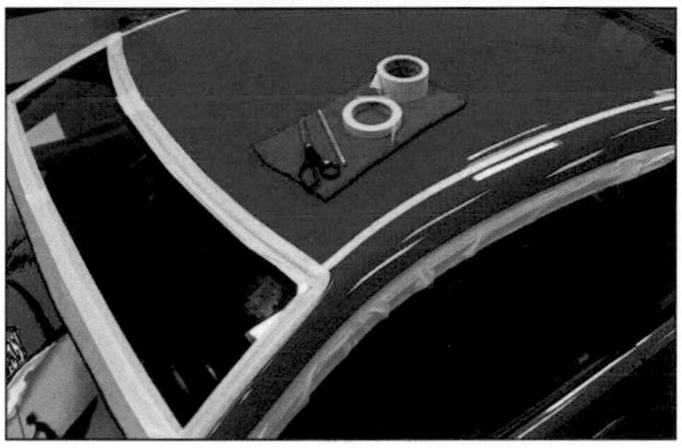

Tape-off all rubber, vinyl and plastic trim

Here you can see all of the rubber, plastic and vinyl, as well as the windshield on a Honda Civic has been thoroughly taped off. Tape anything off that's next to paint. Note that I use a clean, microfiber towel to place my tape, a pair of scissors and a pencil for marking where I want to cut the tape so it's handy but won't harm the finish.

How to reduce the stickiness of the tape

Sometimes you may find yourself working on fragile paint where you

need to be extra careful. Here's a quick way to take some of the stickiness out of painter's tape. Simply place the tape across your cotton t-shirt or cotton pants and like a Lint Remover it will remove some of the stray and loose fibers thus reducing the stickiness of the adhesive.

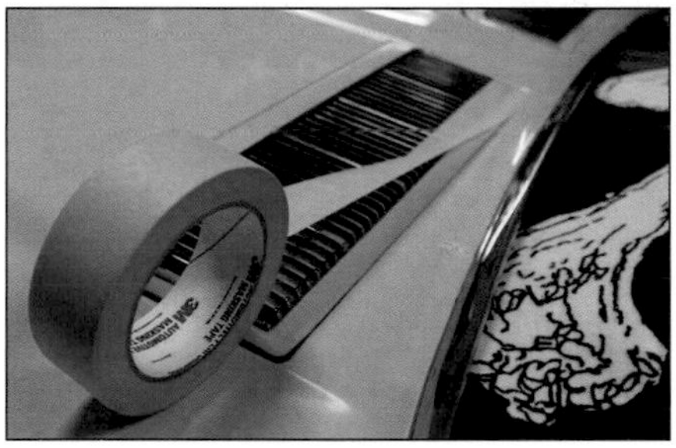

Someone asked me how to easily get the tape onto just the areas you want cover and my answer is you can make it as complicated as you want or as simple as you want. If you want to get complicated here's a simple tip, use a pencil to outline where you want to make your cut, (don't push hard on the tape or you might leave an imprint in the paint), then lift the tape up and back a little and make your cut.

Mark where you want to make the cut, then lift the tape back and carefully cut with scissors

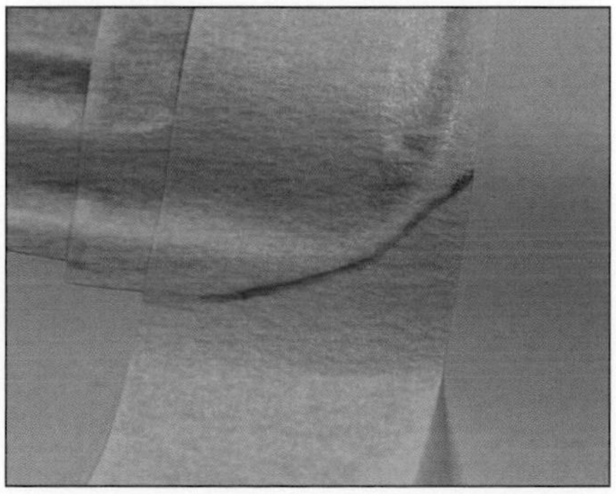

Above I've taped off the rubber gasket around the rear window and also the grille between the louvers and the rubber Whale Tail on a 1994 Porsche 964 Turbo 3.6 Under the deck lid I also covered the engine.

Tape off raised body line

This is especially true for classic cars where body panels don't always fit evenly together.

■ The Beach Towel Tip

On the forum

Here's a tip I use on some cars I detail to cover and protect the plastic surrounding the wiper arms at the back edge of the hood of cars, just before the windshield. I also use it to keep the windshield clean and this is especially important if there is any lettering or graphics on the top of the windshield. If you get spatter around lettering and rub over the lettering to try to get the splatter off you'll lift the corners of the lettering and once this starts it only gets worse with time.

Beach Towels tend to be longer in one direction than the average bath towel; on average, beach towels run around

60" or 70" in length. Where this comes in handy over a bath towel is that your average car, truck or SUV windshield is around 5' to 6' across so a Beach Towel is usually long enough to cover and protect the plastic, wiper arms, and glass in one fell swoop whereas the average bath towel falls short.

This is a stylish Beach Towel I found at Walgreens for around $6.00, my normal towel is white and ugly so I thought this would make for a more fun how-to article. Just to note, you could also use paper or plastic, whatever works for you. I like Beach Towels for a number of reasons that paper and plastic don't offer but I have used both plastic, (2 mil painter's drop cloths), and paper, (usually newspaper but painter's masking paper works great too).

Most new cars, (1990 and newer), have a fair amount of plastic just before the windshield surrounding the wiper

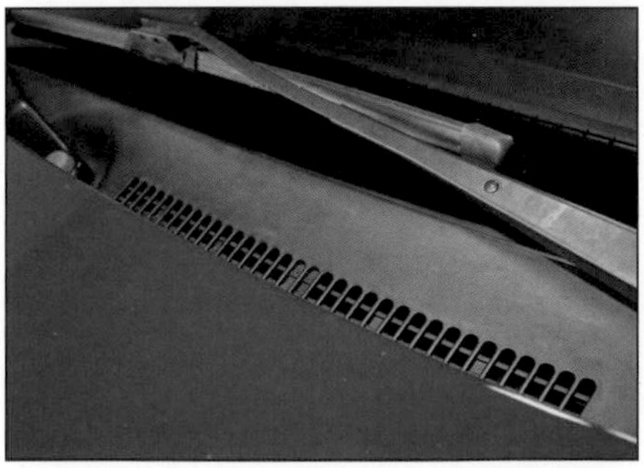

arms. If you get polish splatter onto and into these areas it can be difficult and time consuming to remove.

In most cases, if you're restoring the paint on someone's daily driver, not only is the paint neglected but the plastic is neglected meaning it's weathered, dried and dull and it seems like splatter really likes to stick hard to plastic in this condition.

If you do get splatter on these areas, it's also very unsightly and your customer might not appreciate it if you don't remove it. So with this technique, you never get splatter into and onto these areas in the first place. The old an ounce of prevention idea...

Not only does a Beach Towel work well for this type of job you can also re-wash it and use it again... so it's a green technique...

Start by opening the hood and locating a place to tape one edge of the towel too, make sure the ends of the towel don't bind in the hinge mechanism and don't place dry cloth anywhere on a hot engine where it could be a fire danger or get caught in any moving parts. In other words, use common sense.
After carefully closing the hood, then use some Painter's Tape to affix the towel to the windshield so it doesn't fall down and if you're also taping off other plastic, vinyl or rubber trim, then tape-off these components accordingly.

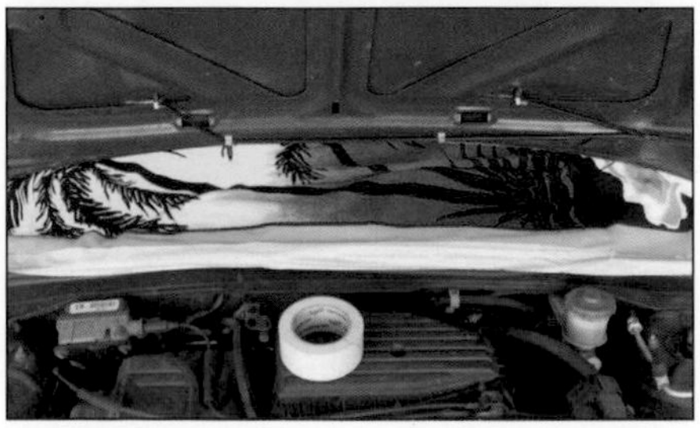

For this Honda, the towel did not reach all the way to the top of the windshield; this is okay, however, because the sling and splatter is mostly an issue for the lower portions adjacent to the hood where the buffing is taking place. You can also use this for the rear window. Side windows are not usually a problem for the glass because the panels are vertical.

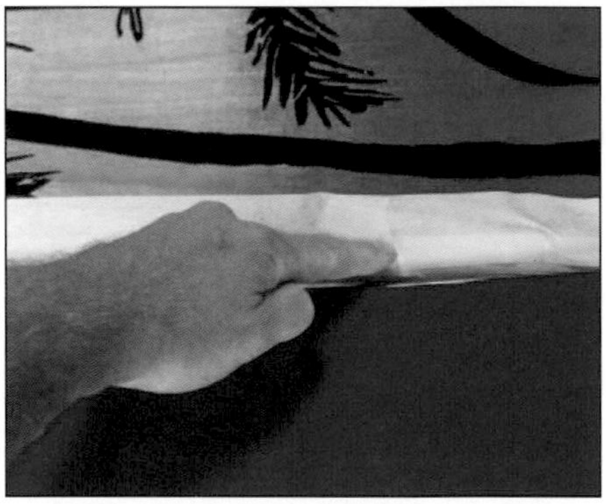

Notice how I've run a couple of strips of wide tape along where the Beach Towel meets the rear edge of the hood.

In some cases, the design of the vehicle means there's no gap or air space between the edge of the hood and the glass or wiper arm area, in these cases, you have to be careful when running your polisher not to run the buffing pad into the Beach Towel because the nap is grippy and your buffing pad could grab it and yank it into itself.

So for cars with a low air-gap or no air-gap between the paint and the area you're trying to cover up, being careful when buffing these areas is important. I also run a couple of strips of tape across this area as a buffing pad that's lubricated with product will just bump into the tape, it won't snag it and possibly pull it off the area and into the pad.

Classic and Antique Vehicles

So many times in my life when I've buffed out a classic car, I find compound and polish residue splattered into impossible to reach areas when I first get to the car and inspect it. A good example of this is the fresh air intake grill usually right before the front of the windshield. Here's an example, the 1969 El Camino I used for this article on Dampsanding.

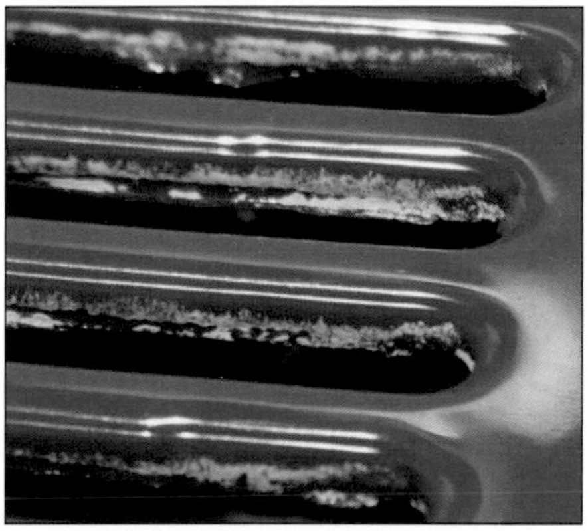

Because the bottom side of the sheet metal where the slots are stamped out are rough and jagged, all the compound and polish residue that was splattered by the rotary buffer has embedded like cement and will be very difficult to fully remove, especially now that it's a few years old. So while this is a very beautiful 1969 El Camino, every time someone looks at the hood area from the side of the car their eyes will be drawn to the very apparent white compound and polish residue that is encrusted where it's hard to reach and remove. Here's how to avoid throwing splatter into areas you can't get to: tape them off.

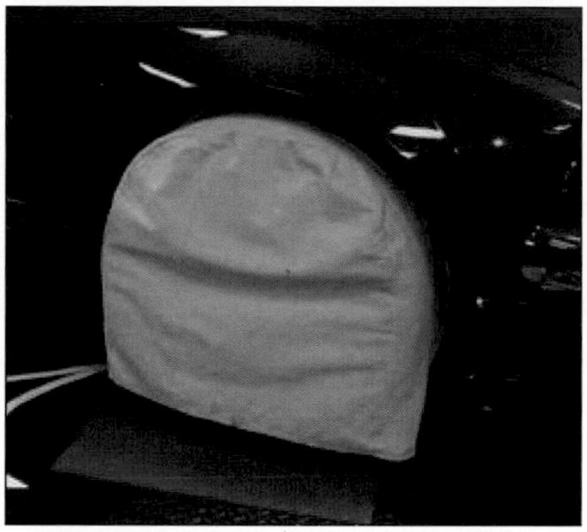

Wheel Maskers

Wheel Maskers are canvas covers with a piece of mild steel rod sewn into the rear perimeter and then placed over wheels and tires to protect them from splatter. Besides protecting the car, they show your customers and potential customers you take your job seriously and pay attention to details. I use them for almost ever car I buff out. If you don't have canvas wheel maskers you can make them from large lawn and leaf plastic bags. I've even made them using newspaper. The last thing I want to do at the end of the day when I'm tired is clean spatter of someone else's wheels and tires.

The Bed Sheet Tip

Believe it or not, a simple flannel or cotton bedsheet comes in real handy for coving up car interiors when it's not an option to put the top up.

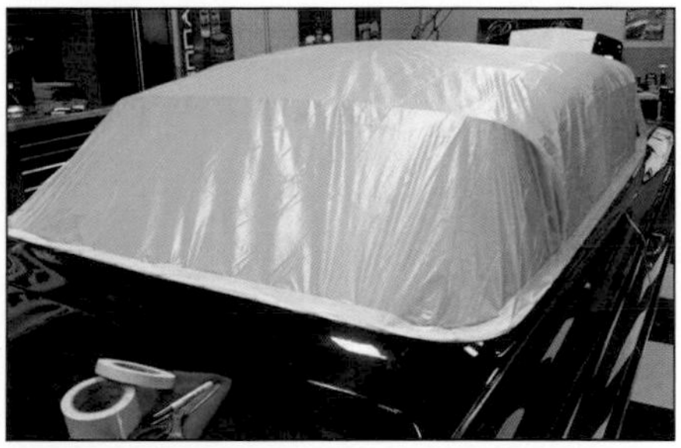

■ **How to cover and protect a convertible top**

If the top is up on a convertible you want to cover it so you don't get polish residue into the weave or grain of the top material, here's how you can do it using tape and a plastic drop cloth. Start by placing a strip of tape around the bottom edge of the convertible top. Next, use painter's tape to attach your protective drop cloth to this tape line already in place.

Here's an example of how I used an inexpensive plastic drop cloth to cover the interior of Nate Truman's Recreation of the Batmobile as I use a rotary buffer to machine buff the single stage paint. Photo Courtesy of MeguiarsOnline.com

■ One more tip... change pads often

Another trick to help you avoid splatter is to have plenty of pads on hand so that if the pad you're using becomes to wet with product you can simply switch to a clean dry pad. This tends to improve buffing performance and reduce the potential for any splatter. Generally speaking, more pads are better no matter what tool you're using.

■ Set-up a work station

Gather all your supplies and assemble them in one easily accessible area. This can be a workbench, a rolling cart or even a folding table. Having all your products, pads and plenty of clean microfiber towels all in one place will help you get the job done faster.

■ Start at the top and work your way down

After you've completed your test spot and dialed-in your approach, the next thing to do is start buffing out the car. Start by buffing out the highest point on the car, which is usually the roof.

■ Divide larger panels into smaller sections

Buffing out a car with any machine is simply a matter of slicing up each panel into smaller sections and then buffing only one section at a time. After finishing one section, move to a new section and overlap a little into the previous section. ■

Here's an example of how I would divide each of the panels of Max's 2012 Mercedes- Benz CLS63 AMG into smaller sections for the correction step.

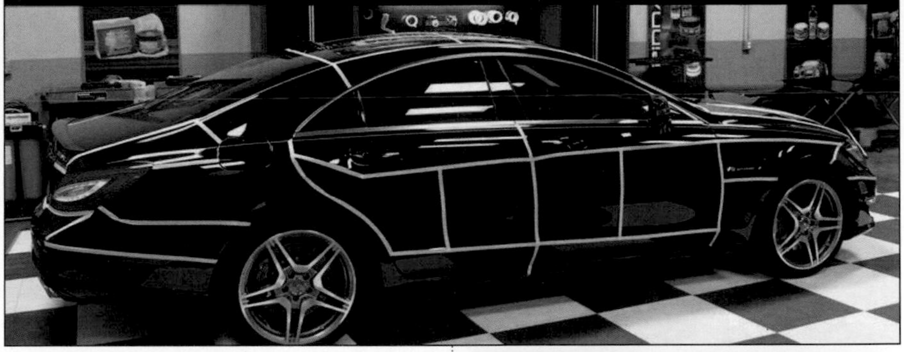

■ The Steps

Most professional detailers will perform one step to the entire car at one time and then move on to the next step.

Step 1 - Correction step
Using the more aggressive pad and product combination that you dialed-in during your test spot, perform this step to the entire car starting with the highest point - the roof. Next, buff the horizontal panels below the roof, usually the hood and trunk lid. After you buff the horizontal panels, tackle the vertical panels. After buffing out the vertical side panels of the vehicle, tackle any paint on the vertical panels of the front and rear of the car. Depending upon the vehicle you're detailing, there may be very little or a lot of paint on the front and rear sections of the vehicle. For example, a lot of modern cars have a grille and a front bumper cover painted the same color as the car. A truck may have very little paint to polish at the front of the vehicle, but there's usually a large, rectangular tailgate to polish at the rear.

In This Section:

- The Steps
- How To Buff Your Car Section By Section
- The Major Correction Step - One Section At A Time
- The Polishing Or Minor Correction Step
- How To Jewel Paint Using A DA Polisher - Optional Step

Step 2 - Polishing step
Perform your second step process to refine the results of the first step, following your original path of travel. For example, if you started on the roof for the first step, start there for the second step.

Step 3 - Sealing step
Whether you're going to apply your choice of wax, paint sealant or a coating for the protection or sealing step, again, start at the highest point and work your way down, following your previous path of travel.

Step 4 - Second coat of wax
A lot of people like to apply two coats of wax or two coats of a paint sealant for two reasons:

1. Uniform coverage - This means to ensure that every square inch of paint was coated. Sometimes, you can accidently miss applying wax to some portions of the paint, especially on light colored cars on which it can be difficult to see there's an actual layer of product being applied.

2. Uniform protection - Applying two thin coats of a wax or paint sealant ensures a uniform layer over the entire surface and thus uniform protection.

Coatings
If you're using a paint coating instead of a traditional car wax or paint sealant, after the polishing step you would clean and prep the paint per manufacturer's directions and apply the coating.

■ How To Buff Your Car Section By Section

Another option is to tackle a detailing project by dividing the car up into sections. Complete one section at a time with all of the steps in the correction process.

A few reasons why to break a car up into sections:

1. Limited time - Instead of spending an entire day buffing out an entire car from start to beginning, divide the car up into smaller, manageable sections. Perform all the steps to just

these sections until you finish with the last step, wiping off the last coat of wax. By doing this, you don't tie up your entire day in the garage working on your car. The next day, or the next weekend, move to a new section and repeat the process.

2. Avoid injury - In other words, don't over-do it. Detailing a car from start to finish whether you work by hand or machine will tax all the muscles in your body, especially if you don't detail cars on a regular basis.

3. Physical limitations - If you have any type of physical limitations, instead of tackling an entire car in one day, divide it into sections. By limiting how much time you invest into detailing your car, you'll also limit your exposure to muscle strain.

4. Reduce exposure to tool vibration - Tool vibration has never bothered me but I know for some people it can tire their grip strength. If this is true for you, spread your car detailing project out over a few weekends.

Here are some common ways to divide a car into sections:

- **Roof -** If the car is a convertible, put the top up and cover it using a plastic drop cloth. With the top up, the interior is protected from splatter and if you cover the top with a drop cloth, you won't get residue into the grain or weave of the convertible top material.
- **Hood or front clip -** The front clip includes the hood, front fenders and any paint around the grill or bumpers.
- **Trunk lid or rear clip** -The rear clip includes the trunk lid and rear two fenders, plus any paint at the rear of the car.
- **Doors/sides -** This includes the sides of the vehicle, including the doors and any other panels.

Mike's Method
Knock out painted roofs first, and then tackle the rest of the car...

When I detail a vehicle, I use a combination of both approaches. Normally, I detail the entire vehicle in one day, starting by completing to entire process to the roof. After the roof is completed, I will then cover it with something soft like a soft flannel bed sheet.

Here's why I do this and why this approach works for me:

1. Save wiping time - When you machine polish the roof of a car, you can't help but throw product splatter onto the paint below. Each time you throw splatter, before you can work on the lower panel, you have to wipe off the splatter. This takes time. In a three step process, you would have to wipe the hood, trunk lid, and anywhere else the splatter lands three times. If you cover the hood and trunk lid with some something and then do the entire multiple-step process to the roof, then you don't waste any time wiping splatter off lower panels.

2. Marketing - If you're detailing cars for money, you know that doing a multiple step process to any car requires a lot of time. This could be anywhere from 10 to 12 hours to a couple of days, depending upon the project.

Now follow me on this:
If while working on the car, you don't have a "finished section", then you have no way to showcase your work and talent to anyone that happens to walk by. This could be the owner or a potential customer. If all they can see is a work in progress, or a car covered in compounding or polishing residue, then there's nothing to get too excited about. If you put the roof through the entire process all the way to wiping off the first application of wax or paint sealant, now anytime someone walks by and comments or asks questions about your work, you can make a "sales presentation" by showcasing your skill and ability.

In my experience, anyone looking at the finished results can usually imagine how the rest of the car is going to look. That puts the "big picture" together, allowing them to appreciate the work you're doing. The flannel bed sheet is covering the roof, because at the point in time at which this picture (shown above) was taken, it had been:

- Dampsanded
- Compounded
- Machine polished twice
- Machine waxed

The reason we covered the finished roof with a soft, flannel bed sheet was so that as we continued to work the lower panels, the bed sheet prevented any airborne dirt, dust or splatter from getting on it.

Personal preference
Of course, It goes without saying that this style of process is personal preference. Each person can find a way that works best for them.

Before you dive in and start the major correction step, you should have already done these things:

- Washed and dried the car
- Inspected the paint visually for swirls, scratches, water spots and oxidation.
- Inspected the paint physically with your sense of touch and the baggie test.
- Performed a test spot and dialed-in a process.
- Decided on an approach to complete the entire vehicle.
- In your mind's eye, divided the car's panels into smaller sections.

If all of the above has been done, you're ready to start the major correction step.

The Major Correction Step - One Section At A Time

Performing the major correction step is just a matter of dividing each panel of a car into smaller sections and buffing one section at a time. After you finish buffing a section, carefully wipe any residue from the paint and move onto a new section. Be sure to overlap a little into the previous section.

Step by step directions

Prime your pad
If you're starting with a clean, dry pad, the first thing you want to do is prime it.

Apply working product to face of pad

Spread product
Next, set the speed setting to around 3 to 4. Place the pad against the paint. Turn the polisher on and spread the product over the area you're going to work.

Increase speed setting
After you have the product spread over

the working area, you need to turn the speed setting up to 5 or 6. You can do this by turning the polisher off and adjusting the variable speed dial or you can do it on the fly with the polisher running.

Caution *– The pad always needs to be in contact with paint when the polisher is on. You don't want to lift the face of the buffing pad off the surface of the paint because you'll throw splatter dots everywhere!*

Wrong technique
Don't place the pad against the paint, turn the polisher on and start making your section passes right away. Start by spreading the product over the area you're going to work. Then, start making your section passes. Spreading your product distributes an even layer of abrasives over the section for even abrading action and thus more uniform swirl removal results.

Start making section passes

- Speed should be on the 5 to 6 setting.
- Place pad against paint
- Turn polisher on and start making slow, overlapping passes. Overlap by 50%.
- Use a slow arm speed.
- Keep pad flat to the surface whenever possible.
- Make 6 to 8 section passes, then turn the polisher off. Make sure the pad stops spinning before you lift it off the paint.
- Remove polish residue and inspect results.
- If defects are gone, clean your pad and move on to next section and overlap a little into the previous section.

The Polishing Or Minor Correction Step

There are two instances when you will use the polishing or minor correction step:

1. After the major correction step
If you've polished the paint using an aggressive compound or polish with a foam cutting, fiber, or even a polishing pad to remove swirls, scratches, water spots and/or oxidation, the next step towards your goal will be to re-polish each square inch of paint using a less aggressive pad and product.
The goal now is to refine the results created during the major correction step to maximize the clarity, gloss and smoothness of the paint.

2. As the only correction step for paint with minor defects
If the paint you're working on is in good to excellent condition, then your test spot would have shown that you could remove these defects using the least aggressive product approach.

This would include a medium to fine finishing polish with either a polishing pad or a finishing pad. Neither an aggressive compound or polish nor an aggressive buffing pad are needed.

For either instance, the procedures are the same. Repeat the same process explained in the major correction step with a less aggressive pad and product and usually a speed setting around the 4 to 5 range.

Step by step directions

Prime your pad
If you're starting with a clean, dry pad, the first thing you want to do is prime it.

Apply working product to face of pad

Spread product
Next, set the speed setting to around 3 to 4. Place the pad against the paint. Turn the polisher on and spread the product over the area you're going to work.

Increase speed setting
After you have the product spread over the working area, you need to turn the speed setting up to 4 or 5. You can do this by turning the polisher off and adjusting the variable speed dial or you can do it on the fly with the polisher running.

***Caution** – The pad always needs to be in contact with paint when the polisher is on. You don't want to lift the face of the buffing pad off the surface of the paint because you'll throw splatter dots everywhere!*

Wrong technique
Don't place the pad against the paint, turn the polisher on and start making your section passes right away. Start by spreading the product over the area you're going to work. Then, start making your section passes. Spreading your product distributes an even layer of abrasives over the section for even abrading action and thus more uniform swirl removal results.

Start making section passes

- Speed should be on the 4 to 5 setting.
- Place pad against paint
- Turn polisher on and start making slow, overlapping passes. Overlap by 50%.
- Use a slow arm speed.
- Make 4 to 5 section passes with firm downward pressure, then reduce pressure and make 2 to 4 more section passes.
- After your last section pass, turn the polisher off. Make sure the pad stops spinning before you lift it off the paint to avoid slinging splatter.
- Carefully wipe off any polish residue and inspect the results. At this point, the paint should look clear and glossy as proven by your test spot.
- Clean your pad and apply fresh product. Move on to a new section and be sure to overlap a little into the previous section.
- Continue this process until you've completed the entire vehicle or the panel or section of the vehicle that you're working on.

Seal or Jewel The Paint
After this step, you are ready to seal the paint using a wax, paint sealant or a coating. Or, if you choose, you can do a second ultra fine polishing step, commonly referred to as "jewelling the paint".

How To Jewel Paint Using A DA Polisher - Optional Step

***Note:** The jewelling step is optional. If you are satisfied with the results from your correction and polishing steps, you can skip the jewelling step and apply a wax, paint sealant or coating.*

Jewelling is another term for final polishing. This means to bring the paint to the highest degree of gloss, shine, depth, and reflectivity. To do this, the paint must be as flat as possible at the microscopic level.

Jewelling - definition
The final machine polishing step in which a soft to ultra soft foam finishing pad with no mechanical abrading ability is used with a high lubricity, ultra fine finishing polish to remove any remaining microscopic surface imperfections. This is performed after the paint has been previously put through a series of machine compounding and polishing procedures to create a near-perfect finish.

Time consuming
Jewelling is time consuming. It would defeat the purpose to rush any part of the jewelling process, including paint preparation.

Work surgically clean – Most Important
Jewelling paint starts with a surgically clean finish. All residues from previous machine polishing steps must be meticulously removed from all the major panels so there's no risk of any leftover residue entering into the jewelling process.

Pads
Jewelling with a DA polisher requires you to use the softest foam pads you can obtain. Ideally, you want to use a foam pad that offers no mechanical abrading ability. Aggressiveness of a foam pad is relative to the hardness of the paint system you're working on.

Below is a list of pads recognized as being very soft and suitable for jewelling for most paint systems.

Lake Country
- 5 1/2" and 6 1/2" CCS Pads
  Black, Blue, Red, Gold
- 5 1/2" and 6 1/2" Flat Pads
  Black, Blue
- 5 1/2" and 6 1/2" Hydro-Tech
  Crimson
- 5 1/2" and 6 1/2" Constant Pressure
  Black

Griot's Garage
- 6" Red Finishing pad

Meguiar's
- 6 1/2" Soft Buff Pads
  Tan Finishing Pad
- 7" Soft Buff Pads
  Black Finishing Pad

Products
Here's a list of fine and ultra fine finishing polishes:

Pinnacle
Advanced Finishing Polish

Wolfgang
Finishing Glaze 3.0

Menzerna
FF 3000 – Final Finish Polish (PO85U)
SF 4000 – Super Finish Polish (PO106FA)
SF 4500 – Super Finish Polish (PO85RD)

Meguiar's
Ultimate Polish
M205 Ultra Finishing Polish

Optimum
Optimum Polish II
Optimum Finish Polish
Optimum Hyper-Polish

Prima
Prima Finish

Mothers
Foam Pad Polish
PowerPolish

Gtechniq
P2 Hologram Removing Polish

Step by step directions

Prime your pad
If you're starting with a clean, dry pad, the first thing you want to do is prime it.

Apply working product to face of pad

Spread product

Next, set the speed setting to around 3 to 4. Place the pad against the paint. Turn the polisher on and spread the product over the area you're going to work.

Increase speed setting
After you have the product spread over the working area, you need to turn the speed setting up to 4 or 6. You can do this by turning the polisher off and adjusting the variable speed dial, or you can do it on the fly with the polisher running.

Caution *– The pad always needs to be in contact with paint when the polisher is on. You don't want to lift the face of the buffing pad off the surface of the paint because you'll throw splatter dots everywhere!*

Wrong technique
Don't place the pad against the paint, turn the polisher on and start making your section passes right away. Start by spreading the product over the area you're going to work. Then, start making your section passes. Spreading your product distributes an even layer of abrasives over the section for even abrading action and thus more uniform swirl removal results.

Start making section passes

- Speed should be on the 4 to 5 setting.

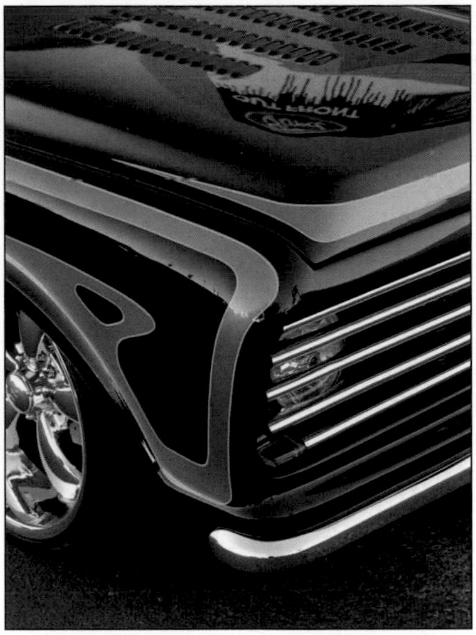

- Place pad against paint
- Turn polisher on and start making slow, overlapping passes. Overlap by 50%.
- Use a slow arm speed.
- Make 4 to 5 section passes with firm downward pressure, then reduce pressure and make 2 to 4 more section passes.
- After your last section pass, turn the polisher off. Make sure the pad stops spinning before you lift it off the paint to avoid slinging splatter dots.
- Carefully wipe off any polish residue and inspect the results. At this point, the paint should look clear and glossy as proven by your test spot.
- Clean your pad and apply fresh product. Move onto a new section and be sure to overlap a little into the previous section.
- Continue this process until you've completed the entire vehicle or the panel or section of the vehicle that you're working on.

Vitally Important
At this stage of the game, you REALLY need to be wiping any and all residues off incredibly carefully. If you've done everything right, then even the slightest, lightest imperfection will show up including wiping or toweling marks. ■

For more information:
How To Remove Dried Wax Using A DA Polisher

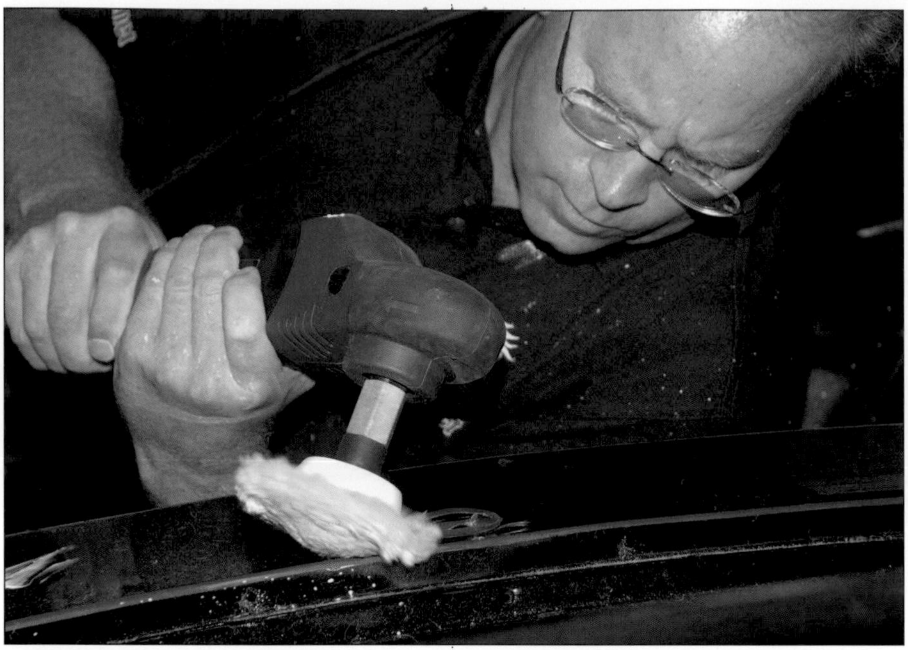

■ The Major Cutting Step

Once you have dialed in a compound/ polish and pad system that works in your Test Spot and you have taped-off or covered up anything you want to protect, you're ready to buff out the rest of the car. I call the first step the cutting step because the abrasives you're using together with the pad and pressure your using are literally cutting into the paint from the direct rotating action of the rotary buffer.

In This Section:

- The Major Cutting Step
- Repeat Test Spot
- Step-by-Step How To Use A Rotary Buffer
- Advanced Technique: Edging
- How To Jewel Paint Using A Rotary Polisher - Optional Step
- Entire Car or Key Panels & Gloss Points
- Finishing out using a DA Polisher
- Marine & RV Detailing with Rotary Buffers
- The 10 @ 10 Technique for picking up a bead of product
- Handles or No Handles
- Surgical Buffing
- Buffing off an edge

■ Repeat the Test Spot

Buffing out an entire car using a rotary buffer is basically repeating the steps you did in your Test Spot to the rest of the car. It's that simple. Dial in your Test Spot and repeat section by section.

■ Step-by-Step How To Use A Rotary Buffer

This is a guide for buffing out either an extremely neglected car or a car after first wetsanding the paint. The first step is the cutting step followed by the polishing step. If the car you're working on has not been wetsanded and/or is not in that bad of condition, you may be able to skip the cutting step and start at the polishing step. Your test spot should let you now how you need to proceed.

Step 1: Divide large panels into smaller section then buff out each section
The largest area you should try to buff would be 2' by 2' max, or about the width of your shoulders squared. As I always say in my best Yoda impersonation, "Let the panel be your guide"

Step 2: Lay down a bead of product on the section you're going to buff
For a large panel, lay down a bead or strip of product about the length and width of a new pencil.

Step 3: Pick up your bead using the 10 @ 10 Technique

Step 4: Spread the product out over the area you're going to work
After you pick up your bead of product, immediately lay your pad flat to the surface move and spread the product out over the area you're going to work.

Step 5: Use firm pressure for the first few passes
After the product is spread out, continue holding the pad flat to the surface and work the product against the paint with slow overlapping passes and firm downward pressure. Firm pressure will engage the abrasives with the paint to force them to take small bites out of it leveling the surface and thus removing the defects.

Step 6: Reduce pressure for the last passes
After abrading the paint with firm

pressure you need to reduce your downward pressure for the remaining few passes till just a little more then the weight of the machine is being used. This applies to both SMAT products and DAT products and the reason for this is to reduce the pressure being applied to everything touching the paint. This would include what's left of the abrasives, the carrying agents the abrasives are suspended in and either the fibers or the foam that makes up the pad.

Step 7: Turn the polisher off and let the pad slow down before lifting it off the surface.
This prevents splatter from spraying everywhere. Most people have to make this mistake a few times before it becomes second nature.

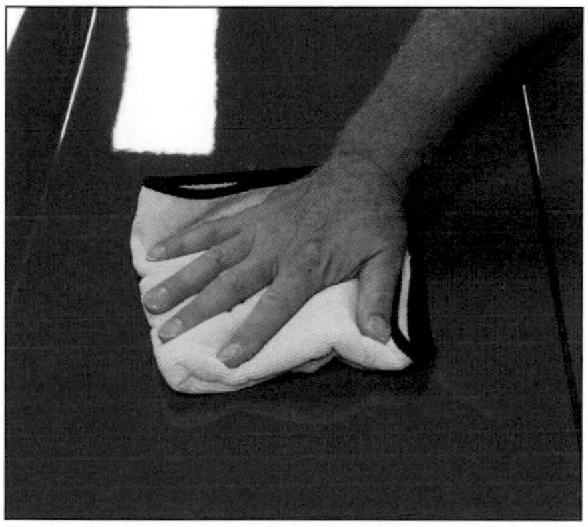

Step 8: Wipe off any residue immediately
Compounds and Polishes don't need to dry and in fact will be easier to wipe-off immediately rather than allowing them to dry. This is also less aggressive to the paint as any wetness left in the residue film will act as a lubricant. I will often use a clean, soft terry cloth towel to wipe-off compounding residues because the larger cotton loop, called

the nap, acts to help slice into and remove compounds better than soft, gentle microfiber towels.

Step 9: Inspect the results
Hopefully if you dialed-in your process during the Test Spot phase the paint will look defect free and you can move on to the next section of paint to buff out.

Continue the cutting step
Continue the cutting step until you've buffed out the entire roof.

Step 10: Make a few Cover Passes
After you have buffed out a panel by buffing out smaller sections of it, wipe the panel spotlessly clean and then clean your pad really well. Now buff out the entire panel as a whole making passes that cover the entire panel; these are called your cover passes.

Long, sweeping cover passes remove any buffing marks from the middle of a panel and help to create a uniform surface level over the entire panel as well as a uniform appearance. After any compounding steps, there may light swirls or haze but that's okay as the next step will remove these.

Choose your style
At this point you need to decide if you're going to use my approach and continue the polishing and waxing steps to the roof or continue working downward and do the cutting step to the entire car. This is personal preference and everyone can find a style that works best for them.

Both approaches work but my preference is to knock out the roof all the way through the entire process and then cover it with a soft flannel sheet to protect it and prevent splatter or any air-borne dust or dirt from accumulating on it while I buff out the rest of the car.

Note: The first step is the most important step
The most important step of any rotary buffing project is the first step. It is the first step that will determine your end-results. If you don't remove the defects in the first step, then you're going to see them at the end of the job. So invest your time into the first step.

Work each quadrant of the panel you're working on carefully, thoroughly and sufficiently to equally remove enough paint over the entire section to remove the defects to the level you're comfortable with. Understand that not all defects can be removed without the risk of removing too much paint and going through the clear on a clear coat finish and exposing the color coat, or going through the color coat of a single stage finish and exposing primer.

After working each section, wipe off and remove any excess product before it dries and move onto a new section. Never apply fresh product to spent product as it will dilute and adulterate the fresh product. Always work clean.

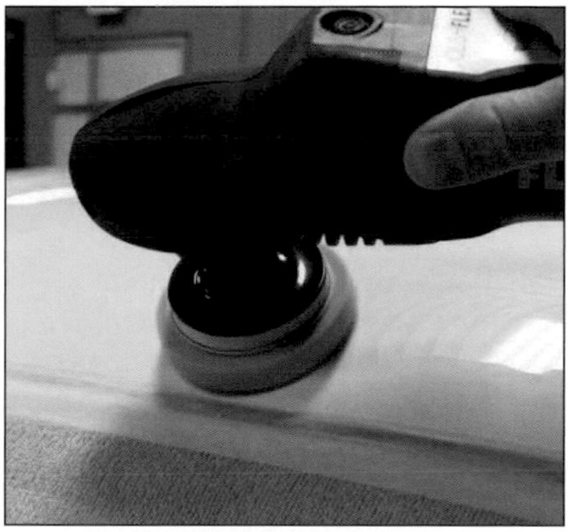

■ Advanced Technique: Edging

Edging means to first buff around the entire edge leaving only the major portions of the panels to buff out. For this you can use smaller pads to make it easier to get close to the edge while maintaining control over the rotary buffer.

Holding the pad flat versus on edge
Anytime you can hold the pad flat, you should hold the pad flat to the surface. This reduces deeper swirls by providing even pressure over the entire face of the pad that is in contact with the paint. This also decreases heat build-up while cutting more paint faster because more surface area is being abraded.

That said, there are times when you have to hold the pad on edge in order to buff curves, sections of paint next to

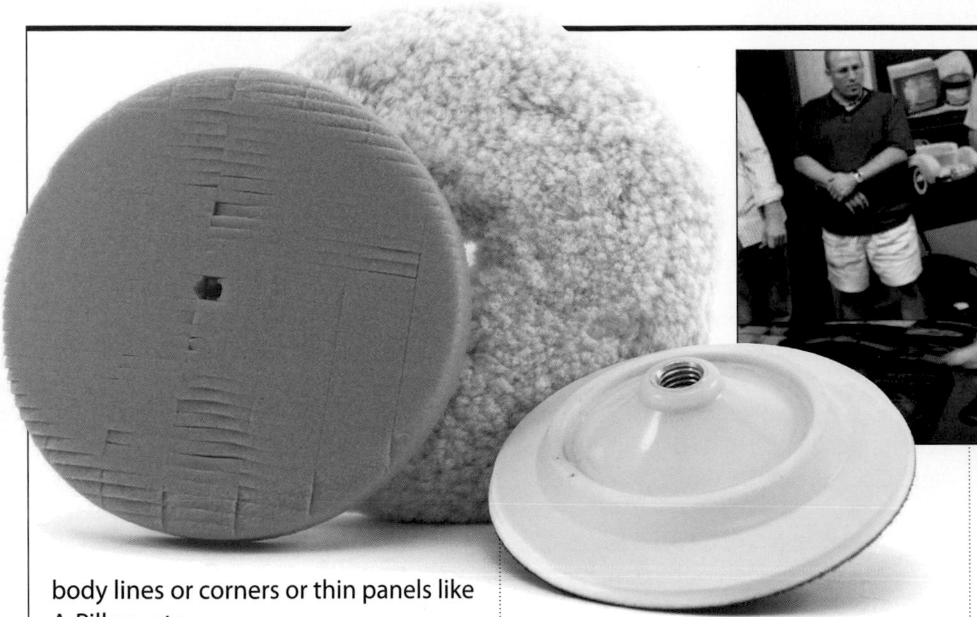

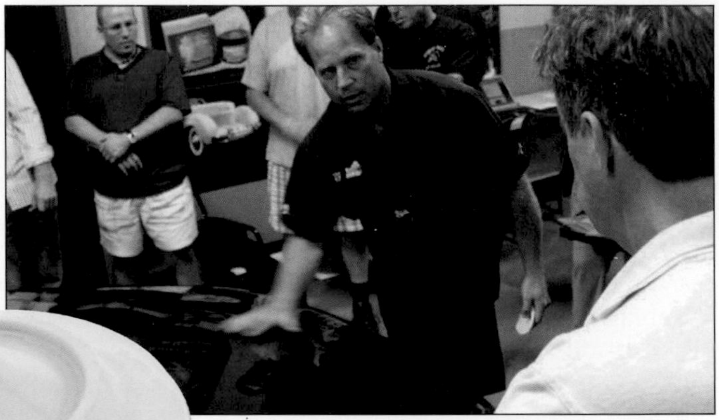

body lines or corners or thin panels like A-Pillars, etc.

My comments

A lot of times if I have to hold a pad on edge, (especially a wool cutting pad), in order to cut a specific section of paint effectively, I will come back and do a few cover passes as best I can over that area with the pad flat to help even out the paint in that area.

Wool Cutting Pads versus Foam Cutting Pads

Wool pads will cut cooler than foam pads because the fibers don't hold the heat in like the dense, thick, uniform surface of foam. Foam provides more cushion but when doing heavy cutting with a foam cutting pad and an aggressive compound you need to be very careful because you can heat the paint up very quickly.

Keep the pad moving

Anytime you're using a rotary buffer you want to keep the pad moving over the surface or you'll generate a lot of heat very quickly and this can lead to either burning through the paint or twisting the paint if buffing on urethane body parts.

Destructive Polishing – Heating the paint up

Getting the paint too hot while buffing is called destructive polishing. Too much heat can paint damage. Rotary buffers have the ability to heat up the paint quicker than any other buffer and can cause visible and invisible permanent, long term damage to the molecular structure of the paint.

Temperature to avoid

I asked two respected chemists, both good friends of mine, as well as two experts on paint technology and buffing procedures, for their opinions on what are the upper temperatures levels to avoid while machine buffing. Their answers were all in a range from 160° Fahrenheit to 180° Fahrenheit.

Black and dark colored paints when exposed to summer sunlight can easily reach temperatures up to 180°. This is just a static temperature and doesn't include an abrasive compound and an aggressive buffing pad being pushed against the paint cutting or abrading it. When the paint is heated and cut aggressively with compounds and cutting pads at too high of a temperature, that's when damage is done.

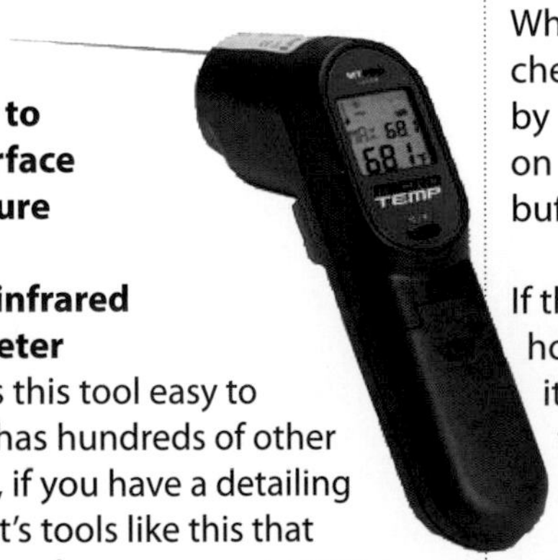

Two ways to gauge surface temperature

1. Get an infrared thermometer

Not only is this tool easy to use but it has hundreds of other uses. Plus, if you have a detailing business, it's tools like this that separate you from your competition while letting your customer know that you take their car and your work seriously. Simply aim and pull the trigger and you'll instantly know the surface temperature.

2. Mike's Fight or Flight Method for Gauging Surface Temperature

The information below is from an article I wrote years ago. It includes a simple method you can use to know if you should stop buffing and allow the paint to cool down. Heat is unavoidable when using a rotary buffer for correction work. The smaller the section your work the greater the risk of getting the paint too hot. It's normal and okay to get paint warm, (because there's nothing you can do about it), but you don't want to get paint too hot and if you do, you want to stop buffing in that section and let the paint cool down.

This method works off your hand's sense of touch and your brain's instincts to protect you. I call it the Fight or Flight Method for Gauging Surface Temperature. Not one of my better titles but descriptive to say the least.

The Fight or Flight Method for Gauging Surface Temperature

When using a rotary buffer, periodically check the temperature of the paint by placing the palm of your hand flat on top of a section you just finished buffing, like this,

If the paint feels warm, BUT it's not so hot that you jerk your hand away, then it's in a temperature range that's safe to buff.

If you place your hand on the paint and your fight or flight instincts take over and you find yourself jerking your hand away from the surface at the speed of light, then the paint is too hot and you should stop buffing that section and allow the paint to cool down. Kind of a caveman approach but you get the idea.

Big Picture
The bigger picture is to check the surface temperature of the paint once in a while because you might surprise yourself at how hot you're getting the paint. You're in control of the rotary buffer and you need pay attention to the surface temperature. This means pausing for a moment to feel the paint.

Different body panel materials like steel, aluminum, fiberglass, composite, etc., will heat up at different rates and will either dissipate or retain heat at different rates, so it's a good idea to check each time you work on a different car. With testing, you can get a feel, (no pun intended), for how long you can buff an average size section before getting the paint too hot.

The Polishing Step
After the cutting step the next thing you want to do is remove any swirls or haze by switching to a foam polishing pad and a Medium Cut to an Ultra Fine Cut Polish. How aggressive or non-aggressive of a pad and polish you choose to use depends upon the hardness or softness of the paint. You determine this when you do your Test Spot.

My comments…
At this point I would be polishing the roof using only the rotary buffer and then applying either a coat of wax, a paint sealant or a coating depending upon which type of protection product I was going to use to seal the paint. For most projects, AFTER the polishing step with the rotary buffer I would do a third polishing step only switch to a dual action polisher. The reason for this is it ensures a swirl-free finish down the road and it doesn't take very long since all you're doing is running the DA Polisher for a few passes over each panel.

Once bitten, twice shy
When I was younger I buffed out a street rod for a customer using only a rotary buffer. At the time, DA Polishers like the Porter Cable did not exist, neither did the Flex 3401 and I did not know about Cyclo polishers. I did all my work with a rotary buffer using the best pads and products available during that time. When I returned the car to the owners the paint was flawless and 100% swirl free. A year and a lot of car washes later, holograms showed up in the paint. The holograms were masked by the polishing oils in the polishes and by a good coat of wax. Had the owners simply "maintained" my work by applying another coat of wax once in a while it would have always looked swirl-free…but they didn't.

What I learned from this was you can't expect other people to know how to take care of their own car's paint. After this experience the Porter Cable DA Polisher was introduced to the car detailing world and ever since then I make it a habit to simply re-polish the paint by changing the action of the tools and avoid any potential for swirls to return that could harm my reputation.

I read posts by other detailers on discussion forums about how all they use is a rotary buffer for all their work and all I can say is good luck with that. You see sometimes it's not about how good you are, it's about how polishable the paint is and unless you're chemically stripping the paint and inspecting to make 100% sure you're not leaving holograms in the finish you don't really know if you are or are not. I cover this topic in depth here:

Hologram Free with a Rotary Buffer

To date, no one has ever challenged what I've written.

Tips for the polishing step
At this point in the game, you need to be using your best microfiber towels to wipe-off and remove polish residues. If you put toweling marks, (a nicer term for scratches), back into the paint while wiping polishing residues off you'll either have to re-polish to remove them or hope your choice of wax, paint sealant or coating masks them. So have plenty of premium quality, clean soft microfiber towels on hand for this step.

See, How to correctly fold use a microfiber towel

■ Step-by-Step How To Jewell Paint using a Rotary Polisher

Jewelling
There is lots of interest on the topic of jewelling using a rotary buffer to create the deepest, wettest looking shine possible. This is an optional step because at this point the paint should already look really good. But for those of you willing to invest the time to completely re-polish out the entire car or just the key panels, here you go…

■ Step-by-Step How To

Step 1: Work surgically clean
At this point you need to make sure the vehicle is surgically clean. Remove all trace residues for any previously used compounds or polishes including removing any splatter out of any cracks and crevices or any place where it could accidently get back onto the panel between the paint and your buffing pad.

You cannot allow any used product to adulterate the jewelling process

Step 2: Start at the top and work downward
Anytime you use a rotary buffer the potential exists to throw splatter. Buff out the top or highest panels first and be sure to re-wipe any lower panels after jewelling the higher panels to remove any splatter from buffing the higher panels. You must work surgically clean throughout the process.

Step 3: Use an Ultra Fine Cut Polish with a soft foam Finishing Pad
The jewelling process is about making

the surface smooth down to the microscopic level. Lake Country and Meguiar's both offer very soft foam finishing pads that work great for jewelling. My preference is a flat face design as you don't want to risk having anything build up in a depression on the pad. A size between 5 inches and 7 inches also works best.

Here are three good pads for jewelling:

- *Meguiars 7" W9207 Soft Buff 2.0 Foam Finishing Pad*
- *5.5" Lake Country Black Flat Finishing Pad or Blue Finessing Pad*
- *6.5" Lake Country Gray Finishing Pad or Blue Finessing Pad*
- *Lake Country Hybrid Black Finishing Pads in either 6.5" or 5"*

The best polish I've used for jewelling is the Menzerna SF 4500. This is an Ultra Fine Cut Polish with plenty of polishing oils to keep the surface lubricated as your pad rotates over the surface.

Step 4: Use a Flexible Backing Plate
A flexible backing plate provides extra cushion aside from what is provided by the pad. When jewelling, you want everything to work for you, and a flexible backing plate is better than a stiff backing plate.

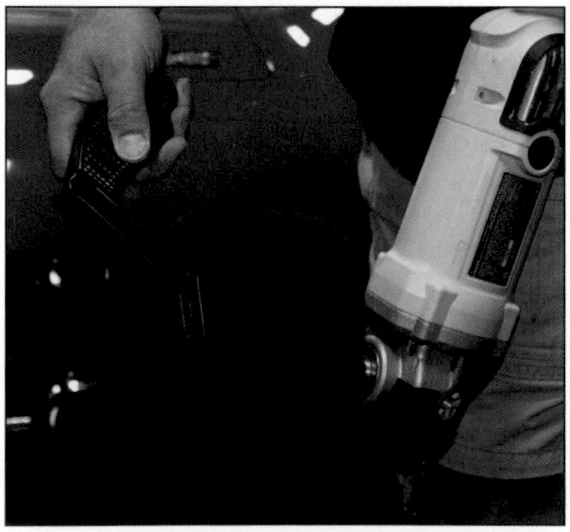

Step 5: Clean your pad before and during the process
Use a nylon Pad Conditioning Brush to ensure the face of the pad is clean before you start and then clean all residues off the face of the pad after buffing each application of polish. You cannot skip a single cleaning step or you're not jewelling.

Step 6: Use a low RPMs
This to me is key, and this is why I really like the new generation of rotary buffers with their ability to rotate pads at 600 RPMs and, in the case of Flex PE14-2-150, even lower. You don't need high RPMs and you don't want high RPMs as this increases the chance for trace holograms to be imparted back into the finish since aggressiveness increases with speed. I personally use either the Flex PE14-2-150 or the DeWalt DWP-849X for jewelling paint. I generally use the speed setting of 600 RPM.

Step 7: Light pressure then reduce to less than the weight of the machine
Start out using light pressure. The Flex PE14 weighs about 5 pounds and both the DeWalt and the Makita weigh in around 6.5 pounds. If you're using the DeWalt or the Makita you won't have to use too much more pressure than the weight of the machine.

Big Picture Buffing
Buff out large sections at a time making your pass over the entire section ending your passes at hard lines like trim or the edge of panel. Try not to stop your pad in the middle of a panel. Make 3-4 passes with a little more than the weight of the machine and then make 2-3 passes with less pressure. You shouldn't be applying much pressure beyond the weight of the machine for the last 2-3 passes.

Do it again...
What I normally do is buff a section using the above procedure and then CAREFULLY wipe off all polishing residues. Clean the face and side of my pad then re-apply fresh product and then do it again. This time, I use just enough weight to maintain soft pressure between the face of the pad and the paint.

■ Entire Car or Key Panels & Gloss Points

Continue these steps to the rest of the car or reserve this step just for the key focal points for the body style you're buffing out. Every body style has its key curves and shapes that make the body style both unique to the marque and beautiful or even sexy to car enthusiasts. If the paint looks awesome after the second step of machine polishing with a foam pad to remove any swirls or haze, then you can cut down your time investment and still reap the reward of a finish that looks dripping wet by jewelling only the key panels and gloss points.

Key Panels = Horizontal panels like hoods that most people look at and inspect when viewing the car.

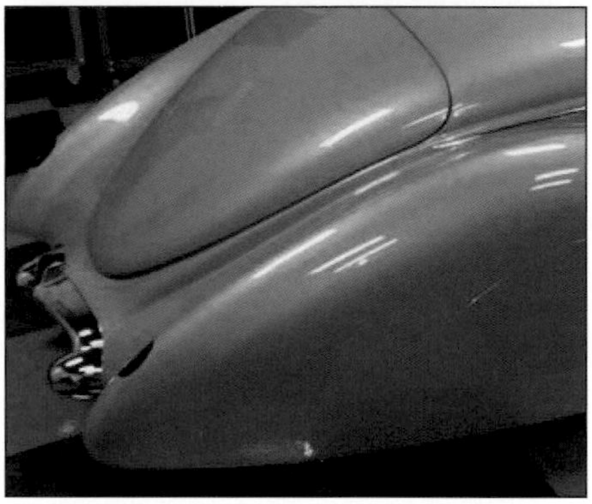

Gloss Points = Any high point whether it's a soft curve or a hard panels.

■ Finishing out using a DA Polisher

As an option, instead of jewelling the paint with a rotary buffer you can use a dual action polisher to ensure no holograms are being left behind, masked by the polishing oils.

In the chapter on using a DA Polisher, see these sections,

- *The Polishing or Minor Correction Step*
- *How To Jewel Paint Using a DA Polisher*

This would include,
- Porter Cable 7424XP
- Griot's Garage DA Polisher
- Meguiar's G110v2, the

- Shurhold DA Polisher, the
- Cyclo Polisher or the
- Flex 3401
- Makita BO6040

Apply Last Step Product
After you finish with your last machine polishing step, at this point you would apply either a non-cleaning finishing wax, a non-cleaning synthetic paint sealant or coating.

■ Marine & RV Detailing with Rotary Buffers

Because of their size and massive surface areas, most detailers that offer Marine & RV detailing will tend to use one-step cleaner/waxes. Think about it, who in their right mind would want to buff out a 37' Grady White or a 40' Motorhome and go around it three times? (Compounding, Polishing & Waxing).

No Market
Most owners of large things like boats and RVs also don't understand the entire swirl issue involved with using a rotary buffer as well as how much time is involved in doing the job right. So they won't pay to have the job done right and thus the market accommodates them by doing production work which means using one-step cleaner/waxes with rotary buffers.

For really oxidized boats and RVs, detailers will do two steps, but this usually means using a heavy cut compound to remove the oxidization followed by a one-step cleaner/wax to restore gloss, shine and to add protection from the elements.

The good news is most boats are white and the majority of the hull is in the water or below eyesight level so it's not an issue like swirled out cars. RV's are another story; hack detailers swirling out clearcoated RVs is a real problem but the problem starts with the market first. Boat and RV owners are not educated on what's involved and thus not willing to pay to have the job done right the first time.

The Flex Option
The Flex 3401 offers a lot of power but not as much as a rotary buffer. It's definitely close and makes a good option for Boats & RVs that are not in bad or neglected condition. For this type of work a one-step cleaner/wax and a soft foam polishing pad will do a great job while leaving a hologram-free finish.

■ The 10 @ 10 Technique for picking up a bead of product

The 10 @ 10 Technique for picking up a bead of product is a technique you can use to pick up your bead of product on the fly with your rotary buffer in a way that pulls the product under and into the face of the buffing pad instead of splattering it all over the place. Just to note, the term bead in detailing talk means a line or strip of product.

Caveman Technique
Some people take their pad and simply spread their product out over the paint with the buffer off and then after spreading it out turn the buffer on and start buffing. This works but it can also throw splatter all over the place. The 10 @ 10 Technique not only works better but it has a cool factor to it that shows anyone watching that you know how to pick up a bead of product like a Pro.

How to use the 10 @ 10 Technique
While holding the rotary buffer in your hands, look at the back of the buffing pad and pretend it's clock. The top is 12:00 O'clock and going clockwise you have the 1, 2, 3, etc. positions on the buffing pad that would correlate with a clock.

What you want to do is bring the rotary buffer up to speed and then lock the trigger into place so you don't have to hold it in the entire time you're buffing. Next, place the buffing pad just in front of your bead of product at the 10 O'clock position. The pad should be spinning but not in contact with the paint.

Lightly touch the buffing pad down so the 3 O'clock position is just making contact with the paint and the 10 O'clock position is raised off the paint about 10 degrees. Now run the buffing pad over the bead of product from right to left drawing the bead in at the 10 O'clock position. (not the 9 O'clock or 11 O'clock posting but the 10 O'clock position).

Since the pad is rotating clockwise, the bead of product will be pulled into and under the pad instead of being thrown away from the pad as splatter.

■ Handles or No Handles

Most rotary buffers come with either what's called a stick handle or a hoop handle. For some reason people think the hoop handle looks cool.

Here's my two cents…

Hoop Handle
The further you move your grip away from the rotary buffer the more you will tax your muscles to control it. That's the facts Jack. Also, if you want to remove the hoop handle to get the body or head of the rotary buffer into a tight area you will need to have the appropriate wrench with you; this is usually a Hex Head Wrench. So lose the hoop hand unless you're just trying to look cool.

Stick Handle
Stick handles give you the option of being able to quickly and easily move the handle from one side to the other without the use of any tools. The stick handle keeps your hand closer to the head of the rotary buffer and with your other hand holding the handle at the back of the tool. This gives you excellent control and leverage over the tool.

No Handle
My personal preference for most buffing work is to use no handle at all

and instead grip the head of the rotary buffer with one hand and hold the rear handle with the other hand. By doing this I'm able to apply pressure directly downward on top of the buffing head and this helps to keep the pad flat to the surface. This option is less tiring to your forearm muscles. The good news is both Flex and DeWALT have figured this is a feature us detailers like and include it in the design of their rotary polishers.

■ Surgical Buffing

When I say surgical buffing I mean extremely accurate or precise. This describes what is needed when buffing tight areas, working on thin panels or buffing around delicate things like pinstripes, lettering, emblems, trim or script. When Doctors do complicated surgeries they use small, lightweight precise instruments like scalpels. The focus needs to be on the procedure and not manhandling a machete.

Compact Size & Lightweight
In order to do surgical buffing, it helps a LOT to have a lightweight compact rotary buffer like the Flex PE14-2-150. A smaller, more compact buffer means that you don't have to support the weight of a full size rotary buffer while trying to guide the buffing pad into small, complicated areas. The compact size means you don't have a large buffing head or body blocking your view or getting in the way of where you need to get your buffer.

Small pads, Extensions & Flexible Backing Plates
In order to do surgical buffing you need a small, lightweight polisher along with small backing plates and pads. You need the small pads to reduce the size of your footprint; that means having a pad that is smaller than the area you're trying to buff. You need an extension to extend the pad away from the body of the tool so the polisher won't block your view of the area being buffed. You'll want a flexible backing plate to provide an interface between the extension and the pad as this enables you to more effectively buff on any contoured surface.

■ Buffing off an edge

This is kind of tricky to type about but here goes. First it's always a good best practice to not buff directly on top of an edge. This is because paint tends to be thinner on high points as it flows downward due to gravity plus there's always the possibility that some other detailer has buffed the car out before you and doesn't practice the best practice.

It's also a good best practice to hold the pad flat to the surface and not hold the pad at an angle so you're only using a portion of the pad on edge. That said, sooner or later all panels come to an end at the end of the panel is an edge. Your goal is to buff the paint up to the edge but not buff with firm pressure directly on top of the edge.

When your rotary buffer is turned on and you're looking down on the back of the buffing pad and backing plate, the pad spins in a clockwise rotation. You need to understand the relationship between the direction the buffing pad is rotating and the way you run the pad next to an edge.

You want the pad touching down in a way that the pad is rotating over and off the edge, not rotating into the edge. See the pictures below as I think they will do a better job of showing you what to do and what not to do. ■

Right Technique – Pad held in a way that it rotates off the edge

Wrong Technique – Pad held so that it rotates into the edge

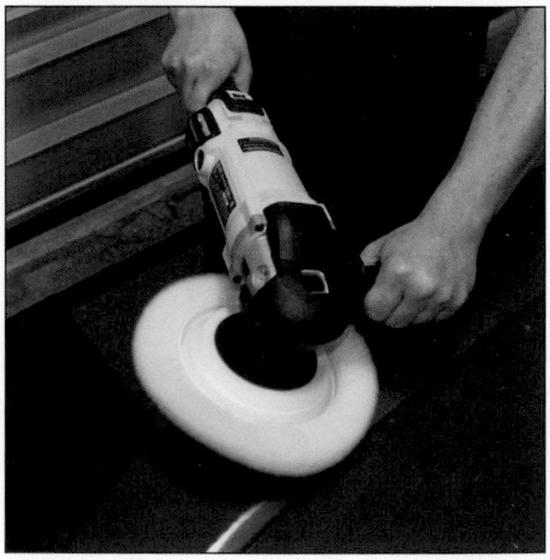

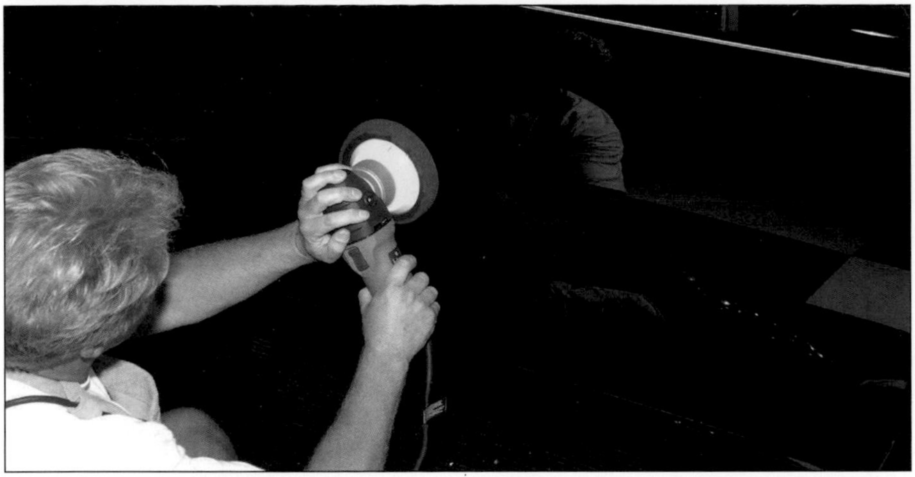

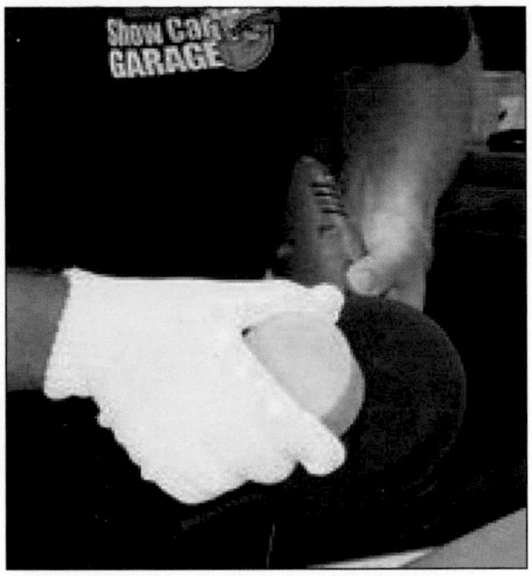

After you've performed any necessary machine polishing steps, it's time to protect the paint by sealing with your choice of a wax, synthetic sealant or coating.

Most people wax their cars for one of two reasons (and usually both).

1. Add a layer of protection
2. Make the paint look good

A quality wax, sealant or coating will do both. Let's take a look at both of these reasons for waxing your car.

1. Add a layer of protection
Modern paint technology is actually very durable and resistant to corrosion and degradation under normal conditions. That said, most people like the idea of applying an additional coating over the paint to provide an extra measure of protection. This coating is considered a sacrificial barrier coating.

Sacrificial Barrier Coating
The primary purpose of a wax or sealant is to act as a sacrificial barrier coating over the surface of your car's paint. Any time anything comes into contact with your car's paint, before it can cause any damage to the paint it first has to get past the layer of wax or paint sealant. When your car's paint is under attack, the layer of wax or paint sealant sacrifices itself. The cost of a new paint job can run into the thousands of dollars, so most people agree that regularly applying a coat of wax is cost-effective preventative maintenance.

In This Section:

- How To Apply Paste Waxes
- How To Apply Liquid Waxes - Kissing The Finish
- How To Apply Cleaner Waxes
- How To Remove Dried Wax
- How To Do The Swipe Test
- The Final Wipe Technique

2. Make the paint look good
Besides adding a layer of protection to the paint, most people like to wax or seal their car's paint to make it look good. Nothing makes your car look better than a fresh coat of wax, especially if the paint is in good to excellent condition to start with. Besides restoring that glossy, factory new look, many people find spending an afternoon washing and waxing their pride and joy a relaxing escape from our hectic, fast-paced world.

■ How To Apply Paste Waxes

Just as the DA polisher does a better job of removing swirls and scratches as compared to working by hand, it also does a better job of applying a well-worked, thin uniform layer of paste wax.

The tricky part
The trick is getting the paste wax onto the pad. Here are several ways to do this:

Physically remove the entire block of paste wax out of the can or jar

This works best with paste waxes that come in plastic jars around 4" in diameter. The wax will stay together and you can easily grip it in your palm.

Microfiber glove
This really works best if you have a clean, microfiber glove on one of your hands. This will enable you to grip the slippery block of wax that slides out of the jar. It will also prevent you from dropping it on the floor, contaminating it or getting wax on your skin.

Knock knock...
To get the wax out of the jar, you need to carefully knock it out. Hold the jar upside down and knock it firmly against your hand with the microfiber glove on it. Sometimes, it helps to lightly heat the outside of the plastic jar with something like a blow dryer as this will loosen the bond and grip created by surface tension when the wax was originally poured into the jar.

After you get the wax out of the jar, you can apply it to the face of your foam finishing pad in two ways:

- **Using your hand.** Simply swipe the wax a few times across the face of a foam finishing pad.

- **Use the power of the polisher.** While holding the block of wax against the face of the pad, blip the on/off button of the polisher for a couple of short bursts. The oscillating/rotating action will quickly transfer wax onto the face of the pad.

After you distribute some wax onto the face of the pad using one of the above techniques, you then want to carefully place the block of wax aside. Either place it back into the jar, or with the lid upside down, rest it inside the lid.

Applying wax using either of the above methods also primes the face of the foam pad so that it is lubricated with wax when you turn on the polisher.

When starting with a clean, dry pad, you'll initially use a little more product. After that, you'll find it takes very little to re-dampen your foam finishing pad with wax to continue working around the car.

Place the face of the pad into the can or jar
If you're using a paste wax in a wide mouth can, you can use a foam finishing pad that's small enough to place inside the can. Simply flip the on/off switch for a couple of short bursts and this will quickly transfer wax onto the face of the foam pad. The benefit to this method is you don't have to remove the wax from the can and it's very fast and easy to do.

Scoop some wax out of the can or jar
This is another option that works just as well. Simply scoop some wax out of the jar or can and then spread it onto the face of the pad as you would use a knife to spread peanut butter over bread. With soft paste waxes this is pretty easy, but it is a little more difficult to do with a hard paste wax.

A lot of people use a handy little tool that's already nearby and that's the flat handle of the backing plate wrench that came with your polisher. It's flat like a butter knife and actually works really well. Just make sure to clean it before sticking it into the can of wax.

Step By Step Directions

After you get wax onto the face of the foam finishing pad, simply apply the wax in the same manner as explained in the chapter for using a liquid wax.

For more information:
liquid wax section

How To Apply Liquid Waxes With A DA Polisher - Kissing The Finish

"Kissing the finish" is a technique you can use to apply a liquid wax which helps keep the wax spreading out over the paint instead of loading up inside your pad. I use this technique when applying any liquid wax or paint sealant. To kiss the finish, touch the face of the foam pad (with wax on it) onto your panel at an angle, thus depositing only a portion of the wax from the pad to one area of the paint. The effect is to have a bunch of dabs of wax on the paint deposited from the face of the pad. Your car's panel will look like it has spots, arcs or lines of product on it.

Step By Step Directions

First, shake shake shake
Always shake liquid car care products thoroughly before applying.

Prime your pad
Next, apply some product onto the face of the pad. Then, using your clean finger, spread the product so the entire face of the pad is dampened with product.

Apply working product
Apply more product to the face of the

pad. For this, I place a circle of product around the outside edge of the buffing pad.

Kiss the finish
Next, touch the edge of the face of the foam pad and deposit some wax to a portion of the panel you're working on. Continue doing this over an entire panel until you've deposited what looks like little arcs or smiles of product onto the paint. After you've kissed the finish in a few places, take what's left and place the face of the foam pad against the paint. Then, turn the polisher on, making passes overlapping by about 50%.

On this El Camino, I can easily reach and work on half of the hood at one time. I used enough wax to coat over half of it and moved the pad over each square inch at least 2 to 3 times to sufficiently work the wax over and into the paint.

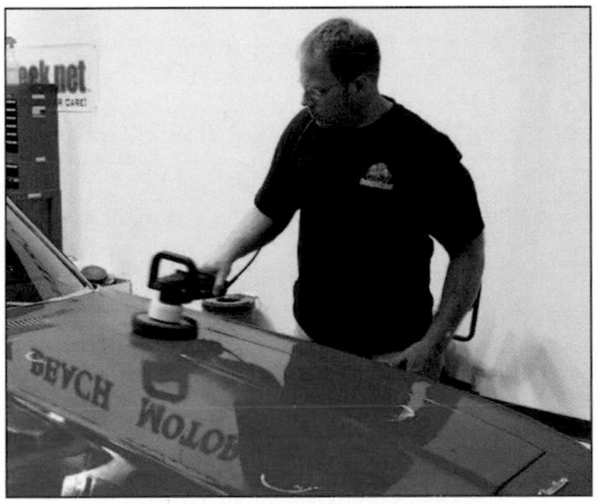

As I came up to a dab of wax where I kissed the finish with my pad, I tilted the polisher, lifting the leading edge of the pad but maintaining constant contact with the trailing edge. I then ran the pad over the dab of wax and then immediately laid the pad flat again to work new territory with this new dab of wax.

Tilt the polisher a little to lift the leading edge of the pad.

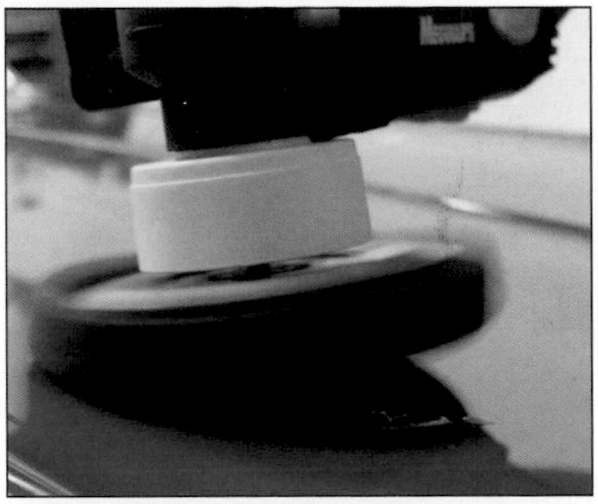

Move the tilted leading edge over the wax to draw and trap the wax between the paint and the pad.

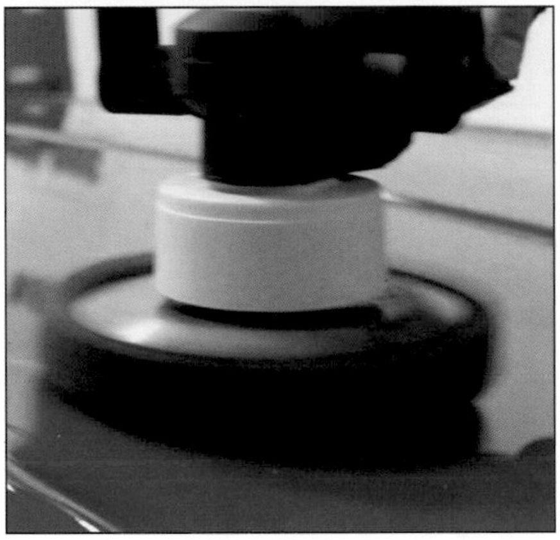

Lay the pad flat and begin working the wax over the paint.

Keep one edge (the trailing edge of the pad) in contact with the paint so it doesn't quickly speed up and throw splatter or fling the pad off the backing plate. Then, move the raised side of the pad quickly over the dab of wax or sealant and quickly lay the pad down flat and continue spreading the product. This should be one seamless, flowing motion.

- **Use a slow to medium arm speed**
  When applying a wax, your goal is to spread out a thin layer of product and also to work the wax over and into the paint. This is best done using a slow to medium arm speed using overlapping motions. Overlap your passes by about 50% and go over each square inch of each panel 2 to 3 times.

- **No limits for work size area** - Unlike removing swirls, you can work a section as far as you can reach as long as you have ample product to spread out.

- **Apply a thin layer** - No matter how you apply your waxes, paint sealants, or coatings, the goal is to always apply a thin layer over the paint. Thick layers of product simply waste money and make wipe-off more difficult.

- **How thin is thin?** - It's common for someone to ask, "How thin is thin?" or, "What does a thin coating look like?"

Both of these are great questions! A thin coating should look like a thin film covering the surface. Because a thin layer is hard to see with your eyes, it's also hard to capture with a camera. But, (shown on page 132) are a few pictures to hopefully give you an idea of what a thin coating looks like.

Apply to the entire car at once
Assuming you have already prepped the paint for application of wax, go ahead and apply your choice of wax or paint sealant to the entire car at one time.

Follow the manufacturer's directions
Manufacturers know their product formulas best, so take a moment to read the directions for application and removal on the label and then follow them as recommended.

■ How To Apply Cleaner Waxes

First, choose the best foam pad for the condition of the paint
A polishing pad, together with the cleaners and abrasives, will offer the right balance of cleaning ability while

A thin coating should look like a thin film covering the surface.

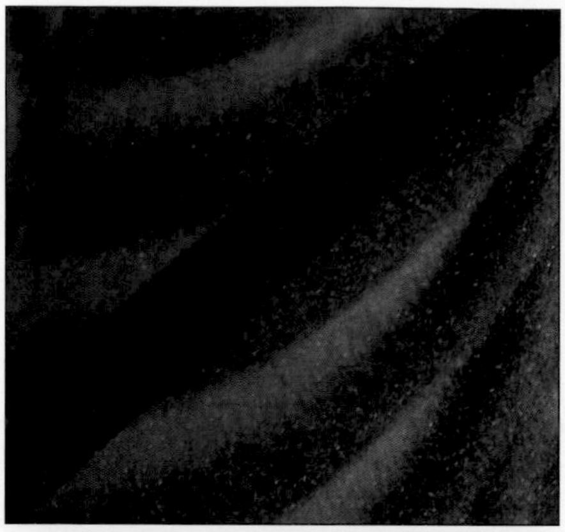

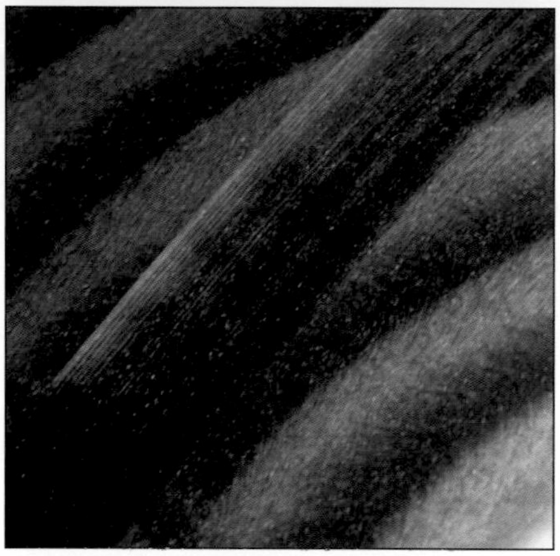

finishing out to a clear, high gloss. If the paint you're working on is in severely neglected condition, you'll have more correction ability using a foam cutting pad, but you do risk leaving some micromarring. Test first and match the right pad to the condition of the paint and the cleaner wax you choose to use.

Step By Step Directions

The key to getting great results on a neglected finish using only a one-step cleaner wax comes down to five techniques or steps:

Speed setting = 5 to 6 on all DA polishers
Be sure to mark your backing plates - you want to see the pad rotating at all times.

1. Use the product heavy or wet
It's only when you're applying finishing waxes and paint sealants that you only use a small amount of wax in order to lay down a thin, uniform coating. When using a cleaner wax by machine, it's just the opposite - you want plenty of cleaning agents and lubrication.

2. Use the section pass technique - only work small sections at a time
Just like doing any correction work with a compound or medium polish, the worse the condition of the paint, the smaller the area you want to work. The better the condition of the paint, the larger the area you can work. However, you normally don't want to go any larger than 2' x 2'. Smaller sections tend to be better as you're focusing more cleaning ability to a smaller section of paint.

3. Overlap your section passes
When starting a new section, be sure to overlap into the previous section for a uniform appearance after final wipe off of the wax residue.

4. Clean your pad on the fly often or switch to a clean, dry pad
If you don't clean your pad often or switch to a clean, dry pad, the residue build-up will interfere with the cleaning agents.

5. Allow the wax to dry before removing
Most cleaner/waxes are also drying waxes, which means you want to use the wet buffing technique. Leave a uniform layer of product on each section you buff so that you end up with an even coating of wax over the entire vehicle. Be sure to read the label for specific instructions from the manufacturer.

How To Do The Swipe Test

To perform the swipe test, take your clean finger and swipe it briskly across a waxed finish. If the paint where you swipe is clear, without any smeary wax left behind, then this is an accurate indicator that the wax is dry and ready to wipe off. If the residue smears and streaks, it has not fully cured and needs more time to set up. If the swipe test shows the wax is still wet, wait a little longer until the paint swipes clear.

How To Remove Dried Wax

There are two ways to remove wax from your car's paint - the normal way (by hand) and by machine.

Benefits to machine removal of wax
Removing wax by machine is personal preference; some people like this technique while others prefer to simply wipe waxes and paint sealants by hand.

Equal pressure
The technique of using a microfiber bonnet over a foam cutting pad provides equal pressure over the entire face of the pad. This removes any pressure points created by your fingertips when wiping off by hand.

Physical advantage
For some people, letting the machine do the work might be a physical advantage versus using their hands, arms and shoulders to wipe the wax off.

- Waxes that dry Removing wax by machine works best if you're using a wax that is supposed to dry first before removing. Be aware that some are formulated to be wipe-on, wipe-off waxes and these are best removed by hand.

- Thin coats Removing dried wax by machine works best when a thin coat is applied.

Products Needed

- **Reversible microfiber bonnets** Microfiber bonnets are almost always reversible. You can use one side until it loads up with dried wax and then remove it, turn it inside out, give it a shake and put back onto your buffing pad. Later, I'll show you my technique for cleaning your bonnet on the fly. Often times, using this technique, you can remove all the wax from an average sized vehicle with just one bonnet.

- **Clean, dry pads for use under the bonnet** - My personal preference has always been to use a firm foam pad because it provides a level of cushion due to the nature of the foam cell wall structure. The cushion offered by foam enables the pad to conform to curves and body lines better than a lambswool pad with a microfiber bonnet over it.

Removing the wax
It doesn't matter where you start, but the normal protocol is to start where you first applied wax and then follow your path of travel. Another way is to start at the top and work your way down. As long as the wax is dry, it's not a huge issue where you start on the various body panels.

Speed setting
Use the high speed setting to remove dried wax. I tend to use the 6 speed setting because you really want all the power the tool has to offer when trying to convince dried wax to give up its grip on the paint.

Downward pressure
You want to use firm, downward pressure when removing the wax. You want the nap of the microfiber slicing into the coating of wax and breaking it up, which cannot be accomplished with only light pressure.

■ A technique for moving from one panel to another panel without turning the polisher off

At the same time you lift the pad off the surface, quickly place your clean hand against the face of the bonnet and keep it there until you're ready to place it against the next panel.

This is safe to do and having the firm pressure of your hand against the pad will keep it from flying off the polisher.

■ A technique for cleaning your bonnet on the fly

As you work your way around the car removing dried wax or paint sealant, you will get a build-up of dried wax residue on the face of the microfiber bonnet.

While you have the option to remove the bonnet and reverse it, I prefer cleaning on the fly. To do this, lift the pad from the paint while holding your fingernails against the bonnet. Apply enough pressure to keep the pad from flying off the polisher but not so much that it stops rotating. This is usually effective enough to remove any dried wax residue from the working face of the microfiber bonnet.

Variation of the bonnet - Just use a microfiber towel
Some people will simply place a clean, dry microfiber towel flat onto the paint and then place a clean, dry buffing pad against the microfiber to remove wax. I'm not a big fan of this method because the microfiber towel can easily work its way out from under the pad, especially if you try this on a vertical panel.

Products for removing wax by machine

Bonnets
- Indigo 6 Inch Microfiber Bonnets 2 pack
- All Bonnets on Autogeek.net

Small, firm dense foam buffing pads
- Lake Country Hydro-Tech 5 1/2" Cyan Cutting Pad

- 5 1/2" Lake Country Flat Yellow Cutting Pad
- 5 1/2" Lake country Flat Orange Light Cutting Pad
- 5 1/2" Lake Country CCS Yellow Cutting Pad
- 5 1/2" Lake country CCS Orange Light Cutting Pad
- 6" Lake Country Purple Kompressor Pad
- 6" Lake Country Orange Kompressor Pad

Small, firm lambswool pads

- 6" Lake Country Lambswool Leveling Pad

The Final Wipe Technique

Note: *The final wiping technique is not for the initial wiping off of a glaze, wax or paint sealant, but instead is to be used after the majority of product has already been removed and now all you're doing is giving the finish a final wipe.*

The Final Wipe
After all the work is done, you usually need to give the paint a final wipe-down. This final wipe is to ensure you didn't miss any spots and to remove any trace residues from the paint.

The technique - slow down
The technique is to wipe the paint down s-l-o-w-l-y using your best, premium quality microfiber polishing towel with gentle, even pressure.

Show car quality work demands focusing on the task at hand and using your best skills and tools to reach the goal of a flawless show car finish. Rushing at the very end doesn't make sense and if you instill swirls and scratches, you're working backwards in the process. Simply put, sometimes you have to slow down to speed up. Using a slow wiping motion will be more effective at removing all microscopic trace residues from the paint. This enables you to reach your goal safely and effectively. ■

I've seen more changes and improvements in the tools, pads and products used in the car detailing and body shop industries in the last few years than over my entire lifetime. Like my good friend and professional detailer Joe Fernandez once said,

"It used to be you actually had to have some experience, skill and talent to create a show car finish"

What Joe meant by that, and I fully agree, is that with today's tools, pads and especially compounds and polishes, just about anyone can turn out professional quality, show car results the very first time they machine polish paint. And that's a big deal because paints are thin and there's not much room for a second chance.

That leads me into the topic of sealing the paint to protect it. You can call it waxing your car or whatever else you like but when you apply a layer of protection, no matter what it is, what you are in effect doing is sealing the paint with a sacrificial barrier coating to protect it.

In This Section:

- Carnauba Car Waxes
- Synthetic Paint Sealants
- Paint Coatings

There are two reasons to seal and protect the paint,

1. Make the paint look beautiful
2. Protect it from attack and deterioration

It's really that simple. If you're reading this book then you fit the description I wrote earlier in the introduction where I said:

Different strokes for different folks
Some of you may look at your car merely as a means of transportation. You are mostly interested in learning how to best protect your investment. Some of you may look at your car as an extension of your personality; you see it as an escape from the daily grind of living in a complicated world. You have a passion for polishing paint and you take it as serious as a heart attack.

Well, people that look at their car as transportation predominantly want to protect it. People that look at their car as an extension of their personality want to both protect it and make it look beautiful. So let's take a look at your options when it comes to sealing the paint.

In an effort to help standardize terms used in the detailing industry, now that paint coatings are mainstream, there are three general categories in the paint protection category.

1. Carnauba Car Waxes
2. Synthetic Paint Sealants
3. Paint Coatings

Car Waxes
Generally defined as any product that contains natural or synthetic waxy type ingredients that are intended to protect the paint and/or add beauty to the paint. These types of traditional waxes will wear off under normal wear-n-tear, repeated washings and exposure to the environment. While the may not be the longest lasting or best protecting options, a premium quality wax will create a beautiful show car finish. For some of us, when working on our pride and joy, the act of applying and removing a traditional Carnauba Finishing Wax is rewarding in and of itself. It can also be a way to escape the rat race if only for a few hours.

Synthetic Paint Sealants
These are generally defined as any protection product that contains man-made or synthetic ingredients that are intended to protect the paint and/or add beauty to the paint. Synthetic paint sealants are known for lasting longer and protecting better than traditional car waxes. I believe this is true as it relates to a reputable, brand name synthetic paint sealant because from experience, you can trust a qualified chemist to manufacture a product that will indeed bond better, protect better and last longer than the traditional

type of car wax. Like car waxes however, synthetic paint sealants will wear off through normal wear-n-tear, repeated washings and exposure to the environment.

Paint Coatings
Generally defined as any paint protection product that contains man-made or synthetic protection ingredients that are intended to permanently bond to the paint to both provide a barrier-coating of protection as well as create a clear, high gloss finish. The products available in this category are considered permanent coatings because like your car's paint, they cannot be removed unless you purposefully remove them or you purposefully neglect them.

Definition of permanent in the context of sealing paint
In the context that we refer to coating as permanent it means that once the coating is properly applied and allowed to cure and set-up, it will not come off under normal circumstances or via normal wear-n-tear such as careful washing. So in this context, a coating is permanent in the same manner your car's paint is permanent.

The paint on your car is not going to come off unless you abrade it, chemically dissolve it or through some other mechanical means, purposefully remove it. In this same way, legitimate paint coatings are not going to come off unless you abrade it, chemically dissolve it or through some other mechanical means, purposefully remove it.

Traditional car waxes and paint sealants will wear off under normal use circumstances or via normal wear-n-tear such as careful washing. So in the context of and in comparison with traditional car waxes and paint sealants, paint coatings are permanent.

Is one better than the other?

Hey great question. Is Coke better than Pepsi? Is a Ford better than a Chevy? It all comes down to personal preference. Carnauba Car Waxes and Synthetic Paint Sealants are by far easier and less complicated to use. You can also remove them easily and switch to something new or add a fresh coat. Not so with coatings. Once the coating is on the paint it's on there to stay. Sure you can remove it but for the most part that means compounding the coating off.

The best way to get more information on any of these categories of products is to become a member of the AutogeekOnline.net discussion forum.

Recommendations
Below you'll find some simple suggestions for some of the more popular products when it comes to performance. Keep in mind the most important aspect of creating a show car finish isn't the wax, sealant or coating, it's the prep work. That is to remove as many of the above and below surface defects as possible before applying your choice of LSP or Last Step Product.

Non-cleaning products
These recommendations are limited to products that contain no cleaners or ingredients intended to clean the surface. If you have already prepped the finish by removing the above surface defects, removing the below surface defects and then polished to a high gloss and you don't want to or need to use a product that cleans as this is working backwards in the process. The goal of creating a show car finish is to always be working forward in the process. Cleaner/Waxes are great products and I'm a huge fan of quality cleaner/waxes but if you're doing a multiple-step process then you want to use a dedicated, non-cleaning product for your last step.

■ Carnauba Car Waxes

Pinnacle Souverän™ Carnauba Paste Wax

This wax is a true joy to work with as it applies easily, wipes off immediately so there is no need to let it dry and it leaves a deep wet shine. I especially like to recommend this product to people with little to no talent when it comes to "touching" their own car's paint because you really can't make a mistake with it since you don't

need to let it dry. Simply apply a thin application by hand or machine and then gently wipe it off using premium quality microfiber towels. Pinnacle Souverän™ Carnauba Paste uses genuine Brazilian Number 1 Carnauba Wax that is further refined into white Ivory Carnauba Wax. It has a buttery smooth texture both in the jar and during application. Because you only apply a thin coat you can easily get 30 to 35 coats per jar. It doesn't need to dry, simply wipe on and then wipe off. It won't leave white stains on black plastic or rubber. It contains no petroleum distillates or cleaners; it is a true show car wax.

Meguiar's M26 Hi Tech Yellow Wax
- *Paste*
- *Liquid*

This wax has been around for over 30 years with continual formula updates to keep it ever up to date with current technology. It's incredibly easy to apply and after allowing it to dry till it swipes clear, it's also incredibly easy to remove - as long as you apply a thin application like you're supposed to do with all finishing waxes. A chemist at Meguiar's once told me M26 is unique because it has the ability to bend light into the paint create a deeper, more clear finish.

Optimum Car Wax

While the name on the label states it's a wax and most people think of a paste wax when they think of a Carnauba Wax, this is actually a thin, spray-on liquid Carnauba wax. OCW contains both Carnauba Wax for gloss and protection but it also contains patented UV inhibitors that migrate into the paint. These are the same type of UV inhibitors used in modern clear coat paint formulas and Dr. David Ghodoussi is a chemist that has worked for many of the major paint manufactures like DuPont, PPG and Sherwin-Williams to create clear coat paint technology. Dr. G as he's referred to on the forums told me that the only way to transfer the UV inhibitors to the paint was via a thin, sprayable liquid. I'm not a chemist and have no desire to become one and I trust Dr. David Ghodoussi so I take his word for it. Besides being the only wax I know of that has patented UV inhibitors it's the only wax I know of that has been independently tested according to ASTM standards and proven to reduce fading and reduction in gloss under controlled testing.

One thing I really like about Optimum Car Wax is you can use it like a spray detailer, that is, you can mist a light coating onto a section of paint, spread around and then buff off to a dry, hard shine. That means most people can use this product without any issues.

Dodo Juice Carnauba Waxes

My good friends PJ and Dom, the Dodo Juice Boys as I like to call them, have really brought the fun back into paste waxes. And to me, having fun waxing your car after all the prep work has been done is the best part. They offer countless varieties with both colorful names and fanciful colors. They take pride in using only the finest ingredients and besides making a complete line of car care products they are also true "car guys" and that's important to me. So if you haven't checked out Dodo Juice Carnauba Waxes, do it.

Mothers California Gold Pure Carnauba Paste Wax

Here's a classic Brazilian Carnauba Paste Wax that has a long-time, strong loyal following for a reason, it works. By that I mean it really creates a deep, warm glossy finish just like you dream about for your car's finish. Besides offering a great Carnauba shine, one of the things I really think Mothers got right was the size of the can for the paste version. Anyone that knows me knows I like to do everything by machine including applying paste waxes and the California Gold Pure Carnauba Paste Wax is large enough you can fit a 5.5" Lake Country Flat Pad into the can and then flip the on/off switch of your DA Polisher to put a little wax on your pad.

■ Synthetic Paint Sealants

Wolfgang Deep Gloss Paint Sealant 3.0

This is what's referred to as a forum favorite with a strong and loyal following because it really does create a deep gloss and a long lasting super slick finish. The appearance it leaves is similar to the gloss and depth of a traditional Carnauba Paste Wax but with the longevity provided by German polymer technology. This synthetic paint sealant is water-based and oxygen activated and to get the maximum performance you need to allow a 12 hour window of time to pass before allowing the finish to get wet to ensure the polymers fully cure and bond to the paint.

#111 Duragloss Clear Coat Polish

Although the name on the label reads like it's an abrasive polish, this is just the way Duragloss names their paint sealants. I'm not sure what they put in here to make it last so long but it's truly a long lasting paint sealant. If water beading is any indication of longevity, then this product ranks at the top. Because it has no abrasives or cleaning agents, it should only be applied to a perfectly prepared finish. The Duragloss company recommends using their #601 Polish Bonding Agent as a prep product to maximize the bonding of the #111 Clear Coat Polish for maximum performance. The application directions say to apply the #601 first and to leave this product on the surface and then apply the #111 directly over it.

Prima Epic Synthetic Wax

This is a really nice synthetic paint sealant that leaves a very slick surface with a wet, glassy look. The product name uses the word "wax" to describe the product but I've been assured by the people at Prima that this is an all-synthetic paint sealant. The manufacturer recommends allowing this to fully dry before removing so use the Swipe Test to check. The Prima company is still somewhat of a sleeper outside of the forum world so if you're looking to try a really nice synthetic paint sealant give Epic a try, and also check out the other products in their line.

Detailer's Poli-Coat Paint Sealant

This is a product that to me is really a good value for your money. It doesn't cost a lot but it sure does last a long time. It contains a bonding agent that aids the protection ingredients to form a strong bond to the paint. It offers all the key features people look for in a synthetic paint sealant. I like to recommend this product to people that just want a straight-forward quality paint sealant that will provide a great shine and durable protection for their daily driver.

Menzerna Power Lock Polymer Sealant

The one thing I really like about this product is how fast it dries and how easy it wipes-off. If you apply a thin coating Power Lock dries fast and wipes off effortlessly to streak-free, super slick shine. Another thing I've noticed about it is consistent performance, that is, it always works great on all paints systems in a wide range of temperatures and humidity. A great show car finish or a staple for production detailing.

Paint Coatings

Gtechniq

Now this company really has some interesting products and there's no way I can even begin to share my reaction the first time I used both the C1 Crystal Lacquer and EXO.

C1 Crystal Lacquer

This is a nano quartz based coating that when applied to the surface becomes a functional part of the surface, meaning its going to last a long time. It makes the surface highly repellent so nothing will bond to it. C1 forms a sub micron crystalline film over the surface that is extremely hard and this makes the surface more scratch and mar resistant. C1 is an excellent option for soft paints. The surface must be polished to perfection and then chemically stripped of any oils or substances that could hinder the C1 from bonding to the surface. To do this, you can use a number of different solvents also used in the body shop industry, but Gtechniq makes this process simple and fool-proof with their own Panel Wipe. After stripping the surface with Panel Wipe, simply apply the C1 Crystal Lacquer.

Application is simple: apply using a small applicator pad to a panel at a time. Immediately after application re-wipe the surface with a clean microfiber towel to smooth out the coating and to remove any excess product. You need to keep the lid on the bottle when not in use as exposure to oxygen will cause the product to harden. Full cure happens after 12 hours.

Video & Pictures - Gtechniq Makeover - 2012 Scion tC 7.0

EXO Ultra Durable Hybrid Coating

This coating is a little bit different than the C1 Crystal Lacquer in that it uses inorganic-organic hybrid materials. The basecoat, the part that will bond to your car's pant is an inorganic hybrid of quartz; the top portion is organic and provides a high gloss, slick feel and appearance. It offers high water and dirt repellency for up to 2 years through a permanent covalent bond to the paint or other surfaces including gel coat, fabric, metal, stone, glass, ceramic and plastic. EXO comes in an aerosol form because the active ingredients cannot be exposed to air or they will harden, so an inert gas is used to suspend and transport the coating until use. The really cool thing about this product is how easy it is to use. Like C1 Crystal Lacquer you first have to perfectly prepare the surface and then chemically strip paint using the Panel Wipe. Then spray EXO onto a soft, flat weave microfiber towel and apply over a panel and then immediately wipe the panel to a high gloss shine.

Video & Pictures: 1965 Fastback Mustang - Gtechniq EXO Show Car Makeover

CarPro Cquartz Ceramic Quartz Paint Protection

CarPro is the company that makes Iron X, the iron remover I shared in the section on washing your car and cleaning your wheels to remove embedded iron particles on the surface. CarPro also offers a number of nanotechnology products that don't just bond to the surface but actually becomes one with the surface. For this reason it won't wear off.

CarPro Cquartz really impressed me the first time I used it as I didn't know what to expect; the finished results were nothing short of amazing. So besides offering nothing short of incredible protection, it also creates a liquid glass shine. Here are some of the features the manufacturer claims Cquartz provides:

- **Ultra hard coating** - CQuartz contains ceramic nano particles, which create an extremely hard finish that is scratch-resistant and durable.
- **Weather-resistance** - CQuartz provides durable protection against rain, sun and salty marine environments. The anti-corrosive coating holds up in all weather conditions.
- **High gloss shine**
- **Water and oil proof finish.**
- **Smooth, dirt repellent surface** - CQuartz's nano particles fill in tiny swirls and imperfections in the paint to make it perfectly smooth. Therefore, dirt and dirty water cannot settle into any crevices. The finish is also resistant to bugs, UV rays, acids, and salts. Plus, the slick surface is anti-static and is easily washed.
- **Anti-Calcium Effect** - CQuartz prevents mineral deposits from bonding to the vehicle's surface so water spots can be wiped off.
- **Detergent-resistant protection** - CQuartz cannot be removed by water, alkaline or other detergents, or by pressure washers. It can last up to two years.
- **Self-cleaning effect** - Most dirt and debris will not stick in the first place, so you may find yourself washing your vehicle much less often.

My comments...

Before applying the Cquartz coating you must first prep the paint by machine buffing to remove all defects. Next you must chemically strip the paint and for this process CarPro offers their own product called Eraser which appears to work really well. Next you apply the product using small, suede microfiber cloths wrapped around a foam block. Next you allow the product to dry for approximately 10 to 20 minutes and then remove. Removal is a little on the difficult side as this product really grips the paint. So take your time to carefully remove the excess using your best microfiber towels so you don't accidently re-instill toweling marks.

Optimum Opti-Coat 2.0 Permanent Paint Coating

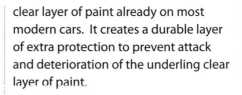

This is another product from Dr. David Ghodoussi at Optimum Polymer Technologies. This is a permanent coating that was previously only available to authorized and approved professional detailers. The primary difference between this version and the pro-version is that this version dries slower to give the enthusiast more time to correctly apply it. Opti-Coat 2.0 is a clear resin coating, similar to the actual clear layer of paint already on most modern cars. It creates a durable layer of extra protection to prevent attack and deterioration of the underling clear layer of paint.

Opti-Coat 2.0 comes in a syringe because the resin technology will harden if exposed to oxygen. Opti-Coat 2.0 kit includes both a removable sealing cap and application tip so that after use it, you can remove the tip and replace the cap to prevent it from drying in the syringe.

Opti-Coat 2.0 creates an incredibly clear, high gloss finish that repels water and all other contaminants and it won't wash off.

One of the unique characteristics about Opti-Coat is that you don't wipe the excess off. You simply apply a thin, uniform coating and you're done. This is called, wipe-on, walk-away technology. This also means you must take care to apply a completely uniform coating with no excess residue because once it dries it's hard like actual clear paint and on some colors you would see the excess. The key to uniform application is to avoid overuse of the product to start with and look at the surface from different angles as you apply. If you see any high points, (this is a term used to mean excess product), simply spread it around or gently wipe it off using a clean, microfiber towel.

Opti-Coat 2.0 must be applied to a thoroughly clean surface. If you're using Optimum polishes like Hyper-Polish, Polish II or Finish, you can simply wipe each panel down using a water dampened microfiber towel. If you're using any other company's polishes or prep products then it's recommended to chemically strip the paint using a 15% IPA/Water solution. ■

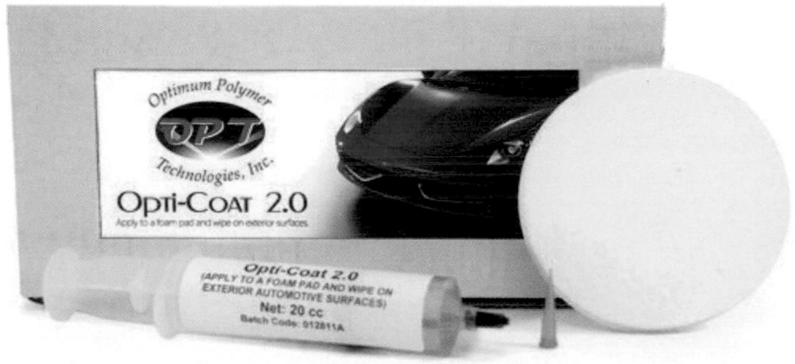

How To Use A Spray Detailer To Maintain Your Car

Spray detailers are for removing:

- Light dust
- Fingerprints
- Smudges

Spray detailers are wonderful, time-saving products if used correctly on paint that's well kept. They enable you to restore that "just detailed" look quickly and easily without having to wash and wax your car. The key is evaluating the condition of your car's paint and making the right judgment as to whether it's safe to use a spray detailer or if the vehicle is too dirty.

How dirty can a car be to safely use a spray detailer without inflicting swirls and scratches in the process?
If the car is only lightly dusty you can safely use a premium quality spray detailer along with high quality towels and proper technique without instilling any swirls or scratches.

How a spray detailer works
A quality spray detailer is supposed to hyper-lubricate the surface to help prevent scratching. A quality spray detailer will encapsulate dirt and dust particulates to help prevent scratching the paint.

Tools needed

- A premium quality spray detailer
- A collection of premium quality microfiber polishing cloths, each folded 4-ways.

How To Use A Spray Detailer

- First, mist the spray detailer over a small section of a panel.
- Next, spread the spray detailer around gently with one side of a microfiber polishing cloth (folded 4-ways).
- Then, quickly turn to the dry side and gently remove the spray detailer and buff the paint in this section to a dry, high shine. You are now finished with this section.
- Before moving onto a new section, re-fold your microfiber polishing towel to expose a clean, dry side. When starting a new section, remember to overlap a little into the previous section. After you've used all eight sides of a single microfiber polishing towel, switch to a fresh, clean microfiber polishing towel.

In This Section:

Two Things That Help A Spray Detailer Do Its Job

1. Use PLENTY of premium quality microfiber polishing towels
Don't try to wipe your entire car down using one or two towels if the goal is to maintain a flawless finish. Use 10 to 12 microfibers for an average sized car. This is not a hard rule, but an average based upon what it takes to do a safe job of wiping the exterior of a car clean while avoiding cross-contamination.

2. Use good technique
Always fold your microfiber polishing towels 4-ways. This will give you eight wiping sides and helps to spread out the pressure from your hand.

How To Use A Spray Wax

There are two general groups of spray-on waxes:

Standalone or dedicated wax
This type of product is an actual replacement or substitute for a normal paste or liquid wax. A spray-on wax in this category can be used as the primary protection product after the paint has been put through a series of compounding and polishing procedures.

Booster wax or maintenance wax
This is a product that's more like a spray detailer with the added bonus of some type of protection ingredients. Products in this category are best used as maintenance products that you use in between normal washing and applications of an actual paste or liquid

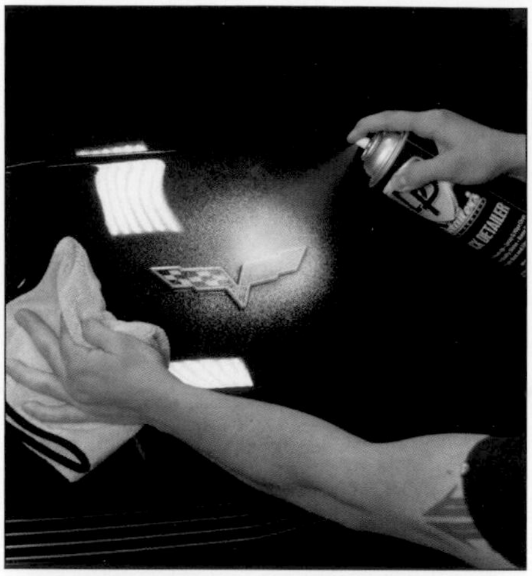

wax. They are not a substitute for a normal coat of wax.

How To Apply

There are two ways to apply a spray-on wax. First consideration should go to the manufacturer's recommendations.

> **1. Wipe off wet** - Mist on, spread around and wipe off
>
> **2. Wipe off dry** - Mist on, spread around, allow to haze, then wipe off

There are different techniques for the two ways to apply these products, which I'll go over below. To start, here are a few guidelines for using spray on waxes:

Always apply to clean vehicle
First, you need to start with a clean car. You can either wash and dry the car, or use one of the other methods mentioned in the washing chapter.

For more information:
📖 *Washing Your Car*

Start at the top and work your way down
When spraying a spray-on wax directly onto the panel, be mindful of overspray, especially around the glass. Most companies don't recommend their waxes for use on glass and especially windshields, but check each company's official recommendations.

Work on a cool surface in the shade
Hot surfaces will make a thin liquid spray-on wax more difficult to spread out and wipe off as the carrying agents

will evaporate quickly. If you do work on a warm surface in direct sun, shrink the size of your work area. This will make it easier to spread and wipe off the product.

Do a test spot
While most people think doing a test spot is only for testing pad and polish combinations, there's nothing wrong with testing out any paint care product to a small area. Make sure you're getting the results you expect and familiarize yourself with the application and removal characteristics of the product.

■ Tips And Techniques for Mist-On & Wipe-Off Spray Waxes:

- Shake product well before and during use.
- Have plenty of clean, soft microfiber towels on hand.
- Wear a microfiber glove on your towel hand.
- Fold your microfiber towels 4-ways to provide eight sides to wipe with and spread out the pressure from your hand.
- Hold sprayer about a foot away from the surface and squeeze trigger firmly. Most quality spray waxes use a nozzle that will atomize the product, but require a firm squeeze to work.
- Spread product over the surface using an overlapping circular motion for large panels, or a back and forth for long, thin for narrow panels.
- After spreading product, turn or fold your microfiber towel to a dry side or portion and wipe residue off until you see a dry, hard shine.
- Move to new section and overlap a little into previous section.

■ Tips And Techniques for Mist-On, Allow To Dry To A Haze & Wipe-Off Spray Waxes:

Trickier to use successfully without the secret technique
Using a spray-on wax that is recommended to be allowed to dry to a haze before removal is a little trickier than using a product that you wipe off immediately.

First, dampen one side of a microfiber towel with the spray-on wax. Then, mist a little wax onto the paint and use the dampened side of your microfiber towel to spread the product. A dampened microfiber towel works best because it's easier to spread out a thin liquid film if your applicator cloth is already wet or dampened with the product you're trying to spread out. If you try to use a dry microfiber towel to try to spread out a thin, liquid film at the same time you're trying to spread the product onto the surface, the dry cloth will absorb the product from the paint at the same time you're trying to leave it behind.

■ Tips

Apply to entire vehicle
Start at the top and continue applying to the rest of the vehicle using your dampened microfiber towel until the entire car is covered with a thin coating of wax.

With a wipe-on, wipe-off spray wax, there's no waiting for the product to dry. A wax that needs to dry to a haze will take about 10 to 20 minutes depending upon temperature, humidity, and wind currents. If you just apply to one section or panel before moving on, you'll be waiting there until the wax dries before you can remove it and move on.

Follow your path of travel
Wipe off the dried wax by starting where you first applied the product. Follow your path of travel, gently and carefully wiping the dried residue off the paint. Be sure to switch to a clean, dry microfiber polishing cloth folded 4 ways to remove the dried film of wax. ■

Spray Detailers

- *Pinnacle Crystal Mist Detail Spray*
- *Wolfgang Instant Detail Spritz*
- *BLACKFIRE Midnight Sun Instant Detailer*
- *Pinnacle XMT Final Finish Instant Detailer*
- *Detailer's Pro Series Final Gloss Quick Detailer*
- *Dodo Juice Red Mist Tropical Protection Detailer*
- *Dodo Juice Time To Dry Drying Detailer*
- *Griot's Garage Speed Shine Detailer*
- *Prima Slick Quick Detail Spray*
- *Finish Kare 425 Extra Slick Final Body Shine*
- *Finish Kare Anti Static Poly wipe Finish Restorer Spray Detailer*
- *Sonus Acrylic Spritz Quick Detail Spray*
- *Meguiar's NXT Speed Detailer*
- *Mothers California Gold Showtime Instant Detailer*
- *Meguiar's #135 Synthetic Spray Detailer*
- *Meguiar's NXT Generation Speed Detailer*
- *Meguiar's #34 Final Inspection*
- *Meguiars Ultimate Quik Detailer*
- *Optimum Instant Detailer & Gloss Enhancer*
- *Optimum Opti-Clean Cleaner & Protectant*
- *Ultima Detail Spray Plus*
- *Poorboy's World Quick Detailer PLUS QD+*
- *Poorboy's World Spray & Gloss*

Spray Waxes

- *1Z Einszett Spray Wax*
- *Pinnacle Souveran Liquid Spray Wax*
- *Pinnacle XMT 360 Spray Wax*
- *Prima Hydro Wax As You Dry Spray*
- *Sonus Carnauba Spritz Quick Detailer*
- *Mothers California Gold Spray Wax*
- *Mothers FX Engineered Spray Wax*
- *Mothers Reflections Advanced Spray Wax*
- *3M Quick Wax*
- *Stoner SpeedBead One-Step Quick Wax*
- *Meguiar's NXT Spray Wax*
- *Meguiar's Ultimate Quik Wax*
- *Optimum Car Wax*
- *Poorboy's World QW+ Quick Wax Plus*

■ Paint Thickness Gauge

Anytime you're abrading the paint by hand or machine, you're removing some measure of paint, this is especially true when using a rotary buffer with a wool pad and a compound. You need to be careful not to remove too much paint at which point you risk buffing through the clear layer on a clear coat paints, or the colored layer of a single stage paints.

Big Picture Indicator
A Paint Thickness Gauge can help you to make what I call the Go or No Go decision. For me it's a "Big Picture Indicator."

■ Factory Paint versus Repaint

When buffing out a car you're either working on factory paint or a repaint. Typically, a repaint is a car that has been repainted after being in an accident or has a custom paint job. As mentioned in the first part of this how-to book, the average clear layer of paint on a factory finish is approximately 2 mils thick. It is only the clear layer that you can work on.

Factory Paint
The overall thickness of a factory finish ranges between a low of 6 mils and a high of 8 mils. If you take some measurements on any of the major panels and they are in the 6 mil range or lower I would suggest being very cautious about using any aggressive pads or products on the finish, especially if the car has been machine buffed in the past. This is just a general rule of thumb; some guys like to live more dangerously than others when it comes to buffing out cars, I for one like to play on the safe side.

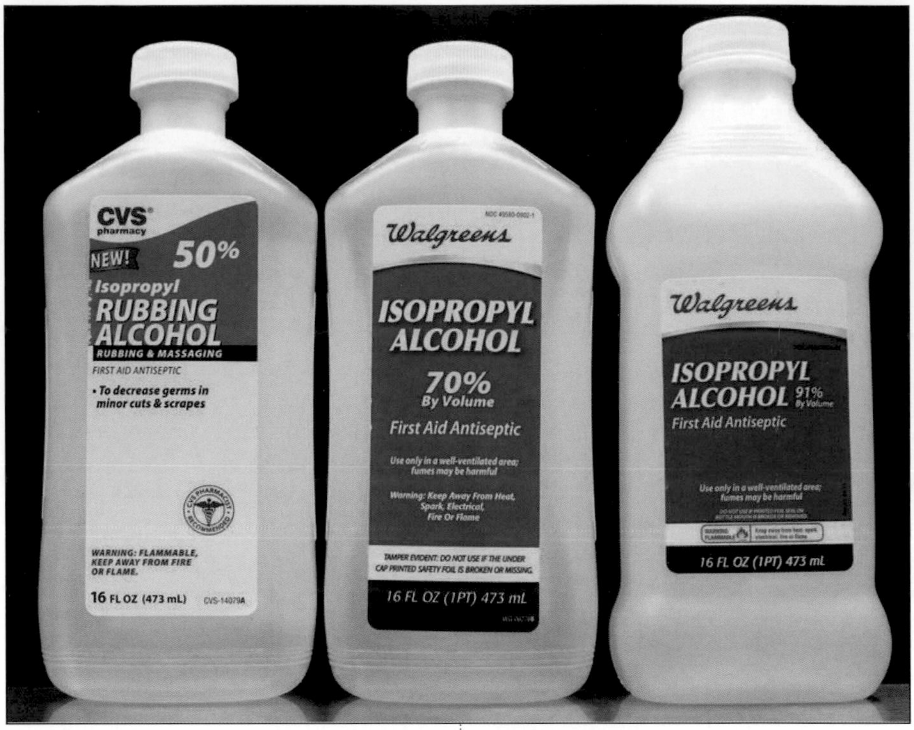

In This Section:

- Paint Thickness Gauge
- Factory Paint versus Repaint
- How to Mix IPA for Inspecting Correction Results
- Chemically removing waxes and/or paint sealants
- How to check your work with IPA
- Non-IPA Options

Repaints
If you're going to work on a car that has been repainted, or that has at least some panels that have been repainted, then measurements for paint thickness can be all over the place and it's possible to get very misleading readings. For example, if a fender has Bondo or extra layers of filling primer, or if much of the original paint was simply scuffed and painted over, you could get a reading showing the paint to be very thick but the clear layer is still very thin. So follow the practice of always using the least aggressive product to get the job done.

Custom Paint Jobs
Custom paint jobs are usually found on SIVs, or Special Interest Vehicles. In most cases, SIVs have a high quality paint job in which the painter has sprayed plenty of paint onto the car. If possible, contact the painter, introduce yourself and let them know you're going to be doing some polishing work to a car they painted. Then, flat out ask them how many coats of clear they sprayed. This will give you an idea if you're working in the safe zone or walking into an accident about to happen. Keep in mind; a lot of custom paint jobs are wetsanded, cut and buffed. The sanding, cutting and polishing work all remove some measure of paint, so take multiple measurements from major panels and use your results to make your Go or No Go decision. And always, no matter what the project, use the least aggressive product to get the job done.

■ How to Mix IPA for Inspecting Correction Results

Most compounds and polishes are made using some type of abrasives, embodied in some type of lubricating carrying agent or base. The lubricating base normally has a lotion-like consistency and can contain some type of oil which reduces scouring of the paint by the abrasives.

The lubricating base is extremely important as it cushions or buffers the abrading action of the abrasives. Too many people discount the lubricating agents as simply fillers and don't understand that without them, they won't be able to remove things like swirls and scratches and leave a better looking finish at the same time.

The problem with lubricating agents is that they can mask or hide any defects in the finish, making it appear as though they've been removed, even though they are still present in the paint. After these lubricating agents or polishing oils wear off, the swirls and scratches show up again, bringing you back to the correction step. One way to make sure you've removed all the defects is to remove the polishing oils and then inspect the paint.

You can remove these polishing oils a number of ways:

- Wipe the paint with a diluted mixture of isopropyl alcohol and water
- Wipe the paint with a product specifically designed to wipe and strip the paint
- Wash the car using a detergent soap
- Wipe the paint using mineral spirits

My recommendation is to read through this section and then test out and decide which approach works best for you.

WARNING *- Do not chemically strip FRESH PAINT. This means paint that is less than 30 days old. Fresh paint has not fully cross-linked, dried and hardened. Introducing any type of solvent to the surface and allowing it to dwell could have a negative effect on the paint. This does not affect a new car because the paint on a new car was baked on at the factory before the car rolled off the assembly line.*

Note: *This is NOT an official recommendation by Mike Phillips or Autogeek. It is an attempt to clear up any confusion on the topic of chemically stripping paint with the common products used for this procedure. If you choose to chemically strip paint, all the risk is yours. Any time you use a new product or procedure, it's a great idea to first test in an inconspicuous area and check the results before moving forward.*

What NOT to do

Most recommendations I've heard use one of two options:

- Use it straight out of the bottle
- Dilute IPA 1:1 (50%) with water
  If you simply dilute the commonly found bottles if IPA by 50%, here's what you'll get:
- Diluting 91% IPA 1:1 (50%) = a 45% dilution of IPA to water solution.
- Diluting 70% IPA 1:1 (50%) = a 35% dilution of IPA to water solution.
- Diluting 50% IPA 1:1 (50%) = a 25% dilution of IPA to water solution.

TOO STRONG!

After talking to chemists in this industry, they all felt that these dilution levels were overkill and too strong for removing residues after compounding and/or polishing paint.
Most quality name brand compounds and polishes are water soluble and don't need a strong solution of isopropyl alcohol to dissolve, emulsify and loosen any leftover residues on the surface.

The most common dilution levels you can purchase over the counter are 50%, 70% and 91% isopropyl alcohol.

After talking at length with 3 seasoned chemists in the car wax industry, they all agreed that an approximate 10% dilution of IPA to water solution was a good range for chemically stripping paint for inspection.

High-solid clear coat paints are "alcohol friendly", meaning products like isopropyl alcohol can and will penetrate, soften, wrinkle and/or stain the paint. To avoid any of these problems, a 10% dilution of IPA to water solution is recommended and adequate to remove any compounding and polishing residues without risking any danger to your car's paint.

How to Mix IPA for Inspecting Correction Results

Here are the easiest ways to mix an approximate 10% solution for the most popular concentrations of isopropyl alcohol available at the retail level.

- 91% IPA To mix a 32 ounce spray bottle Pour 4 ounces of 91% IPA into a 32 ounce spray bottle and top the rest of the bottle off with water. This will make 32 ounces of 11.375% IPA to water solution.
- 70% IPA To mix a 32 ounce spray bottle Pour 8 ounces of 70% IPA into a 32 ounce spray bottle and top the rest of the bottle off with water. This will make 32 ounces of 17.5% IPA to water solution.
- 50% IPA To mix a 32 ounce spray bottle Pour 8 ounces of 50% IPA into a 32 ounce spray bottle and top the rest of the bottle off with water. This will make 32 ounces of 12.5% IPA to water solution.

For what it's worth...

Common household glass cleaners have been used for years as a convenient way to strip the finish to inspect correction results, often times because it's a commonly found product in a detailing environment. Most glass cleaners that use alcohol are around the 10% range or lower.

My personal recommendation for IPA *- If you want to chemically strip paint to remove any compound or polish residues so that you can accurately see the true condition of the paint after any correction steps, then I recommend using a 10% dilution of IPA to water solution. This is a safe approach to remove any residues that may be masking the true results of your process to the paint without the risk of causing any harm.*

Checking your test spot vs checking the entire car *- Theoretically, if you use IPA to chemically strip your test spot and the results look good, duplicating the same correction process over the rest of the panels should yield the same results as seen in your test spot. Assuming all the panels have the same type of paint, then you shouldn't have to continue stripping all the paint on each panel. Keep doing the same work you did for your test spot and trust your skills and abilities - consistent work yields consistent results.*

■ Chemically removing waxes and/or paint sealants

Note: *This article addresses IPA dilution strength for removing compounding and/or polishing lubricating oils (sometimes called "fillers") during the paint correction process. You can also use this to try to remove any previously applied wax or paint sealant, but isopropyl alcohol may not effectively remove some polymer products. To remove any previously applied wax or paint sealant, I recommend using a light* *paint cleaner or a fine polish applied by hand or machine. A light paint cleaner or abrasive polish will effectively remove any previously applied wax or paint sealant AND leave the paint looking clear and glossy.*

If you're dead set on chemically stripping the paint, then a combination of using both a 10% solution of IPA to water followed by wiping with mineral spirits should remove any previously applied wax or paint sealant.

■ How to check your work with IPA

Removing compound and polish residue
Now that you have a safely diluted mixture of IPA and water, if you want to check your work during any of the correction steps, the first thing you want to do is to wipe off any visible residue. After you've wiped a panel clean, you're ready to chemically strip the paint for inspection.

Simply mist some of the IPA mixture onto the area and spread it using a clean microfiber towel folded 4-ways. Work the product gently over the paint, turn the towel to a dry side and wipe until the surface is dry and clear.

Safety precautions *- Always wear the appropriate safety gear when working with chemicals. This includes safety glasses, protective gloves and a shop apron.*

My comments... *In the last year, I used some 70% IPA to chemically strip paint while doing some polish comparisons. I had used painters tape to tape off specific sections for the test. After wiping the area with straight 70% IPA, some of the IPA penetrated between the tape and the paint, allowing it to dwell while I continued testing. When I removed the tape, there was a visible spot where the clear coat paint wrinkled from being exposed to the high concentration of IPA for too long.*

Removing previously-applied wax or paint sealant
To remove previously-applied wax or paint sealant, simply mist some of the IPA mixture onto the area and spread it around using a clean microfiber towel folded 4-ways. Work the product gently over the paint, turn to a dry side and wipe until the surface is dry and clear.

■ Non-IPA Options

Menzerna Top Inspection
Formulated specifically to remove compound and polish residues for inspecting correction results.

Griot's Garage Pre-Wax Cleaner
Formulated to be used after compounding and polishing to prepare the surface for wax or paint sealant.

Griot's Garage Paint Prep
Formulated to remove previously applied waxes, silicones and oils either before doing any correction work with compounds and polishes, or before application of wax or paint sealant.

Optimum Power Clean All Purpose Cleaner
A good all-around all purpose cleaner that can be used for a variety of cleaning purposes, including stripping paint.

While these products are sometimes recommended for stripping paint, the manufacturers recommend that after applying these products, the paint should be rinsed with water to remove any residues. As such, they are not spray-on / wipe-off products.

Odorless mineral spirits - Mineral spirits are another option for chemically stripping an automotive finish. Odorless mineral spirits are best for this application as the process for removing the odors also removes a lot of nasty substances through further refining of the product. Mineral spirits will tend to wipe easier than most other options and leave a more clear finish.

Percent volatile - When discussing mineral spirits, the idea has been brought up that they may leave behind a film that could, like compound or polish residues, mask defects and thus defeat the purpose of stripping the finish after correction work. I brought this up with two of my chemist friends and they both said that it's not an issue,

but if you want to be sure, choose a brand of mineral spirits that states the "percent volatile" is 100%.

All-purpose cleaners and/or degreasers - All-purpose cleaners and degreasers are more complex in their formulas in that they contain more ingredients to give them the ability to clean or dissolve a wide spectrum of substances like grease, oil, road grime, etc. It's this expanded ability that makes all-purpose cleaners and degreasers excellent for cleaning things like engine compartments, but this same ability makes them riskier to use on a delicate, clear coat finish because they can stain or dull paint.

Personal thoughts on inspecting correction work
I tend to use a combination of all of the above. I don't have an allegiance to just a specific product or process, but instead which product I will use may depend upon what I'm trying to accomplish, or even simpler, what's closest to my hand at the time I'm working on a project. ■

On the Autogeek.net Store:

- Menzerna Top Inspection
- Griot's Garage Paint Prep
- Griot's Garage Pre-Wax Cleaner
- Optimum Power Clean All Purpose Cleaner
- Black Nitrile Gloves
- Show Car Garage Apron
- Autogeek 32 ounce Heavy Duty PVC Clear Spray Bottle
- Spraymaster Trigger Sprayer - Chemical Resistant Spray Head

Time to put what you've learned into practice! Just go through the steps:

- Wash and dry the car.
- Inspect and evaluate the condition of the finish – Check for above and below surface defects.
- Determine your goal - this tells you which pads and products you'll need
- Remove above-surface bonded contaminants if discovered.
- Remove swirls, scratches and water spots using a dedicated correction step or use a one-step cleaner wax.
- Polish the paint to a high gloss if you choose to do a multiple-step procedure.
- Seal the paint with a coat or two of your favorite wax, paint sealant or coating.
- Maintain your car's finish and all your hard work using spray detailers and spray-on waxes.

Feel free to share your before and after pictures in the Show and Shine section of AutogeekOnline.net.

■ Conclusion

There's a lifetime of tips and techniques jammed into this how-to book, with the intended goal of sharing knowledge that I have gained over years of experience.

Creating a show car finish starts with knowledge
The information in this book is real and based upon a lifetime of polishing paint and teaching others. Your job is to absorb this information and save years of time learning everything through testing and practice via trial and error.

The best news of all is, after reading this how-to book, if you should have any questions, you'll find answers on our AutogeekOnline.net discussion forum. Feel free to start a thread and ask any questions that you may have. A host of incredibly sharp, friendly and helpful forum members and I will go out of our way to see you through to success.

I can also be reached via phone at Autogeek's headquarters, but prefer to answer questions on the public forum. This is simply because if you have a question, odds are that others have the same question and by using the forum to interact, more people benefit.

So read through this how-to book, take what you've learned out into your garage, and start doing some testing to dial in a successful system that creates the results you wish to achieve.

See you on the forum!
Mike Phillips
www.AutogeekOnline.net
1-800-869-3011 x206

A

Abrasive Particulate
Any small, hard, sharp particle, normally referred to as it relates with the potential and ability to instill swirls and scratches into clearcoat paints.

Aggressive Cut Compound
A very aggressive liquid or paste that uses some type of abrasive technology to cut or abrade paint quickly. In the body shop world, compounds are used to remove sanding marks. In the detailing world, compounds are used to remove deep below-surface defects like swirls, scratches and water spot etchings. Depending upon the abrasive technology and the application method and material, some automotive compounds can remove down to 1000 grit sanding marks. Of course, topcoat hardness is an important factor that affects a compound's effectiveness.

AIO *see Cleaner Wax*

Air Currents
Spinning buffing pads create air-currents on the surface. It's possible for this air current to draw any loose dirt particles into the buffing process, trapping them between the paint and the pad, potentially inflicting swirls and scratches throughout the entire finish.

Ample
An amount of product that is fully sufficient to meet the needs of the buffing process.

Arm Speed
How fast or slow you move the polisher over the paint.

B

Backing Plate
An interface that attaches to the free floating spindle bearing assembly of a polisher by using a 5/16" arbor. The other side has hook material for attaching buffing pads as a part of a hook and loop pad attachment system.

Basecoat/Clearcoat
A two part paint system in which the color coat is sprayed over the body panels and the clear layer is sprayed on top. In most cases, the color coat offers no gloss or shine and is matte in appearance. The clearcoat layer of paint creates the gloss and brings out the full richness of color.

Bodyshop Safe
Products that are bodyshop safe contain no ingredients that could contaminate a fresh paint environment by introducing substances that would cause surface adhesion problems on body panels to be sprayed with fresh paint.

Buffing Cycle
The buffing cycle is the amount of time you are able to work a product before the abrasives have broken down.

Burning-through
Burning-through occurs when an area is buffed for so long that enough paint is removed from the clear layer of paint to expose the colored layer. When working on a single stage paint, if you burn through the colored coat, you'll expose the primer.

C

Carnauba Car Wax
A product that contains some type of naturally occurring waxy substance intended to protect the paint while creating a clear, glossy finish. Carnauba wax is the most commonly used naturally occurring wax found in car wax formulations. This category of traditional waxes will wear off under normal wear and tear, repeated washings and exposure to the environment. It should be reapplied on a regular basis to maintain a protective coating on the surface of the paint.

Circle Pattern
An alternative way to add working product to the face of the pad. When using the circle pattern, apply your product to the outside edge to help prevent your pad from becoming saturated in the center.

Clay Haze
Marring or scratching left in the paint, typically from the use of an aggressive clay.

Cleaner Wax *also called an AIO*
A cleaner wax or All-In-One (AIO) is a one-step product formulated using a blend of chemical cleaners and often some type of abrasives, with some type of protection ingredients that will remain on the surface after the cleaning action is finished and the residue is wiped from the paint.

Clear Coat Failure
Clear coat failure is when the clear layer of paint either delaminates from the basecoat and peels off or when it deteriorates by first turning an opaque whitish color. Clear coat failure cannot be fixed by applying any type of compound or polish. The only remedy is to repaint the affected area or the entire car.

Cobweb Swirls *also called Spiderweb*
This term comes from the appearance of swirls in the paint which can look like a spider's cobweb. These swirls have a circular or radial pattern to them when the paint is highlighted with a strong focused point of bright light.

Correction
The process of removing below-surface defects like swirls and scratches, normally using an abrasive medium polish or true compound with a cutting or polishing pad. For shallow defects, a fine polish can also be used.

Crater Etching
Usually a round or irregular shaped depression in the paint where some type of liquid or other substance has dwelled long enough to eat into or dissolve enough of the paint coating to leave a void.

Creeping Out
Using a folded microfiber towel, gently begin moving outward from a shiny spot, taking wax off in little bites using small, overlapping circular motions.

D

Dampsander
Any tool that can be used with sanding and finishing discs to dampsand paint to remove orange peel and other surface defects.

DA Polishers (Dual Action)
A generic term for polishers that offer both rotating and oscillating action.

Dampsanding
Dampsanding is simply a variation of wetsanding that uses less water with sanding discs that are designed specifically for this process.

Dry Buffing
There are some products on the market whose manufacturers recommend buffing the product until it dries. As the product dries, you'll tend to see some dusting as the product residue becomes a powder and the paint will have a hard, dry shine to it.

E

Edging
Buffing along an edge before buffing out the rest of the major portions of the panel. By edging a panel first, you don't have to buff near the edges as closely when you switch over to a larger pad to buff out the panel.

F

Fine Cut Polish
A liquid or paste that uses some type of abrasive technology to cut or abrade the paint, but is less aggressive than a true medium polish. Depending upon the abrasive technology and the application method and material, some fine polishes can remove down to 2500 grit sanding marks while still finishing LSP ready. Topcoat hardness is an important factor that affects a fine polish's effectiveness.

Fingermarks
A type of scratch pattern left in the paint by the pressure from your fingertips. Usually caused by pressing down on some type of applicator pad when using a product that's either too aggressive to be used by hand or not safe for clear coat paints.

Forced Rotation Dual Action Polishers
A tool that uses a direct drive gear mechanism to both rotate and oscillate a buffing pad at the same time. There is no slippage with this type of drive mechanism as there is with a free floating spindle bearing assembly.

Free Floating Spindle Bearing Assembly
A unique drive mechanism that will simultaneously rotate and oscillate a buffing pad, enabling the user to safely remove swirls, scratches, oxidation and water spots. If too much downward pressure is applied, or if the tool is held so that more pressure is applied to an edge of the buffing pad, the pad will simply stop spinning, preventing you from burning through the paint or instilling swirls.

G

Glaze or Pure Polish - Non-Abrasive Products
Historically, the term glaze is used to describe a bodyshop safe, hand-applied liquid used to fill-in and mask fine swirls while creating a deep, wet shine on fresh paint.

Grabby
The characteristic where it feels

like the pad is grabbing the paint as you're trying to glide it over the surface instead of moving over the surface smoothly. Pad and product combinations that are grabby make controlling the polisher more difficult and will tire you out faster. Also see Buffer Hop.

Grit Guard Inserts
A plastic insert that fits into the bottom of a 5-gallon bucket and traps dirt that comes off your wash mitt. The design includes a plastic grill that dirt and other abrasive particles can fall past to the bottom of the bucket. The grill is suspended about two inches off the bottom by four vanes. These vanes help to trap dirt particles by preventing the water at the bottom from swirling around, thus preventing dirt particles from rising back above the grill where they could potentially get onto your wash mitt.

H

Hard Water Spots
Hard water spots are mineral deposits left behind on the paint surface. These minerals are either dissolved or embodied in water, and when the water evaporates, it leaves the physical minerals behind on the surface.

■ I

Impermeable
A material that will not allow substances such as fluids or gasses to pass through it.

IPA
Isopropyl alcohol, also called rubbing alcohol. Easily found in most drug stores in varying dilution strengths. Mixed with water to chemically strip paint to remove any fillers or polishing oils so you can more accurately inspect the true results of an abrading process.

■ J

Jewelling
The final machine polishing step in which a soft to ultra soft foam finishing pad with no mechanical abrading ability is used with a high lubricity, ultra fine finishing polish to remove any remaining microscopic surface imperfections. This is performed after the paint has been previously put through a series of machine compounding and polishing procedures to create a near-perfect finish.

■ K

Kissing the Finish
To kiss the finish, touch the face of the foam pad (with wax on it) onto your panel at an angle, thus depositing only a portion of the wax on the pad to one area of the paint. This technique helps keep the wax spreading out over the paint instead of loading up inside your pad.

■ L

LSP = Last Step Product
The last product to be applied to and removed from the paint before the final wipe.

LSP Ready
Paint that is ready to be sealed with a car wax, a paint sealant or a coating. This means that all above-surface bonded contaminants and the majority of below-surface defects have been removed, leaving behind a predominantly defect-free surface.

■ M

Medium Cut Polish
A liquid or paste that uses some type of abrasive technology to cut or abrade the paint, but is less aggressive than a true cutting compound. Depending upon the abrasive technology and the application method and material, some medium polishes can remove down to 2000 grit sanding marks and finish LSP ready. Topcoat hardness is an important factor that affects a medium polish's effectiveness.

Mil
Metric unit of measurement that equals one ten thousandth of a millimeter. When measuring paint coatings, mils or microns are the two most commonly used units.

■ N

Non-Reticulated Foam = Closed Cell Foam
Closed cell foam means the cell wall structure is closed. This makes the foam non-porous. While it's not impossible for air and liquids to flow through it, it is more difficult.

Normal Car Wash
A normal car wash is simply the more traditional method of using a hose and bucket to wash your car. This system works well, but it also uses a lot of water and in some geographical areas, this may not be allowed.

■ O

OEM = Original Equipment Manufacturer
While the word "equipment" can make you think of a part or component, it can also refer to the manufacturer of an entire vehicle.

Outgassing
The process in which solvents and other additives work their way out of the paint to the surface where they can evaporate.

Oxidation
Oxidation is the loss of at least one electron when two or more substances interact. When your car's paint is exposed to oxygen and moisture, the oxygen molecules interact with the paint resin, causing free radicals to be eliminated.

■ P

Paint Cleaner
A liquid, paste or cream that relies primarily on chemical cleaning agents to remove any light topical contamination or surface impurities to restore a clean, smooth surface. Used as part of a process to prepare a painted finish for application of a wax, paint sealant or coating. Paint cleaners are for very light cleaning and are not

normally intended to be used like an abrasive polish to remove below-surface defects.

Paint Coatings
Generally defined as any paint protection product that contains man-made or synthetic protection ingredients that are intended to permanently bond to the paint to provide a barrier-coating of protection and create a clear, high gloss finish. The products available in this category are considered permanent coatings, because like your car's paint, they cannot be removed unless you purposefully remove or neglect them.

Paint System
A paint system refers to both a brand and type of paint. There are different manufacturers for automotive paints, each with their own proprietary formulas for their paint lines.

Panel
Generally defined as a complete component of the car body.

Permeable
A material that can be penetrated, usually by liquids as it applies to car detailing.

pH
A measurement of the acidity or alkalinity of a solution in a range of 0 to 14, with the number 7 representing a neutral rating. The numbers 8 to 14 represent increasing alkalinity and numbers 0 to 6 represent decreasing acidity.

Pre-Wax Cleaner
Similar or the same as a paint cleaner. Most pre-wax cleaners are complimentary products in that they are part of a specific brand's system in which the pre-wax cleaner is matched to a wax or paint sealant. There's a chemical synergistic compatibility to ensure maximum performance between products that might not be achieved using products from outside the brand.

Priming A Pad
Applying, spreading and working product into the face of a buffing pad.

Priming the pad ensures 100% of the face of the pad is loaded with abrasives and/or cleaning agents so that you maximize abrading and cleaning ability.

■ R

Reticulated Foam = Open Cell Foam
Open cell foam means the cell wall structure is open, meaning the membranes are missing, leaving only the framework in place. This allows liquids and gasses to pass through easily.

RIDS = Random Isolated Deeper Scratches
This type of scratch comes from normal wear and tear. RIDS are like tracers in that they are deeper scratches that show up after the shallow scratches have been removed through a machine or hand buffing process, usually with a compound or paint cleaner. After the shallow swirls and scratches have been removed, any deeper scratches that remain will now show up because there are no longer thousands of lighter, more shallow scratches camouflaging them.

Road Grime
Usually a film on the outside of the car that is a mixture of oils and dirt.

Rotary Buffer
A tool that uses a direct drive gear mechanism to rotate a buffing pad in a single circular direction.

■ S

Sacrificial Barrier Coating
The primary purpose of a wax or sealant is to act as a sacrificial barrier coating over the surface of your car's paint. Any time anything comes into contact with your car's paint, before it can cause any damage to the paint it first has to get past the layer of wax or paint sealant. When your car's paint is under attack, the layer of wax or paint sealant sacrifices itself.

Seal
To coat over a painted surface using a car wax, paint sealant or coating with the intended purpose of creating a uniform protective sacrificial barrier-coating.

Section
A section is a portion of a panel. For example, when using a DA Polisher to buff out the hood on a medium size passenger car, you'll usually slice the hood up into 4 to 6 sections.

Section Pass
A section pass is when you move the polisher back and forth with enough single overlapping passes to cover the entire section one time.

Single Pass
A single pass is when you move the

polisher from one side of the section you're buffing to the other.

Single Stage Paint
Paint with pigment mixed into it that is used for a final top coat. Most single stage paints were used before the 1980s and were either a lacquer or enamel type paint. They will tend to oxidize easily if not regularly maintained with polishing and waxing. They tend to be easier to remove swirls and scratches out of because they tend to be softer than basecoat/clearcoat paints.

Splatter Dots
Little dots of product sprayed outward. These are usually caused by accidently lifting a pad wet with product from the surface of a panel before allowing the pad to stop spinning.

Spray Detailer
A high lubricity spray and wipe product used for restoring shine and gloss while safely removing light dust, fingerprints and smudges.

Synergistic Chemical Compatibility = System Approach
Using all the polishing products from a single manufacturer to complete the entire buffing process.

Synthetic Paint Sealant
A product that contains some type of man-made or synthetic protection ingredients to protect the paint while creating a clear, glossy finish.

Swath
The width and length of a single wipe over the surface of paint with your hand on a folded microfiber towel, usually while you're wiping off a coat of wax or paint sealant.

Swirls
Scratches that appear to be circular when exposed or highlighted by a bright source of light.

■ T

Tape Line
A tape line is used when inspecting the results of a buffing process. By only working on one side of the tape line, you make it easy to detect changes in before and after condition of the paint.

Terry Cloth
Cotton toweling that uses a nap or loop of cotton for the design of the weave.

Test Spot
A small area in which pads, products and tools are tested to establish a proven buffing procedure before detailing the entire vehicle.

Topcoat Hardness
A measure of how hard or soft the top layer of paint is as it relates to removing defects. Topcoat hardness is an unknown variable, and an important reason to do a test spot before buffing out any car.

Topping
The practice of applying a different type of wax or paint sealant over an initial application of a wax or paint sealant to either create a thicker and more durable layer of protection or to create a deep, wet-look shine.

Tracers
Tracers are deeper scratches left by the hand sanding process, usually in straight lines because most people move their hand in a back and forth motion when wet sanding. Tracers show up after the paint is compounded and all shallow scratches have been removed. Remaining in the paint are the deeper sanding marks and these are called tracers.

■ U

Ultra Fine Cut Polish
A liquid or paste that uses some type of abrasive technology to cut or abrade the paint, but is less aggressive than a true fine polish. Depending upon the abrasive technology and the application method and material, some ultra fine polishes can remove down to 2500 grit sanding marks while still finishing out LSP ready. Topcoat hardness is an important factor that affects an ultra fine polish's effectiveness.

UMR = Uniform Material Removal
Buffing a panel, section by section in a methodical and controlled manner, to remove a uniform amount of material equally from the surface.

■ W

Water Insoluble
Not able to be broken down or liquefied easily using water. Waxes and paint sealants, by their nature, are insoluble.

Water Soluble
Able to be broken down or liquefied using water. Most compounds and polishes are water soluble and are easy to wash from the car, microfiber towels and from buffing pads.

Water Spots - Type I
These are mineral deposits, or what people commonly call hard water spots. They can be the remains of minerals suspended in city water or well water that are left behind after the water evaporates from the finish. This can happen if hard water is allowed to dry on paint, whether it is from sprinkler water, acid rain, or other water sources.

Water Spots - Type II
These are actual etchings or craters in paint, caused by something corrosive in a water source landing on the finish without being removed before etching occurred.

Water Spots - Type III
These are spots that look dull and faded and are found primarily on single stage paints. They are usually found after a water source pools on the paint and is allowed to dwell on the surface.

Waterless Car Wash
A waterless car wash is a high lubricity pre-mixed spray detailer used to heavily saturate a panel. The panel is then carefully wiped to remove any dirt or road grime.

Wet Buffing Technique
Maintaining a wet film of product on the surface while the pad is in contact with the paint.

Working Product
Product that is applied to the face of a foam buffing pad that has already been primed.